QMW LIBRARY
23 0937860 6

KU-140-546

The Prince of Poets

The Prince of Poets

ESSAYS ON EDMUND SPENSER

edited by
JOHN R. ELLIOTT, JR.

1968

NEW YORK
New York University Press
LONDON
University of London Press Limited

Library of Congress catalog card number: 68–16827
Manufactured in the United States of America

Acknowledgments

"Edmund Spenser," by William Butler Yeats. Reprinted from "The Cutting of an Agate," *Essays and Introductions* by permission of The Macmillan Company, M. B. Yeats and A. P. Watt and Son, Ltd. Copyright © 1961 by Mrs. W. B. Yeats.

"The Faery Queen," by Virginia Woolf, from *The Moment and Other Essays* by Virginia Woolf. Copyright © 1948 by Harcourt Brace & World, Inc. and reprinted with their permission. Acknowledgment is also made to Leonard Woolf and Hogarth Press Ltd. for permission to reprint.

"On Chaucer and Spenser," by William Hazlitt. Excerpts reprinted from *Lectures on the English Poets,* Everyman's Library, J. M. Dent & Sons, 1908. The essay was first printed in 1818.

"Spenser," by James Russell Lowell. Excerpts reprinted from *The Complete Writings of James Russell Lowell,* Houghton Mifflin, 1904, Vol. V. The essay was first printed in 1875.

"Spenser, the Poet and Teacher," by Edward Dowden. Excerpts reprinted from *The Complete Works in Verse and Prose of Edmund Spenser,* edited by Alexander B. Grosart; Hazell, Watson and Vinney, Vol. I, 1884.

"Spenser's Philosophy," by W. L. Renwick. Reprinted from *Edmund Spenser: An Essay on Renaissance Poetry* by permission of Edward Arnold Ltd. and St. Martin's Press, Inc. Copyright © 1925 by Edward Arnold Ltd.

"Colin Clout," by William Nelson. Reprinted from *The Poetry of Edmund Spenser* by permission of William Nelson and Columbia University Press. Copyright © 1963 by Columbia University Press.

"The Amoretti: Most Goodly Temperature," by Louis L. Martz. Reprinted from *Form and Convention in the Poetry of Edmund Spenser, Selected Papers from the English Institute,* edited by William Nelson, by permission of Columbia University Press. Copyright © 1961 by Columbia University Press.

"Thought's Astonishment and the Dark Conceits of Spenser's *Amoretti*," by Robert Kellogg. Reprinted from *Renaissance Papers 1965* by permission of Robert Kellogg and The Southeastern Renaissance Conference. The essay has been specially revised by the author for this volume.

"Spenser and the Epithalamic Convention," by Thomas M. Greene. Reprinted from *Comparative Literature,* Vol. IX by permission of Thomas M. Greene and Comparative Literature.

"From Earthly Love to Heavenly Love," by Robert Ellrodt. Reprinted from *Neoplationism in the Poetry of Spenser* by Robert Ellrodt by permission of Robert Ellrodt and Librarie Droz. Copyright © 1960 by Robert Ellrodt.

"Gothic Unity in *The Faerie Queene,*" by Richard Hurd from *Letters on Chivalry and Romance,* London, 1762.

"Preface to *The Faerie Queene*," by John Upton. Reprinted from *The Faerie Queen,* edited by John Upton, London, 1758, Vol. I.

"Allegory in *The Faerie Queene*," by Graham Hough. Reprinted from *A Preface to "The Faerie Queene,"* by Graham Hough by permission of W. W. Norton & Company, Inc., and Gerald Duckworth & Co., Ltd. Copyright © 1962 by Graham Hough.

"The Nature of Spenser's Allegory," by A. C. Hamilton, reprinted from The Structure of Allegory in *"The Faerie Queene,"* by permission of The Clarendon Press, Oxford. Copyright © 1961 by The Clarendon Press.

"The Cave of Mammon," by Frank Kermode. Reprinted from *Elizabethan Poetry,* edited by John Russell Brown and Bernard Harris, *Stratford-Upon-Avon Studies 2,* by permission of Edward Arnold Ltd. and St. Martin's Press, Inc. Copyright © 1966 by Edward Arnold Ltd.

"The Image of Britomart," by Thomas P. Roche, Jr. Reprinted from *The Kindly Flame: A Study of the Third and Fourth Books of Spenser's Faerie Queene,* by Thomas P. Roche, Jr. by permission of Princeton University Press and Thomas P. Roche, Jr. Copyright © 1964 by Princeton University Press.

"Mutabilitie and the Cycle of the Months," by Sherman Hawkins. Reprinted from *Form and Convention in the Poetry of Edmund Spenser, Selected Papers from the English Institute,* edited by William Nelson, by permission of Columbia University Press. Copyright © 1961 by Columbia University Press.

For my Mother and Father

Introduction

PERHAPS no major English poet has received a more appreciative re-reading in recent times than Edmund Spenser. For years relegated to the dusty shelf reserved for authors politely honored but seldom read, Spenser has been one of the chief beneficiaries of our renewed interest in and understanding of Renaissance art. With the discovery by modern readers of the intellectual complexity and artistic coherence of literary forms that once seemed merely naïve and disordered, Spenser has emerged from the shadow of Marlowe, Shakespeare, and Donne to lay claim once again to his title as "the Prince of Poets in his Tyme."

Modern scholarship and criticism are rich in documents supporting this claim, as the essays presented here demonstrate. They also reveal, however, that Spenser has been restored to his rightful position only after long years of exile, during which he has suffered equally from the contempt of enemies and the zeal of friends. While to his own age Spenser seemed a model of the noblest aspirations of English poetry, such nobility soon went out of fashion, and Spenser's was only one of the many aristocratic heads to fall victim to the modern revolution in taste. Until very recently Spenser was read, when he was read at all, only for that worst of reasons—because he was thought to be "important"—and C. S. Lewis may well have been right in wondering whether a hundred people, or even ten, not officially connected with English studies had voluntarily opened a copy of *The Shepherds Calender* during his lifetime.

Undoubtedly, a major cause of this neglect lay in the barriers which modern taste had erected to an appreciation of Spenser's work. The average twentieth-century reader has tended to be scornful of the great subjects of Spenser's poetry—spiritual purity, moral virtue, idealized love—and unresponsive to the imaginary world of shepherds, knights, and magicians in which Spenser embodied them. But a more important cause of Spenser's neglect has been the widespread misunderstanding of the purposes that he sought to achieve in his poetry. This misunderstanding dates back to the nineteenth-century Romantic critics, by whom Spenser was dubiously enshrined as "the poet's poet," that is, the poet of dreams, of unreality, of pure beauty uncontaminated by the actualities of real life. For Keats and Hazlitt, for Hunt and Lowell, such a conception of Spenser's art was more often than not a complimentary one, for it coincided with their own views of what poetry ought to be like. For modern readers, on the other hand, trained to value realism and intellectual subtlety in literature, the image of Spenser as the literary grandfather of Keats and Tennyson was unlikely to enhance his reputation.

Recent scholarship, however, has demonstrated that the Romantic image of Spenser was a false one—or at best a very incomplete one. A glance at the contents of Part I of this volume, for instance, will reveal that to his contemporaries, at least, Spenser seemed anything but the poet of intuitive flights of fancy. Even before the publication of *The Faerie Queene* Spenser had established a reputation for "great learning," "morall wysenesse," and "deepe conceit." Drayton remembered him not as an idle dreamer but as "grave morall Spencer." Indeed, if literary paternity is to be claimed as a measure of a poet's quality, we should remember that it was the most learned writer of the age, Milton, who considered Spenser to be "a better teacher than Scotus or Aquinas." In addition, Spenser was esteemed nearly as highly for his mastery of the rhetoric which subserved his grave subjects—his "decorum" in "personages, matter, and speech." While the musical elegance and the imaginative richness of his style did not go unnoticed, it was plainly as a philosophical poet, skilled in the rhetorical expression of "meaning," that Spenser was considered by his contemporaries.

With the recognition of the historical inaccuracy of the Romantic conception of Spenser, modern readers are now better prepared to read him on his own terms. Yet even when the imaginary barriers between us and Spenser's poetry have been cleared away, some very real ones still remain. If Spenser's purposes were not so different from those of modern poets as has been supposed, his methods were very different indeed, and the "meaning" which Spenser's contemporaries valued so highly in his poetry may well elude us unless we make some effort to recognize these differences. Where today, for instance, a narrative writer normally attempts to represent abstract forces or ideas by imitating as closely as possible their operation on real people living in a recognizably real world, Spenser works the other way around: he habitually removes real personages and real events into a deliberately artificial world of poetic symbol and convention. Let us consider an example. In the "April Eclogue" of *The Shepherds Calender* two shepherds express their sympathy for their love-sick friend, Colin Clout, who has been rejected by "fayre Rosalind." In memory of happier times, one of them, Hobbinol, agrees to sing a song of Colin's in praise of "fayre Eliza, Queene of shepheardes." The song begins by asking the Nymphs and Muses to sing a song in praise of fair Eliza, and proceeds to explain that she is the daughter of Pan and Syrinx, that she is crowned with flowers, that she puts both Phoebus and Cynthia to shame with her beauty, and that she is attended by the Muses, the Graces, the "Ladyes of the lake," and the virgin shepherdesses who present her with twelve different kinds of flowers. Colin's, or Hobbinol's, song ends by dismissing the "daintie Damsells" and asking Dame Eliza to thank them for her song.

The modern reader, while admitting that this is all very pretty, is likely to exclaim, "But why didn't Spenser tell us what Queen Elizabeth was *really* like?" The answer is that Spenser *has* told us what Queen Elizabeth was "really" like—only Spenser's conception of the real is what we today would call the ideal. What Queen Elizabeth stands for is more important, and more "real," to Spenser than what in fact she might actually be. His method is to abstract the essence of her queenliness and of her virginity, and to express this essence through images which relate for their meaning, not representationally to things in the real world, but symbolically to Ideas in the ideal world. Eliza, for instance, is not the daughter of Henry VIII, but of Pan, the "shepeheards God." Her crown is not of stones but of flowers signifiying Victory and Peace. Although there are, to be sure, some images in the "April Eclogue" which seem to refer directly to actual historical events, even these carry a symbolic, idealized meaning as well. For example, the mixture of the red rose and the white in Eliza's cheek is an obvious reference to the settlement of the Wars of the Roses by the accession of the Tudors. By Spenser's time, however, this event had taken on an almost mythical quality and was itself a standard literary symbol of the more general order and harmony of the ideal state.

Moreover, details in the "April Eclogue" which seem confusing or simply erroneous when taken mimetically become consistent and intelligible when considered in the light of Spenser's Platonic theory of poetry. The twelve flowers presented to the Queen by the shepherdesses, for instance, could never actually be found together in nature, for in reality they bloom in different seasons. But their significance lies precisely in their unreality: the ideal realm ruled by "Dame Eliza" is a golden world, independent of time and space, unaffected by seasonal change. Again, Spenser cannot seem to make up his mind as to who is the "author" of the song: is it Colin? is it Hobbinol? or is it the Muses whom Eliza is directed to thank for it? The question is, however, irrelevant, for the song has very little to do with its fictional author, whoever he may be. We are asked to read it—or listen to it—not for what it tells us about the character who "wrote" it, but for what it tells us about itself. The mimetic framework which introduces the song only serves to distance it from its supposed author: it was wont to be sung by Colin, is now sung by Hobbinol, and itself pretends to be sung by the Muses. The final effect is of a communal hymn in which the inhabitants of Eliza's realm, both real and imagined, join in the praise of their ruler. Insofar as the song does illuminate the character of its "author," in the way that we should normally expect of mimetic fiction, it does so by illustrating the unfortunate gap between Colin's infatuation with the "real" Rosalind and his former ability to conceive and venerate the ideal image of the Virgin Queen.

The recent revival of interest in Spenser by academic scholars, then, has this to commend it, that it has addressed itself to an understanding of the conventional modes of thought and expression in Spenser's poetry and has tried to recapture the point of view of those contemporary readers who reacted to it so enthusiastically. In order to reacquaint the modern reader with Spenser's poetic idiom, the majority of the essays in this collection are historically oriented, descriptive and interpretive rather than critical or "appreciative." The theory of poetry in the Renaissance, intellectual currents such as

Protestantism and Neoplatonism, the function of the pastoral, the conventions of the sonnet sequence and of the epithalamion, the nature and purpose of allegory—all of these are subjects central to an understanding of what Spenser was about in his poetry and that readers today are likely to want some instruction in. Such instruction is widely scattered in scholarly books and journals, and I have tried to bring together here the best and most pertinent of it.

It would be only too comforting, however, to pretend that when all problems of interpretation have been solved, all our questions as readers of poetry will be answered. To understand all may be indeed to excuse all, and we will certainly be more sympathetic readers of Spenser when we understand him better, but the question of critical judgment remains. Here it is not enough to appeal to the opinion of Spenser's own age against the ignorance or eccentricity of succeeding ones, for from the beginning Spenser's poetry has received conflicting evaluations. In spite of their sympathy with his aims, even Spenser's contemporaries often judged his practice harshly. Both Sidney and Jonson, for example, vigorously objected, though for different reasons, to the most original and characteristic element of Spenser's style, his use of archaic diction. A more general and damaging criticism was Gabriel Harvey's condemnation of the "Gothic" irregularity of the narrative structure in *The Faerie Queene*—an issue that was again much debated in the eighteenth century (see the essays by Upton and Hurd) and that is still in dispute today (see the essays by Hamilton and Hough). The judgment on Spenser of Restoration critics, with their orientation towards classicism and realism, was largely a negative one, and even the Romantics' adulation of "the poet's poet" was tempered by occasional annoyance with his artificialities and improbabilities, and by suspicion of a style which, as they thought, valued sound more than sense. In our own day the New Critics (though none has written at any length about him) have charged Spenser with all that they consider most damnable in poetry—abstract statement, allegory, "poetic" diction—and have placed him, along with Milton and Tennyson, outside what they consider to be the mainstream of English poetry. On the other hand, there has been in every age abundant recognition of the power and charm exercised by Spenser's poetry on readers of all types, whether they value moral wisdom, with Ralegh and Milton; or supernatural enchantment, with Cowley; or prosodic music, with Dryden; or ethereal serenity, with Wordsworth and Hazlitt; or vividness of imagery, with Hunt; or scope of imagination, with Virginia Woolf. In these matters, as in all matters of taste and opinion, each reader must be his own final judge. The essays that follow in this volume will help him to be an informed judge and to prevent the critical dogmas of the present or the past from imposing a barrier between the reader and his experience of Spenser's poetry.

These essays have been selected and arranged as well with a number of more specific purposes in mind. Part I, "The Poet's Poet," reprints the most important references to Spenser by other poets and men of letters from Sir Philip Sidney to Virginia Woolf. Aside from the intrinsic interest of the judgments passed by fellow practitioners of Spenser's craft, this section also provides an epitome of the history of Spenser's reputation from his own day to the early part of our century. While the history of a poet's reputation often throws more light on the taste of succeeding ages than on the actual quality of his work, in the case of Spenser the conflicting opinions recorded by literary history have been curiously similar in all ages and are still very much present in current discussions of his poetry. As we have noted, the argument in the eighteenth century between Upton and Hurd over the "unity" of *The Faerie Queene* is virtually restated in the conflicting views of Hamilton and Hough. Part I thus serves as a helpful introduction to the later sections of the volume. Part II includes two of the most eloquent examples of the Romantic interpretation of Spenser, from critics on either side of the Atlantic—William Hazlitt and James Russell Lowell. Part III presents two of the milestones in the modern scholarly attempt to place Spenser in the culture of the sixteenth century. The essay of Edward Dowden was in fact revolutionary when it appeared in 1884, and W. L. Renwick's study is an even more extensive attempt at an historical understanding of the poet. Part IV presents a selection of recent essays on Spenser's poems other than *The Faerie Queen,* concentrating on those which have retained the greatest appeal—*The Shepherds Calender,* the *Amoretti* and *Epithalamion,* and the *Four Hymns.* The longest section of this volume, Part V, is quite properly devoted to Spenser's chief work, *The Faerie Queene.* Since detailed commentary on even all the major parts of so vast a poem could obviously not be contained here, I have preferred a more varied course. The first four essays in the section—those by Hurd, Upton, Hough, and Hamilton—deal generally with Spenser's epic, discussing matters, especially Spenser's use of allegory, which are relevant to the poem as a whole. They thus serve to introduce the reader to problems he may expect to encounter wherever he should pick the poem up. I have then selected three essays—those by Kermode, Roche, and Hawkins—which discuss particular portions of the poem in such a way as to illustrate patterns of thought and poetic techniques typical of the work as a whole. The result, hopefully, is a balanced collection which will aid and stimulate the reader. Readers who wish to follow any of these subjects further may consult the Selected Bibliography at the end of the volume.

I am grateful to the authors of copyrighted materials for permission to reprint their work, and to the original publishers in each case. The texts printed here are from the earliest or authoritative editions and are reproduced without change, unless requested by authors, with the exception of the regularization and occasional expansion of footnote material. Omissions in the text are indicated in all cases; occasional editorial explanations have been bracketed.

I am grateful also to the following for advice and encouragement of various sorts: Robert Kellogg, Oliver Steele, Albert R. Cirillo, Harry Berger, Jr., René Graziani, Bruce Rosenberg, Allan Orrick. A research grant from the Humanities Institute of the University of California facilitated preparation of this volume.

Santa Barbara, California
January 20, 1968

Contents

PART II The Critics' Poet

PART III The Scholars' Poet

PART IV The Minor Poems

PART V *The Faerie Queene*

I. The Poets' Poet

Gabriel Harvey

IN GOOD FAITH I had once againe nigh forgotten your *Faerie Queene:* howbeit by good chaunce, I haue nowe sent hir home at the laste, neither in better nor worse case, than I founde hir. And must you of necessitie haue my iudgement of hir in deede? To be plaine, I am voyde of al iudgement if your *Nine Comedies,* whereunto in imitatiom of *Herodotus,* you giue the names of the *Nine Muses* * (and in one mans fansie not vnworthily) come not neerer *Ariostoes Comedies,* eyther for the finenesse of plausible Elocution, or the rarenesse of Poeticall Inuention, then that *Eluish Queene* doth to his *Orlando Furioso,* which notwithstanding, you wil needes seeme to emulate, and hope to ouergo, as you flatly professed yourself in one of your last Letters . . . But I wil not stand greatly with you in your owne matters. If so be the *Faerye Queene* be fairer in your eie than the *Nine Muses,* and *Hobgoblin* runne away with the Garland from *Apollo:* Marke what I saye, and yet I will not say that I thought, but there an End for this once, and fare you well, till God or some good Aungell putte you in a better minde.

—Letter to Spenser (1580)

* [This work has not survived—ed.]

Sir Philip Sidney

THE SHEAPHEARDS KALENDER hath much Poetrie in his Eglogues: indeede worthy the reading, if I be not deceiued. That same framing of his stile to an old rustick language I dare not alowe, sith neyther *Theocritus* in Greeke, *Virgill* in Latine, nor *Sanazar* in Italian did affect it.

—"An Apologie for Poetrie" (1583)

William Webbe

. . . BUT NOWE yet at the last hath England hatched vppe one Poet of this sorte, in my conscience comparable with the best in any respect: euen Master *Sp:* Author of the *Sheepeheardes Calender,* whose trauell in that peece of English Poetrie I thinke verely is so commendable, as none of equall iudgment can yeelde him lesse prayse for hys excellent skyll and skylfull excellency shewed foorth in the same then they would to eyther *Theocritus* or *Virgill,* whom in mine opinion, if the coursenes of our speeche (I meane the course of custome which he woulde not infringe) had beene no more let vnto him then theyr pure natiue tongues were vnto them, he would haue (if it might be) surpassed them. What one thing is there in them so worthy admiration whereunto we may not adioyne some thing of his of equall desert? Take *Virgil* and make some little comparison betweene them, and iudge as ye shall see cause.

Virgill hath a gallant report of *Augustus* couertly comprysed in the first *Æglogue;* the like is in him of her Maiestie, vnder the name of *Eliza. Virgill* maketh a braue coloured complaint of vnstedfast freendshyppe in the person of *Corydon;* the lyke is him in his 5 *Æglogue.* Agayne, behold the pretty Pastorall contentions of *Virgill* in the third *Æglogue;* of him in the eight *Eglogue.* Finally, either in comparison with them, or respect of hys owne great learning, he may well were the Garlande, and steppe before the best of all English Poets that I haue seene or hearde; for I thinke no lesse "deserueth" (thus sayth *E. K.* in hys commendations) "hys wittinesse in deuising, his pithinesse in vttering, his complaintes of loue so louely, his discourses of pleasure so pleasantly, his Pastrall rudenes, his Morrall wysenesse, his due obseruing of *decorum* euery where, in personages, in season[s], in matter, in speeche, and generally in all seemely simplicity of handling hys matter and framing hys wordes." The occasion of his worke is a warning to other young men, who, being intangled in loue and youthful vanities, may learne to looke to themselues in time, and to auoyde inconueniences which may breede if they be not in time preuented. Many good Morrall lessons are therein contained, as the reuerence which young men owe to the aged, in the second *Eglogue:* the caueate or warning to beware a subtill professor of freendshippe, in the fift *Eglogue:* the commendation of good Pastors, and shame and disprayse of idle and ambitious Goteheardes, in the seauenth: the loose and retchlesse lyuing of Popish Prelates, in the ninth: the learned and sweete complaynt of the contempt of learning vnder the name of Poetry, in the tenth. There is also much matter vttered somewhat couertly, especially the abuses of some whom he would not be too playne withall: in which, though it be not apparent to euery one what hys speciall meaning was, yet so skilfully is it handled, as any man may take much delight at hys learned conueyance, and picke out much good sence in the most obscurest of it. Hys notable prayse deserued in euery parcell of that worke, because I cannot expresse as I woulde and as it should, I wyll cease to speake any more of, the rather because I neuer hearde as yet any that hath reade it, which hath not with much admiration commended it. One only thing therein haue I hearde some curious heades call in question, *viz:* the motion of some vnsauery loue, such as in the sixt *Eglogue* he seemeth to deale withall, which (say they) is skant allowable to English eares, and might well haue beene left for the Italian defenders of loathsome beastlines, of whom perhappes he learned it: to thys obiection I haue often aunswered (and I thinke truely) that theyr nyce opinion ouer shooteth the Poets meaning, who though hee in that as in other thinges immitateth the auncient Poets, yet doth not meane, no more did they before hym, any disordered loue, or the filthy lust of the deuillish *Pederastice* taken in the worse sence, but rather to shewe howe the dissolute life of young men, intangled in loue of women, doo neglect the freendshyp and league with their olde freendes and familiers. Why (say they) yet he shold gyue no occasion of suspition, nor offer to the viewe of Christians any token of such filthinesse, howe good soeuer hys meaning were: wherevnto I oppose the simple conceyte they haue of matters which concerne learning or wytt, wylling them to gyue Poets leaue to vse theyr vayne as they see good: it is their foolysh construction, not hys wryting that is blameable. Wee must prescrybe to no wryters (much lesse to Poets) in what sorte they should vtter theyr conceyts. But thys wyll be better discussed by some I hope of better abillity.

—"A Discourse of English Poetrie" (1586)

Thomas Nashe

AND SHOULD the challange of deepe conceit be intruded by any forrainer, to bring our English wits to the touchstone of Art, I would preferre diuine Master *Spencer,* the miracle of wit, to bandie line by line for my life, in the honour of England, against Spaine, France, Italy, and all the world.

—Preface to Greene's *Menaphon* (1589)

Sir Walter Ralegh

The prayse of meaner wits this worke like profit brings,
As doth the Cuckoes song delight when Philumena sings.
If thou hast formed right true vertues face herein:
Vertue her selfe can best discerne, to whom they writen bin.
If thou hast beauty praysd, let her sole lookes diuine
Iudge if ought therein be amis, and mend it by her eine.
If Chastitie want ought, or Temperaunce her dew,
Behold her Princely mind aright, and write thy Queene anew.
Meane while she shall perceiue, how far her vertues sore
Aboue the reach of all that liue, or such as wrote of yore:
And thereby will excuse and fauour thy good will:
Whose vertue can not be exprest, but by an Angels quill.
  Of me no lines are lou'd, nor letters are of price,
  Of all which speak our English tongue, but those of thy deuice.

—Dedicatory Sonnet to *The Faerie Queene* (1590)

Joseph Hall

But let no rebell *Satyre* dare traduce
Th'eternall *Legends* of thy *Faery Muse,*
Renowmed *Spencer:* whome no earthly wight
Dares once to emulate, much lesse dares despight.
Salust of *France* and *Tuscan Ariost,*
Yeeld vp the *Lawrell girlond* ye haue lost:

And let all others willow weare with mee,
Or let their vndeseruing *Temples* bared bee.
—*Virgidemiae* (1597)

The Return From Parnassus (anonymous)

Ingenioso: Good men and true, stand togither: heare your censure.
What's thy iudgement of *Spencer*?
Iudicio: A sweeter Swan then euer song in Poe,
A shriller Nightingale then euer blest
The prouder groues of selfe admiring Rome!
Blith was each vally, and each sheapeard proud,
While he did chaunt his rurall minstralsie;
Attentiue was full many a dainty eare;
Nay, hearers hong vpon his melting tong,
While sweetly of his Faiery Queene he song,
While to the waters fall he tun'd her fame,
And in each barke engrau'd Elizaes name.
And yet, for all this, vnregarding soile
Vnlac't the line of his desired life,
Denying mayntenance for his deare releife;
Carelesse ere to preuent his exequy,
Scarce deigning to shut vp his dying eye.
Ingenioso: Pity it is that gentler witts should breed,
Where thick skin chuffes laugh at a schollers need.
But softly may our honours ashes rest,
That lie by mery *Chaucers* noble chest.
—Part II (1601)

Michael Drayton

Grave morrall *Spencer* after these came on
Then whom I am perswaded there was none
Since the blind *Bard* his *Iliads* up did make,
Fitter a taske like that to undertake,
To set downe boldly, bravely to invent,
In all high knowledge, surely excellent.
—"Of Poets and Poesie" (1627)

Ben Jonson

Spencer, in affecting the Ancients, writ no Language: Yet I would have him read for his matter; but as *Virgil* read *Ennius.*
—*Timber* (1640)

John Milton

THAT VERTUE therefore which is but a youngling in the contemplation of evill, and knows not the utmost that vice promises to her followers, and rejects it, is but a blank vertue, not a pure; her whitenesse is but an excrementall whitenesse; Which was the reason why our sage and serious Poet *Spencer,* whom I dare be known to think a better teacher then *Scotus* or *Aquinas,* describing true temperance under the person of *Guion,* brings him in with his palmer through the cave of Mammon, and the bowr of earthly blisse that he might see and know, and yet abstain.

—*Areopagitica* (1644)

Sir William Davenant

Spencer MAY STAND here as the last of this short File of Heroick Poets; Men, whose intellectuals were of so great a making, (though some have thought them lyable to those few censures we have mention'd) as perhaps they will in worthy memory out-last even Makers of Laws, and Founders of Empires, and all but such as must therefore live equally with them, because they have recorded their Names; and consequently with their own hands led them to the Temple of Fame. And since we have dar'd to remember those exceptions which the Curious have against them; it will not be expected I should forget what is objected against *Spencer;* whose obsolete language we are constrain'd to mention, though it be grown the most vulgar accusation that is lay'd to his charge. . . . But this vulgar exception shall onely have the vulgar excuse; which is, that the unlucky choise of his *Stanza* hath by repetition of Rime brought him to the necessity of many exploded words.

If we proceed from his Language to his Argument, we must observe with others, that his noble and most artfull hands deserv'd to be employ'd upon matter of a more naturall, and therefore of a more usefull kind. His Allegoricall Story (by many held defective in the Connexion) resembling (me thinks) a continuance of extraordinary Dreams; such as excellent Poets, and Painters, by being overstudious, may have in the beginning of Feavers: And those morall visions are just of so much use to Humane application, as painted History, when with the cousenage of lights it is represented in Scenes, by which we are much lesse inform'd then by actions on the Stage.

—"A Discourse Upon *Gondibert*" (1650)

Abraham Cowley

BUT, HOW THIS LOVE OF POETRY came to be produced in me so early is a hard question: I believe I can tell the particular little chance that filled my head first with such Chimes of Verse, as have never since left ringing there: For I remember when I began to read, and to take some pleasure in it, there was wont to lie in my Mothers Parlour (I know not by what accident, for she her self never in her life read any Book but of Devotion) but there was wont to lie *Spencers* Works; this I happened to fall upon, and was infinitely delighted with the Stories of the Knights, and Giants, and Monsters, and brave Houses, which I found every where there: (Though my understanding had little to do with all this) and by degrees with the tinckling of the Rhyme and Dance of the Numbers, so that I think I had read him all over before I was twelve years old, and was thus made a Poet as irremediably as a Child is made an Eunuch.

—"Of Myself" (1656)

John Dryden

NOW IF IT MAY BE PERMITTED ME TO GO BACK AGAIN, to the Consideration of *Epique* Poetry, I have confess'd, that no Man hitherto has reach'd, or so much as approach'd to the Excellencies of *Homer* or of *Virgil; . . .* The *English* have only to boast of *Spencer* and *Milton,* who neither of them wanted either Genius, or Learning, to have been perfect Poets; and yet both of them are liable to many Censures. For there is no Uniformity in the Design of *Spencer:* He aims at the Accomplishment of no one Action: He raises up a Hero for every one of his Adventures; and endows each of them with some particular Moral Virtue, which renders them all equal, without Subordination or Preference. Every one is most Valiant in his own Legend; only we must do him that Justice to observe, that Magnanimity, which is the Character of Prince Arthur, shines throughout the whole Poem; and Succours the rest, when they are in Distress. The Original of every Knight, was then living in the Court of Queen *Elizabeth:* And he attributed to each of them that Virtue, which he thought was most conspicuous in them: An Ingenious piece of Flattery, tho' it turn'd not much to his Account. Had he liv'd to finish his Poem, in the six remaining Legends, it had certainly been more of a piece; but cou'd not have been perfect, because the Model was not true. But Prince *Arthur,* or his chief Patron, Sir *Philip Sidney,* whom he intended to make happy, by the Marriage of his *Gloriana,* dying before him, depriv'd the Poet, both of Means and Spirit, to accomplish his Design: For the rest, his Obsolete Language, and the ill choice of his Stanza, are faults but of the Second Magnitude: For notwithstanding the first he is still Intelligible, at least, after a little practice; and for the last, he is the more to be admir'd; that labouring under such a difficulty, his Verses are so Numerous, so Various, and so Harmonious, that only Virgil, whom he profestly imitated, has surpass'd him, among the *Romans;* and only Mr. *Waller* among the *English.*

—"Discourse on Satire" (1692)

Alexander Pope

. . . SPENSER has been ever a favourite poet to me: he is like a mistress, whose faults we see, but love her with them all.

—Letter to John Hughes (1715)

Thomas Warton

Thro Pope's soft song tho' all the Graces breathe,
And happiest art adorn his Attic page;
Yet does my mind with sweeter transport glow,
As at the root of mossy trunk reclin'd,
In magic *Spenser's* wildly-warbled song
I see deserted Una wander wide
Thro' wasteful solitudes, and lurid heaths,
Weary, forlorn; than when the fated fair
Upon the bosom bright of silver Thames
Launches in all the lustre of brocade,
Amid the splendors of the laughing Sun.

—"The Pleasures of Melancholy" (1747)

William Wordsworth

. . . And that gentle Bard,
Chosen by the Muses for their Page of State—
Sweet Spenser, moving through his clouded heaven
With the moon's beauty and the moon's soft pace,
I called him Brother, Englishman, and Friend!
—*The Prelude,* Book III (1850)

The name of Spenser, whose genius is of a higher order than even that of Ariosto, is at this day scarcely known beyond the limits of the British Isles. And if the value of his works is to be estimated from the attention now paid to them by his countrymen, compared with that which they bestow on those of some other writers, it must be pronounced small indeed.

The laurel meed of mighty conquerors
And poets *sage*

are his own words; but his wisdom has, in this particular, been his worst enemy; while its opposite, whether in the shape of folly or madness, has been *their* best friend. But he was a great power; and bears a high name: the laurel has been awarded to him.
—"Essay Supplementary to the Preface to *Lyrical Ballads*" (1815)

John Keats

SPENSER! a jealous honourer of thine,
A forester deep in thy midmost trees,
Did last eve ask my promise to refine
Some English that might strive thine ear to please.
But Elfin Poet 'tis impossible
For an inhabitant of wintry earth
To rise like Phoebus with a golden quill
Fire-wing'd and make a morning in his mirth.
It is impossible to escape from toil
O' the sudden and receive thy spiriting:
The flower must drink the nature of the soil
Before it can put forth its blossoming:
  Be with me in the summer days and I
  Will for thine honour and his pleasure try.
—Sonnet (1818)

Samuel Taylor Coleridge

YOU WILL TAKE especial note of the marvellous independence and true imaginative absence of all particular space or time in the Faery Queene. It is in the domains neither of history or geography; it is truly in land of Faery, that is, of mental space. The poet has placed you in a dream, a charmed sleep, and you neither wish, nor have the power, to inquire where you are, or how you got there. . . .

Lastly, the great and prevailing character of Spenser's mind is fancy under the conditions of imagination, as an ever present but not always active power. He has an imaginative fancy, but he has not imagination, in kind or degree, as Shakespeare and Milton have; the boldest effort of his powers in this way is the character of Talus. Add to this a feminine tenderness and almost maidenly purity of feeling, and above all, a deep moral earnestness which produces a believing sympathy and acquiescence in the reader, and you have a tolerably adequate view of Spenser's intellectual being.

—Lectures of 1818

Leigh Hunt

AN OLD LADY, to whom Pope one day read some passages out of Spenser's *Faerie Queene,* said that he had been entertaining her with a "gallery of pictures." Probably he had been reading some of the allegories, or the description of the pictures in the Enchanted Chamber; but the words would apply to the *Faerie Queene* in general. Spenser has been called, and justly, the "most poetical of poets"; not because his poetical faculty is in itself greater than that of some others, but because he is invariably, and (not to use the word in an invidious sense) *merely* poetical. His morals are deep or superficial, as the case may happen: they are those of the age. His politics are aristocratical, and are being daily refuted. But his delight in nature, in the voluptuous and the beautiful, is true and unceasing. The moment he enters upon his task, we see him, like a poetical boy let loose in a field, looking about with a determination to enjoy everything he beholds; to turn his back upon everything real, or what is exclusively called so, however he may pretend to bear it in mind; and to give himself up to the dreams of books, of romances, of mythology, of whatsoever is remote from the prose of human affairs.

But though Spenser beheld the beautiful with the eyes of a true and great poet, and could felicitously express its inner nature, there was an indolence and (not to speak it offensively) a sensuality in his temperament, resembling that of a man addicted to lying on the grass and weaving dreams of pleasure, which disposed him to content himself, if not with the surface of what he beheld, yet with the beauty of its forms and the vivacity of its colors; and hence, if in one sense of the word he is the most poetical of poets, he is in every sense the most pictorial of them—the painter of the poets—or, if you will, the poet for the painters; for while he has the power of conveying those impressions of the invisible, and illustrations of one thing by another, which are the innermost part of the magic of poetry, and the despair of its sister art, he is in the habit of soothing his senses and delighting his eyes by painting pictures as truly to be called such, as any that came from the hands of Titian and Raphael. It is easy to show that he took a painter's as well as poet's delight in color and form, lingering over his work for its corporeal and visible sake, studying contrasts and attitudes, touching and retouching, and filling in the minutest parts; in short, writing as if with a brush instead of a pen, and dipping with conscious eyes into a luxurious palette. Spenser's muse is dressed in the garments of a sister who is only less divine than herself; and the union of the two produces an enchantment, never perhaps to be perfectly met with elsewhere.

—"A New Gallery of Pictures" (1833)

William Butler Yeats

[SPENSER] was born in London in 1552, nineteen years after the death of Ariosto, and when Tasso was about eight years old. Full of the spirit of the Renaissance, at once passionate and artificial, looking out upon the world now as craftsman, now as connoisseur, he was to found his art upon theirs rather than upon the more humane, the more noble, the less intellectual art of Malory and the Minstrels. Deafened and blinded by their influence, as so many of us were in boyhood by that art of Hugo that made the old simple writers seem but as brown bread and water, he was always to love the journey more than its end, the landscape more than the man, and reason more than life, and the tale less than its telling. . . .

One cannot think that he should have occupied himself with moral and religious questions at all. He should have been content to be, as Emerson thought Shakespeare was, a Master of the Revels to mankind. I am certain that he never gets that visionary air which can alone make allegory real, except when he writes out of a feeling for glory and passion. He had no deep moral or religious life. He has never a line like Dante's "His Will is our Peace," or like Thomas à Kempis's "The Holy Spirit has liberated me from a multitude of opinions," or even like Hamlet's objection to the bare bodkin. He had been made a poet by what he had almost learnt to call his sins. If he had not felt it necessary to justify his art to some serious friend, or perhaps even to "that rugged forehead," he would have written all his life long, one thinks, of the loves of shepherdesses and shepherds, among whom there would have been perhaps the morals of the dovecot. One is persuaded that his morality is official and impersonal—a system of life which it was his duty to support—and it is perhaps a half understanding of this that has made so many generations believe that he was the first Poet Laureate, the first salaried moralist among the poets.

—*Poems of Spenser* (1902)

Virginia Woolf

THE QUESTION ASKS ITSELF how Spenser, himself imprisoned in so many impediments of circumstance, remote from us in time, in speech, in convention, yet seems to be talking about things that are important to us too? Compare, for example, his perfect gentleman with Tennyson's Arthur. Already, much in Tennyson's pattern is unintelligible; an easy butt for satire. Among living writers again, there is none who is able to display a typical figure. Each seems limited to one room of the human dwelling. But with Spenser, though here in this department of our being, we seem able to unlock the door and walk about. We miss certain intensities and details; but on the other hand we are uncabined. We are allowed to give scope to a number of interests, delights, curiosities, and loves that find no satisfaction in the poetry of our own time. But though it would be easy to frame a reason for this and to generalize about the decay of faith, the rise of machines, the isolation of the human being, let us, however, work from the opposite point of view. In reading *The Faery Queen* the first thing, we said, was that the mind has different layers. It brings one into play and then another. The desire of the eye, the desire of the body, desires for rhythm, movement, the desire for adventure—each is gratified. And this gratification depends upon the poet's own mobility. He is alive in all his parts. He scarcely seems to prefer one to another. We are reminded of the old myth of the body which has many organs, and the lesser and the obscure are as important as the kingly and important.

Here at any rate the poet's body seems all alive. A fearlessness, a simplicity that is like the movement of a naked savage possesses him. He is not merely a thinking brain; he is a feeling body, a sensitive heart. He has hands and feet, and, as he says himself, a natural chastity, so that some things are judged unfit for the pen. "My chaster muse for shame doth blush to write." In short, when we read *The Faery Queen,* we feel that the whole being is drawn upon, not merely a separate part.

—"The Faery Queen" (pub. 1948)

II. The Critics' Poet

William Hazlitt

On Chaucer and Spenser

. . . SPENSER, as well as Chaucer, was engaged in active life; but the genius of his poetry was not active: it is inspired by the love of ease, and relaxation from all the cares and business of life. Of all the poets, he is the most poetical. Though much later than Chaucer, his obligations to preceding writers were less. He has in some measure borrowed the plan of his poem (as a number of distinct narratives) from Ariosto; but he has engrafted upon it an exuberance of fancy, and an endless voluptuousness of sentiment, which are not to be found in the Italian writer. Farther, Spenser is even more of an inventor in the subject matter. There is an originality, richness, and variety in his allegorical personages and fictions, which almost vies with the splendor of the ancient mythology. If Ariosto transports us into the regions of romance, Spenser's poetry is all fairyland. In Ariosto, we walk upon the ground, in company, gay, fantastic, and adventurous enough. In Spenser, we wander in another world, among ideal beings. The poet takes and lays us in the lap of a lovelier nature, by the sound of softer streams, among greener hills and fairer valleys. He paints nature, not as we find it, but as we expected to find it; and fulfills the delightful promise of our youth. He waves his wand of enchantment—and at once embodies airy beings, and throws a delicious veil over all actual objects. The two worlds of reality and of fiction are poised on the wings of his imagination. His ideas, indeed, seem more distinct than his perceptions. He is the painter of abstractions, and describes them with dazzling minuteness. In the mask of Cupid he makes the god of love "clap on high his coloured winges *twain*": and it is said of Gluttony, in the Procession of the Passions, "In green vine leaves he was right fitly clad."

At times he becomes picturesque from his intense love of beauty; as where he compares Prince Arthur's crest to the appearance of the almond tree:

> Upon the top of all his lofty crest,
>   A bunch of hairs discolour'd diversely
> With sprinkled pearl and gold full richly drest,
>   Did shake and seem'd to daunce for jollity;
> Like to an almond tree ymounted high
>   On top of green Selenis all alone,
> With blossoms brave bedecked daintily;
>   Her tender locks do tremble every one
> At every little breath that under heav'n is blown.

The love of beauty, however, and not of truth, is the moving principle of his mind; and he is guided in his fantastic delineations by no rule but the impulse of an inexhaustible imagination. He luxuriates equally in scenes of Eastern magnificence, or the still solitude of a hermit's cell—in the extremes of sensuality, or refinement. . . .

The finest things in Spenser are, the character of Una, in the first book; the House of Pride; the Cave of Mammon, and the Cave of Despair; the account of Memory, of whom it is said, among other things,

> The wars he well remember'd of King Nine,
> Of old Assaracus and Inachus divine;

the description of Belphoebe; the story of Florimel and the Witch's son; the Gardens of Adonis, and the Bower of Bliss; the Mask of Cupid; and Colin Clout's vision, in the last book. But some people will say that all this may be very fine, but that they cannot understand it on account of the allegory. They are afraid of the allegory as if they thought it would bite them: they look at it as a child looks at a painted dragon, and think it will strangle them in its shining folds. This is very idle. If they do not meddle with the allegory, the allegory will not meddle with them. Without minding it at all, the whole is as plain as a pike-staff. It might as well be pretended that we cannot see Poussin's pictures for the allegory, as that the allegory prevents us from understanding Spenser. For instance, when Britomart, seated amidst the young warriors, lets fall her hair and discovers her sex, is it necessary to know the part she plays in the allegory, to understand the beauty of the following stanza?

> And eke that stranger knight amongst the rest
>   Was for like need enforc'd to disarray,
> Tho' when as vailed was her lofty crest,
>   Her golden locks that were in trammels gay
> Upbounden, did themselves adown display,
>   And raught unto her heels like sunny beams
> That in a cloud their light did long time stay;
>   Their vapour faded, shew their golden gleams,
> And through the persant air shoot forth their azure streams.

Or is there any mystery in what is said of Belphoebe, that her hair was sprinkled with flowers and blossoms which had been entangled in it as she fled through the woods? Or is it necessary to have a more distinct idea of Proteus than that which is given of him in his boat, with the frighted Florimel at his feet, while

> . . . the cold icicles from his rough beard
> Dropped adown upon her snowy breast!

. . . In reading these descriptions, one can hardly avoid being reminded of Rubens's allegorical pictures; but the account of Satyrane's taming the lion's whelps and lugging the bear's cubs along in his arms while yet an infant, whom his mother, so naturally, advises to "go seek some other play-fellows," has even more of this high picturesque character. Nobody but Rubens could have painted the fancy of Spenser; and he could not have given the sentiment, the airy dream that hovers over it!

With all this, Spenser neither makes us laugh nor weep. The only jest in his poem is an allegorical play upon words, where he describes Malbecco as escaping in the herd of goats, "by the help of his fayre horns on hight." But he has been unjustly charged with a want of passion and of strength. He has both in an immense degree. He has not indeed the pathos of immediate action or suffering, which is more properly the dramatic; but he has all the pathos of sentiment and romance—all that belongs to distant objects of terror, and uncertain, imaginary distress. His strength, in like manner, is not strength of will or action, of bone and muscle, nor is it coarse and palpable—but it assumes a character of vastness and sublimity, seen through the same visionary medium, and blended with the appalling associations of preternatural agency. We need only turn, in proof of this, to the Cave of Despair, or the Cave of Mammon, or to the account of the change of Malbecco into Jealousy. . . .

It is not fair to compare Spenser with Shakespeare, in point of interest. A fairer comparison would be with *Comus;* and the result would not be unfavorable to Spenser. There is only one work of the same allegorical kind, which has more interest than Spenser (with scarcely less imagination): and that is the *Pilgrim's Progress.* The three first books of the *Faerie Queene* are very superior to the three last. One would think that Pope, who used to ask if any one had ever read the *Faerie Queene* through, had only dipped into these last. The only things in them equal to the former are the account of Talus, the Iron Man, and the delightful episode of Pastorella.

The language of Spenser is full, and copious, to overflowing: it is less pure and idiomatic than Chaucer's, and is enriched and adorned with phrases borrowed from the different languages of Europe, both ancient and modern. He was, probably, seduced into a certain license of expression by the difficulty of filling up the molds of his complicated rhymed stanza from the limited resources of his native language. This stanza, with alternate and repeatedly recurring rhymes, is borrowed from the Italians. It was peculiarly fitted to their language, which abounds in similar vowel terminations, and is as little adapted to ours, from the stubborn, unaccommodating resistance which the consonant endings of the northern languages make to this sort of endless sing-song. Not that I would on that account part with the stanza of Spenser. We are, perhaps, indebted to this very necessity of finding out new forms of expression, and to the occasional faults to which it led, for a poetical language, rich and varied and magnificent beyond all former, and almost all later, example. His versification is, at once, the most smooth and the most sounding in the language. It is a labyrinth of sweet sounds, "in many a winding bout of linked sweetness long drawn out," that would cloy by their very sweetness, but that the ear is constantly relieved and enchanted by their continued variety of modulation—dwelling on the pauses of the action, or flowing on in a fuller tide of harmony with the movement of the sentiment. It has not the bold dramatic transitions of Shakespeare's blank verse, nor the high-raised tone of Milton's; but it is the perfection of melting harmony, dissolving the soul in pleasure, or holding it captive in the chains of suspense. Spenser was the poet of our waking dreams; and he has invented not only a language, but a music of his own for them. The undulations are infinite, like those of the waves of the sea: but the effect is still the same, lulling the senses into a deep oblivion of the jarring noises of the world, from which we have no wish to be ever recalled.

James Russell Lowell

Spenser

DURING THE PERIOD when Spenser was getting his artistic training, a great change was going on in our mother tongue, and the language of literature was disengaging itself more and more from that of ordinary talk. The poets of Italy, Spain, and France began to rain influence and to modify and refine not only style but vocabulary. Men were discovering new worlds in more senses than one, and the visionary finger of expectation still pointed forward. There was, as we learn from contemporary pamphlets, very much the same demand for a national literature that we have heard in America. This demand was nobly answered in the next generation. But no man contributed so much to the transformation of style and language as Spenser; for not only did he deliberately endeavor at reform, but by the charm of his diction, the novel harmonies of his verse, his ideal method of treatment, and the splendor of his fancy, he made the new manner popular and faithful. We can trace in Spenser's poems the gradual growth of his taste through experiment and failure to that assured self-confidence which indicates that he had at length found out the true bent of his genius,—that happiest of discoveries (and not so easy as it might seem) which puts a man in undisturbed possession of his own individuality. Before his time the boundary between poetry and prose had not been clearly defined. His great merit lies not only in the ideal treatment with which he glorified common things and gilded them with a ray of enthusiasm, but far more in the ideal point of view which he first revealed to his countrymen. He at first sought for that remoteness, which is implied in an escape from the realism of daily life, in the pastoral,—a kind of writing which, oddly enough, from its original intention as a protest in favor of naturalness, and of human as opposed to heroic sentiments, had degenerated into the most artificial of abstractions. But he was soon convinced of his error, and was not long in choosing between an unreality which pretended to be real and those everlasting realities of the mind which seem unreal only because they lie beyond the horizon of the everyday world, and become visible only when the mirage of fantasy lifts them up and hangs them in an ideal atmosphere. As in the old fairy tales, the task which the age imposes on its poet is to weave its straw into a golden tissue; and when every device has failed, in comes the witch Imagination, and with a touch the miracle is achieved, simple as miracles always are after they are wrought.

Spenser, like Chaucer a Londoner, was born in 1553. Nothing is known of his parents, except that the name of his mother was Elizabeth; but he was of gentle birth, as he more than once informs us, with the natural satisfaction of a poor man of genius at a time when the business talent of the middle class was opening to it the door of prosperous preferment. In 1569 he was entered as a sizar at Pembroke Hall, Cambridge, and in due course took his bachelor's degree in 1573, and his master's in 1576. He is supposed, on insufficient grounds, as it appears to me, to have met with some disgust or disappointment during his residence at the University.[1] Between 1576 and 1578 Spenser seems to have been with some of his kinsfolk "in the North." It was during this interval that he conceived his fruitless passion for the Rosalinde, whose jilting him for another shepherd, whom he calls Menalcas, is somewhat perfunctorily bemoaned in his pastorals. Before the publication of his *Shepherds Calender* in 1579, he had made the acquaintance of Sir Philip Sidney, and was domiciled with him for a time at Penshurst, whether as guest or literary dependant is uncertain. In October, 1579, he is in the household of the Earl of Leicester. In July, 1580, he accompanied Lord Grey de Wilton to Ireland as Secretary, and in that country he spent the rest of his life, with occasional flying visits to England to publish poems or in search of preferment. His residence in that country has been compared to that of Ovid in Pontus. And, no doubt, there were certain outward points of likeness. The Irishry by whom he was surrounded were to the full as savage, as hostile, and as tenacious of their ancestral habitudes as the Scythians [2] who made Tomi a prison, and the descendants of the earlier English settlers had degenerated as much as the Mix-Hellenes who disgusted the Latin poet. Spenser himself looked on his life in Ireland as a banishment. In his "Colin Clout's Come Home Again" he tells us that Sir Walter Ralegh, who visited him in 1589, and heard what was then finished of the *Faerie Queene,*

> 'Gan to cast great liking to my lore
> And great disliking to my luckless lot,
> That banisht had myself, like wight forlore,
> Into that waste, where I was quite forgot.
> The which to leave thenceforth he counselled me,
> Unmeet for man in whom was aught regardful,
> And wend with him his Cynthia to see,
> Whose grace was great and bounty most rewardful.

But Spenser was already living at Kilcolman Castle (which, with 3,028 acres of land from the forfeited estates of the Earl of Desmond, was confirmed to him by grant two years later), amid scenery at once placid and noble, whose varied charm he felt profoundly. He could not complain, with Ovid, "Non liber hic ullus, non qui mihi commodet aurem," for he was within reach of a cultivated society, which gave him the stimulus of hearty admiration both as poet and scholar. Above all, he was fortunate in a seclusion that prompted study and deepened meditation, while it enabled him to converse with his genius disengaged from those worldly influences which would have disenchanted it of its mystic enthusiasm, if they did not muddle it ingloriously away. Surely this sequestered nest was more congenial to the brooding of those ethereal visions of the *Faerie Queene* and to giving his "soul a loose" than

> The smoke, the wealth, and noise of Rome,
> And all the busy pageantry
> That wise men scorn and fools adore.

Yet he longed for London, if not with the homesickness of Bussy-Rabutin in exile from the Parisian sun, yet enough to make him joyfully accompany Ralegh thither in the early winter of 1589, carrying with him the first three books of the great poem begun ten years before. Horace's *nonum prematur in annum* had been more than complied with, and the success was answerable to the well-seasoned material and conscientious faithfulness of the work. But Spenser did not stay long in London to enjoy his fame. Seen close at hand, with its jealousies, intrigues, and selfish basenesses, the court had lost the enchantment lent by the distance of Kilcolman. A nature so prone to ideal contemplation as Spenser's would be profoundly shocked by seeing too closely the ignoble springs of contemporaneous policy, and learning by what paltry personal motives the noble opportunities of the world are at any given moment endangered. It is a sad discovery that history is so mainly made by ignoble men. . . .

Spenser once more visited England, bringing with him three more books of the *Faerie Queene,* in 1595. He is supposed to have remained there during the two following years. In 1594 he had been married to the lady celebrated in his somewhat artificial *amoretti.* By her he had four children. He was now at the height of his felicity; by universal acclaim the first poet of his age, and the one obstacle to his material advancement (if obstacle it was) had been put out of the way by the death of Lord Burleigh, August, 1598. In the next month he was recommended in a letter from Queen Elizabeth for the shrievalty of the county of Cork. But alas for Polycrates! In October the wild kerns and gallowglasses rose in no mood for sparing the house of Pindarus. They sacked and burned his castle, from which he with his wife and children barely escaped.[3] He sought shelter in London, and died there on the 16th January, 1599, at a tavern in King Street, Westminster. He was buried in the neighboring Abbey, next to Chaucer, at the cost of the Earl of Essex, poets bearing his pall and casting verses into his grave. . . .

There are two ways of measuring a poet, either by an absolute æsthetic standard, or relatively to his position in the literary history of his country and the conditions of his generation. Both should be borne in mind as coefficients in a perfectly fair judgment. If his positive merit is to be settled irrevocably by the former, yet an intelligent criticism will find its advantage not only in considering what he was, but what, under the given circumstances, it was possible for him to be.

The fact that the great poem of Spenser was inspired by the *Orlando* of Ariosto, and written in avowed emulation of it, and that the poet almost always needs to have his fancy set agoing by the hint of some predecessor, must not lead us to overlook his manifest claim to originality. It is not what a poet takes, but what he makes out of what he has taken, that shows what native force is in him. Above all, did his mind dwell complacently in those forms and fashions which in their very birth are already obsolescent, or was it instinctively drawn to those qualities which are permanent in language and whatever is wrought in it? There is much in Spenser that is contemporary and evanescent; but the substance of him is durable, and his work was the deliberate result of intelligent purpose and ample culture. The publication of his *Shepherds Calender* in 1579 (though the poem itself be of little interest) is one of the epochs in our literature. Spenser had at least the originality to see clearly and to feel keenly that it was essential to bring poetry back again to some kind of understanding with Nature. His immediate predecessors seem to have conceived of it as a kind of bird of paradise, born to float somewhere between heaven and earth, with no very well defined relation to either. It is true that the nearest approach they were able to make to this airy ideal was a shuttlecock, winged with a bright plume or so from Italy, but, after all, nothing but cork and feathers, which they bandied back and forth from one stanza to another, with the useful ambition of *keeping it up* as long as they could. To my mind the old comedy of *Gammer Gurton's Needle* is worth the whole of them. It may be coarse, earthy, but in reading it one feels that he is at least a man among men, and not a humbug among humbugs.

The form of Spenser's *Shepherds Calender,* it is true, is artificial, absurdly so if you look at it merely from the outside,—not, perhaps, the wisest way to look at anything, unless it be a jail or a volume of the *Congressional Globe,*—but the spirit of it is fresh and original. We have at last got over the superstition that shepherds and shepherdesses are any wiser or simpler than other people. We know that wisdom can be won only by wide commerce with men and books, and that simplicity, whether of manners or style, is the crowning result of the highest culture. But the pastorals of Spenser were very different things, different both in the moving spirit and the resultant form from the later ones of Browne or the *Piscatory Eclogues* of

Phineas Fletcher. And why? Browne and Fletcher wrote because Spenser had written, but Spenser wrote from a strong inward impulse —an instinct it might be called—to escape at all risks into the fresh air from that horrible atmosphere into which rhymer after rhymer had been pumping carbonic-acid gas with the full force of his lungs, and in which all sincerity was on the edge of suffocation. His longing for something truer and better was as honest as that which led Tacitus so long before to idealize the Germans, and Rousseau so long after to make an angel of the savage.

Spenser himself supremely overlooks the whole chasm between himself and Chaucer, as Dante between himself and Vergil. He called Chaucer master, as Milton was afterwards to call *him*. And, even while he chose the most artificial of all forms, his aim—that of getting back to Nature and life—was conscious, I have no doubt, to himself, and must be obvious to whoever reads with anything but the ends of his fingers. It is true that Sannazaro had brought the pastoral into fashion again, and that two of Spenser's are little more than translations from Marot; but for manner he instinctively turned back to Chaucer, the first and then only great English poet. He has given common instead of classic names to his personages, for characters they can hardly be called. Above all, he has gone to the provincial dialects for words wherewith to enlarge and freshen his poetical vocabulary.[4] I look upon the *Shepherds Calender* as being no less a conscious and deliberate attempt at reform than Thomson's *Seasons* were in the topics, and Wordsworth's *Lyrical Ballads* in the language of poetry. But the great merit of these pastorals was not so much in their matter as their manner. They show a sense of style in its larger meaning hitherto displayed by no English poet since Chaucer. Surrey had brought back from Italy a certain inkling of it, so far as it is contained in decorum. But here was a new language, a choice and arrangement of words, a variety, elasticity, and harmony of verse most grateful to the ears of men. If not passion, there was fervor, which was perhaps as near it as the somewhat stately movement of Spenser's mind would allow him to come. . . . But in general it is not so much the sentiments and images that are new as the modulation of the verses in which they float. The cold obstruction of two centuries thaws, and the stream of speech, once more let loose, seeks out its old windings, or overflows musically in unpractised channels. The service which Spenser did to our literature by this exquisite sense of harmony is incalculable. His fine ear, abhorrent of barbarous dissonance, his dainty tongue that loves to prolong the relish of a musical phrase, made possible the transition from the cast-iron stiffness of *Ferrex and Porrex* to the Damascus pliancy of Fletcher and Shakespeare. It was he that

> . . . Taught the dumb on high to sing,
> And heavy ignorance aloft to fly:
> That added feathers to the learned's wing,
> And gave to grace a double majesty.

I do not mean that in the *Shepherds Calender* he had already achieved that transmutation of language and meter by which he was afterwards to endow English verse with the most varied and majestic of stanzas, in which the droning old alexandrine, awakened for the first time to a feeling of the poetry that was in him, was to wonder, like M. Jourdain, that he had been talking prose all his life,—but already he gave clear indications of the tendency and premonitions of the power which were to carry it forward to ultimate perfection. . . .

Undoubtedly Spenser wished to be useful, and in the highest vocation of all, that of teacher, and Milton calls him "our sage and serious poet, whom I dare be known to think a better teacher than Scotus or Aquinas." And good Dr. Henry More was of the same mind.[5] I fear he makes his vices so beautiful now and then that we should not be very much afraid of them if we chanced to meet them; for he could not escape from his genius, which, if it led him as philosopher to the abstract contemplation of the beautiful, left him as poet open to every impression of sensuous delight. When he wrote the *Shepherds Calender* he was certainly a Puritan, and probably so by conviction rather than from any social influences or thought of personal interests. There is a verse, it is true, in the second of the two detached cantos of "Mutability," "Like that ungracious crew which feigns demurest grace," which is supposed to glance at the straiter religionists, and from which it has been inferred that he drew away from them as he grew older. It is very likely that years and widened experience of men may have produced in him their natural result of tolerant wisdom which revolts at the hasty destructiveness of inconsiderate zeal. But with the more generous side of Puritanism I think he sympathized to the last. His rebukes of clerical worldliness are in the Puritan tone, and as severe a one as any is in *Mother Hubberds Tale,* published in 1591.[6] There is an iconoclastic relish in his account of Sir Guyon's demolishing the Bower of Bliss that makes us think he would not have regretted the plundered abbeys as perhaps Shakespeare did when he speaks of the winter woods as "bare ruined choirs where late the sweet birds sang":

> But all those pleasant bowers and palace brave
> Guyon broke down with rigor pitiless,
> Ne ought their goodly workmanship might save
> Them from the tempest of his wrathfulness,
> But that their bliss he turned to balefulness;
> Their groves he felled, their gardens did deface,
> Their arbors spoil, their cabinets suppress,
> Their banquet-houses burn, their buildings rase,
> And of the fairest late now made the foulest place.

But whatever may have been Spenser's religious opinions (which do not nearly concern us here), the bent of his mind was toward a Platonic mysticism, a supramundane sphere where it could shape universal forms out of the primal elements of things, instead of being forced to put up with their fortuitous combinations in the unwilling material of mortal clay. He who, when his singing robes were on, could never be tempted nearer to the real world than under some subterfuge of pastoral or allegory, expatiates joyously in this untrammelled ether:

> Lifting himself out of the lowly dust
> On golden plumes up to the purest sky.

Nowhere does his genius soar and sing with such continuous aspiration, nowhere is his phrase so decorously stately, though rising to an enthusiasm which reaches intensity while it stops short of vehemence, as in his *Hymns to Love and Beauty,* especially the latter. There is an exulting spurn of earth in it, as of a soul just loosed from its cage.

I shall make no extracts from it, for it is one of those intimately coherent and transcendentally logical poems that "moveth altogether if it move at all," the breaking off a fragment from which would maim it as it would a perfect group of crystals. Whatever there is of sentiment and passion is for the most part purely disembodied and without sex, like that of angels,—a kind of poetry which has of late gone out of fashion, whether to our gain or not may be questioned. Perhaps one may venture to hint that the animal instincts are those that stand in least need of stimulation. Spenser's notions of love were so nobly pure, so far from those of our common ancestor who could hang by his tail, as not to disqualify him for achieving the quest of the Holy Grail, and accordingly it is not uninstructive to remember that he had drunk, among others, at French sources not yet deboshed with absinthe. Yet, with a purity like that of thrice-bolted snow, he had none of its coldness. He is, of all our poets, the most truly sensuous, using the word as Milton probably meant it when he said that poetry should be "simple, sensuous, and passionate." A poet is innocently sensuous when his mind permeates and illumines his senses; when they, on the other hand, muddy the mind, he becomes sensual. Every one of Spenser's senses was as exquisitely alive to the impressions of material, as every organ of his soul was to those of spiritual beauty. Accordingly, if he painted the weeds of sensuality at all, he could not help making them "of glorious feature." It was this, it may be suspected, rather than his "praising love," that made Lord Burleigh shake his "rugged forehead." Spenser's gamut, indeed, is a wide one, ranging from a purely corporeal delight in "precious odors fetched from far away" upward to such refinement as

> Upon her eyelids many graces sate
> Under the shadow of her even brows,

where the eye shares its pleasure with the mind. He is court-painter in ordinary to each of the senses in turn, and idealizes these frail favorites of his majesty King Lusty Juventus, till they half believe themselves the innocent shepherdesses into which he travesties them.

In his great poem he had two objects in view: first, the ephemeral one of pleasing the court, and then that of recommending himself to the permanent approval of his own and following ages as a poet, and especially as a moral poet. To meet the first demand, he lays the scene of his poem in contemporary England, and brings in all the leading personages of the day under the thin disguise of his knights and their squires and lady-loves. He says this expressly in the prologue to the second book:

> Of Faery Land yet if he more inquire,
> By certain signs, here set in sundry place,
> He may it find; . . .
> And thou, O fairest princess under sky,
> In this fair mirror mayst behold thy face
> And thine own realms in land of Faery.

Many of his personages we can still identify, and all of them were once as easily recognizable as those of Mademoiselle de Scudéry. This, no doubt, added greatly to the immediate piquancy of the allusions. The interest they would excite may be inferred from the fact that King James, in 1596, wished to have the author prosecuted and punished for his indecent handling of his mother, Mary Queen of Scots, under the name of Duessa.[7] To suit the wider application of his plan's other and more important half, Spenser made all his characters double their parts, and appear in his allegory as the impersonations of abstract moral qualities. When the cardinal and theological virtues tell Dante, "Noi siam qui ninfe e in ciel siamo stelle," the sweetness of the verse enables the fancy, by a slight gulp, to swallow without solution the problem of being in two places at the same time. But there is something fairly ludicrous in such a duality as that of Prince Arthur and the Earl of Leicester, Arthegall and Lord Grey, and Belphœbe and Elizabeth.

> In this same interlude it doth befall
> That I, one Snout by name, present a wall.

The reality seems to heighten the improbability, already hard enough to manage. But Spenser had fortunately almost as little sense of humor as Wordsworth, or he could never have carried his poem on with enthusiastic good faith so far as he did. It is evident that to him the land of Faery was an unreal world of picture and illusion, "The world's sweet inn from pain and wearisome turmoil," in which he could shut himself up from the actual, with its shortcomings and failures:

> The ways through which my weary steps I guide
> In this delightful land of Faery
> Are so exceeding spacious and wide,
> And sprinkled with such sweet variety
> Of all that pleasant is to ear and eye,
> That I, nigh ravisht with rare thoughts' delight,
> My tedious travail do forget thereby,
> And, when I 'gin to feel decay of might,
> It strength to me supplies, and cheers my dullëd spright.

Spenser seems here to confess a little weariness; but the alacrity of his mind is so great that, even where his invention fails a little, we do not share his feeling nor suspect it, charmed as we are by the variety and sweep of his measure, the beauty or vigor of his similes, the musical felicity of his diction, and the mellow versatility of his pictures. In this last quality Ariosto, whose emulous pupil he was, is as Bologna to Venice in the comparison. That, when the personal allusions have lost their meaning and the allegory has become a burden, the book should continue to be read with delight, is proof enough, were any wanting, how full of life and light and the other-worldliness of poetry it must be. As a narrative it has, I think, every fault of which that kind of writing is capable. The characters are vague, and, even were they not, they drop out of the story so often and remain out of it so long, that we have forgotten who they are when we meet them again; the episodes hinder the advance of the action instead of relieving it with variety of incident or novelty of situation; the plot, if plot it may be called,

> . . . That shape has none
> Distinguishable in member, joint, or limb,

recalls drearily our ancient enemy, the Metrical Romance; while the fighting, which in those old poems was tediously sincere, is between shadow and shadow, where we know that neither can harm the other, though we are tempted to wish he might. Hazlitt bids us not mind the allegory, and says that it won't bite us nor meddle with us if we do not meddle with it. But how if it bore us, which after all is the fatal question? The truth is that it is too often forced upon us against our will, as people were formerly driven to church till they began to look on a day of rest as a penal institution, and to transfer to the Scriptures that suspicion of defective inspiration which was awakened in them by the preaching. The true type of the allegory is the *Odyssey,* which we read without suspicion as pure poem, and then find a new pleasure in divining its double meaning, as if we somehow got a better bargain of our author than he meant to give us. But this complex feeling must not be so exacting as to prevent our lapsing into the old *Arabian Nights* simplicity of interest again. The moral of a poem should be suggested, as when in some medieval church we cast down our eyes to muse over a fresco of Giotto, and are reminded of the transitoriness of life by the mortuary tablets under our feet. The vast superiority of Bunyan over Spenser lies in the fact that we help make his allegory out of our own experience. Instead of striving to embody abstract passions and temptations, he has given us his own in all their pathetic simplicity. He is the Ulysses of his own prose-epic. This is the secret of his power and his charm, that, while the representation of what *may* happen to all men comes home to none of us in particular, the story of any one man's real experience finds its startling parallel in that of every one of us. The very homeliness of Bunyan's names and the every-dayness of his scenery, too, put us off our guard, and we soon find ourselves on as easy a footing with his allegorical beings as we might be with Adam or Socrates in a dream. Indeed, he has prepared us for such incongruities by telling us at setting out that the story was of a dream. The long nights of Bedford jail had so intensified his imagination, and made the figures with which it peopled his solitude so real to him, that the creatures of his mind become *things,* as clear to the memory as if we had seen them. But Spenser's are too often mere names, with no bodies to back them, entered on the Muses' muster-roll by the specious trick of personification. There is, likewise, in Bunyan, a childlike simplicity and taking-for-granted which win our confidence. His Giant Despair,[8] for example, is by no means the Ossianic figure into which artists who mistake the vague for the sublime have misconceived it. He is the ogre of the fairy tales, with his malicious wife; and he comes forth to us from those regions of early faith and wonder as something beforehand accepted by the imagination. These figures of Bunyan's are already familiar inmates of the mind, and, if there be any sublimity in him, it is the daring frankness of his verisimilitude. Spenser's giants are those of the later romances, except that grand figure with the balances in the second canto of Book V, the most original of all his conceptions, yet no real giant, but a pure eidolon of the mind. As Bunyan rises not seldom to a natural poetry, so Spenser sinks now and then, through the fault of his topics, to unmistakable prose. Take his description of the House of Alma, for instance:

> The master cook was cald Concoctiön,
> A careful man, and full of comely guise;
> The kitchen-clerk, that hight Digestiön,
> Did order all the achates in seemly wise.

And so on through all the organs of the body. The author of Ecclesiastes understood these matters better in that last pathetic chapter of his, blunderingly translated as it apparently is. This, I admit, is the worst failure of Spenser in this kind; though, even here, when he gets on to the organs of the mind, the enchantments of his fancy and style come to the rescue and put us in good humor again, hard as it is to conceive of armed knights entering the chamber of the mind, and talking with such visionary damsels as Ambition and Shamefastness. Nay, even in the most prosy parts, unless my partiality deceive me, there is an infantile confidence in the magical powers of Prosopopœia which half beguiles us, as of children who *play* that everything is something else, and are quite satisfied with the transformation.

The problem for Spenser was a double one: how to commend poetry at all to a generation which thought it effeminate trifling,[9] and how he, Master Edmund Spenser, of imagination all compact, could commend *his* poetry to Master John Bull, the most practical of mankind in his habitual mood, but at that moment in a passion of religious anxiety about his soul. *Omne tulit punctum qui miscuit utile dulci* was not only an irrefragable axiom because a Latin poet had said it, but it exactly met the case in point. He would convince the scorners that poetry might be seriously useful, and show Master Bull his new way of making fine words butter parsnips, in a rhymed moral primer. Allegory, as then practised, was imagination adapted for beginners, in words of one syllable and illustrated with cuts, and would thus serve both his ethical and pictorial purpose. Such a primer, or a first intallment of it, he proceeded to put forth; but he so bordered it with bright-colored fancies, he so often filled whole pages and crowded the text hard in others with the gay frolics of his pencil, that, as in the Grimani missal, the holy function of the book is forgotten in the ecstasy of its adornment. Worse than all, does not his brush linger more lovingly along the rosy contours of his sirens than on the modest wimples of the Wise Virgins? "The general end of the book," he tells us in his Dedication to Sir Walter Ralegh, "is to fashion a gentleman of noble person in virtuous and gentle discipline." But a little further on he evidently has a qualm, as he thinks how generously he had interpreted his promise of cuts: "To some I know this method will seem displeasant, which had rather have good discipline delivered plainly in way of precepts or sermoned at large, as they use, than thus cloudily enwrapped in allegorical devices." Lord Burleigh was of this way of thinking, undoubtedly, but how could poor Clarion help it? Has he not said,

> And whatso else *of virtue good or ill,*
> Grew in this garden, fetcht from far away,
> Of every one he takes and tastes at will,
> And on their pleasures greedily doth prey?

One sometimes feels in reading him as if he were the pure sense of the beautiful incarnated to the one end that he might interpret it to our duller perceptions. So exquisite was his sensibility, that with him sensation and intellection seem identical, and we "can almost say his body thought." This subtle interfusion of sense with spirit it is that gives his poetry a crystalline purity without lack of warmth. He is full of feeling, and yet of such a kind that we can neither say it is mere intellectual perception of what is fair and good, nor yet associate it with that throbbing fervor which leads us to call sensibility by the physical name of heart.

Charles Lamb made the most pithy criticism of Spenser when he called him the poets' poet. We may fairly leave the allegory on one side, for perhaps, after all, he adopted it only for the reason that it was in fashion, and put it on as he did his ruff, not because it was becoming, but because it was the only wear. The true use of him is as a gallery of pictures which we visit as the mood takes us, and where we spend an hour or two at a time, long enough to sweeten our perceptions, not so long as to cloy them. He makes one think always of Venice; for not only is his style Venetian, but as the gallery there is housed in the shell of an abandoned convent, so his in that of a deserted allegory. And again, as at Venice you swim in a gondola from Gian Bellini to Titian, and from Titian to Tintoret, so in him, where other cheer is wanting, the gentle sway of his measure, like the rhythmical impulse of the oar, floats you lullingly along from picture to picture.

> If all the pens that ever poet held
> Had fed the feeling of their master's thoughts,
> And every sweetness that inspired their hearts
> Their minds and muses on admirëd themes,
> If all the heavenly quintessence they still
> From their immortal flowers of poesy,
> If these had made one poem's period,
> And all combined in beauty's worthiness;
> Yet should there hover in their restless heads
> One thought, one grace, one wonder at the best,
> Which into words no virtue can digest.[10]

Spenser at his best has come as near to expressing this unattainable something as any other poet. He is so purely poet that with him the meaning does not so often modulate the music of the verse as the music makes great part of the meaning and leads the thought along its pleasant paths. No poet is so splendidly superfluous as he; none knows so well that in poetry enough is not only not so good as a feast, but is a beggarly parsimony. He spends himself in a careless abundance only to be justified by incomes of immortal youth. . . .

His natural tendency is to shun whatever is sharp and abrupt. He loves to prolong emotion, and lingers in his honeyed sensations like a bee in the translucent cup of a lily. So entirely are beauty and delight in it the native element of Spenser, that, whenever in the *Faerie Queene* you come suddenly on the moral, it gives you a shock of unpleasant surprise, a kind of grit, as when one's teeth close on a bit of gravel in a dish of strawberries and cream. He is the most fluent of our poets. Sensation passing through emotion into revery is a prime quality of his manner. And to read him puts one in the condition of revery, a state of mind in which our thoughts and feelings float motionless, as one sees fish do in a gentle stream, with just enough vibration of their fins to keep themselves from going down with the current, while their bodies yield indolently to all its soothing curves. He chooses his language for its rich canorousness rather than for intensity of meaning. To characterize his style in a single word, I should call it *costly*. None but the daintiest and nicest phrases will serve him, and he allures us from one to the other with such cunning baits of alliteration, and such sweet lapses of verse, that never any word seems more eminent than the rest, nor detains the feeling to eddy around it, but you must go on to the end before you have time to stop and muse over the wealth that has been lavished on you. . . .

In the world into which Spenser carries us there is neither time nor space, or rather it is outside of and independent of them both, and so is purely ideal, or, more truly, imaginary; yet it is full of form, color, and all earthly luxury, and so far, if not real, yet apprehensible by the senses. There are no men and women in it, yet it throngs with airy and immortal shapes that have the likeness of men and women, and hint at some kind of foregone reality. Now this place, somewhere between mind and matter, between soul and sense, between the actual and the possible, is precisely the region which Spenser assigns (if I have rightly divined him) to the poetic susceptibility of impression, "To reign in the air from the earth to highest sky." Underneath every one of the senses lies the soul and spirit of it, dormant till they are magnetized by some powerful emotion. Then whatever is imperishable in us recognizes for an instant and claims kindred with something outside and distinct from it, yet in some inconceivable way a part of it, that flashes back on it an ideal beauty which impoverishes all other companionship. This exaltation with which love sometimes subtilizes the nerves of coarsest men so that they feel and see, not the thing as it seems to others, but the beauty of it, the joy of it, the soul of eternal youth that is in it, would appear to have been the normal condition of Spenser. While the senses of most men live in the cellar, his "were laid in a large upper chamber which opened toward the sunrising." . . .

Other poets have held their mirrors up to Nature, mirrors that differ very widely in the truth and beauty of the images they reflect; but Spenser's is a magic glass in which we see few shadows cast back from actual life, but visionary shapes conjured up by the wizard's art from some confusedly remembered past or some impossible future; it is like one of those still pools of medieval legend which covers some sunken city of the antique world; a reservoir in which all our dreams seem to have been gathered. As we float upon it, we see that it pictures faithfully enough the summer clouds that drift over it, the trees that grow about its margin, but in the midst of these shadowy echoes of actuality we catch faint tones of bells that seem blown to us from beyond the horizon of time, and looking down into the clear depths, catch glimpses of towers and far-shining knights and peerless dames that waver and are gone. Is it a world that ever was, or shall be, or can be, or but a delusion? Spenser's world, real to him, is real enough for us to take a holiday in, and we may well be content with it when the earth we dwell on is so often too real to allow of such vacations. It is the same kind of world that Petrarca's Laura has walked in for five centuries with all ears listening for the music of her footfall.

The land of Spenser is the land of Dream, but it is also the land of Rest. To read him is like dreaming awake, without even the trouble of doing it yourself, but letting it be done for you by the finest dreamer that ever lived, who knows how to color his dreams like life and make them move before you in music. . . .

Three of Spenser's own verses best characterize the feeling his poetry gives us:

> Among wide waves set like a little nest,
> Wrapt in eternal silence far from enemies,
> The world's sweet inn from pain and wearisome turmoil.

We are wont to apologize for the grossness of our favorite authors sometimes by saying that their age was to blame and not they; and the excuse is a good one, for often it is the frank word that shocks us while we tolerate the thing. Spenser needs no such extenuations. No man can read the *Faerie Queene* and be anything but the better for it. Through that rude age, when Maids of Honor drank beer for breakfast and Hamlet could say a gross thing to Ophelia, he passes serenely abstracted and high, the Don Quixote of poets. Whoever can endure unmixed delight, whoever can tolerate music and painting and poetry all in one, whoever wishes to be rid of thought and to let the busy anvils of the brain be silent for a time, let him read in the *Faerie Queene*. There is the land of pure heart's ease, where no ache or sorrow of spirit can enter.

Notes

1. This has been inferred from a passage in one of Gabriel Harvey's letters to him. But it would seem more natural, from the many allusions in Harvey's pamphlets against Nash, that it was his own wrongs which he had in mind, and his self-absorption would take it for granted that Spenser sympathized with him in all his grudges. Harvey is a remarkable instance of the refining influence of classical studies. Amid the pedantic farrago of his omni-sufficiency (to borrow one of his own words) we come suddenly upon passages whose gravity of sentiment, stateliness of movement, and purity of diction remind us of Landor. These lucid intervals in his overweening vanity explain and justify the friendship of Spenser. Yet the reiteration of emphasis with which he insists on all the world's knowing that Nash had called him an ass, probably gave Shakespeare the hint for one of the most comic touches in the character of Dogberry.

2. In his prose tract on Ireland, Spenser, perhaps with some memory of Ovid in his mind, derives the Irish mainly from the Scythians.

3. Ben Jonson told Drummond that one child perished in the flames. But he was speaking after an interval of twenty-one years, and, of course, from hearsay. Spenser's misery was exaggerated by succeeding poets, who used him to point a moral, and from the shelter of his tomb launched many a shaft of sarcasm at an unappreciative public. Phineas Fletcher in his *Purple Island* (a poem which reminds us of the *Faerie Queene* by the supreme tediousness of its allegory, but in nothing else) set the example in the best verse he ever wrote: "Poorly, poor man, he lived; poorly, poor man, he died." Gradually this poetical tradition established itself firmly as authentic history. Spenser could never have been poor, except by comparison. The whole story of his later days has a strong savor of legend. He must have had ample warning of Tyrone's rebellion, and would

probably have sent away his wife and children to Cork, if he did not go thither himself. I am inclined to think that he did, carrying his papers with him, and among them the two cantos of *Mutability,* first published in 1611. These, it is most likely, were the only ones he ever completed, for, with all his abundance, he was evidently a laborious finisher. When we remember that ten years were given to the elaboration of the first three books, and that five more elapsed before the next three were ready, we shall waste no vain regrets on the six concluding books supposed to have been lost by the carelessness of an imaginary servant on their way from Ireland.

4. Sir Philip Sidney did not approve of this: "That same framing of his style to an old rustic language I dare not allow, since neither Theocritus in Greek, Vergil in Latin, nor Sannazaro in Italian did affect it." (*Defence of Poesy.*) Ben Jonson, on the other hand, said that Guarini "kept not decorum in making shepherds speak as well as himself could." (*Conversations with Drummond.*) I think Sidney was right, for the poets' Arcadia is a purely ideal world, and should be treated accordingly. But whoever looks into the glossary appended to the *Calender* by E. K. will be satisfied that Spenser's object was to find unhackneyed and poetical words rather than such as should seem more on a level with the speakers. See also the *Epistle Dedicatory.* I cannot help thinking that E. K. was Spenser himself, with occasional interjections of Harvey. Who else could have written such English as many passages in this *Epistle*?

5. [Henry More (1614–1687), poet and philosopher, who called *The Faerie Queene* "as richly fraught with divine Morality as Phansy"—ed.]

6. Ben Jonson told Drummond "that in that paper Sir W. Ralegh had of the allegories of his *Faerie Queene* by the Blatant Beast the Puritans were understood." But this is certainly wrong. There were very different shades of Puritanism, according to individual temperament. That of Winthrop and Higginson had a mellowness of which Endicott and Standish were incapable. The gradual change of Milton's opinions was similar to that which I suppose in Spenser. The passage in *Mother Hubberd* may have been aimed at the Protestant clergy of Ireland (for he says much the same thing in his *View of the State of Ireland*), but it is general in its terms.

7. Had the poet lived longer, he might perhaps have verified his friend Ralegh's saying, that "whosoever in writing modern history shall follow truth too near the heels, it may haply strike out his teeth." The passage is one of the very few disgusting ones in the *Faerie Queene*. Spenser was copying Ariosto; but the Italian poet, with the discreeter taste of his race, keeps to generalities. Spenser goes into particulars which can only be called nasty. He did this, no doubt, to pleasure his mistress, Mary's rival; and this gives us a measure of the brutal coarseness of contemporary manners. It becomes only the more marvelous that the fine flower of his genius could have transmuted the juices of such a soil into the purity and sweetness which are its own peculiar properties.

8. Bunyan probably took the hint of the Giant's suicidal offer of "knife, halter, or poison," from Spenser's "swords, ropes, poison," in *Faerie Queene,* Bk. I. C. ix. I.

9. See Sidney's *Defence,* and Puttenham's *Art of English Poesy,* I.viii.

10. Marlowe's *Tamburlaine,* Part I. Act V. 2.

III. The Scholars' Poet

Edward Dowden

Spenser, the Poet and Teacher

IN ENGLAND of the age of Elizabeth what place is filled by the poetry of Spenser? What blank would be made by its disappearance? In what, for each of us who love that poetry, resides its special virtue? Shall we say in answer to these questions that Spenser is the weaver of spells, the creator of illusions, the enchanter of the Elizabethan age; and that his name is to us a word of magic by which we conjure away the pain of actual life, and obtain entrance into a world of faery? Was Spenser, as a poet of our own time names himself, "the idle singer" of his day—that day not indeed "an empty day," but one filled with heroic daring and achievement? While Ralegh was exploring strange streams of the New World, while Drake was chasing the Spaniard, while Bacon was seeking for the principles of a philosophy which should enrich man's life, while Hooker, with the care of a wise master-builder, was laying the foundation of polity in the national Church, where was Spenser? Was he forgetful of England, forgetful of earth, lulled and lying in some bower of fantasy, or moving in a dream among imaginary champions of chivalry, distressed damsels, giants and dragons and satyrs and savage men, or shepherds who pipe and shepherdesses who dance for ever in a serene Arcady?

Assuredly it was not thus that a great Englishman of a later age thought of Spenser. When Milton entered upon his manhood, he entered upon a warfare; the peaceful Horton days, days of happy in-gathering of varied culture, days of sweet repose amid rural beauty, were past and gone; and he stood with loins girt, prepared for battle on behalf of liberty. And then, in London, when London was a vast arsenal in which weapons were forging for the defence of truth and freedom, Milton in his moment of highest and most masculine ardor, as he wrote his speech on behalf of unlicensed printing, thought of Spenser. It was not as a dreamer that Milton thought of him. Spenser had been a power with himself in youth, when he, "the lady of his college," but such a lady as we read of in *Comus,* grew in virginal beauty and virginal strength. He had listened to Spenser's "sage and solemn tunes,"

> Of turneys and of trophies hung;
> Of forests and enchantments drear,
> Where more is meant than meets the ear.

And now, in his manhood, when all of life has grown for him so grave, so glorious with heroic effort, Milton looks back and remembers his master, and he remembers him not as an idle singer, not as a dreamer of dreams, but as "our sage and serious Spenser, whom I dare to name a better teacher than Scotus or Aquinas."

A teacher—what is the import of this? "The true use of Spenser," says a poet of our own day, Mr. J. R. Lowell, "is as a gallery of pictures which we visit as the mood takes us, and where we spend an hour or two at a time, long enough to sweeten our perceptions, not so long as to cloy them." And again: "Whenever in the *Faerie Queene* you come suddenly on the moral, it gives you a shock of unpleasant surprise, a kind of grit, as when one's teeth close on a bit of gravel in a dish of strawberries and cream." This, then, is the *Faerie Queene*—a dish of strawberries and cream mixed up unfortunately with a good deal of grit. And as for the allegory, we may "fairly leave it on one side"; [1] Spenser employed it to "convince the scorners that poetry might be seriously useful, and show Master Bull his new way of making fine words butter parsnips, in a rhymed moral primer." Shall we accept this view, or that of Milton—"a better teacher than Scotus or Aquinas"? Was Spenser such a teacher "sage and serious" to his own age? If so, does he remain such a teacher for this age of ours?

Let us put the question in another way, and inquire, What was the highest function which an English poet in the second half of the sixteenth century could fulfill? The death of the medieval world and the birth of the modern world had been the achievements of Italy. In Italy the fire of intellectual life had been gathered as on a hearth, and its flame leaped highest; it was from Italy that the light and warmth diffused themselves to other lands. To Italian seamen we owe the discovery of the New World: Columbus was a Genoese, John Cabot was a Venetian. To Italian students we owe the rediscovery of the Old World of classical art, poetry, and eloquence. The great thinkers of Greece were no longer denaturalized in the interests of an effete scholastic system; the pillars of the Parthenon were not employed to prop the crumbling walls of a chapter-house. Plato became at least an equal master with Aristotle, and in Plato the humanists found that beauty and enthusiasm which were needed to arouse and satisfy the imaginative reason. At the same time the architecture of Italy passed from its period of free and varied experiment—experiment nobly inventive—to its period of fulfilled attainment. To the first thirty years of the sixteenth century belong the painters who represent the culmination of the great art-movement of Italy. Life in that southern land seemed like a blossoming plant with petals deep of dye and rich in floating perfume; like a flame, swift, delicate, and aspiring.

But there was a dark side to the Italian Renaissance. The Church and the world had alike too much forgotten that true humanism includes a noble morality. In Rome, at the heart of Christendom, were fraud, avarice, ambition, violence, foul living, effeminacy. And the Church possessed no monopoly of vices. A tendency to materialism in philosophy coincided in point of time with a practical cynicism as to what is most spiritual in human conduct and character. Sensuality was elaborated into an art. "The immorality of the Italians," says Mr. Symonds, making a just distinction, "was not that of beasts; it rather resembled that of devils."

In such a moral environment had appeared for a short time a man possessed by the old prophetic fire. Over against Lorenzo, with his splendor and his culture, arose the face—a brand under the darkness of the cowl—and the harsh condemnatory voice of Savonarola. It was no part of Savonarola's mission to assail, like Luther, the dogma of the Church; he was a reformer of morals, not of faith; and he remained a monk. He came as a prophet to announce a judgment. When his voice rang in the Duomo "the walls re-echoed with sobs and wailings." The painter could no longer paint, the man of culture could no longer trifle, while the awful issues of life and death were pending. Fra Bartolommeo bore his studies of the nude to the pyre, and flung them among the other vanities doomed to destruction. Pico della Mirandula, the young scholar who at thirty had mastered all learning, shuddered as he listened to the voice of the preacher; he forsook the world, and wore the frock and hood of St. Dominic. So wrought on tender and beautiful souls the truths set forth by Savonarola. But Savonarola fell; Christ was no longer king of Florence, and Italy went its way to an age of impotence and shame.

Now the question arose, "How is this revival of learning, this new enthusiasm about beauty, this new and strong delight in man and in the life of man, to fare with the nations of the North?" Will those nations side with Lorenzo and the humanists, or with Savonarola and his Puritans? Or is it possible to reconcile these two contending forces? . . .

Might it not be that some man at once of fine imaginative genius and of fine moral temper was destined to arise, who should bring into harmony the best elements of the religious movement and the best elements of the artistic movement? Some preparation, as it were, for the advent of such a writer had been made. The question between the churches in England was virtually settled; the nation, working in its own large practical way, had found a faith. An Englishman born about the middle of the sixteenth century might enter upon a heritage of belief; the moral and spiritual forces of the time were organized, and were strong; they had not yet stiffened into conventions or decayed into traditions. It was in some respects a happy time for a young man of aspiring moral temper. From day to day the national life of England was mounting to the fullness of the flood. In the Queen the nation had found an ideal center; loyalty to her became identical with loyalty to England. Much of the homage which at first strikes us as servility was like the devotion of a soldier to his banner: on the English banner was inscribed "Elizabeth." The overgrown power of Spain lay open to attack like a huge galleon hung upon by some persistent and persecuting seadog. The spirit of adventure and enterprise was astir. In the little seaports bronzed mariners told marvelous tales of islands in far ocean, and trackless rivers, and mines of silver, and a city of gold. In town and country there was more of mirth and merrymaking than had been known since Chaucer's pilgrims jingled their reins Canterburyward. The great nobles gathered around their sovereign, and were proud to bear their part in the pageantry of a court. Gay fashions of dress were imported from the Continent. Ideas were attired in fantastic forms of speech on the lips of peeress and of page: when the tide of life runs free it must have its little laughing eddies. We know how, in the history of an individual man or woman, when shock has followed shock of anguish or of joy, if these do not overwhelm and crush the spirit, they render it coherent and ardent, they transform it from a state of cold abstraction into one molten, glowing mass. So it was with the English nation in the sixteenth century: shock had followed shock; it passed from its period of struggle and pain, of hesitancy and division, to a period of coherence and ardor, when it became natural to think greatly of man, to have a passionate faith in human goodness, a passionate apprehension of evil, to hope high things, to dare and to achieve noble and arduous things.

The time had come for England to possess her poet. It could not be a matter of doubt after the year 1579 who that poet was. Spenser did not introduce himself to the world with a fanfare of trumpets, as about to celebrate a triumph. He did not even place his name upon the title-page of the *Shepherds Calender*. He styled himself "Immerito" (the Undeserving):

> I never list presume on Parnasse hill,
> But piping low in shade of lowly grove
> I play to please myself, all be it ill.

Yet he could not but be conscious of high powers; and the friend who introduced the volume to English readers, while commenting on the author's diffidence in choosing the pastoral form, compares him to a young bird who proves his wings before making a higher and wider flight: "So flew Vergil, as not yet well feeling his wings. So flew Mantuane, as not being full sumd. So Petrarque. So Boccace."

In the *Shepherds Calender* we discern much of the future writer of the *Faerie Queene*. It contains the poetical record of his personal griefs as a lover; it expresses his enthusiasm for his art as a poet; his loyalty to the crown as a servant of the Queen; his loyalty to the

Reformation as an English churchman; his delight in natural beauty, and in the fairness of woman. It is now gay and sportive, now staid and serious; sensuous ardor and moral wisdom are united in it; the allegorical form in miniature is already employed; it exhibits a mode of idealized treatment of contemporary public affairs not dissimilar in essentials from that afterwards put to use in his romantic epic. The pastoral, with its ideals of peace and simplicity, possessed a singular charm for Europe in the high-wrought and artificial age of the Renaissance. It had a charm for Spenser; but his is not the Arcadian pastoral of Sannazaro and Sidney. Colin and Cuddie keep their flocks upon the hills of Kent; the disdainful Rosalinde, "the widow's daughter of the glen," is a North-country lass. Spenser's power of taking up real objects, persons and incidents, of plunging these in some solvent of the imagination, and then of re-creating them—the same and not the same—is manifest throughout. Everything has been submitted to the shaping power of the imagination; everything has been idealized; yet Spenser does not remove from real life, does not forsake his own country and his own time; he does not shrink from taking a side in controversies then troubling the English Church; he is primarily a poet, but while a poet, he also aspires to be what Milton named him—a teacher. In these poems the little archer, Love, shoots his roguish shafts; Pan is the patron of shepherds; Cynthia sits crowned upon the grassy green. The poet freely appropriates what pleases his fancy in classical or neoclassical mythology; yet at heart he is almost Puritan. Not indeed Puritan in any turning away from innocent delights; not Puritan in casting dishonor on our earthly life, its beauty, its splendor, its joy, its passion; but Puritan as Milton was when he wrote *Lycidas,* in his weight of moral purpose, in his love of a grave plainness in religion and of humble laboriousness in those who are shepherds under Christ.

The tenth eclogue of the *Calender,* that for the month of October, is especially characteristic of its author. In it, as stated in the argument, is set out "the perfect pattern of a poet." In what way does Spenser conceive of poetry? We know how in periods which are not creative, periods which are not breathed upon by new divine ideas, which are not driven by the urge of strong emotions, poetry comes to be looked on as primarily an art, or even as an accomplishment, and it is treated as if its function were to decorate life much as the artistic upholsterer decorates our houses. At such a time great regard is had to the workmanship of verse exclusive of the burden and inspiration of the song, and elegant little specimens of mosaic or of enameling are turned out of the workshops of skilled artists; until the thing descends into a trade. In the creative periods there is not less devotion to form and workmanship; but the devotion is of a less self-conscious kind, because generative powers work in the poet with a rapturous blindness of love, and he thinks of himself less as a master of technique (though he is also this) than as a man possessed by some influence out of and beyond himself, some dominant energy of Nature or of God, to which it is his part to submit, which he cannot lay claim to as if it were an attainment of skill, and which he dare not call his own. At such times poetry aims at something more than to decorate life; it is spoken of as if it possessed some imperial authority, a power to bind and to loose, to sway man's total nature, to calm, to regulate and restrain, and also to free, to arouse, to dilate the spirit—power not to titillate a particular sense, but to discipline the will and mold a character. In such a tone of high assumption Spenser speaks of poetry. About this time he heard much of experiments in new and ingenious forms of English verse. Sidney and Dyer, Drant and Gabriel Harvey, were full of a scheme for introducing classical meters into our poetry, and Spenser was for a while taken by the scheme. He could not at such a time, he did not ever, despise the craftsman's part of poetry; yet while he thinks of poetry as an art, in the same moment it appears to him to be "no art, but a divine gift and heavenly instinct not to be gotten by labor and learning, but adorned with both; and poured into the wit by a certain 'Ενθουσιασμος and celestial inspiration." When in the eclogue the needy poet complains that Apollo is a poor paymaster, Piers replies in the spirit of Sidney when he maintains that the highest end of literature is to instruct and incite men to virtuous action:

Cuddie, the prayse is better than the price,
The glory eke much greater than the gayne;
O! what an honor it is to restraine
The lust of lawless youth with good advice,
Or pricke them forth with pleasaunce of thy vaine,
Whereto thou list their trayned wills entice.

Soon as thou gynst to set thy notes in frame,
O, how the rurall routes to thee doe cleave!
Seemeth thou dost their soule of sense bereave;
All as the shepheard that did fetch his dame
From Plutoes balefull bowre withouten leave,
His musicks might the hellish hound did tame.

From the eclogue which contains this pronouncement as to the end of poetry, it appears that Spenser already was meditating verse of a loftier kind, and was even now aware that he should before long change his "oaten reeds" for trumpets:

Abandon, then, the base and viler clowne;
Lift up thy selfe out of the lowly dust,
And sing of bloody Mars, of wars, of giusts;
Turne thee to those that weld the awful crowne,
To doubted knights, whose woundlesse armour rusts,
And helmes unbruzed wexen daily browne.

The *Faerie Queene* is here almost promised. Was this to be a mere romance of adventures, like Ariosto's *Orlando,* but unsupported by the wit and worldly wisdom of an Ariosto? Or did Spenser conceive his great poem as something more than a play of fancy? Did he conceive it as capable of winning that praise which he declares in the *Shepherds Calender* to be the true glory of art?

The *Shepherds Calender* was dedicated

To him who is the president
Of Noblesse and of chevalree,

to Philip Sidney, "the noble and virtuous Gentleman, most worthy of all titles both of learning and chevalrie." It was possibly on the enforcement of Sidney that Spenser undertook his task "to sing of knights and ladies gentle deeds." Now, although we have to regret the loss of the work entitled *The English Poet,* in which Spenser treated of his own art, there remains to us the admirable essay by Sidney written in defence of poetry against the well-meant but ill-considered attack of the playwright-turned-precisian, Stephen Gosson. . . . In Sidney's reply to Gosson's attack on poetry he inquires what is the end or object of the life of man, and he answers—as Aristotle had answered in the *Nicomachean Ethics*—it is virtuous action. He compares, with reference to their tendency to lead men to an active virtue, three branches of human learning—philosophy, history, poetry; and his contention is that to poetry must be assigned the highest place. Philosophy enlightens the intellect, but does not move the will; it is weak in its influence on conduct because it deals too exclusively with abstract truth; it lays down the rule, but omits to give the example. History fails for an opposite reason: it deals too exclusively with concrete fact; it gives the example, but the example unilluminated by its principle. Poetry excels them both, giving as it does neither precept apart from example, nor the example apart from the precept or principle, but both together; and thus it not only enlightens the intellect, but vivifies the emotions and moves the will.

In the spirit of Sidney's *Apologie for Poetry* Spenser conceived and wrote the *Faerie Queene*. It is an attempt to harmonize the three divisions of learning discussed by Sidney—history, moral philosophy, poetry; and to make the first and second of these subserve the greatest of the three. The end of the whole is virtuous action; Spenser would set forth an ideal of human character, and incite men to its attainment. He thought of his poem, while never ceasing to be a true poem, as if it were, in a certain sense, a study in ethics. One day Spenser's friend Bryskett in his cottage near Dublin gathered about him a circle of distinguished acquaintances, and conversing on the subject of ethics, which he wished were worthily handled in English, "whereby our youth might speedily enter into the right course of vertuous life," he turned to Spenser with an embarrassing request—that Spenser should forthwith proceed to deliver a discourse on the virtues and vices, and give the company a taste of true moral philosophy. Spenser naturally excused himself, and pleaded on his own behalf that, though he could not improvise a lecture on ethics, he had actually in hand a work which might in some sort satisfy his friend's desire:

> For sure I am, that it is not unknowne unto you, that I have already undertaken a work tending to the same effect, which is in heroical verse under the title of a *Faerie Queene* to repre-

> sent all the moral vertues, assigning to every vertue a Knight to be the patron and defender of the same, in whose actions and feats of arms and chivalry the operations of that vertue, whereof he is the protector, are to be expressed, and the vices and unruly appetites that oppose themselves against the same, to be beaten down and overcome.

"A poet at that time," says the Dean of St. Paul's,[2] commenting on this passage, "still had to justify his employment by presenting himself in the character of a professed teacher of morality." But this is hardly in accordance with the facts. It was not as a professed teacher of morality that Chaucer had told his *Canterbury Tales;* it was not as a professed teacher of morality that Marlowe wrote his *Hero and Leander,* or Shakespeare his *Venus and Adonis.* "Every great poet," said Wordsworth, "is a teacher: I wish either to be considered as a teacher, or as nothing." May it not be that Spenser had higher thoughts than of justifying his employment? May not he, like Wordsworth, but unlike Chaucer and Marlowe, have really aimed at edification—such edification as is proper to a poet? "You have given me praise," Wordsworth wrote to John Wilson, "for having reflected faithfully in my poems the feelings of human nature. I would fain hope that I have done so. But a great poet ought to do more than this: he ought, to a certain degree, to rectify men's feelings, to give them new compositions of feeling, to render their feelings more sane, pure, and permanent, in short, more consonant to nature and the great moving spirit of things." To render men's feelings more sane, pure, and permanent—this surely was included in the great design of the *Faerie Queene;* it was deliberately kept before him as an object by Spenser—"our sage and serious Spenser, whom I dare to name a better teacher than Scotus or Aquinas."

How, then, should we read the *Faerie Queene*? Is it poetry? or is it philosophy? Are we merely to gaze on with wide-eyed expectancy as at a marvelous pageant or procession, in which knights and ladies, Saracens and wizards, anticks and wild men pass before our eyes? or are these visible shows only a rind or shell, which we must break or strip away in order to get at that hidden wisdom which feeds the spirit? Neither of these things are we to do. The mere visible shows of Spenser's poem are indeed goodly enough to beguile a summer's day in some old wood, and to hold us from morning to evening in a waking dream. The ethical teaching of Spenser extracted from his poetry is worthy a careful study. Raphael drew his fainting Virgin Mother as a skeleton in his preparatory study, and the student of Raphael may well consider the anatomy of the figure, because whatever an artist has put into his work, that a critic may try to discover in it. So the moral philosophy of Spenser even apart from his poetry may rightly form a subject of study. But the special virtue of the *Faerie Queene* will be found only by one who receives it neither as pageantry nor as philosophy, but in the way in which Spenser meant that it should be received—as a living creature of the imagination, a spirit incarnate, "one altogether," "of a reasonable soul and human flesh subsisting."

There are, indeed, portions of the *Faerie Queene* which are not vital—which are, so to speak, excrementitious. In a short poem—the expression of a moment of lyrical excitement—a single line, a single word which is not vital, destroys the integrity of the piece. But a poem which has taken into itself the writer's entire mind during long years cannot but be like a wide landscape that includes level with rise, and sandy patches with verdurous tracts. It seems inevitable that in such comprehensive works as the *Divine Comedy,* the *Paradise Lost,* the two parts of *Faust,* the *Faerie Queene,* the stream of pure imagination should sometimes well out of rocky masses of intellectual argument or didactic meditation. The dullest portions of Spenser's poem are those in which he works with most self-consciousness, piecing together definite meanings to definite symbols; where his love of beauty slumbers and his spirit of ingenuity awakes; where his ideas do not play and part and gather themselves together and deploy themselves abroad, like the shifting and shredding of clouds blown by soft upper airs, but are rather cut out with hard edges by some process of mechanism. When in the "Legende of Temperance" the poet allegorizes Aristotle's doctrine that virtue is a mean betwixt the extremes of excess and of defect, our distaste for Elissa and Perissa would surely content the moralist, were it not that our feeling towards their virtuous sister is hardly less unfriendly. From the "Castle of Alma" we should not be ill-pleased if the master-cook, Concoction, and the kitchen-clerk, Digestion, were themselves ignobly conveyed away (if allegory would permit such a departure) by that nether gate, the Port Esquiline.

These lapses and declensions we may pardon and forget. Upon the whole the *Faerie Queene,* if nothing else, is at least a labyrinth of beauty, a forest of old romance in which it is possible to lose oneself more irrecoverably amid the tangled luxury of loveliness than elsewhere in English poetry. . . . Now, this sensibility to beauty—the beauty of earth and sky, the beauty of man and woman—does it bring with it any peculiar dangers, any temptations and seductions? Every noble sensibility, every high faculty of man, it may be answered, brings with it some peculiar danger. Spenser certainly was conscious of risks attending this sensibility to beauty. Puritanism was also aware of these risks; and Puritanism, when it had attained to full strength, said, "Lest thy right eye offend thee straightway pluck it out." Spenser said, "See that it offend thee not." Ascetic in the best sense of that word Spenser assuredly was: he desired to strengthen every part of our nature by heroic discipline, and to subordinate the lower parts to the higher, so that, if strong, they might be strong for service, not for mastery. But Spenser was almost as free as Wordsworth from asceticism in its evil sense, and for the same reason as Wordsworth. To Spenser and to Wordsworth it could not seem desirable to put out the right eye, because to both the eye was an inlet of divine things for the uses of the spirit. With respect to beauty, Spenser's teaching is that true beauty is always sacred, always ennobling to the spirit which is itself sane and pure, but the sensual mind will put even beauty to sensual uses. And he declares further that there is a forged or feigned beauty, which is no more than a fair illusion covering inward foulness and shame. The true beauty, according to Spenser, may be recognized by a certain illuminating quality; it is not mere pasture for the eye; rather it smites the gazer, long accustomed to the dimness of common things, as if with sudden and exquisite light; it is indeed a ray derived from God, the central Luminary of the universe.

But neither the Aristotelian doctrine of the mean, nor Platonic conceptions of love and beauty, serve best to protect and deliver us from the temptations of sense as set forth in Spenser's poetry. By his enthusiasm on behalf of the noblest moral qualities, by his strenuous joy in presence of the noblest human creatures—man and woman—Spenser breathes into us a breath of life, which has an antiseptic power, which kills the germs of disease, and is antagonistic to the relaxed fiber, the lethargy, the dissolution, or disintegrating life-in-death of sensuality. Any heroism of man or woman is like wine to gladden Spenser's heart; we see through the verse how it quickens the motion of his blood. A swift, clear flame of sympathy, like an answering beacon lit upon the high places of his soul, leaps up in response to the beacon-fire of chivalric virtue in another soul, even though it be an imagined one, summoning his own. The enchantress Acrasia in her rosy bower is so bewitchingly fair and soft that it goes hard with us to see her garden defaced and herself rudely taken captive. Or it would go hard with us did we not know the faithfulness and soft invincibility of Amoret, the virgin joy and vigor of Belphœbe, the steadfastness and animating trust in Una's eyes—or had we not beheld the face of Britomart shining beneath her umbriere like day-dawn to a belated wanderer, and then all that is vain and false and sensual becomes to us what those ignoble knights of Malecasta were to the warrior virgin—no more than shadows:

> All were faire knights and goodly well beseene,
> But to faire Britomart they all but shadows beene.

We have no need to inspect the rout of monsters degraded from manhood by Acrasia's witchcraft. Britomart has clean delivered us from Acrasia.

And so we are brought back to the statement that the high distinction of Spenser's poetry is to be found in the rare degree in which it unites sense and soul, moral seriousness and the Renaissance appetite for beauty. Herein lay his chief lesson for men of his own time. To incite and to conduct men to an active virtue is not only the express purpose of the *Faerie Queene,* but as far as a poem can render such service, the *Faerie Queene* doubtless has actually served to train knights of holiness, knights of temperance, knights of courtesy. Spenser, although an ardent patriot of the time of Elizabeth, or rather because he was an ardent patriot, did not flatter his own age. He believed that the world had declined from its high estate, and fearing that things might tend to worse, he observed anxiously the wrong-doings of the time. He speaks very plainly in *Mother Hubberds Tale* of vices in the court, the church, the army. He desired to serve his country and his age, as other great Englishmen were doing, and yet in his own proper way. Now, Spenser expected little—perhaps even less than Shakespeare—from the people; the doctrine of equality he held, as Shakespeare also held, to be a dangerous and misleading cry of demagogues; Spenser expressly argues against that idea in his "Legend of Justice." Liberty he held to consist in obedience to highest law; that people, he thought, is wise and happy which follows its appointed leaders. What Spenser's political faith would be, if he were now living, we may surmise, but cannot assert. Living in the age of great monarchies, he was monarchical and aristocratic. He admired heroic personalities, and he found some of these among the gentle and noble persons of England. He had known Sidney; he served under Lord Grey. When he conceived and planned this vast poem, of which only six out of the twenty-four contemplated books were written, it was with a design which doubtless seemed to Spenser the best suited and the most needful to his own time; his end, as he declared to Ralegh, was "to fashion a gentleman or noble person in vertuous and gentle discipline." He desired to see at the head of affairs in England a company of noble Englishmen serving for no selfish ends, but following honor in the highest sense of that word—the "Gloriana" of the *Faerie Queene*.

Thus, with all its opulence of color and melody, with all its imagery of delight, the *Faerie Queene* has primarily a moral or spiritual intention. While Spenser sees the abundant beauty of the world, and the splendor of man and of the life of man, his vision of human life is grave and even stern. For life he regards as a warfare, a warfare needing all our foresight, strength, and skill. Thus to a certain point Spenser's conception of life may be said to be the Puritan conception; it is certainly the reverse of the Epicurean conception. Nor is the combat between good and evil in Spenser's poem one in which victory is lightly or speedily attainable; the sustaining thought is that victory is possible. There is a well-known painting by Raphael of the Archangel Michael slaying the Dragon; the heavenly avenger descends like a young Apollo, with light yet insupportable advance, and in a moment the evil thing must be abolished. There is a little engraving by Albert Dürer which contrasts strangely with that famous picture. It represents the moment of St. George's victory; the monster, very hideous and ignoble, has bitten the dust and lies impotent. But is the victor elated? He is too weary for much elation, too thankful that the struggle is ended; he rests for a short space, still mounted on his heavy German stallion; we can perceive that other combats await him, and that the battle with evil is a battle that lasts a lifetime. Spenser's conception of the strife with wrong comes nearer to that of Dürer than to that of Raphael. . . .

Spenser's conception of life was Puritan in its seriousness; yet we think with wonder of the wide space that lies between the *Faerie Queene* and our other great allegory, the *Pilgrim's Progress.* To escape from the City of Destruction and to reach the Celestial City is Christian's one concern; all his recompense for the countless trials of the way lies upon the other side of the river of death. His consuming thought is this: "What must I do to be saved?" Spenser is spiritual, but he is also mundane; he thinks of the uses of noble human creatures to this world in which we move. His general end in the poem is "to fashion a gentleman or noble person in vertuous and gentle discipline." "A grand self-culture," I have elsewhere said, "is that about which Spenser is concerned; not, as with Bunyan, the escape of the soul to heaven; not the attainment of supernatural grace through a point of mystical contact, like the vision which was granted to the virgin knight, Galahad, in the medieval allegory. Self-culture, the formation of a complete character for the uses of earth, and afterwards, if need be, for the uses of heaven—this was subject sufficient for the twenty-four books designed to form the epic of the age of Elizabeth. And the means of that self-culture are of an active kind—namely, warfare—warfare, not for its own sake, but for the generous accomplishment of unselfish ends." Bunyan, with whom the visionary power was often involuntary, who would live for a day and a night in some metaphor that had attacked his imagination, transcribed into allegory his own wonderful experience of terrors and of comfort. Spenser is more impersonal: he can refashion Aristotle in a dream. But behind him lies all the sentiment of Christian chivalry, and around him all the life of Elizabethan England; and from these diverse elements arises a rich and manifold creation, which, if it lacks the personal, spiritual passion of Bunyan's allegory, compensates by its moral breadth, its noble sanity, its conciliation of what is earthly and what is divine. "A better teacher than Scotus or Aquinas." We have seen to some small extent what Spenser sought to impress upon the mind of his own age. He strove, in his own way as poet, to make the national life of England a great unity—spiritual, yet not disdaining earth or the things of earth. He strove, as far as in him lay, to breed a race of high-souled English gentlemen, who should have none of the meanness of the libertine, none of the meanness of the precisian. But the contending parties of the English nation went their ways—one party to moral licentiousness and political servility, the other to religious intolerance and the coarse extravagances of the sectaries. Each extreme ran its course. And when the Puritan excess and the Cavalier excess had alike exhausted themselves, and England once more recovered a portion of her wisdom and her calm, it had become impossible to revert to the ideals of Spenser. Enthusiasm had been discredited by the sectaries until it had grown to be a byword of reproach. The orgies of the Restoration had served to elevate common decency into something like high virtue. After the Puritan excess and the Cavalier excess, England recovered herself not by moral ardor or imaginative reason, but by good sense, by a prosaic but practical respect for the respectable, and by a utilitarian conviction that honesty is the best policy.

"A better teacher than Scotus or Aquinas." Yet we are told by the Dean of St. Paul's, that in giving himself credit for a direct purpose to instuct, Spenser "only conformed to the curiously utilitarian spirit which pervaded the literature of the time." It is the heresy of modern art that only useless things should be made beautiful. We want beauty only in playthings. In elder days the armor of a knight was as beautiful as sunlight, or as flowers. "In unaffected, unconscious, artistic excellence of invention," says one of our chief living painters,[3] "approaching more nearly to the strange beauty of nature, especially in vegetation, medieval armor perhaps surpasses any other effort of human ingenuity." What if Spenser wrought armor for the soul, and, because it was precious and of finest temper, made it fair to look upon? That which gleams as bright as the waters of a sunlit lake is perhaps a breastplate to protect the heart; that which appears pliant as the blades of summer grass may prove at our need to be a sword of steel.

Notes

1. With which contrast Coleridge's words, "No one can appreciate Spenser without some reflection on the nature of allegorical writing"; and Mr. Ruskin's painstaking attempt in *Stones of Venice* to interpret the allegory of Book I.

2. [R. W. Church—ed.]

3. Mr. G. F. Watts.

W. L. Renwick

Spenser's Philosophy

THE BASIC FACT of the Renaissance, so difficult to isolate, has been held to be the escape of human reason from the bonds of authority. It would be true also to say that it was the escape of human temperament from the bonds of reason, from the habit of categorical division which is the mark of the legalistic mind of the Middle Ages. The medieval man kept things separate, and attended to one at a time. The Griselda of the Clerk's Tale, for instance, offends a modern reader by her lack of proper pride; the Clerk's Tale, however, is not about proper pride, but about patience. So also the passivity of Emily in the Knight's Tale is sometimes cited as a social document, evidence for the position of women in the Middle Ages, but the Knight's Tale is not about the relations of a young lady with two young men who are fighting over her, nor about her ideas or emotions, but about the relations of two friends who find themselves in enmity, and about the proper conduct of their quarrel. On the larger scale, the simple emotion of the *Acta Sanctorum* is divided from the austere logic of the *Summa Theologiæ;* Guillaume de Lorris expounds a law that is neither Canon nor Civil, but chivalric; the religious emotion of the story of the Saint Graal does not affect the ethics of the story of Tristram and Iseult in the same book. This separation of human functions and interests could not last for ever, and when it weakened there began the Renaissance, the discovery of man as a whole, indivisible, mind and body and soul together—the discovery of the central inclusive fact of Life. On one hand the evasion of temperament broke down the dominion of medieval intellectualism, leading philosophy away from metaphysics, which exercised only logic, to ethics, which implies the cooperation with intellect of intuition and feeling; and on the other hand it removed ethics from the sole jurisdiction of dogmatic and inexpugnable ecclesiasticism, to be examined in the light of thought and experience. Men discovered that their own actions and emotions were really the most interesting subject in the world, and felt they were not receiving the serious attention they deserved. Scholastic philosophy ignored them, the Church pronounced judgment upon them, sometimes in accordance with an ascetic ideal too high for the ordinary mortal and sometimes in accordance with clerical aims which the world's honesty condemned, and the secular literature of chivalry dealt with them only in the limited sphere of social convention.

Love between man and woman, for example, could not be discussed by scholastic philosophers with any profit to lovers. The Church regarded sex as an evil—even if it were a necessary evil—and recognized its existence only by imposing restrictions on it. The chivalric poets treated of it without regard to ethics at all: Sir Gawaine's reason for refusing to commit adultery, for instance, is purely social—it would be discourteous to the husband, who is his host.[1] But this was one of the great human facts whose interest the Renaissance felt pressing, and it had to be considered in all its bearings. So also with Justice and Temperance and Glory, and all the other vital factors in man's existence; they escaped the categories of truth and falsehood, of holiness and sinfulness, of good form and bad form, not because these categories did not apply, but because they all applied. Taken separately in the medieval manner, they were too narrow and too rigid, and so men turned to the classics, where the conditions of man's life and the factors of his destiny are treated under wider and more elastic terms of good and evil. In the classics, again, a less dogmatic theory of the state, the ideas of civic duty and of expediency, the political virtues and vices, were included among those conditions and factors, and the sense of beauty and its cultivation in art, disregarded by the Schoolmen and denounced by the Church, but very living in the eager temperament, permeated all the thought and expression of the ancients. Few of the humanists, perhaps, and few of their disciples, could have formulated what it was that satisfied them in Plato and Cicero and Vergil, but the instinct, however obscure, was powerful, and when the new poets set themselves to school to the classics it was to acquire not only the finer art, but this wider scope, this adequacy to life as a whole, which even the best of the vernacular poets had missed. The humanists led them to Lucretius, the poet who was a philosopher, and to Plato, the philosopher who was a poet, and they, proposing to themselves the creation of a philosophic poetry, a poetry which should treat of human life in all its aspects and under all the categories of judgment, sought wisdom from the philosophers just as they sought guidance in their art from the critics.

One of the purposes of the new poetry was to bring into circulation among the modern peoples the treasures of the world's thought, for the sake of whatever use the peoples might make of them. The ideas of the philosophers formed part of Spenser's academic training, and part of the *materies* which it was his duty to treat in his dissimilar English manner. He incorporates into his own poems, accordingly, fragments from philosophic as well as from other writers, and for the same variety of reasons. When, for instance, he insets into his somewhat medieval description of the Court of Venus the first thirty-odd lines of the *de Rerum Natura* of Lucretius,[2] the passage has no special Epicurean significance; the procedure is purely literary. In this Book Spenser was treating largely of Love. For the complete presentation of his theme he had been studying Lucretius, and when his poetic precedents called for a hymn to Venus, he imitated this excellent one. Here the literary motive is clear enough, but less purely artistic imitations cause endless doubt and difficulty, which can be overcome only by tactful consideration by the reader of each example as it occurs. A fragment of Aristotle or Seneca or Plato may be borrowed, not only for its beauty, but because it expressed more or less clearly some feeling which Spenser was trying to make explicit, and it may be borrowed just as a phrase or a story might be borrowed from Vergil or Ariosto. The use of quotations may be proof of study, but is not necessarily proof of intellectual discipleship, still less of complete acceptance of a system of thought. Nor did quotations necessarily come direct from their originals, for many phrases and arguments had done duty many times, and not always the same duty or in the same connection.

By an ordinary process, again—and we have seen Spenser bear his part in it—technical expressions, divorced from their original bearing, pass into the common stock of allusion, and thence, losing precision of reference and meaning by the way, into the common stock of current speech. It is one of the difficulties that confront the student of the Renaissance that the process was then both rapid and voluminous. Many common words and phrases, now almost empty of content, may at any occurrence in Renaissance work be understood as having their original connotation, or their modern, or anything between, and this is particularly noticeable in the work of Spenser, who kept a loose grip on language, and is apt, moreover, to use the technical terms of philosophy just as he uses those of law or of falconry, but with scarcely the same precision. In such a passage as the following, for instance, the term "Idea" is explicitly the technical term of Platonism:

> Faire is the heaven . . .
> More faire is that, where those Idees on hie
> Enraunged be, which Plato so admired.[3]

When in the *Hymne of Heavenly Love* the poet speaks of "th' Idee" of God's "pure glorie,"[4] the difficulty of the conception may be caused by loose thinking—he means, presumably, the divine glory as seen in itself, not in an earthly reflection. In two of the *Amoretti,* however, the term appears to mean an image or representation in the mind:

> Within my hart, though hardly it can shew
> thing so divine to vew of earthly eye,
> the fayre Idea of your celestial hew
> and every part remaines immortally.[5]

> Ne ought I see, though in the clearest day,
> when others gaze upon theyr shadows vayne:
> but th' onely image of that heavenly ray
> whereof some glance doth in mine eie remayne,
> of which beholding the Idaea playne
> through contemplation of my purest part
> with light thereof I feed my love-affamisht hart.[6]

These have been taken as a confession of Platonic faith, the record of progress from desire of beauty seen in the flesh to desire of beauty conceived in the intellect. The first, however, is a well-known commonplace, used by Marot [7] and derived from Serafino da Aquila. The second is closely related not only to Sonnet XXXV, but to Petrarch's Sonnet LXXI and Canzone XII, and still more to one of Bembo's *Rime:*

> Mentre 'l fero destin me toglie, et vieta
> Veder Madonna, e tiemmi in altra parte
> La bella immagin sua veduta in parte
> Il digiun pasce, e i miei sospiri acqueta.[8]

The Platonic source of Spenser's phrasing is obvious—he might not, perhaps, have disclaimed a Platonic sub-intention—but the use of the term "idea" to mean "image" can be paralleled in Ronsard and Montaigne, and the employment of philosophical tags in many of Ronsard's sonnets, as here:

> . . . O lumière enrichie
> D'un feu divin qui m'ard si vivement
> Pour me donner et force et mouvement
> Estes-vous pas ma seule Entelechie? [9]

which is not an Aristotelian psalm, but a compliment to his lady's eyes. If, finally, Spenser intended the full Platonic significance to be attached to these sonnets, then he was a bad or at least a reluctant Platonist, for surely the philosopher should rejoice at his achievement of a step nearer the One, and here Spenser mourns.

It is not safe to argue Spenser's adherence to a system of philosophy upon such uncertain evidence, and as for more extensive borrowings, let the warning of three quotations suffice. "It is easie to verifie," says Montaigne, "that excellent authors, writing of causes, do not only make use of those which they imagine true, but eftsoones of such as themselves believe not: always provided they have some invention and beautie. They speake sufficiently, truly and profitably, if they speake ingeniously. We cannot assure ourselves of the chiefe cause: we hudle up a many together, to see whether by chance it shall be found in that number."[10] According to Ronsard, as we have seen, the aim of the poet is "to imitate, invent, and represent the things which are, or can be, or which the Ancients believed to be true."[11] And after discussing the variety of knowledge required by Ariosto for his heroic poem, Pigna continues: "And since in such variety of different professions there may be opinions of many philosophers, with which he comes in contact, he is here a Stoic, there a Platonist, and on one hand one opinion is followed, on another, another."[12] Literary imitation and the careful exhibition of wide scholarship might almost be supposed to account for the appearance in Spenser's work of philosophic matter, were it not that deep thought was required of the new school of poetry, and that one of his purposes in *The Faerie Queene,* and that not the least important, was "to fashion a gentleman or noble person in vertuous and gentle discipline." Holding such a purpose, he did not attempt to construct an original independent theory of morality. He lived in days before it was necessary to gain a reputation as moralist by showing that unchastity is chastity or that purity of soul is best manifested in a Russian debauch. True to his classical training and to the profound common sense of his English character, trying to arrive at the central truth, the essential common factor which all men must recognize, he attempted rather an exposition of the general consensus of the best ethical doctrine. Such a purpose required all the course of philosophic reading on which his Cambridge studies entered him, as well as his native and inherited instincts.

The method of *The Faerie Queene* is, to display each virtue completely in all its forms and phases, not as a simple characteristic, but as defined by the various trials and experiences operating to its perfection, by the various actions proper to its possession, and, negatively, by the diverse vices and defects opposed to it. A single exemplar is not enough. Guyon and the Palmer present Temperance arising from two different moral bases, highmindedness and restraint; Britomart and Belphœbe and Amoret, different conceptions of chastity—that which depends on strength and faithfulness, that which is a noble fastidiousness removed from common frailty, and that which is a natural attribute of womanly character. Spenser drives home his lesson by repeated variations, adding additional illustrations by additional characters and episodes. Sir Calidore, to take the simplest instance, represents Courtesy: his principal task is to restrain malice and evil speaking—the "Male-Bouche" of the chivalric allegorists—he also teaches mercy and mildness, championship of woman, tenderness to the sick, politeness to honest inferiors.[13] Cruelty, haughtiness, inhospitality, treachery, insincerity, are his opposites, though not necessarily his personal opponents in the story.[14] Tristram and the Hermit show that Courtesy, though rightly "named of court," belongs to "the gentle blood" and not to worldly position; the Savage Man, that goodwill and right instinct are its primary conditions. Incidental illustrations are given in the old knight Aldus, who tempered his grief for his son's wounds

> . . . and turned it to cheare
> To cheare his guests, whom he had stayed that night
> And make their welcome to them well appeare,[15]

and in the quaint worldly-wise diplomacy of Calidore's explanation of the lady Priscilla's absence from home.[16] Courtesy, again, is allied to Justice in Prince Arthur's punishment of Turpine,[17] its place in the sphere of Love illustrated by the episode of Mirabella,[18] its interpretation extended by the vision of the Graces and Colin Clout's explanation.[19] Nor does this very rapid analysis by any means exhaust the complexity of Spenser's conception, which appears often in a phrase or even a pregnant word.

To frame and exhibit this complex conception of the virtues, then, required more than the current body of conventional social habit, and so Spenser draws upon the philosophers. The Sixth Book, as might be expected, contains least matter from classical sources: there are evident reminiscences of Seneca in many places,[20] but Chaucer and the romancers,[21] and the example of the best contemporaries, were authorities enough for Courtesy. Books which deal with more difficult questions, and questions which have been treated of by many minds, display a greater variety of sources, and Spenser evidently made a special study of the main authorities for each Book. It is only in the Sixth Book that Senecan borrowings appear in any quantity; the Stoic doctrine of the right of suicide, for instance, is mentioned only to be condemned by the Red Cross Knight.

The Bible contributes much matter and phrase to the First

Book, as well as the methods already noticed, because it is the authority for Holiness, as Aristotle is for Temperance and for Justice; but "in the multitude of professions" other authorities are quoted, and the complete ethical conception—for be it noted that even Holiness is an ethical conception, with only the slightest mystical infusion in the last canto—the complete conception is built up of many fragments drawn from many sources. The Books of Chastity and Friendship, which really deal with Love, are drawn from Lucretius as well as from the Nicomachean Ethics: that Spenser follows Aristotle generally in the Book of Justice by no means precludes his following Boethius or Plato, the Hebrew prophets, the institutes of chivalry, or the police system of contemporary Ireland, in any one passage. Some of Spenser's debts to the philosophers have been studied, and there is matter enough for more, but unfortunately none of these separate studies, though valuable in themselves, can give a proper idea of Spenser's philosophy, for the character of his thought, here as elsewhere, can be appreciated better through a rough grasp of his peculiar mixture of sources than by a complete study of one.

The difficulty—and the interest—arises from his equal acceptance of all available authorities: it should not be increased by over-simplification, by trying to confine Spenser to a school. He could accept all the ancient schools, all "that the Ancients believed to be true," just because they were all equally superseded by revealed religion. The fundamental fact about his ethics is that they were those of a Christian, a Protestant Christian with a tendency—not an indulged tendency—towards Calvinism. Like all the modern world, he inherited much ancient philosophy in the tradition of the church and of society, which made easier the interfusion of one with another, but where he deliberately seeks the aid of the Schools it is as supplementary to the teaching of the Church of England, and borrowings should be read only for their value at the moment and not as committing Spenser to an alien, still less to a pagan system. He draws upon Seneca, and at the same time upon the Epistle of St. James, upon Aristotle, and upon the Apocrypha, the Prophets, the Book of Job, the Revelation of St. John. All are intimately mingled together, but the Bible of all books was his principal source, as it was the foundation of his faith.

This attempt to combine the best of all the philosophies within a predominant Christianity, the intimacy with which the various borrowings are mingled, and the occasional confusion which results, are typical of the time, not only of the poets, but also of professed philosophers. The men of the Renaissance, unlike those of the French Revolution, were not seeking for a simplification; they had, as we have seen, just escaped from one, and they rejoiced in the variety and complexity of life, of human activities and possibilities, of human thought. They were somewhat bewildered and confused by that variety, those possibilities, but they faced them. There was no one dominant or leading philosophy as there was in the thirteenth century or even in the nineteenth, and no system could be evolved until the intellectual excitement had calmed: only Calvin succeeded in working out a complete system, and his system, confined to the sphere of theology, excludes many considerations very important to the average thinker of the time. Calvin succeeded because he worked by pure logic, but in this he was alone in his time: his contemporaries could not keep their temperament out of their thinking, and their doctrines, and the choice of authority to support them, are not the result of severe process. Thinking to them was an art and an indulgence, and it is by strength of temperament rather than by novelty of thought, that that passionate thinker Giordano Bruno is the typical Renaissance philosopher. Bruno has been held to have influenced Spenser, but they worked toward different ends, Bruno in ardent speculation, Spenser in solid ethics. The phrases of Bruno may appear in Spenser, but the ideas they hold in common are not those peculiar to Bruno, but those which they could both find in Lucretius and Plato, and even the phrases are uncertain, for both phrase and idea were of the common stock of the time. The curious mixture of schools, and the loose handling and uncertain application of terms and formulas taken from various and often from conflicting sources, resulted from the attempt to gather and reconcile all the philosophies and to relate the mass to Christianity. It is the same process, though in the wider sphere and with much less security in outcome, as we have seen in the critical thought of the new poets, and it is to be found in such popular philosophical works as that of Leone Hebreo, and in commentaries like that of Loys le Roy on the Symposium, work which may be only of historical interest, but must not therefore be neglected.

All these men were strongly affected by Platonism, for the reconciliation of ancient philosophies with Christian doctrine began with the Platonic Academy of Florence. Why Platonism was so attractive to the Renaissance mind is sufficiently clear from what has gone before—in Plato's works temperament and intellect move in harmony, humane feeling and exalted speculation, ethics and the spiritual universals, somehow interpenetrate and are fused into one. There was some common ground in the unrecognized Platonic element in the tradition of the Church, and still more community in the temper of thought, for Plato was not only the philosopher who taught, like the Church, that earth is but the shadow of heaven, but the philosopher of Love and Beauty and Desire, the poet-philosopher of the beautiful, spiritual tales. Platonism, then, was cultivated, compressed, and spread abroad. The treatises of Ficino, Politian, Pico della Mirandola—especially his commentary on the Platonic *canzone* of Benevieni—passed the tenets of the Florentine school into the mind of all Europe. To put it bluntly, Platonism was the fashion. It marched well with Petrarchism, it certainly was inspiring, and it could be romanced about. There would be room for surprise if Spenser had not caught this fashion along with all the others of his time: where he found the material for the *Hymnes in Honor of Love and Beauty* is more difficult. He certainly knew some of Plato's works at first hand, and used them, but the systematic method of the *Hymnes* is of the Renaissance. Ficino, the master of all Renaissance Platonists, would be his master also, but the phrase of Lucretius, "Mother of love and of all worlds delight," [22] was already brought into Platonic exposition by Loys le Roy; [23] Bruno's *degli Heroici Furori* may have supplied some of the matter, and so may Bembo's *Asolani,* and Castiglione's *Corteggiano* (newly translated by Sir Thomas Hoby), and Leone Hebreo, and Pico, and Benevieni. It is more likely that Spenser knew all these than that he did not: in any one of them he would find all or nearly all he required for the *Hymnes,* and his slight uncertainties of thought are probably due to this, that he was versifying the common floating conception—though not far from his books—rather than one hammered out in his mind.

In Italy the Church had to restrain the growing cult of systematized Neoplatonism, for though the intention was to reconcile it with Christian dogma, the Platonism tended to swallow up the Christianity. In France and England Neoplatonism did not antagonze the Churches, for the Reformation had preceded its introduction, and the fact of open conflict upon well-defined grounds forced men to take a side for one Church or another and attached them the more passionately to the central tenets of their creed. The infusion of Platonism into the thought of Christian men could do no harm, for there was no possibility of competition and no possible place for paganism. In the dedicatory epistles prefixed to the *Fowre Hymnes* Spenser apologizes for those in honor of Love and Beauty as having been written "in the greener times of my youth," and in the *Hymnes* of Heavenly Love and Heavenly Beauty he attempts to sanctify his old Neoplatonism by treating the Neoplatonic scheme as a myth, to symbolize the progress of the Christian soul. The attempt, though productive of some beautiful phrases, is neither very lucid philosophy nor very downright theology; it required more logic than Spenser cared to spend in a poem; but it shows that the Platonic fashion ceased to prevail with a man isolated from fashion and deeply engaged in the war of the Churches. Platonism attracted him, always, as it attracted many of his contemporaries, more as an emotion than as a creed—in which he was perhaps the nearer Plato.

For the purposes of *The Faerie Queene* the Neoplatonists were less useful than the practical teachers of ethics like Aristotle and Seneca: which means, of course, that Spenser was less interested in the Neoplatonists. When Castiglione wrote his treatise *Il Corteggiano,* he, like Spenser, intended it "to fashion a gentleman or noble person in vertuous and gentle discipline," and when he broached the inevitable problem of the relation of the sexes he put into the mouth of Bembo, as the author of the *Asolani,* a brief resumé of Platonic doctrine, telling how the lover progresses from desire of beauty in one human embodiment to desire of that beauty divorced from flesh, so to desire of universal beauty, and so to God, Who is Beauty Itself. Now this is just what Spenser did not do in the poem into which he poured all he knew and felt and learned about the good life. In view of a common tendency among writers on this subject it is necessary to premise that to derive from Plato any and every conception of love higher than the brute instinct is a libel on mankind. There have been honorable souls in other states than Athens, and one element in the Platonic temperament, the yearning mood, the vague desire for far-away or half-imagined beauty, is common to all youth and to many peoples—to Kormak the Icelander, and Jaufré Rudel, and many an old poet of Germany and Ireland. "Platonic Love" as a deliberately accepted and conclusive ethic flourished in Italy, and, with Maurice Scève, in the Italianate city of Lyons: it may be doubted whether it suited the solid mind of the North, except as a scholarly elegance. The exaltation of beauty into something divine flattered the Renaissance temperament—almost gave an excuse for indulgence—and the spiritualization of love was easily grafted on the tradition of *amour courtois* to make a courtly refinement. But that very tradition carried a principle hostile to the Neoplatonic scheme. Under Renaissance Neoplatonism the only duty of woman is to be beautiful, to awaken desire, and then to disappear, leaving the desire to be nursed into an ecstasy in which she has no place: this cannot be reconciled with the principle of personal loyalty, the first clause of the law of *amour courtois* as it was the basis of the whole medieval system. And behind the principle of personal loyalty lies the secular instinct of the North, obvious enough for a stranger like Tacitus to have observed it, giving the woman her equal share in a love which exists for both man and woman together, and exists by virtue of their being man and woman.

Plato contributed largely to Spenser's thought, but he was not the only source of principle, nor was he the final authority. He enforced the truth that love is a spiritual activity, but the complementary truth that love is a primary function of the animate universe, essential to its continuance, was set forth with equal force by Lucretius, and these two principles were reconciled for Spenser in the final authority, the teaching of the Church of England, defined in the Marriage Service of the Prayer Book. Heavenly Love and Earthly are not eternal antagonists, but complements one of the other, and so the story of Chastity is a love story. All Spenser's virtues are positive fighting virtues, and Chastity among them: its representative is neither nun nor sage, but a redoubtable knight who is also a woman in love, destined to the honorable estate of matrimony and the procreation of a noble line; for chastity is nothing other than truth and honor in the question of sex, sanctified by the spirit of God, Who is Love, and serving the world as His agent. Chastity is attended by Prudence, but depends on its own strength and courage. It is as free from the asceticism of the Middle Ages and the asceticism of the Neoplatonists as it is from the frauds and counterfeits, the weaknesses and the perversions it combats, for its end is not in the solitary individual soul, but in the universe, through love, of which it is the necessary condition.

This is the mark of Spenser's Puritanism. His removal from Cambridge took him out of the ecclesiastical controversies about vestments and altar-tables into a wider sphere of thought, but the essential of Puritanism remained with him, the sense of personal responsibility which cannot be transferred to priest or king. In his preaching of this doctrine he was, perhaps, as well in the example of his art, the master of Milton, who in a famous passage of *Areopagitica* dared think him "a better teacher than Scotus or Aquinas." False Puritanism is distinguished by its negations, but the true Puritan is not an ascetic, undergoing privations as a sacrifice or in self-distrust, but an athlete and a soldier, disciplining himself against indulgences which would unfit him here and now for his duty, and for the reward to be earned, not by the privations, but by the duty accomplished. The individual is responsible for himself, for his own destiny, and for more than his own: he is a combatant in the eternal strife between good and evil for the dominion of a universe in which spiritual and material are one. His victories and his defeats affect the universe as a whole, and he is never fighting alone. Ethics, then, takes a large place in Puritan thought, as the rule of a daily life which is an activity of the universe.

Individual human conduct, though perhaps concerned in any one instance with small material conditions, extends into the great movement which is ultimately spiritual, just as the individual human life is part of the universal. In his study of love as the law of life Spenser extends ethics into speculation, for in it there is some hint of a solution to the problem which recurs through all his work, the problem of change. The mutability of things, the brevity of life, the inevitable end of human beauty and greatness, haunted the Renaissance as it haunted the Middle Ages; but unlike the medieval poets Spenser was not content to accept it only as tragedy or as a subject for moralizing, for the problem was enlarged, made more poetic in being made more philosophical, by Lucretius. On this note *The Faerie Queene,* as we have it, closes, and we do not know how

Spenser proposed to treat the Legend of Constancy, but it is in all his thought. His astronomical knowledge, however incomplete, destroyed for him even the poetic fiction of the changeless stars: [24] all earth was involved in change. That he learned to accept as a universal law: substance is constant, form changes according to universal law; and Universal Law is God.

> What wrong then is it, if that when they die,
> They turne to that, whereof they first were made?
> All in the powre of their great Maker lie:
> All creatures must obey the voice of the most hie.[25]

That is the theological statement, in a passage based on the second chapter of the first Book of Samuel and on Lucretius: it is stated again in the sixth canto of the Third Book, in the famous myth of the Garden of Adonis, compiled from the *Phaedrus,* the *Tabula* ascribed to Cebes, Aristotle *de Anima,* Lucretius, and the Book of Genesis. Here the principle of continuance in change is the Venus of Lucretius, presiding over procreation, and representing "nothing other than the power of God." Thus Love is doubly sanctified, matter and spirit are reconciled, and the tragedy of mutability is resolved, not by blind submission or by abstention, but by comprehension.

That is one solution of the problem of change: form begets form in perpetuity according to the will of the Creator; but man cannot forget that which was, and in a universe of unceasing change his desire is for stability. In the last resort the only permanence is with God:

> When I bethinke me on that speech whyleare
> Of Mutabilitie, and well it way,
> Me seemes that though she all unworthy were
> Of the Heav'ns Rule, yet very sooth to say,
> In all things else she beares the greatest sway:
> Which makes me loath this state of life so tickle,
> And love of things so vaine to cast away
> Whose flowring pride, so fading and so fickle,
> Short Time shall soon cut down with his consuming sickle.

Then gin I thinke on that which Nature sayd,
Of that same time when no more change shall be,
But stedfast rest of all things, firmely stayd
Upon the pillours of Eternity,
That is contrayr to Mutabilitie;
For all that moveth doth in Change delight:
But thence-forth all shall rest eternally
With Him that is the God of Sabaoth hight:
O! that great Sabaoth God, grant me that Sabaoths sight.[26]

But the positive spirit of England, of the time and the man, would not allow Spenser to wait in mystical contemplation for the coming of the Kingdom of Heaven. In this world of change men must strive for such stability as may be won by the strength of their virtues, and so the ethical ideal returns with renewed importance and validity. Yet Puritanism did not make Spenser a rebel. Just as the individual must be a well-disposed member of the universal life, so he must be a well-disposed citizen, for the state and the universe are maintained by order and control. The lesson of *The Faerie Queene* is the same throughout: society must be held together by concord or Friendship, the individual must be controlled by Temperance, the state by Justice. The recurrent victory of the trained and disciplined knights over "the rascal many" was more than an inheritance from the aristocratic Middle Ages, or an echo of Tudor statesmanship, or a memory of Irish insurrections. All these were in Spenser's mind, but they were contained within the greater idea, the necessity of stability. The rabble is crushed because it is a rabble, incapable of constant policy of united action.

Spenser's political attitude is thus similar to that of Shakespeare, and for good cause. As *Paradise Lost* proclaims the individualism of the seventeenth century, so *The Faerie Queene* sums up the lesson of English history for a century and a half. There was reason in the adulation of Queen Elizabeth: she stood for the sixteenth-century virtues as Queen Victoria for those of the late nineteenth, and she had given England something approaching civil and religious stability for over thirty years when the first part of *The Faerie Queene* was published. In English history Shakespeare saw the clash of personality and the permanence of England: Spenser, less interested in the dramatic personality than in the idea of movement, saw the eternal vicissitude of things exemplified, and the need for stability enforced. Partly this may be the reflection of the official mind, largely it is the conclusion of the philosophical temper. The great vision of Spenser is the vision of Mutability, the alteration of the stars in their courses, the succession of the months and seasons and centuries, the cycle of birth and death, the sequence of kings and dynasties, all subject to the universal law.

> For all that lives, is subject to that law:
> All things decay in time, and to their end do draw.[27]

Yet there is the permanent factor:

> That substance is eterne, and bideth so,
> Ne when life the decayes, and forme does fade,
> Doth it consume, and into nothing go,
> But chaunged is, and often altred to and fro.
>
> The substance is not chaunged, nor altered,
> But th' only forme and outward fashion.[28]

So in every particle of existence, in man, in society, in the state, the temporary form is important as a phase of the permanent, and must therefore be brought to its best mode and noblest function.

Here, then, is justified the cultivation of all the activities of human life which was the contribution of the Renaissance to the progress of the world. Spenser could not set aside the material for the sake of the spiritual, nor could he live in the material in despite of God. All knowledge, art, beauty, emotion, government, manners, were important as promoting the fine fashioning of the universal substance, and as fashioning it towards permanence, for permanence is possible only in perfection. We do not know what were the twelve virtues which together made up Magnificence, but they were not merely theological virtues. The six we have are Holiness, a spiritual virtue; Temperance and Chastity, personal virtues; Justice, a political virtue; Friendship and Courtesy, social virtues; and all these are shown to be intimately interrelated and equally required of the inclusive virtue of Magnificence. This complete and balanced cultivation of all the powers of man was the ideal of the Renaissance: Sidney displayed it in his life, Shakespeare dramatically, Spenser philosophically. The great man must be competent in each function, must possess the capacity for thought, the capacity for feeling, and the capacity for action, all trained and cultivated, and all in equilibrium. Hamlet, Lear, Othello are subjects of tragedy because one of their capacities is overbalanced, though it may be only for the time, by the others: Spenser's ideal knights are victorious, because they are in possession and in control of all three. The only permanence is in perfection—that is, in God—but something may be done on earth by the careful maintenance of equilibrium. Thus Temperance is the personal ideal which gives its due place to all the faculties of mind and body by refusing dominion to any one, Justice the political ideal which gives its due rights to each unit of the state, prescribes to each its duties and keeps each within its rights and its duties, Courtesy the social ideal which gives each man his due of proper regard in his degree and restrains the overbearing and the ungracious.

How much of this Spenser learned from Aristotle is very obvious, as his debt to Plato is obvious, but as we have seen, he was thirled to neither of them. The attempts that have been made to discover the source of the Twelve Virtues in Aristotle or in his commentators have all been unsuccessful, and it would be more surprising to find than to miss it. Some credit must be given to Spenser: just as the new poets combated the notion that all the world's store of poetic power has been expended on the earlier races, so they would have claimed for the modern age some power of thought, if only because Christianity had reoriented many of the ancient problems. There were to be twelve Books in *The Faerie Queene* because that was the correct number for an epic poem, not because there were any twelve virtues; and the phrase of Spenser "the twelve private morall vertues, as Aristotle hath devised," is best and most simply understood to mean "the twelve moral virtues which are such as Aristotle would call *private* virtues." Artistic motives must be kept in mind as well as philosophic, and temperament as well as reason. Thus Plato appealed to the spiritual and artistic nature of the poet, and Lucretius to his feeling for this world that is caught in the whirl of change—and, since temperament must judge of temperament, one reader at least feels that the deeper communion of spirit was between Spenser and Lucretius, that there is a depth of tone in the Lucretian passages of *The Faerie Queene* more moving and more heartfelt than the somewhat shrill straining of the *Hymnes* of Love and Beauty. But if one name be asked for, as of him who most formed the thought, and the habit of thought, of Spenser, then it were best, here also, to turn back to his early training, and there, of all thinkers that he would be made to study, we find the prose idol of the humanists, Cicero. *The Faerie Queene,* with much in it *de Natura Deorum,* is the *de Officiis* and the *de Finibus* of the Renaissance, deriving the elements of a complex civic and personal ideal from the opinions of many philosophers, aiming at stability and the proper distribution of rights and duties in an uncertain world, with a backward glance at the pristine virtues of the past and yet a wide outlook on the universe, preaching the search for "what order may be, what it may be that is seemly and fitting, a measure in speech and action," observing man's relations with God, with his fellows, and with the state.

Spenser was not a mere critic of life, but a constructive idealist, and intent on a possible ideal. All his virtues, as has been said, are positive fighting virtues, and go to build up the positive ideal of Magnificence, magnanimity. Magnificence seems vague and uncertain. The place of Prince Arthur in the epic-romance was never quite clearly worked out; his appearances are fitfull and unrelated, and this naturally obscures the expression of the virtue he represents, but we know that Magnificence includes all the others, and its difficulty is due to its complexity. The Renaissance would forgo nothing and would shirk nothing, but endeavored to combine in one comprehensive plan of life all personal and political good, religion, learning, and all arts and elegances. It is the most complex ideal that any poet ever attempted to express, inclusive of all that Vergil ceded to Greece and all he claimed for Rome, all the gifts and graces of Chaucer's knight and squire and clerk and parson, and all the art of Vergil and Chaucer with them. Intellect and feeling had to combine in it, and to combine equally. Spenser's philosophy lacked the lucidity and system of severe intellectual process, but at least it did not attain lucidity and system by a severe process of exclusion of all that might interfere with its security. And among all our philosophic poets that may be said of Spenser alone.

Notes

1. *Gawaine and the Green Knight,* lines 1773–75.

2. Book IV.x.44–47.

3. *Hymne of Heavenly Beautie,* 78–83.

4. *Hymne of Heavenly Love,* 284.

5. *Amoretti,* XLV.

6. *Amoretti,* LXXXVIII.

7. Elegie XVI, 72–99.

8. Ed. of 1548, fol. 31v. "While cruel fate seizes me and forbids me to see my Lady, and keeps me in another place, her fair image seen in part feeds my hunger and quiets my sighs."

9. *Amours.*I.lxviii.

10. III.vi: *Of Coaches,* tr. Florio.

11. *Abrégé de l'art Poétique François,* ed. Blanchemain, VIII, 321.

12. G.-B. Pigna, *I Romanzi* (1554), p. 81.

13. VI.i.40 ff.; ii.14; ii.47–48; ix.6–7, 18.

14. Crudor, Briana, Maleffort, Turpine, Blandina.

15. Canto VI.iii.6.

16. Canto VI.iii.12–19.

17. Canto VI.vi. 18–vii.27.

18. Canto VI.vii.27–viii.30.

19. Canto VI.x.21–24.

20. Cf. i.12, 5–6 and Seneca, Ep. XXXV; vi.6 ff., and Ep. VIII.L, LXVIII; vi.14, and Ep. IX, XXV, LXIII; ix.20 ff., and Ep. II, IV; etc.

21. Alluded to, III.1. Cf. Wife of Bath's Tale, 257–60; *Rose,* 2196–97 *et passim.*

22. *Hymne in Honor of Beautie,* 16.

23. 1559. Du Bellay translated the verse quotations for him.

24. Introduction to Book V; VII.vii.49–55.

25. V.ii.40.

26. VII.viii—the last fragment of *The Faerie Queene.*

27. III.vi.40.

28. III.vi.37–38.

IV. The Minor Poems

William Nelson

Colin Clout

SPENSER CHOSE to present himself to the literary public of England under the pen name "Immerito," the Worthless One:

> I never lyst presume to Parnasse hyll,
> But pyping lowe in shade of lowly grove,
> I play to please my selfe, all be it ill. (*June,* 70–72)

His election of the pastoral form, traditionally the most humble of the literary "kinds," bears out the pose of the hesitant beginner, uncertain of his abilities. And the concluding Envoy

> Goe lyttle Calender, thou hast a free passeporte,
> Goe but a lowly gate emongste the meaner sorte

echoes the well-worn formula of self-depreciation which introduces or concludes Chaucer's *Troilus,* Lydgate's *Troy Book* and *Fall of Princes,* Hawes's *Pastime of Pleasure,* and other considerable works. The poet of this tradition claims no status, he is not a competitor of the great authors, he lacks skill and training. He has written his book at command, or to eschew that idleness which might lead him to worse sins, and he hopes only that his reader will forgive his errors and correct what is amiss. Perhaps, too, his labor will turn some man to good. These disclaimers may be as conventionally rhetorical and as meaningless as "your humble servant" but their general acceptance in the late Middle Ages together with the conception of the poet's role that goes with them contrasts sharply with the humanist exaltation of the poet as civilizer of mankind.

The pastoral is a humble genre; paradoxically, Spenser's choice of it to introduce himself as the "new poet" betrays his soaring ambition. He had decided to make of his career an *imitatio Vergilis*. Cuddie sets forth the model in the October eclogue:

> Indeede the Romish Tityrus, I heare,
> Through his Mecœnas left his Oaten reede,
> Whereon he earst had taught his flocks to feede,
> And laboured lands to yield the timely eare,
> And eft did sing of warres and deadly drede,
> So as the Heavens did quake his verse to here. (ll. 55–60)

As Vergil's pastorals prepared the way first for the *Georgics* and then for his great heroic poem, so Spenser, "following the example of the best and most auncient Poetes," begins with the pastoral, "as young birdes, that be newly crept out of the nest, by little first to prove theyr tender wyngs, before they make a greater flyght." Within a few months of the publication of the *Calender* Spenser had already finished a part of *The Faerie Queene* substantial enough to be sent to Harvey for criticism.

Although under his pastoral name of Colin, Spenser usually maintains the modest posture of a shepherd "boy," his rustic companions are lavish in his praise. The dramatic form of the eclogues may make us forget momentarily that it is the poet who makes Hobbinol say:

> I sawe Calliope wyth Muses moe,
> Soone as thy oaten pype began to sound,
> Theyr yvory Luyts and Tamburins forgoe:
> And from the fountaine, where they sat around,
> Renne after hastely thy silver sound.
> But when they came, where thou thy skill didst showe,
> They drewe abacke, as halfe with shame confound,
> Shepheard to see, them in theyr art outgoe. (*June*, 57–64)

And Perigot:

> O Colin, Colin, the shepheards joye,
> How I admire ech turning of thy verse
> (*August*, 190–91)

And Cuddie:

> For Colin fittes such famous flight to scanne:
> He, were he not with love so ill bedight,
> Would mount as high, and sing as soote as Swanne.
> (*October,* 88–90)

In *December,* even Colin admits the excellence of his verse:

> And if that Hobbinol right judgement bare,
> To Pan his owne selfe pype I neede not yield.
> For if the flocking Nymphes did folow Pan,
> The wiser Muses after Colin ranne. (ll. 45–48)

It is not the mere charm of his song that distinguishes Colin; the "wiser Muses" are led by other allurements. Pan and Cuddie may be content to "feede youthes fancie, and the flocking fry" but Colin's aim is higher. The same Envoy which humbly urges "Goe lyttle Calender" begins in a nobler vein:

> Loe I have made a Calender for every yeare,
> That steele in strength, and time in durance shall outweare:
> And if I marked well the starres revolution,
> It shall continewe till the worlds dissolution.
> To teach the ruder shepheard how to feede his sheepe,
> And from the falsers fraud his folded flocke to keepe.

The echo of the "Romish Tityrus" who "taught his flocks to feede" dares the comparison of Spenser with Vergil and makes it clear that the didactic intention of the *Calender* is not merely that of turning some man to good but the betterment of the commonwealth.[1]

Appropriately, therefore, the form of the first publication of *The Shepheardes Calender* was intended to impress the reader with a sense of the importance of the work. This collection of English poems by an unknown author was equipped with apparatus proper to an edition of a Latin classic: an introduction pointing out the singular merits of the poem, a disquisition on the nature and history of its genre, a glossary and notes. No English poet had ever been announced so pretentiously. There were four more printings in quarto, the last in 1597, after which the *Calender* was incorporated into the many editions of Spenser's collected works.

The identity of E. K., who is responsible for the editorial apparatus, is not known. There was an Edward Kirke at Pembroke Hall during Spenser's residence, and in October, 1579, a Mistresse Kerke collected and forwarded Spenser's mail. But little more is recorded of the former and nothing of the latter, so that even if they could be linked with the editor of the *Calender* the student of Spenser's poem would not be enlightened.[2] However, we do know something about E. K., both from the book itself and from references to him in Spenser's correspondence with Harvey. He claims friendship with the poet and some knowledge of his personal affairs, and he exhibits respectful admiration for Harvey to whom he addresses his dedicatory epistle. In the year following the publication of the *Calender* he was engaged in preparing an edition of another of Spenser's poems. Spenser writes to Harvey:

> I take best my *Dreames* shoulde come forth alone, being growen by meanes of the Glosse, (running continually in maner of a Paraphrase) full as great as my *Calendar*. Therein be some things excellently, and many things wittily discoursed of E. K. and the Pictures so singularly set forth, and purtrayed, as if Michael Angelo were there, he could (I think) nor amende the best, nor reprehende the worst.[3]

Unfortunately, the *Dreames* never did come forth, alone or otherwise. But if E. K. was the authorized editor of that work it seems not unlikely that he was of the *Calender* also, and that Spenser knew and approved of his introduction and notes before its publication.

Nevertheless, E. K. is not a reliable guide to the meaning of the *Calender*. Sometimes he obfuscates intentionally: in *May,* for instance, "Algrind" (transparently Archbishop Grindal) is glossed pointlessly—or as a sly joke—"the name of a shepheard." Sometimes he errs in interpreting Spenser's archaic words and in citing his sources. In larger matters, however, what W. L. Renwick justly calls the "stiffness" of E. K.'s mind makes his comment of doubtful value.[4] Pompously proud of his learning, he is more concerned with pointing out "a pretty epanorthosis" or arguing that "eclogue" should be written "aeglogue" than with explaining to the reader "the generall dryfte and purpose" of the work he is editing. Indeed, he may not have understood that drift. His Argument for the October eclogue describes Cuddie as "the perfecte paterne of a Poete, which finding no maintenaunce of his state and studies, complayneth of the contempte of Poetrie, and the causes thereof." This is, in fact, Cuddie's complaint and the complaint of pastoral poems on the same subject since the time of Theocritus, but it is not what this poem says, nor is Cuddie, obviously a foil for Colin, in any sense "the perfecte paterne of a Poete." Perhaps misreadings of this kind explain why Spenser thinks E. K.'s remarks are more often witty than excellent.

But E. K.'s criticism is sometimes excellent indeed. In defining the quality which makes the newness of the new poet, he writes: "For what in most English wryters useth to be loose, and as it were ungyrt, in this Authour is well grounded, finely framed, and strongly trussed up together." It is precisely the fine framing and strong trussing up together that distinguishes Spenser, not only from the "rakehelly rout" of his contemporaries, but also from most poets before him and after. The search for a unity, in particular a unity of the most various and even discordant elements, a unity both of form and substance, is one of the dominant characteristics of Spenser's poetry. And when the elements are considered in terms of time and change, the sought-for One becomes changeless eternity, not in opposition to the mutable but comprising it and arising from it. Hobbinol tells us in *April* that Colin tuned his lay unto the water's fall. A waterfall, single though composed of diverse and conflicting currents, stable though never the same, is no poor figure for the kind of poetry Spenser wanted to write and the conception of the world that he wanted to express.

Spenser was at least twenty-five years old when the *Calender* appeared, so that it can scarcely be described as a product of his immaturity. But in comparison with the work of his later years its contrivance is obvious enough to betray the direction of his poetic bent. He was familiar with the body of pastoral poetry, classical and Renaissance in origin. The form as he knew it had little to do with the beauty of growing things or the charm of the countryside. Particularly in its Renaissance development the pastoral standpoint required the poet to weigh the world of everyday, the world of court and city, by reducing its complexity and confusion to a conventional simplicity: simple loves, songs, and tasks, simple jealousies, ambitions, and responsibilities. So Spenser uses the form. But he elected to deviate from typical pastoral practice in several ways, most radically in the plan of his poem. Vergil's *Bucolics* consists of ten eclogues (from *eclogae,* selections); the number has no significance. Spenser's pastorals are twelve in number, firmly trussed up with the round of the year. Since the twelve eclogues, as the title page announces, are "proportionable to the twelve monethes," Spenser entitled them *The Shepheardes Calender,* "applying an olde name to a new worke." The old name is that of the *Kalendar & Compost of Shepherds,* a curious compilation which is an ancestor of innumerable "farmers' almanacs." Translated from a fifteenth-century French original in 1503 and again in 1506 and 1508, it proved hugely popular, edition succeeding edition until as late as 1656. Like its successors, the *Kalendar* contained in addition to an almanac proper a treasury of moral instruction and useful information: analyses of the vices and virtues; expositions of the paternoster, the creed, and the commandments; compendious dissertations on astronomy, physiology, and anatomy. Spenser took from it not only his title but the idea of illustrating each of his eclogues with a woodcut labeled with the astrological sign appropriate to the month.[5] He may also have noticed the chapter (No. 33) entitled "Of the commodity of the twelve months of the year with the twelve ages of man," though the notion of a correspondence between the succession of seasons and the course of human life is no doubt as old as man himself.

"We are entitled to assume," writes an editor of *The Shepheardes Calender,* "that Spenser invented the Calendar-scheme because he had written some eclogues, rather than that he invented the scheme in the air and then proceeded to write eclogues."[6] The title to this assumption rests, first, on the fact that some of the eclogues make no mention of the season, and second, on evidence tending to show that Spenser did not compose them in the order in which they appear. E. K. provides no note or gloss for that part of *August* following line 138, so that it seems likely that Colin's sestina (ll. 151–89) was interpolated after the editorial work had been completed. Again, in the November eclogue, Colin tells us that Phoebus has "taken up his ynne in Fishes haske" [a] yet the maker of the woodcuts knew that in November the sun is in the astrological sign Sagittarius, not Pisces, and so too did Spenser himself when he came to write the Cantos of Mutabilitie. Probably, Spenser decided for some reason to make a February eclogue do for November and carelessly failed to change the text accordingly. For these reasons, a number of scholars have undertaken to reconstruct the order in which Spenser composed the parts of the *Calender,* the result being an equal number of different hypothetical sequences.

But it must be the rare poet who begins with the first line of his poem and finishes with the last. In the absence of Spenser's own testimony it is impossible to decide whether he thought of a *Calender* because he had written some eclogues or whether he invented the scheme "in the air." In fact, he would so have invented it if he remembered the famous instruction of Geoffrey of Vinsauf which his "master" Chaucer quotes in *Troilus and Criseyde* (Book I, ll. 1065–69):

> For everi wight that hath an hous to founde
> Ne renneth naught the werk for to bygynne
> With rakel [b] hond, but he wol bide a stounde,
> And sende his hertes line out fro withinne
> Aldirfirst his purpos for to wynne.

The question to be answered, at least for the purpose of understanding Spenser's meaning, is whether the book is one poem or twelve, whether the title is merely the consequence of a process of "practical bookmaking" or concerns the substance of the work. The history of the composition of a poem, however interesting biographically, is one thing; the structure of a poem is another. It is the structure to which I shall attend.

Geoffrey of Vinsauf's house has a plan, but it does not have a beginning or an end. There is a strong tendency among critics to insist upon progression or development of some kind as essential

[a] haske: basket, creel.
[b] rakel: hasty.

to all literary constructions. Plots must be resolved, characters "grow," ideas reveal themselves. Under the influence of this tendency, some students of the *Calender* have tried to find a "story" in it: a tale of the love of Colin for Rosalind, a poet's autobiography. There is no such story. Spenser's *Calender* does not bring us from the beginning of the year to its end; it is a circle rather than a straight line.

Although Spenser is not as rigid an architect as some of his critics, the theme of time and man pervades his poem and constitutes its principal subject.[7] The dimension of time is here employed, not primarily to expose the idea of mutability, but to examine human states in terms of their past and their future. *January* and *December,* unlike the other eclogues, are soliloquies. In *January* Colin complains of the futile waste of his life:

> Thou barrein ground, whome winters wrath hath wasted,
> Art made a myrrhour, to behold my plight:
> Whilome thy fresh spring flowrd, and after hasted
> Thy sommer prowde with Daffadillies dight.
> And now is come thy wynters stormy state,
> Thy mantle mard,[c] wherein thou maskedst late.
>
> Such rage as winters, reigneth in my heart,
> My life bloud friesing with unkindly cold:
> Such stormy stoures do breede my balefull smart,
> As if my yeare were wast, and woxen old.
> And yet alas, but now my spring begonne,
> And yet alas, yt is already donne. (ll. 19–30)

As *January* recalls the spring and foreshadows *December,* so *December* recapitulates: "Whilome in youth, when flowrd my joyfull spring." Throughout the *Calender,* the matter of growth, maturity, and decay repeatedly asserts itself. *February* is a debate between youth and age; *March* presents the innocent youth as yet unacquainted with the pangs of love; *May* contrasts Palinode, who wishes he could help the ladies bear the Maybush, with Piers:

[c] mard: marred.

For Younkers [d] Palinode such follies fitte,
But we tway bene men of elder witt. (ll. 17–18)

In *June* Colin rejects beauty and delight:

And I, whylst youth and course of carelesse yeeres
Did let me walke withouten lincks of love,
In such delights did joy amongst my peeres:
But ryper age such pleasures doth reprove,
My fancye eke from former follies move
To stayed steps. (ll. 33–38)

September shows us the fortune-seeking Diggon Davie returned from his travels ragged, despondent, and bitter. In *October* Cuddie compares his youthful song-making with the improvidence of the grasshopper of the fable. In *November* Colin sings of the death of Dido: spring is the time of merriment, autumn of the mournful muse.

As the examples I have given suggest, the poles which form the *Calender* are not simply youth and age. With youth Spenser associates susceptibility to love, freedom from care, delight in song, ambitious striving. With maturity and age come pain and disillusionment in love, a profound sense of responsibility, rejection of pleasure, disappointment in life's harvest. From eclogue to eclogue, these subsidiary contraries receive greater or less emphasis, yet each recurs often enough to give unity to the whole. As the thematic stress changes, so does the pastoral conception itself. Sometimes the shepherd is primarily a lover, sometimes a poet, sometimes a priest, yet he is always all of these.

The confrontation of youth and age is most direct in the February eclogue. The introductory dialogue between the shepherd boy Cuddie and the ninety-year-old Thenot recalls the soliloquy of the young-old loving-unloved Colin of *January*. Cuddie's green love has not yet reached the point of pain:

. . . Phyllis is myne for many dayes:
I wonne her with a gyrdle of gelt,[e]

[d] Younkers: youngsters.
[e] gelt: gilt(?).

Embost with buegle[f] about the belt.
Such an one shepeheards woulde make full faine:
Such an one would make thee younge againe.

But Thenot answers:

Thou art a fon,[g] of thy love to boste,
All that is lent to love, wyll be lost. (ll. 64–70)

Cuddie and his flock are miserable in the bitter winter. But Thenot has learned the lesson of the Stoics: he makes no complaint of cold or heat, he is no foeman to Fortune,

. . . ever my flocke was my chiefe care,
Winter or Sommer they mought well fare. (ll. 23–24)

Cuddie may be careless, his youthful pride to be paid for with "weeping, and wayling, and misery," but he is alive, budding, about to flower. So too is his "brag" bullock:

His hornes bene as broade, as Rainebowe bent,
His dewelap as lythe, as lasse of Kent.
See howe he venteth into the wynd.
Weenest of love is not his mynd? (ll. 73–76)

Thenot, like his sheep, is dried up, crooked, fruitless:

Thy Ewes, that wont to have blowen bags,
Like wailefull widdowes hangen their crags:[h]
The rather[i] Lambes bene starved with cold,
All for their Maister is lustlesse and old. (ll. 81–84)

Thenot concludes the eclogue with his tale of the Oak and the Briar. Of all the stories told by the Kentish shepherd Tityrus (Chaucer, of

[f] buegle: glass bead.
[g] fon: fool.
[h] crags: necks.
[i] rather: younger.

course, though the tale is none of his) there is "none fitter then this to applie."

The application is obvious enough. An ancient Oak, once a goodly tree but now barren and decaying, is challenged by a Briar, proudly thrusting upward, gay with blossoms, the delight of shepherds' daughters and of nightingales. When the Briar complains to the Husbandman that the great old tree tyrannizes over him, cutting off his light and blighting his flowers, the Oak is cut down. But the Briar's glee is short-lived: winter comes, and the unprotected Briar, burdened by snow, falls to the ground,

> . . . is trodde in the durt
> Of cattell, and brouzed, and sorely hurt.
> Such was thend of this Ambitious brere,
> For scorning Eld. (ll. 235–38)

Curiously, in *The Ruines of Time* Spenser uses the figure of an aged tree that will not suffer new growth near it to condemn the overshadowing Burghley. Here, since Thenot tells the story, the reader's sympathy goes to the Oak. The reverence—perhaps superstitiously—due to age cannot save it from decay and destruction. But youth, though it wants to live free of control, though it envies the prestige and authority which maturity brings, nevertheless depends upon maturity for its existence. The moral is not unlike that of Menenius' fable of the belly and the members: as plebeians cannot live without the nobility, so youth cannot live without age. Cuddie, naturally, thinks it a lewd tale of little worth.

In *December* the mature Colin faces his own youth. The contrasts of *February* reappear: the young man "Like Swallow swift" wanders carelessly, thinking his spring will last forever; with time comes pain, an application to things of "ryper reason," a profound sense of responsibility. And again, youth destroys age. As Shakespeare has it in Sonnet LXXIII,

> In me thou seest the glowing of such fire,
> That on the ashes of his youth doth lye,
> As the death bed, wheron it must expire,
> Consum'd with that which it was nurrisht by.

The rage of love, kindled in the young man's breast by the god of shepherds ("But better mought they have behote[j] him Hate"), blasts the promised harvest. On this dark note the *Calender* ends.

Much of the December eclogue is imitated from Clement Marot's *Eglogue au Roy*. The theme of love the destroyer, however, is Spenser's addition. It is one of the most important of the threads which bind the *Calender*. Although Cuddie thinks love is mere delight, Thenot knows it to be folly. In *August* Perigot complains,

> So learnd I love on a hollye eve
>
> That ever since my hart did greve. (ll. 121–23)

Willy, in the March eclogue, is childish enough to suggest that

> . . . we little Love awake,
> That nowe sleepeth in Lethe lake,
> And pray him leaden our daunce. (ll. 22–24)

His companion, Thomalin, is wiser through experience. Cupid, in seeming play, once hit him with his shaft:

> . . . then I little smart did feele:
> But soone it sore encreased.
> And now it ranckleth more and more,
> And inwardly it festreth sore,
> Ne wote I, how to cease it. (ll. 98–102)

The change of love from honey to gall reflects a change in the god of love himself. When Willy is told of the poison in Cupid's arrows, he remembers,

> . . . once I heard my father say,
> How he him caught upon a day,
> (Whereof he wilbe wroken[k])

[j] behote: called.
[k] wroken: revenged.

Entangled in a fowling net,
Which he for carrion Crowes had set,
  That in our Peeretree haunted.
Tho sayd, he was a winged lad,
But bowe and shafts as then none had:
  Els had he sore be daunted. (ll. 106–14)

Perhaps the fowling net is intended to make the reader think of the gin in which Vulcan trapped Venus and Mars, the pear tree to remind him of the tree of Eden or the one into which May climbed in Chaucer's tale. But the point of the episode is that Love, who once upon a time went about without weapons, in all innocence, now is armed with a venomous sting. Leo Spitzer reads the moral of the tale, "Rejoice not in spring, be not young!—for this is hybris, and nemesis must follow!" [8]

Colin's love for Rosalind is of this day, and the armed Cupid has taken his revenge. In youth, the heat of heedless lust engendered the flame:

Tho would I seeke for Queene apples unrype,
To give my Rosalind. (*June,* 43–44)

The happiness of such a love is fragile. It is destroyed by the discovery that Rosalind is disdainful ("dangerous," the medieval lover would say) and worse, fickle. The remainder is pain and waste: the harvest burnt, friendship for Hobbinol sacrificed, the shepherd's pipe broken. And the sheep in Colin's care suffer too:

Thou feeble flocke, whose fleece is rough and rent,
Whose knees are weake through fast and evill fare:
Mayst witnesse well by thy ill governement,
Thy maysters mind is overcome with care.
Thou weake, I wanne: thou leane, I quite forlorne:
With mourning pyne I, you with pyning mourne.
(*January,* 43–48)

The case is general. As Willy says in *August:* "Never knewe I lovers sheepe in good plight."

As the amorous shepherd cares little for his sheep, so the preoccupied pastor neglects his flock. Neither Theocritus nor Vergil would have thought of associating rustic and priest, but the authority of the Bible and the weight of medieval tradition made the connection inevitable. Out of that tradition emerged an ideal portrait of the priest: simple, humble, pure, completely dedicated to the care of his congregation. The ideal, like all ideals, served as a principal weapon of satire, as it did for Chaucer at his most bitter:

> For if a preest be foul, on whom we truste,
> No wonder is a lewed man to ruste;
> And shame it is, if a prest take keep,
> A shiten shepherde and a clene sheep.[9]

In the formal pastoral of the Renaissance, the equation of priest and shepherd appears as early as Petrarch, and it occurs in the eclogues of Spenser's English predecessors in the genre, Alexander Barclay and Barnabe Googe. For the Protestant, the analogy was particularly attractive because it supported both his demand for a return to the religion of the apostles and his attack upon the pomp and pride of Rome.[10]

May, July, and *September* are the eclogues principally devoted to the shepherd-priest. *February* is usually included with these, but the argument for its interpretation in this sense seems to me tenuous. The best support for such a reading of the eclogue is found in the lines which describe the old Oak as it is about to be felled:

> . . . it had bene an auncient tree,
> Sacred with many a mysteree,
> And often crost with the priestes crewe,
> And often halowed with holy water dewe.
> But sike fancies weren foolerie,
> And broughten this Oake to this miserye.
> For nought mought they quitten him from decay.
>
> (ll. 207–13)

The crossing and the holy water suggest that by the Oak Spenser may intend Catholicism or in some sense the old religion (though a Protestant would insist that his was the religion of the apostles and Catholicism a latter-day distortion). Once such an identification is accepted, a variety of allegories can be drawn out of Thenot's fable. The most plausible of these interprets the tale as a warning to those religious radicals who, in their zeal for reform, would uproot all of the old and leave the new Tudor growth without the protection of established tradition. But Spenser may have meant no more than a passing shot at Roman rites as equivalent in vanity to the pagan magic of Druid oak-worshipers. Following Professor Renwick, I am inclined to accept E. K.'s description of the eclogue as "a discourse of old age" "rather morall and generall, then bent to any secrete or particular purpose."[11]

The subject of *May* is the dedication of the priest to his calling. Piers—his name suggests Langland's Piers the Plowman and his numerous successors of the fifteenth and sixteenth centuries—is of the line of Chaucer's poor Parson. For Piers, the life of a true "shepherd" must be altogether unworldly, altogether unlike the life of a layman. The apostles, the first Christians, had no concern with possessions, with pleasures, with ambitions. Like them, the modern shepherd must give himself up wholly to the watch of his flock, to the protection of the faith. The slightest relaxation leads to disaster, for the Enemy is wily beyond measure. To this effect Piers tells the fable of the foolish Kid whom a false Fox deceives and devours. Palinode, as his name declares (but what an odd name for a shepherd!), takes the contrary position. A shepherd is a man as other men are. The goods of the world are God-given and given to be enjoyed. The carping precisian, constantly scolding other shepherds, does more harm than good, bringing shame upon the whole calling. To these arguments Piers answers uncompromisingly:

> . . . what concord han[l] light and darke sam? [m]
> Or what peace has the Lion with the Lambe?
>
> (ll. 168–69)

There are suggestions in Piers's fable that the Fox is to be identified with Catholicism: he carries a bag of bells, baubles, and glass trifles

[l] han: have.
[m] sam: together.

and he swears by "sweete Saint Charitee." E. K.'s account of the eclogue, in fact, asserts that Piers and Palinode represent "two formes of pastoures or Ministers, or the protestant and the Catholique." But the intention is surely wider than the latter alternative. Rome may be a manifestation of Satan, but the ways of error are countless. Nor is the debate as one-sided as the identification of the speakers with Protestantism and Catholicism would demand. It is true that Piers's contention is the weightier and the more emotionally charged. But Palinode's part is not specious. In *September,* Hobbinol, of whom Spenser obviously approves, is made to speak very much in Palinode's vein:

> Ah Diggon, thilke same rule were too straight,
> All the cold season to wach and waite.
> We bene of fleshe, men as other bee,
> Why should we be bound to such miseree?
> What ever thing lacketh chaungeable rest,
> Mought needes decay, when it is at best. (ll. 236–41)

As Spenser uses it, the dialogue of a pastoral poem is not a Socratic demonstration but a valid disagreement in which the speakers explore what may best be said on either part.

The debate of *July* is between pride (or aspiration) and humility (or laziness). The symbol of the former is the hill upon which the goatherd Morrel sits; that of the latter the shepherd Thomalin's lowly plain. In the eighth eclogue of Baptista Mantuanus (Baptista Spagnuoli), the principal source of *July,* it is the peasant on the hill who persuades. Spenser gives the stronger argument to his opponent. Morrel may claim that the great god Pan dwelt upon Mount Olivet, but Thomalin knows that the "saints" of yore "lived in lowlye leas." Such was Abel

> That whilome was the first shepheard,
> and lived with little gayne:
> As meeke he was, as meeke mought be,
> simple, as simple sheepe. (ll. 127–30)

And such, too, were Moses and Aaron and the twelve brothers who founded the tribes of Israel. The ideal is that of Piers:

> But shepheard mought be meeke and mylde,
> well eyed, as Argus was,
> With fleshly follyes undefyled,
> and stoute as steede of brasse. (ll. 153–56)

The butt of Thomalin's satire is also that of Piers's, the self-seeking prelate whose great possessions and concern with power leave him no interest in the welfare of his flock. Catholic priests are of this kind, as Palinode, who has been to Rome, testifies. But the eclogue as a whole is not merely a diatribe against Catholicism. Thomalin's exemplary tale is of Algrind, the good shepherd, who once sat on a hill and suffered therefor:

> For sitting so with bared scalpe,
> an Eagle sored hye,
> That weening hys whyte head was chalke,
> a shell fish downe let flye:
> She weend the shell fishe to have broake,
> but therewith bruzd his brayne,
> So now astonied with the stroke,
> he lyes in lingring payne. (ll. 221–28)

Aeschylus' mishap is here applied to Archbishop Grindal in one of the indubitable topical references of the *Calender*. Grindal, Archbishop of Canterbury, was suspended by Queen Elizabeth in 1577, two years before the publication of Spenser's poem, for his refusal to carry out harsh measures against extreme Puritans. Morrel prophesies his restoration:

> . . . his hap was ill,
> but shall be bett in time. (ll. 229–30)

Although Algrind was no Roman, he rose to high place and was struck down. The eclogue is concerned only in part with a condemnation of ambitious priests. It is also a warning against the temptation and the danger of the heights.

September is more obscure—or more confused—than the other eclogues of this group. It begins with a variant of the ambition theme: Diggon Davie has sought to better his state in "forrein costes" but has found only misery and loss. His foil is the temperate philosopher Hobbinol:

> Content who lives with tryed state,
> Neede feare no chaunge of frowning fate. (ll. 70–71)

Diggon's complaint turns into a violent denunciation of the greedy, proud, false shepherds whom he encountered in his travels. In some passages those shepherds are clearly the "Popish prelates" to whom E. K. refers, in others they appear to be intended more generally as bad priests in high places. Diggon's fable, like that of Piers in *May,* emphasizes the wiliness of the Enemy and the necessity for sleepless watch. Its hero is Roffy: John Young, Bishop of Rochester (*episcopus Roffensis*), whose secretary in 1578 was Edmund Spenser. Because the Kid in the May story is foolish and unwary, the Fox escapes with his prey, and because Roffy is "wise, and as Argus eyed," the Wolf of *September* is caught and killed.

This body of religious satire seems hard to reconcile with the loves of Cuddie, Perigot, and Colin. But Spenser forges the link. The unfortunate Kid of the May eclogue is as heedlessly lustful as Cuddie:

> His Vellet[n] head began to shoote out,
> And his wreathed hornes gan newly sprout:
> The blossomes of lust to bud did beginne,
> And spring forth ranckly under his chinne. (ll. 185–88)

The good shepherd Abel is contrasted with Helen's Paris:

> But nothing such thilk shephearde was,
> whom Ida hyll dyd beare,
> That left hys flocke, to fetch a lasse,
> whose love he bought to deare:
> For he was proude, that ill was payd,
> (no such mought shepheards bee)
> And with lewde lust was overlayd:
> tway things doen ill agree. (*July,* 145–52)

[n] Vellet: velvet, the soft skin covering the growing horns.

As there was a time when Cupid went unarmed, so there was a golden age of Christianity before priests became greedy and proud. But innocence is gone and both shepherd-lover and shepherd-priest are the worse for it.

Colin himself is the principal shepherd-poet. The woodcuts for the four eclogues in which he appears all show him with a shepherd's pipe. In *January, June,* and *December,* the pipe lies shattered at his feet; in *November* Colin plays upon it his dirge for Dido as Thenot puts a laurel crown on his head. The motif of the broken pipe is the dominant one. The January eclogue announces it: since Rosalind scorns Colin's rustic muse he will sing no more. In *June* the restless, tormented Colin is contrasted with his friend Hobbinol, content with his lot:

> O happy Hobbinol, I blesse thy state,
> That Paradise hast found, whych Adam lost.

Hobbinol urges his friend to join him in his delicious dale, to leave the hills which have bewitched him. But Colin cannot recover the Eden he has lost. Once, in his youth, when he walked "withouten lincks of love," he was able to enjoy the delights of Hobbinol's paradise, to sing sweet rhymes and roundelays. But time and pain have killed his bent for such song, and his only ambition now is to make complaint so bitter that it will pierce the heart of heartless Rosalind. In *December* Colin again recalls his early song, framed "Unto the shifting of the shepheards foote," the youthful promise of his poetry, and the blighting of that promise by Rosalind's falseness. Now his Muse is hoarse and weary, and he hangs his pipe upon a tree (though the woodcut shows it broken on the ground).

It is the October eclogue which is principally devoted to the shepherd-poet. Because of its elevation of the subject to a new and exalted level and because of its resumption of the themes that bind the *Calender* together, it constitutes the focus of the whole. Theocritus had written about the poet unrewarded and so had Vergil, Baptista Mantuanus, and many others. Cuddie's part in the eclogue is imitated from Baptista, but Piers's speeches are for the most part Spenser's own. Cuddie, like Colin, has abandoned song, but not because of a broken heart:

> The dapper ditties, that I wont devise,
> To feede youthes fancie, and the flocking fry,
> Delighten much: what I the bett for thy? (ll. 13–15)

The "Delighten much" was a signal to Spenser's readers—where was the rest of the "delight and teach" formula? When Piers offers glory as a reward, Cuddie takes it to mean words of praise, nothing but smoke and wind. Once, indeed, there was a time when poetic genius might fulfill itself: through the help of Maecenas, Vergil (the "Romish Tityrus") grew from the writing of pastorals to the composition of the useful *Georgics,*

> And eft did sing of warres and deadly drede,
> So as the Heavens did quake his verse to here. (ll. 59–60)

But the modern poet lacks both means and subject matter. Maecenas is dead, and there is no longer a "mighty manhode" to celebrate in these degenerate, easeful times.

Piers and Cuddie are such poles apart that they can talk only at cross purposes. For Piers, the honor of virtuous action, not earthly fame, is the reward for the poet who inspires men to noble deeds and keeps them from evil ways:

> O what an honor is it, to restraine
> The lust of lawlesse youth with good advice:
> Or pricke them forth with pleasaunce of thy vaine,
> Whereto thou list their trayned ° willes entice. (ll. 21–24)

As Milton puts it in *Lycidas,* the payment for the homely, slighted shepherd's trade cannot be canceled by the blind Fury slitting the thin-spun life: "Of so much fame in Heaven expect thy meed." Like Cuddie, Piers believes that as the true poet matures he reaches higher. His ascent begins on the Vergilian path: when the pastoral mode is outgrown the poet should "sing of bloody Mars, of wars, of giusts." But now Piers looks to a step beyond:

° trayned: trapped.

Turne thee to those, that weld the awful crowne,
To doubted Knights, whose woundlesse armour rusts,
And helmes unbruzed wexen dayly browne. (ll. 40–42)

The rusted armor, like Mercilla's rusted sword in the fifth book of *The Faerie Queene,* represents a power the potentiality of which is enough to keep the peace. For subject matter Piers offers, not the embattled warriors whose absence Cuddie regrets, but those who, like Elizabeth and the great Earl of Leicester ("That first the white beare to the stake did bring"), make England so feared that none dares attack it. Nor is this the pinnacle of poetic achievement. When Cuddie protests that poetry finds no favor among the great in these corrupt times, Piers breaks into an apostrophe to "pierlesse Poesye":

. . . where is then thy place?
If nor in Princes pallace thou doe sitt:
(And yet is Princes pallace the most fitt)
Ne brest of baser birth doth thee embrace.
Then make thee winges of thine aspyring wit,
And, whence thou camst, flye backe to heaven apace.
(ll. 79–84)

As poetry is divine in origin, so its final subject is the divine. And now the eclogue takes a new turn.

Though Cuddie's vision is limited, he is able to sense both the height of Piers's conception and his own inadequacy to it:

For Colin fittes such famous flight to scanne:
He, were he not with love so ill bedight,
Would mount as high, and sing as soote as Swanne.
(ll. 88–90)

The bitter experience of the shepherd-lover makes it impossible for him to attain the poetic summit, the song of heaven. The result, as Cuddie sees it, is the barren waste of *January* and *December.* But for Piers, love is not a blight. "Ah fon," he says (I take it that the "fool" is Colin):

> . . . for love does teach him climbe so hie,
> And lyftes him up out of the loathsome myre:
> Such immortall mirrhor, as he doth admire,
> Would rayse ones mynd above the starry skie.
> And cause a caytive corage to aspire,
> For lofty love doth loath a lowly eye. (ll. 91–96)

Love the destroyer is here faced with love the creator. The opposition is central to the poet's thinking, but I must here leave it adumbrated, as the poet does.

In some sense, Colin is of course Master Edmund Spenser, the gifted young poet deeply concerned with the calling he had elected and its relation to the world about him. But Spenser's harvest was not burnt up, his career a failure and at an end in 1579; in fact, it is clear from his correspondence with Harvey that the publication of the *Calender* had spurred his poetic activity and that he was full of hopes for advancement. Hobbinol is as surely Gabriel Harvey. Spenser's portrait of him as the wise, contented philosopher does not, in truth, fit with what Nashe has to say about Harvey nor with our own impression drawn from Harvey's writings, but Nashe and we may be wrong, or Spenser may. However, we may be secure in doubting that Dr. Harvey ever sent Edmund Spenser "His kiddes, his cracknelles, and his early fruit." Hobbinol's pastoral love for Colin gives us no reason to suppose (or not to suppose) that Harvey was homosexually inclined. The search for Rosalind's identity has wasted infinite scholarly effort. Of all the speculations on the subject, the most remarkable is that which identifies her with Queen Elizabeth, partly on the ground that "Elisa R" taken together with the first syllable of "England" (with the "g" changed to "d" for euphony) is an anagram for *Rasilende,* "a name close in sound and spelling to *Rosalind*." [12] Both E. K. and Harvey's letters suggest that there was indeed a living Rosalind, but who she was and what relationship she bore to the Rosalind of the *Calender* no one knows. Cuddie, too, appears to have some connection with an Elizabethan person but our knowledge ends with that statement. In any case, it has proved impossible to read a biography of Spenser from *The Shepheardes Calender.*

In the tradition, as old as Vergil, which made the pastoral eclogue an appropriate vehicle for political comment, some of the shepherds of the *Calender* allude to public figures of the time. Roffy and Algrin, or Algrind, as has been said, refer to Bishop Young and Archbishop Grindal. Perhaps Morrel (of *July*) is Aylmer or Elmer, Bishop of London, whom Martin Marprelate ragged so unmercifully a decade later. Diggon Davie (*September*) may allude to Richard Davies, Bishop of St. David's, and Thomalin (*March* and *July*) to Thomas Cooper, Bishop of Lincoln.[13] If Spenser intended the identification of Morrel, Diggon Davie, and Thomalin with these bishops he was bold enough to criticize the morality of very powerful men indeed, a risky matter for a young poet to meddle with but something of which he was quite capable, as we know from his later attacks on Cecil. Even the undoubted reference to Grindal's suspension is evidence of that rashness of spirit of which his friend Harvey accused him.

Under other names of the poem Spenser eulogizes the great of the realm. Even E. K. admits that Elisa represents the Queen—rude shepherds, he points out, would be incapable of knowing her right name. (Drayton achieves originality of a kind by having his shepherds call her "Beta.") Lobbin, who appears in *Colin Clouts Come Home Againe* as the Earl of Leicester, may also have the same meaning in the November eclogue where he mourns the loss of Dido, though diligent research has failed to discover an appropriate Dido. Pan presents a problem of a different kind. He is always identifiable from context, but the identity in one place is that of Henry VIII (with Syrinx as Anne Boleyn?), in another a poet less meritorious than Colin, and in yet another God Himself.

The names Spenser chooses for the people of the *Calender* are not usual ones. Most Renaissance pastoralists, including Spenser's English predecessors Alexander Barclay and Barnabe Googe, were content to use the names made familiar by Theocritus and Vergil: Codrus, Daphnis, Phyllis, Menalcas, Tityrus. Clement Marot is an exception. He calls himself Colin, which Spenser imitates by adopting "Colin Clout," the pseudonym of the English satirist John Skelton. "Thenot" also comes from Marot. Spenser's Willy and Piers are plain English, harmonious with the rustic setting. But what can be made of Hobbinol, Wrenock, Palinode, and Roffy? Evidently Spenser wished to avoid on the one hand the classicism of the traditional names and on the other the commonness of the everyday. Names like these sound rude and are therefore fitting but they are not banal. Drayton follows Spenser's example, calling his shepherds Batte, Gorbo, Olcon, and Motto.

The point has some relevance to the larger question of Spenser's choice of a literary vocabulary. As he would not name his characters Daphnis and Phyllis, so he rejected the Latinate words that the English humanist tradition condemned as "inkhorn" and "smelling of the lamp." But he rejected, also, the kind of English that the humanist tradition advocated, a "standard" language which admitted only the oldest of the new and the newest of the old. For the purposes of poetry, such a language is dull and prosy, as Aristotle and Coleridge and many others have recognized. The principle of decorum, too, forbade the speech of Spenser's London to his rustics. They might have spoken a dialect, but the effect, for Spenser's audience, would have been merely ridicule. The only instance of sixteenth-century literary use of dialect for other than humorous or grotesque effect that I can think of is Shakespeare's *Henry V*, and in this case the exception really proves the rule: one of the principal points of the play is that under a true king true Englishmen who speak oddly or eat leeks are nevertheless Englishmen and those who think otherwise will find language and vegetable rammed down their throats. Spenser's solution is to mix with a basically normal vocabulary words already archaic or becoming so, words made to sound archaic by such means as the addition of the perfective prefix "y" ("yglaunst," "yshrilled"), and dialectal words which he and his London readers may have thought archaic. The result is a flavor of the antique and the rude in which sometimes the one predominates and sometimes the other. In poems written after *The Shepheardes Calender* the flavor remains, though it becomes rather less rude and much less sharp. E. K. is at pains to defend Spenser's practice on the principle of decorum and on a variety of other grounds: it reflects the poet's inheritance of the national tradition of Chaucer and other English "ancients"; the antiquity of the words "maketh the style seeme grave, and as it were reverend"; because of their harshness the words serve as discords in music to make the contrasting harmony sweeter; and their return to English usage recovers for the language "good and naturall English words, as have ben long time out of use and almost cleane disherited." Sir Philip Sidney, to whom the poem was dedicated, was not impressed with these arguments: "That same framing of his stile to an old rustick language I dare not alowe, sith neyther Theocritus in Greeke, Virgill in Latine, nor Sanazar in Italian did affect it." [14] On precisely the same ground of authoritative precedent Dryden and Pope praise Spenser for his imitation of Theocritus' use of a Doric dialect. Ben Jonson says that Spenser "writ no language" and Samuel Johnson thinks that if the shepherds of the *Calender* found it necessary to discourse on theology they might at least have taken the time to learn English. Others have come to the conclusion that Spenser is the father of English as a language of poetry.[15] That his adventure in vocabulary was a success may be doubted; that it was bold cannot.

In his verse forms, too, Spenser departs from the tradition. Following Vergil's example, the neo-Latin pastoralists of the Renaissance accepted the hexameter as their proper meter. Alexander Barclay's English eclogues are all in pentameter couplets except for a stanzaic elegy. Barnabe Googe holds faithfully to the fourteener. In contrast, there are thirteen different verse forms in the *Calender*. According to Renwick, "Of these three or four were common in his time; two at least were entirely new inventions, three were new rhyme-arrangements, two new importations, one an imitation of Chaucerian couplet peculiar to this book; and only three of the thirteen were ever used by Spenser again." [16] This variety is unique in collections of formal eclogues, apart, that is, from imitations of Spenser. But it does have a precedent in Sannazaro's Arcadian romance, a mingling of prose and verse in which there are examples of the canzone, the sestina, terza rima, and other forms.[17] The precedent is an important one since it suggested to Sidney the use of a great number of verse forms for the poems in his own *Arcadia*. At about the same time—it is impossible to tell which is earlier—both Sidney and Spenser were exploring the range of metrical possibilities for pastoral poetry. The explorations had very different results.

In Sidney's *Arcadia,* the first poem of the "Eclogues" which conclude Book I is itself a medley of meters and complex rhyme schemes. It is followed by three poems in unrhymed quantitative verse: elegiacs, sapphics, and hexameters. The last of the eclogues of Book I is a long poem in stanzas rhyming *abababcc*. Elsewhere in the

Arcadia are sestinas, unrhymed, double, and rhymed; dizains with a "crown" (the last line of each stanza is the first of the next); an echo poem; and more classical experiments: anacreontics, asclepiads, phaleucians.

With the exception of the sestina, to which Spenser gives a twist of his own, none of these ingenuities appears in the *Calender*. There is no quantitative verse at all, though Spenser was strongly attracted to the idea and discussed it with Harvey and with Sidney himself in 1580. Perhaps he thought so learned a kind of composition would be inappropriate in a pastoral. There are only three poems in complex verse forms in the *Calender,* and all are attributed to Colin, the nightingale of shepherds: the lay of Elisa, the sestina of *August,* and the elegy on Dido. The rest of the *Calender* is written in couplets or in simple stanzaic patterns.

It is not so much the number of the metrical forms in the *Calender* that is remarkable; it is rather their range. The sestina in which Colin gravely laments the pain of his love is set against the breathless rustic roundelay of Perigot and Willy. At one end of Spenser's scale are the long, flowing stanzas in praise of Elisa and in memory of Dido, mixing long and short verses, the rhyme schemes formally binding the units together, the complex but lucid syntax providing integrity of substance for the whole. These forms, no doubt inspired by French or Italian models, Spenser later elaborated to create the magnificent structures of his *Epithalamion* and *Prothalamion.* At the other end of his scale are the rude, lurching couplets of *February, May,* and *September.*

The lines of these eclogues are deliberately rough:

Hobbinol: Diggon Davie, I bid her[p] god day:
Or Diggon her is, or I missaye.
Diggon: Her was her, while it was daye light,
But now her is a most wretched wight.
For day, that was, is wightly[q] past,
And now at earst[r] the dirke night doth hast.

(*September,* 1–6)

[p] her: him.
[q] wightly: swiftly.
[r] at earst: at once.

The irregular stress and the alliteration suggest that Spenser was imitating such revivals or survivals of Anglo-Saxon versification as *Piers Plowman* and Dunbar's *Tretis of the Tua Mariit Wemen and the Wedo.* Some scholars have thought that Spenser's model was Chaucer as he would have been read in the sixteenth century, with final *e*'s silent. But such a reading, while it would have been more irregular than Chaucer intended, would not have resulted in the harshness of the *February* verse nor would it account for the insistent running of the letter. Whatever its derivation, the experiment was a most daring one. The generation of poets before Spenser had aspired to a perfectly regular alternation of strong and weak stresses. Sidney's line is usually free from the monotonous regularity of his predecessors, but he takes no such liberties as Spenser does. Even his attempts at quantitative verse merely substitute one kind of rule for another, while the verse of *February, May,* and *September* follows no usual rule at all. The justification for Spenser's practice must lie in the traditional Englishness of his line and in the principle of decorum as the Renaissance understood it. Since the matter of these eclogues is harsh and unpleasant, the manner should grate. The association of roughness of versification with satiric content was reinforced by the example of Juvenal. John Skelton, who claims Juvenal as his inspiration, defends his own peculiar cacophonies:

> For though my rime be ragged,
> Tattered and jagged,
> Rudely rayne beaten,
> Rusty and moughte eaten,
> If ye take well therwith,
> It hath in it some pyth.[18]

And at the end of the century the satirist Hall makes the point explicitly:

> It is not for every one to rellish a true and naturall Satyre, being of it selfe besides the native and in-bred bitternes and tartnes of particulers, both hard of conceipt, and harsh of stile.[19]

It is among the "moral" eclogues, as E. K. classifies them, "which for the most part be mixed with some Satyrical bitternesse" that *February, May,* and *September* belong.

Twelve years after the publication of *The Shepheardes Calender* Spenser took up the pastoral form once more. *Colin Clouts Come Home Againe,* a title evidently intended to recall the earlier poem, repeats few of its radical experiments. The vocabulary avoids grotesque harshness, the rustic-antique appearing only in an occasional "ne" for "no," "leasing" for "lie," "yshrilled" and the like. Some of the old names of the *Calender*—Cuddy, Hobbinol, Lobbin—are retained, perhaps because of their association with real people; the others are euphonious: Marin, Alexis, Melissa. There are no violent contrasts in verse form, no jagged lines, and no display pieces. Yet the poet has not reversed direction. His aims, both poetic and didactic, are similar to those he attempted in the *Calender,* but his means have become more subtle.

The unity of *Colin Clouts Come Home Againe* is ingeniously supported by the structure of its verse. The effect of calm, unbroken flow is created by quatrains usually though not always coinciding with the syntax but organized principally as sweeping verse paragraphs. The casual reader may not even be aware of the quatrains, for Spenser disguises the pattern by beginning with seven lines linked terza rima fashion and ending with five lines rhyming *ababa.* A pervasive pastoral atmosphere arises from the simple innocence of the speakers: Colin's fearful wonder at sea and ship, Cuddy's ignorance of the existence of any land besides his own, Corylas' belief that love is to be found only among shepherds, the amazement of the whole company at the description of Cynthia's court. A single narrative device frames the whole: Colin, like Diggon Davie in the September eclogue, tells the story of his travels to a far land.

These unifying characteristics bind together a tremendous variety of mood and subject. The tone ranges from the rhapsodic to the bitter, the extremes emphasized by the comments of Colin's auditors:

> Colin (said Cuddy then) thou hast forgot
> Thyself, me seemes, too much, to mount so hie:
> Such loftie flight, base shepheard seemeth not,
> From flocks and fields, to Angels and to skie. (ll. 616–19)

Ah Colin (then said Hobbinol) the blame
Which thou imputest, is too generall,
As if not any gentle wit of name,
Nor honest mynd might there be found at all.
(ll. 731–34)

Colin repeats his story of the love of the rivers Bregog and Mulla as he sang it in friendly competition with the Shepherd of the Ocean; he tells of his voyage over the sea, of incomparable England, of the poets and ladies of the court, of the great and bountiful Queen Cynthia, of the false courtier, of love counterfeit and true, of the proud Rosalind. The effect would be merely chaotic were it not for the easy run of the verse, the skillfully handled transitions, and the repeated reference to the pastoral setting of Colin's discourse.

The portrait of the poet Colin is done with delicate strokes. In the art of singing he is the peer of the Shepherd of the Ocean:

He pip'd, I sung; and when he sung, I piped,
By chaunge of turnes, each making other mery,
Neither envying other, nor envied,
So piped we, untill we both were weary. (ll. 76–79)

His rustic companions "stand astonisht at his curious skill." But they do not proclaim him superior to Pan and the Muses. They wonder, rather, that so great a shepherdess as Cynthia should trouble to listen to him, "a simple silly Elfe." If his songs of Cynthia will not be forgotten it is because "her great excellence,/ Lifts me above the measure of my might." When he is brought to consider the poets of her court he confidently assumes the role of judge and adviser. But because he is an outsider he avoids direct competition with them, and he is even able to praise Palin "Albe he envie at my rustick quill." The pastoral pose, while it permits Colin the appearance of humility, sets him apart from the others and in an important sense above them, since he alone is a free man, unimpeded by ambition and the necessity for timeserving.

As in the *Calender,* shepherd-poet is also shepherd-lover. Since the philosophy of love which Colin expounds with such ecstasy foreshadows its fuller statement in the *Fowre Hymnes* it will be considered later. The triangle involving Rosalind and Hobbinol, however, relates directly to that of the *Calender*. The situation remains superficially the same: Colin still despairs, Rosalind scorns, Hobbinol vainly reasons. But Rosalind is no longer faithless, and her pride is not merely destructive since it is just and praiseworthy:

> Not then to her that scorned thing so base,
> But to my selfe the blame that lookt so hie:
> So hie her thoughts as she her selfe have place,
> And loath each lowly thing with loftie eie. (ll. 935–38)

Piers says in *October* that "lofty love doth loath a lowly eye" and reasons that it should therefore raise the poet's mind "above the starry skie." Colin of the *Calender* has not learned this lesson and as the poem ends he abandons his shepherd's pipe. The new Colin will continue to sing:

> Yet so much grace let her vouchsafe to grant
> To simple swaine, sith her I may not love:
> Yet that I may her honour paravant,[8]
> And praise her worth, though far my wit above.
> (ll. 939–42)

And this grace will bring some ease to his cureless pain.

The matter of religion, so important a subject in the *Calender*, scarcely appears at all. In its place is the court as seen by a shepherd, also part of the stock of Renaissance pastoral. With precise tact, Colin manages to explain his rejection of that court while at the same time glorifying Cynthia's bounty ("Her deeds were like great clusters of ripe grapes") and praising the noble wits and gracious ladies who surround her. For "all the rest" are proud, lewd double-dealers, and the simple swain, not daring to adventure himself among them, prefers to return to his sheep:

> . . . it is no sort of life
> For shepheard fit to lead in that same place. (ll. 688–89)

[8] paravant: preeminently.

Like Colin, Spenser went back to what he considered the rudely barbarous isolation of Ireland from the sophisticated barbarities of the court. Whether he did so at his own choice, like Colin, or because the displeasure of Cecil made his position untenable is not a matter that this poem can decide. The sensitive and intelligent man of the Renaissance must always have been ambivalent about the pursuit of a career at court. On the one hand, the "disordered thrust" (as Daniel puts it) of ambitious striving was incompatible with contemplative study; on the other, the principal justification of contemplative study was the service it could render to the state. This was the dilemma of Thomas More: in the first book of *Utopia* Hythlodaye rejects the suggestion that he become adviser to a king; within a year of the publication of that work More entered royal service. It was the dilemma of Thomas Wyatt who wrote a satire on court life addressed to his friend Sir John Poins during a brief interval in his lifelong service as diplomat:

> But here I ame in Kent and Christendome
>   Emong the muses where I rede and ryme;
>   Where if thou list, my Poynz, for to come,
> Thou shalt be judge how I do spend my tyme.

The answer is Wyatt's, too:

> Yet woll I serve my prynce, my lord and thyn,
>   And let theim lyve to fede the panche [t] that list.[20]

As *The Shepheardes Calender* sets that which is against that which was, so *Colin Clouts Come Home Againe* subjects the most civilized of institutions to the scrutiny of the rustic. In both, the grand movement is circular: the *Calender* begins and ends in winter, Colin Clout leaves his home in the country and returns to it. In both, corruption is a principal theme, of pristine innocence in the one and of simple truth in the other. But the past and the pasture are offered not as solutions but as touchstones by which this time and this world may be tested. The *Calender* proclaims that the old right religion

[t] panche: paunch.

"may again retorne" (which Milton thought prophetic) and that true love should raise the poet's spirit above the dust. *Colin Clouts Come Home Againe* says of Elizabeth's England:

> . . . all good, all grace there freely growes,
> Had people grace it gratefully to use:
> For God his gifts there plenteously bestowes,
> But gracelesse men them greatly do abuse. (ll. 324–27)

The poet's task is to grapple with error, not escape from it.

Notes

1. The last lines of this Envoy disclaim the ambition to compete with "Tityrus" or with "the Pilgrim that the Ploughman playde a while." I take Tityrus in this context to mean Vergil, although the name is used for Chaucer in the February eclogue and Vergil is specifically "the Romish Tityrus" in *October.* The Plowman-Pilgrim must refer to the Chaucerian (not for Spenser pseudo-Chaucerian) *Plowman's Tale* in which the Plowman does indeed play the Pilgrim for a while. Some scholars understand "Tityrus" to mean Chaucer and the Plowman Langland. A. C. Hamilton, who holds this view, reads Spenser's line as a reference to a Pilgrim (i.e., Langland's Piers) who played the role of a Plowman ("The Visions of *Piers Plowman* and *The Faerie Queene,*" in *Form and Convention in the Poetry of Edmund Spenser: Selected Papers from the English Institute,* ed. William Nelson [New York, 1961], pp. 2–3).

2. It is sometimes conjectured that E. K. is Spenser himself, and the idea dies hard. See D. T. Starnes, "Spenser and E. K.," *Studies in Philology,* XLI (1944), 181–200.

3. *Works,* IX, 18.

4. *The Shepherd's Calendar,* ed. W. L. Renwick (London, 1930), p. 173.

5. The woodcuts themselves resemble those in contemporary editions of Vergil's *Bucolics.* See, for example, *Opera Virgiliana* (Lyons, 1529), fols. XVII ff. These cuts are said to reproduce those in the edition of Jean Grüninger, Strasbourg, 1502, and appear in many sixteenth-century editions of Vergil.

6. *The Shepherd's Calendar,* ed. Renwick, p. 167.

7. Other scholars have come to different conclusions about the structure of the poem. A. C. Hamilton ("The Argument of Spenser's *Shepheardes Calender,*" *ELH,* XXIII [1956], 171–82) contends that Spenser's argument is "the rejection of the pastoral life for the truly dedicated life in the world" (p. 181). R. A. Durr ("Spenser's Calendar of Christian Time," *ELH,* XXIV [1957], 269–95)

proposes that the governing subject of the poem is "the contrast between good and bad shepherds" (p. 270) and asserts that "the only meaningful division of the *Calender* must therefore be that between the flesh and spirit, *amor carnis* and *amor spiritus,* between love of self and world and love of neighbor and God" (p. 274).

8. L. Spitzer, "Spenser, *Shepheardes Calender, March,* ll. 61–114, and the Variorum Edition," *Studies in Philology,* XLVII (1950), 499.

9. General Prologue to *The Canterbury Tales,* ll. 501–504.

10. I use the large term "Protestant" here although I am aware that not all of those who rejected the authority of the Pope also rejected religious practices lacking scriptural warrant. A desire for the purification of the church, however, is not exclusively "Puritan." I prefer to reserve that label to describe the party that wished to alter or supplant the episcopal system.

11. See also L. S. Friedland, "Spenser as Fabulist," *Shakespeare Association Bulletin,* XII (1937), 97 ff., and the same author's "Spenser's Fable of 'The Oake and the Brere,' " *ibid.,* XVI (1941), 52–57, and "A Source for Spenser's 'The Oak and the Brier,' " *Philological Quarterly,* XXXIII (1954), 222–24.

12. P. E. McLane, *Spenser's "Shepheardes Calender"* (Notre Dame, 1961), p. 32.

13. *Ibid.,* pp. 188–234 and *passim.*

14. "An Apology for Poetry," in *Elizabethan Critical Essays,* ed. G. Gregory Smith (Oxford, 1904), I, 196.

15. See *Works,* VII, 614 ff.

16. W. L. Renwick, *Edmund Spenser* (London, 1925; reprinted 1957), p. 98.

17. Sannazaro's *Arcadia* is suggested as a model for Spenser's use of a variety of metrical schemes by Francesco Viglione, *La Poesia Lirica di Edmondo Spenser* (Genoa, 1937), p. 170.

18. *Colin Clout,* ll. 53–58.

19. *The Collected Poems of Joseph Hall,* ed. A. Davenport (Liverpool, 1949), p. 97. At this time the word *satire* was thought to be derived from *satyr,* so that a rude, uncivilized manner was considered essential to the form.

20. *Collected Poems of Sir Thomas Wyatt,* ed. Kenneth Muir (London, 1949), pp. 187, 192.

Louis L. Martz

The *Amoretti:* "Most Goodly Temperature"

MOST OF US, I imagine, have at one time or another felt some degree of disappointment in reading Spenser's *Amoretti.* These sonnets have often seemed rather tame and flat when compared with Sidney's or with Shakespeare's, or even with Drayton's best: our sage and serious Spenser, perhaps, lacked the wit and compression necessary for distinguished work within the sonnet medium; his melody, his craft, his emblematic techniques, his strong idealism may not be adequate to lift the *Amoretti* very far above their heavy reliance on the Petrarchan conventions.

At the same time we may tend to agree with the argument strongly advanced by J. W. Lever in one of the most recent, and one of the best, interpretations of the *Amoretti:* that the sonnets show irreconcilable inconsistencies in the presentation of the heroine. In most of the poems we find a "lofty conception" of the lady as angelic, divine, purely virtuous; and yet in many others she is represented as cruel, murderous, savage, guileful, tormenting. As a result, Mr. Lever finds here "an attempted blending of two collections of sonnets, differing in subject-matter, characterization, and general conception." He believes that we can best deal with the sequence "by setting apart those sonnets which evidently belong to an earlier phase and run counter to the general stream of thought and feeling"; he singles out "at least some eighteen sonnets best considered apart from the main group"—all of them relating to the cruel "Tyrannesse." [1]

Moreover, it has sometimes been charged that the series is lacking in proportion: the change in the lover's mood occurs too quickly at the second New Year, and the happy sonnets that follow are outweighed by the mass of earlier complaints. And finally, we have the problems raised by the ending of the sequence, which many readers have found abrupt and disconcerting, as the mood suddenly turns from contentment to distress, in the last four sonnets, and we are left with the puzzling group of anacreontic verses between us and the great *Epithalamion*.

All these objections are so closely related that to deal with one is to deal with all. Let me start with the last. A careful study of the opening sonnet will be of great help here, for Sonnet I, as prologue and dedication to the whole, seems to link directly with the last three sonnets and to give us both the physical and the emotional setting in which all the sonnets should be read. The poet first addresses those happy leaves of paper which are about to receive his lady's touch:

> Happy ye leaues when as those lilly hands,
> which hold my life in their dead doing might
> shall handle you and hold in loues soft bands,
> lyke captiues trembling at the victors sight.

And hold in loues soft bands: the phrase implies more than her physical touch; the poet seems assured that his poems will be welcomed and cherished by her love. He does not need to beg her to read them; he knows that she will read them:

> And happy lines, on which with starry light,
> those lamping eyes will deigne sometimes to look
> and reade the sorrowes of my dying spright,
> written with teares in harts close bleeding book.
> And happy rymes bath'd in the sacred brooke,
> of *Helicon* whence she deriued is,
> when ye behold that Angels blessed looke,
> my soules long lacked foode, my heauens blis.

My soules long lacked foode: he has been absent from her "blessed looke" for a long while, it seems, and these poems are now being sent off to her, a record of the whole courtship up to this point of their separation. But the poet does not endure this separation in doubt and anguish. He is writing now from a standpoint in which he can review his sorrows with the calm assurance of a mutual affection, an assurance, a poise, a security of mind represented in this poem's highly symmetrical constuction. "Happy ye leaues . . . / And happy lines . . . / And happy rymes"; and then the final couplet, binding all together:

> Leaues, lines, and rymes, seeke her to please alone,
> whom if ye please, I care for other none.

All this seems to point toward the situation, mood, and tone of the last three sonnets (87, 88, 89), unless we choose to read them in an unjustified relation to Sonnet 86, where the poet tells how a "Venemous toung," "with false forged lyes," "in my true loue did stirre vp coles of yre." But the ending of this sonnet may be taken to suggest the failure of the slanderer [2]

> . . . that didst with guile conspire
> in my sweet peace such breaches to haue bred.

And there is no indication in the three following sonnets that his lady's anger has continued or that these slanders have caused the separation here recorded. There is no sign that he is in disgrace, that he is barred from her presence by anger and disdain. He has simply left the presence of his love and he now spends the time "with expectation," in a state of mind that "maketh euery minute seeme a myle" (Sonnet 87). For all we know, the separation may have been caused by preparations for their wedding. All we know is that, for a time, he has "lackt the comfort of that light" that radiates from his lady's presence, and must maintain himself by "beholding the Idaea" of her radiance:

> with light thereof I doe my selfe sustayne,
> and thereon feed my loue-affamisht hart. (Sonnet 88)

The situation, then, seems to be much the same as that implied by "my soules long lacked foode" in Sonnet 1. Finally, the series comes to rest in Sonnet 89, where the lover's sorrow is presented as deriving from the temporary separation of two assured mates:

Lyke as the Culuer on the bared bough,
  Sits mourning for the absence of her mate:
  and in her songs sends many a wishfull vow,
  for his returne that seemes to linger late.
So I alone now left disconsolate,
  mourne to my selfe the absence of my loue:
  and wandring here and there all desolate,
  seek with my playnts to match that mournful doue:
Ne ioy of ought that vnder heauen doth houe,
  can comfort me, but her owne ioyous sight:
  whose sweet aspect both God and man can moue,
  in her vnspotted pleasauns to delight.
Dark is my day, whyles her fayre light I mis,
  and dead my life that wants such liuely blis.

The most appropriate sequel to such a mood of "expectation" is the joyful *Epithalamion* that Spenser has given us; I do not feel the abruptness and uncertainty that some have found in the conclusion of the *Amoretti*. One touch of slander cannot spoil this kind of love; and indeed Sonnet 86 presents only one of several futile threats to the lovers' security which Spenser deals with toward the end of his sequence. Separation is one threat, which the whole sequence strives to overcome. The envy of the world, in Sonnet 85, is another threat, coming from those witless cuckoos who "when I doe praise her, say I doe but flatter." His recurrent sense of his own unworthiness, in Sonnet 82, is still another. Sonnets 83 and 84, if read in a paired relationship, suggest the discontents arising from his own "hungry eyes" and "greedy couetize"; these unruly tendencies are suppressed, or at least controlled, in Sonnet 84 by vowing:

Let not one sparke of filthy lustful fyre
  breake out, that may her sacred peace molest:
  ne one light glance of sensuall desyre
  Attempt to work her gentle mindes vnrest.

Instead, he will attempt to convert such rude emotions into "pure affections" and "modest thoughts"; and he concludes, rather ruefully,

but speake no word to her of these sad plights,
which her too constant stiffenesse doth constrayn.
Onely behold her rare perfection,
and blesse your fortunes fayre election.

Sonnet 83, of course, is the notorious repetition of Sonnet 35; this repetition has been taken as evidence that the sequence was hastily gathered together, and therefore as a justification for questioning the contents and arrangement of the first edition, our only authority. It is certainly possible that Spenser simply forgot to cross out the sonnet in one place after changing its position and revising one word. On the other hand, the sonnet is appropriate in either place, and its double occurrence might be taken, not as a slip, but as a reprise: a designed reminiscence and recurrence of an earlier mood of pining and complaint.

In any case, these varied threats to contentment seem entirely appropriate after the long rich climax of almost unalloyed happiness that has run from Sonnet 63, where he at last descries "the happy shore," down through the culmination of her praise in Sonnet 81, with its balanced, symmetrical blazon of his lady's beauty, both in body and in spirit:

Fayre is my loue, when her fayre golden heares,
with the loose wynd ye wauing chance to marke:
fayre when the rose in her red cheekes appeares,
or in her eyes the fyre of loue does sparke.
Fayre when her brest lyke a rich laden barke,
with pretious merchandize she forth doth lay:
fayre when that cloud of pryde, which oft doth dark
her goodly light with smiles she driues away.
But fayrest she, when so she doth display
the gate with pearles and rubyes richly dight:
throgh which her words so wise do make their way
to beare the message of her gentle spright.
The rest be works of natures wonderment,
but this the worke of harts astonishment.

The only qualifications to his happiness here are slight, and very easily overcome: her fear of losing her liberty (Sonnet 65); a suggestion that he is too "meane a one" for her (Sonnet 66); several intimations of mortality (Sonnets 72, 75, 79); and one mild lamentation of her absence (Sonnet 78). Spenser, I think, greatly strengthens the *Amoretti* at the very close by bringing his joy within a harsher context of worldly reality. Their love is not impaired by these threats, but it learns to live within the world, as it must. The great *Epithalamion* then emerges happily out of its own triumphant accommodation with the world. (It will be evident that I have only one solution to offer for the intervening anacreontics: ignore them.)

But what of the other alleged disproportions and inconsistencies in the sequence? These too, I feel, tend to disappear within a dominant tone of assurance and poise and mutual understanding that controls the series. This peculiar and highly original relationship between the lover and his lady may be our best key to the whole sequence. It involves a variety of closely related issues: how does the lover characterize himself? what attitudes does he adopt toward the lady? what sort of audience does she provide? how does she receive his addresses? It is worth while to examine first the nature of this lady, for she talks and acts more than most of these heroines do. Most Petrarchan ladies, as Pope might say, "have no characters at all"; and even Sidney's Stella, though she comes to display considerable adroitness in damping her lover's ardors, remains for most of the sequence a black-eyed effigy around which Astrophel performs his brilliant Portrait of the Lover as a very young dog.

But Spenser's lady has a very decided and a very attractive character.[3] First of all, it is clear that the lover's tributes to "her mind adornd with vertues manifold" (Sonnet 15), her "deep wit" (Sonnet 43), her "gentle wit, and vertuous mind" (Sonnet 79), her "words so wise," "the message of her gentle spright" (Sonnet 81)—it is clear that all these tributes to her mental powers are very well deserved. Quite early in the sequence, in the paired Sonnets 28 and 29, we find the lady wittily turning the tables on her lover in a dialogue that throws a bright light on their peculiar relationship. In Sonnet 28 the lover has noticed that she is wearing a laurel leaf, and this sign, he says, "giues me great hope of your relenting mynd," since it is the poet's own symbol; he goes on to warn her of the fate that befell proud Daphne when she fled from the god of poetry, and he ends with the witty turn:

> Then fly no more fayre loue from Phebus chace,
> but in your brest his leafe and loue embrace.

Then in Sonnet 29 the lady pertly carries on this play of wit:

> See how the stubborne damzell doth depraue
> my simple meaning with disdaynfull scorne:
> and by the bay which I vnto her gaue,
> accoumpts my self her captiue quite forlorne.
> The bay (quoth she) is of the victours borne,
> yielded them by the vanquisht as theyr meeds,
> and they therewith doe poetes heads adorne,
> to sing the glory of their famous deedes.

All right, he says, since she claims the conquest, "let her accept me as her faithfull thrall":

> Then would I decke her head with glorious bayes,
> and fill the world with her victorious prayse.

I do not see how this interchange can be taken as anything but smiling and good-humored, yes, even humorous, in our sense of the word. The phrase "stubborne damzell" tells us a great deal about the poet's tone here: it is intimate, smiling, affectionate, respectful, reproachful, and courtly, all at once: it strikes exactly the tone that an older man, of experience and wisdom (someone a bit like Emma's Mr. Knightley) might adopt toward a bright and beautiful and willful young lady for whom he feels, not awe, but deep admiration and affection. It is an attitude that also implies considerable hope and confidence that his suit will in time be rewarded. It is an attitude that finds a fulfillment and perfect counterpart later on, after his acceptance, in the gentle wit of Sonnet 71, which even Mr. Lever takes as "affectionate banter" (p. 130). This is the sonnet where the lady, in a witty reversal of the poet's complaints, has woven into her embroidery a fable of the Bee and the Spyder; the poet picks up the imagery with joy and develops it with a deeply affectionate humor. Indeed, throughout the sequence she is certainly one of the most smiling and "chearefull" ladies to appear in any English sequence, and I doubt that her smiles are outdone anywhere on the Continent. Sonnets 39 and 40, wholly devoted to her smiling and her "amiable cheare," are only the most sustained of many indications of her "sweet eye-glaunces" and her "charming smiles" (Sonnet 71). In view of this it is hard to see why readers have insisted upon taking the whole sequence so solemnly. Sonnet 16, very early in the game, is enough in itself to tell us otherwise, with its playful, deliberately hyperbolic, and clearly smiling use of the Alexandrian Cupid:

> One day as I vnwarily did gaze
> on those fayre eyes my loues immortall light:
> the whiles my stonisht hart stood in amaze,
> through sweet illusion of her lookes delight;
> I mote perceiue how in her glauncing sight,
> legions of loues with little wings did fly:
> darting their deadly arrowes fyry bright,
> at euery rash beholder passing by.
> One of those archers closely I did spy,
> ayming his arrow at my very hart:
> when suddenly with twincle of her eye,
> the Damzell broke his misintended dart.
> Had she not so doon, sure I had bene slayne,
> yet as it was, I hardly scap't with paine.

Now the meaning of "twincle" as a wink, a nod, a hint, was current in Elizabethan usage; a damsel with a twinkle would seem to hold here every modern connotation. At the same time, the strong colloquialism of the last two lines seems to warn us with a similar twinkle not to take this lover's professions of grief too solemnly.

But what then shall we make of Mr. Lever's eighteen excommunicated sonnets, along with others of this kind, where the lady commits those "huge massacres" with her eyes, and as a "cruell warriour"

greedily her fell intent poursewth,
Of my poore life to make vnpittied spoile.
(Sonnet 11)

Many of these are done with such extravagant exaggeration of the conventional poses that they strike me as close to mock-heroic. These are the conventions of love, the poet seems to say; these are the usual rituals of courtship; he will gladly pay these tributes, and even over-pay them, since this is what his delightful damsel seems to expect, and she thoroughly deserves this state; at the same time a girl of her deep wit will know exactly how to take them, in the spirit offered. She can be expected to respond with a smile and a witty rejoinder, as she does in Sonnet 18, herself outdoing the Petrarchan poses:

But when I pleade, she bids me play my part,
and when I weep, she sayes teares are but water:
and when I sigh, she sayes I know the art,
and when I waile, she turnes hir self to laughter.

We can begin to see, then, the kind of relationship in which these charges of cruelty are uttered; we can begin to anticipate the sort of tone that the lover will tend to adopt in paying his conventional tributes.

Spenser's title is in itself a clue: *Amoretti,* the diminutive form, implying a relationship of intimate affection; it might be translated as: "intimate little tokens of love." [4] At the same time, the Italian title seems to draw a special attention to the great Continental tradition from which the sequence takes its themes, its imagery, its form. A complete definition might read: *Amoretti,* "intimate little tokens of love made out of ancient materials deriving, primarily, from Italy."

And so we have:

Vnrighteous Lord of loue what law is this,
That me thou makest thus tormented be?
the whiles she lordeth in licentious blisse
of her freewill, scorning both thee and me.

See how the Tyrannesse doth ioy to see
the huge massacres which her eyes do make:
and humbled harts brings captiues vnto thee,
that thou of them mayst mightie vengeance take.
But her proud hart doe thou a little shake
and that high look, with which she doth comptroll
all this worlds pride bow to a baser make,
and al her faults in thy black booke enroll.
That I may laugh at her in equall sort,
as she doth laugh at me and makes my pain her sport.
(Sonnet 10)

The tone here is very hard to describe. It would be too much to call it parody, and yet the postures seem to be deliberately judged by the presence of some degree of smiling. It would be too much to call the sonnet comic, and yet, if we temper the term rightly, there is an element of comedy here, though not so broad as in the sonnet with the "twincle." At the same time, of course, a great many of these sonnets of complaint are delivered in a straightforward manner, and others allow little more than the glimmer of a smile to break through in the last line or two. I am arguing only that the series is frequently touched with an element that we might call humor, parody, or comedy; it is a light touch, but it is, I think, sovereign. Among the sixty sonnets that come within the first year of courtship, it is possible to single out at least fifteen that seem clearly to display this transforming humor (for example: Sonnets 10, 12, 16, 18, 20, 24, 26, 28, 29, 30, 32, 33, 37, 43, 46, 48, 50, 57); and their presence is bound to have considerable effect upon our reading of all the other sonnets of complaint. As prime examples I would instance Sonnet 30, where Spenser drives into absurdity the old Petrarchan cliché: "My loue is lyke to yse, and I to fyre"; or Sonnet 32, where the homely image of the "paynefull smith" beating the iron with "his heauy sledge" prepares the way for an account of how the lover's "playnts and prayers" beat futilely "on th' anduyle of her stubberne wit";

What then remaines but I to ashes burne,
and she to stones at length all frosen turne?

Lines such as these, so close to parody, need not be taken as utterly inconsistent with those other sonnets, such as 7, 8, and 9, where the poet praises his lady's angelic virtue, with that famous tribute to her eyes:

> Then to the Maker selfe they likest be,
> whose light doth lighten all that here we see.
>
> (Sonnet 9)

Does the opening line of the next sonnet (10)—"Vnrighteous Lord of loue what law is this, / That me thou makest thus tormented be?"—conflict with that exalted view of the lady? On the contrary, the poet seems to be making a clear distinction between those essential qualities deriving from the heavenly Maker, and those "cruelties" demanded by conventional Cupid, the unrighteous Lord of love, the adversary of the "glorious Lord of lyfe" who in Sonnet 68 teaches the lovers their devout lesson of love.

These two aspects of the lady's portrait (essence and appearance) are frequently considered together in the same sonnet, where their incongruity is fully recognized, as in Sonnet 31, which concludes:

> But did she know how ill these two accord,
> such cruelty she would have soone abhord.

Or again, in Sonnet 24, we find the same awareness of this contradiction, in a mode closer to the comic:

> When I behold that beauties wonderment,
> And rare perfection of each goodly part:
> of natures skill the onely complement,
> I honor and admire the makers art.
> But when I feele the bitter balefull smart,
> which her fayre eyes vnwares doe worke in mee:
> that death out of theyr shiny beames doe dart,
> I thinke that I a new *Pandora* see. . . .

But it all ends with a playful suggestion:

But since ye are my scourge I will intreat,
that for my faults ye will me gently beat.

Likewise in Sonnet 26 we have that witty series of playful epigrams, all stressing his lady's double aspect:

Sweet is the Rose, but growes vpon a brere;
Sweet is the Iunipere, but sharpe his bough;
sweet is the Eglantine, but pricketh nere;
sweet is the firbloome, but his braunches rough.
Sweet is the Cypresse, but his rynd is tough,
sweet is the nut, but bitter is his pill;
sweet is the broome-flowre, but yet sowre enough;
and sweet is Moly, but his root is ill.
So euery sweet with soure is tempred still,
that maketh it be coueted the more.

And in Sonnet 45 we have, fully developed, the view that her essential being is belied by her proud and tyrannic aspects; here the lover, with a tone of excessive courtesy, urges the lady to stop looking in her mirror, "Your goodly selfe for euermore to vew," and instead to seek within her lover's "inward selfe" the image of her "semblant trew":

Within my hart, though hardly it can shew
thing so diuine to vew of earthly eye:
the fayre Idea of your celestiall hew,
and euery part remaines immortally:
And were it not that through your cruelty,
with sorrow dimmed and deformd it were:
the goodly ymage of your visnomy,
clearer than christall would therein appere.
But if your selfe in me ye playne will see,
remoue the cause by which your fayre
beames darkned be.

In still other sonnets the lover attempts to make a virtue of necessity by converting her twofold aspect into an example of "most goodly temperature": "Myld humblesse mixt with awfull maiesty" (Sonnet 13):

> Was it the worke of nature or of Art,
> which tempred so the feature of her face,
> that pride and meeknesse mixt by equall part,
> doe both appeare t'adorne her beauties grace?
>
> (Sonnet 21)

In short, the sonnets that deal with the proud and cruel fair form an indispensable part of the series; they represent the due and proper acknowledgment of all the usual forms of tribute:

> Bring therefore all the forces that ye may,
> and lay incessant battery to her heart,
> playnts, prayers, vowes, ruth, sorrow, and dismay,
> those engins can the proudest loue conuert.
> And if those fayle fall downe and dy before her,
> so dying liue, and liuing do adore her.

Sonnet 14 thus foretells the use of every possible mode of Petrarchan approach, and the series thoroughly fulfills the promise, in many various modes: exalted, solemn, tender, touched with the edge of a smile, tinged with a hint of wit, or broadly comic.

Then, as we come close to the point where the lover discovers his acceptance, we find the rich variety of all the earlier sonnets summed up for us in Sonnet 54, which is perhaps more important than any other individual sonnet for an understanding of the sequence:

> Of this worlds Theatre in which we stay,
> My loue lyke the Spectator ydly sits
> beholding me that all the pageants play,
> disguysing diuersly my troubled wits.
> Sometimes I ioy when glad occasion fits,
> and mask in myrth lyke to a Comedy:
> soone after when my ioy to sorrow flits,
> I waile and make my woes a Tragedy.

Those lines provide the best possible answer to any who might doubt the presence of mirth and comedy in the sequence; but more important is the way in which this sonnet indicates the complete recognition of the lover that he is deliberately playing many parts, staging "all the pageants" in an ancient festival of courtship, adopting all the masks that may catch his lady's eye and prove his devotion.

> Yet she beholding me with constant eye,
> delights not in my merth nor rues my smart:
> but when I laugh she mocks, and when I cry
> she laughes, and hardens euermore her hart.
> What then can moue her? if nor merth nor mone,
> she is no woman, but a sencelesse stone.

But actually these pageants have achieved their end; the festival of courtship is nearly over, and only a few sonnets later (63, 64) the lover receives his due acknowledgment from this thoroughly composed and constant young lady. The lover's own assurance that he will soon be openly accepted appears to be suggested just before the end of the year's courtship, in the paired Sonnets 58 and 59, which constitute some kind of dialogue on the lady's self-assurance. Some have thought that the heading of Sonnet 58, "By her that is most assured to her selfe," belongs rather with Sonnet 59, which may be taken as the lady's reply to the lover's query in the immediately preceding lines:

> Why then doe ye proud fayre, misdeeme so farre,
> that to your selfe ye most assured arre?

In my original version of this paper I tended to accept this point of view; but William Nelson and Leicester Bradner have convinced me that the word "By" in this heading must be used in the old sense of "concerning," as Gascoigne used it in the headings to several of his poems.[5] Thus the poet has composed a pair of sonnets on this problem: rebuke and palinode; and he has phrased the second in a way that allows it to be taken as a representation of the lady's point of view. She does not misdeem; she knows precisely what she is doing:

> Thrise happie she, that is so well assured
> Vnto her selfe and setled so in hart:
> that nether will for better be allured,
> ne feard with worse to any chaunce to start,
> But like a steddy ship doth strongly part
> the raging waues and keepes her course aright:
> ne ought for tempest doth from it depart,
> ne ought for fayrer weathers false delight.

Here is the sage and serious lady, the poet's proper mate, who in Sonnet 75 so wisely rebukes her lover's efforts to write her name in the sand; but now at the close of Sonnet 59 the sternness changes to a promising smile:

> Most happy she that most assured doth rest,
> but he most happy who such one loues best.

That compact final line assumes a quiet understanding between this lover and his lady. For how can he be happy who loves such a one, unless she will return his love with all the power of her constancy? In fact, if we allow for a colloquial looseness in the use of relative pronouns, we may find a double meaning in the word "who." He is indeed most happy who such a one loves best.

The next four sonnets, in many ways, represent the full peripeteia of the series. Sonnet 60 formally marks the anniversary of their courtship (something like a "whole years work" has been mentioned in Sonnet 23: we may take the intervening sonnets as a full memorial of that year); and at the same time we are told the lover's age: he is forty. This revelation (which seems to astound and dismay even graduate students) explains a great deal that may have puzzled us about the lover's manner and tone; it confirms our impression that the foregoing sonnets are written from the broad, experienced view of maturity, written with a witty and mature consciousness that has mastered all the modes of courtship. He is in love; he knows his lady's nature; and although he would be grieved if she should reject him, he never really accepts this possibility.

The presence of this assured attitude throughout the series is clearly demonstrated by the two sonnets (33 and 80) in which he alludes to his writing of *The Faerie Queene*. In the first of these he tells his friend Lodwick that he finds it impossible to work upon the poem, for his troubles with his proud lady have completely distracted him:

> How then should I without another wit,
> thinck euer to endure so taedious toyle?
> sins that this one is tost with troublous fit,
> of a proud loue, that doth my spirite spoyle.

Since this comes directly after the witty Sonnet 32, we may well suspect a strong degree of posturing in this boyish excuse; and our suspicion is borne out in Sonnet 80, where it appears that he has in fact been working on the poem all the while; he has completed six books, and he now asks leave to rest at this convenient half-way point, "and gather to my selfe new breath awhile."

> Till then giue leaue to me in pleasant mew,
> to sport my muse and sing my loues sweet praise:
> the contemplation of whose heauenly hew,
> my spirit to an higher pitch will rayse.
> But let her prayses yet be low and meane,
> fit for the handmayd of the Faery Queene.

There is no danger that this discreet lover will ever lose his strong sense of duty and propriety.

This attitude of mature consciousness (or middle-aged discretion, if you will) has been conveyed throughout by the poise and harmony of Spenser's poetical techniques. The steady beat of his intricate rime-scheme is varied only in Sonnet 8, where we may feel that the Shakespearean form serves to stress, by emphatic variation, the goodly temperature that his lady has already begun to develop in this lover:

> You frame my thoughts and fashion me within,
> you stop my toung, and teach my hart to speake,
> you calme the storme that passion did begin,
> strong thrugh your cause, but by your vertue weak.

This balance and symmetry of structure, firmly represented in the first sonnet, recurs at frequent intervals throughout the series: Sonnet 56, a lament for her cruelty, displays a structure very similar to that of Sonnet 1; and there are many varieties of such tightly balanced construction, as in the comparisons of Sonnets 9 and 26. Here is another reason why the assertions of his "bitter balefull smart" are taken as a tribute, not as an emotional fact. The statements of his suffering are artifacts presented as adornments, offerings, and "moniments." Meanwhile Spenser's tactful deployment of archaic diction and his frequent reminiscence of the old-fashioned alliterative verse both contribute to the total impression of a lover who has a deep respect and affection for the ancient, traditional, formal modes of utterance.

And now, at the moment of full peripeteia, Sonnet 61 retracts all charges laid against her pride and cruelty, and casts the full weight of the lover's adoration toward the celebration of her divine essence:

> The glorious image of the makers beautie,
>   My souerayne saynt, the Idoll of my thought,
>   dare not henceforth aboue the bounds of dewtie,
>   t'accuse of pride, or rashly blame for ought.
> For being as she is diuinely wrought,
>   and of the brood of Angels heuenly borne:
>   and with the crew of blessed Saynts vpbrought,
>   each of which did her with theyr guifts adorne;
> The bud of ioy, the blossome of the morne,
>   the beame of light, whom mortal eyes admyre:
>   what reason is it then but she should scorne
>   base things that to her loue too bold aspire?
> Such heauenly formes ought rather worshipt be,
>   then dare be lou'd by men of meane degree.

So then in Sonnet 62 the New Year begins again, "with shew of morning mylde," "betokening peace and plenty to ensew." This outer "chaunge of weather," as he suggests, betokens a change of inner weather, in which both lover and lady cease their pageants and return each other's love without a mask. In Sonnet 63 he clearly descries "the happy shore," and in Sonnet 64 the great sequence of joy is fully launched with his ritual celebration of their kiss, recalling, as Israel Baroway has pointed out,[6] the poetical techniques of the Song of Solomon—though we should add that Spenser gives to these techniques his own witty turns:

> Her lips did smell lyke vnto Gillyflowers,
> her ruddy cheekes lyke vnto Roses red:
> her snowy browes lyke budded Bellamoures,
> her louely eyes lyke Pincks but newly spred,
> Her goodly bosome lyke a Strawberry bed,
> her neck lyke to a bounch of Cullambynes:
> her brest lyke lillyes, ere theyr leaues be shed,
> her nipples lyke yong blossomd Iessemynes.

So all the modes of being from earth to heaven are now woven together into a full Spenserian harmony. His love moves to the steady measure of the calendar, both secular and religious. The reprise of the New Year's motif, recalling Sonnet 4, and the reprise of the Spring song in Sonnet 70, recalling both Sonnet 4 and Sonnet 19, place the lovers' lives in tune with the seasons of nature; meanwhile the great Easter sonnet (68), recalling the "holy season fit to fast and pray" of Sonnet 22, places the whole series in a firm accord with the lessons of the Lord of life. And finally, climax of harmony, we have Sonnet 74, where the unity of life is celebrated through the symbolism of the three Elizabeths: his mother, his queen, and his lady. Only a poet so persistently harmonious as Spenser could have managed to arrange so perfect an accord of filial piety, courtly fealty, and virtuous betrothal.

Most goodly temperature indeed: in that one phrase Spenser has given us the best possible account of the *Amoretti,* as he leads us back to the ancient roots and affiliations of the word *temperature: temperatura, temperatus, temperatio;* signifying, in the terms of my Latin dictionary: a due mingling, fit proportion, proper combination, symmetry, a regulating power, an organizing principle.

Notes

1. *The Elizabethan Love Sonnet* (London: Methuen, 1956), pp. 97–102.

2. See Janet Spens, *Spenser's Faerie Queene* (London: Arnold, 1934), p. 104.

3. See Hallett Smith, *Elizabethan Poetry* (Cambridge: Harvard University Press, 1952), pp. 166–67.

4. This translation was suggested by my friend Thomas Bergin.

5. See *OED,* "By": A. *prep.,* IV, 26; and George Gascoigne, *A Hundreth Sundrie Flowres,* ed. by C. T. Prouty (Columbia: University of Missouri, 1942), poems 10, 12, 14, pp. 114–16.

6. "The Imagery of Spenser and the *Song of Songs,*" *JEGP,* XXXIII (1934), 23–45; esp. pp. 39–40.

Robert Kellogg

Thought's Astonishment and the Dark Conceits of Spenser's *Amoretti*

SPENSER'S *Amoretti and Epithalamion* is a poetic account of a courtship and marriage. Because the poet himself is thought to have married his second wife, Elizabeth Boyle, sometime before November 19, 1594, the date on which the *Amoretti and Epithalamion* was entered in the Stationers' Register for publication, his book has been interpreted as the description of actual events and of Spenser's emotional response to them.[1] Indeed, if they are read by canons of nineteenth-century realism and poetic sincerity, Spenser's lyrics do seem to provide a glimpse into the depths of the passionate heart, as well as a chronology of the poet's most private affairs. Since there was an actual Elizabeth Boyle and an actual courtship and marriage, the *Amoretti and Epithalamion* must, of course, have stood in some sort of relationship to those actualities. It may even have been a most delightful and sophisticated relationship indeed. But of the actualities we know nothing beyond their existence.[2] We have only the fictional account. A relevant critical response to the *Amoretti and Epithalamion* must perforce restrict itself to an examination of the poems themselves and the literary tradition of which they form a part. I should like in this essay to consider only the *Amoretti,* as being the more difficult of the two major parts of the book and as raising more urgently the question of the degree to which we may be justified in viewing the poems as a record of personal experience.

In accordance with Renaissance conventions of the love lyric, stretching back in time through Petrarch to the troubadours, the speaker in the *Amoretti* identifies himself as a poet. From Sonnet 1 onward he is conscious of a double identity; he is both lover and poet:

> Leaves, lines and rymes, seeke her to please alone,
> Whom if ye please, I care for other none.[3]

On occasion he refers to himself in a third role, that of religious devotee:

> There I to her as th' author of my blisse,
> Will builde an altar to appease her yre. (Sonnet 22)

We need not be quick to identify this fictional poet-lover-worshipper with the historical Edmund Spenser. These are rhetorical voices which from time immemorial have characterized the lyric speaker. They are, of course, not the only ones. There are the shepherds, soldiers, students, watchmen, children, farmers, animals, gods, and countless others whose voices we hear in various lyric types and individual poems. But in its daily affairs our culture grants to three kinds of imagination (the Renaissance would have called them three kinds of madness) a special license to express their visions of things inaccessible to the sense of ordinary men. These three kinds of imagination are the artistic, the erotic, and the religious.[4] And writers of lyric verse have assumed the masks and the license of the poet, the lover, and the religious worshipper in order to create the illusion that their fictions are authentic. For thousands of years it has been conventional to write religious and erotic poetry *as if* it were the record of actual events impinging upon the poetic imagination. Sidney's famous line, " 'Fool,' said my Muse to me, 'look in thy heart, and write!' " exemplifies neatly the explicit characterization of the speaker in the Renaissance sonnet sequence as both a lover and a poet. The line does not signal, as it is sometimes said to do, Sidney's liberation from outworn literary tradition, for its statement of reliance upon emotional experience goes back at least as far as Bernart de Ventadorn's twelfth-century lyric *Chantar no pot gaire valer*.[5]

If the first step in describing the speaker of the *Amoretti* is merely a precaution against identifying him too directly with the historical Edmund Spenser, the second step will have to be an accounting for the unmistakably personal references in the poems. The speaker does not simply assume the mask of any poet; like Chaucer's narrators, he assumes the mask of his own creator. We learn in Sonnet 74 that the speaker's mother, mistress, and queen, like Spenser's are all named Elizabeth. In Sonnet 33, addressing Spenser's friend Lodowick Bryskett, and again in Sonnet 80, the speaker admits to having neglected his work on the *Faerie Queene* while he suffered the agonies of love. And, finally, the historical Edmund Spenser was, in 1593, of an age with the forty-year-old speaker of Sonnet 60.[6] If we must grant that this much is true of both Spenser and his lyric persona, how much else do the two have in common? Did Spenser actually get caught in a shower leaving Elizabeth's one day (Sonnet 46)? Did he actually write her name upon the strand (75)? Did she actually respond so wittily when he gave her a branch of laurel (29)? We would like to believe all of these things actually happened. But it matters little, for we believe in them the way we believe in any realistic fiction: they are probable, they may well have happened.

Some things in the *Amoretti* we would not like to believe. We would not like to believe that the author of the *Faerie Queene* was ever so abjectly enamored that his mistress could despise and disdain him with haughty cruelty for months on end, only to receive the renewed pledges of devotion which he sent with his modest requests for better treatment in the future.

> So doe I weepe, and wayle, and pleade in vain,
> Whiles she as steele and flint doth still remayne. (18)

> In vaine I seeke and sew to her for grace,
> And doe myne humbled hart before her poure:
> The whiles her foot she in my necke doth place,
> And tread my life downe in the lowly floure. (20)

> But since ye are my scourge I will intreat,
> That for my faults ye will me gently beat. (24)

> How long shal this lyke dying lyfe endure,
> And know no end of her owne mysery? (25)

Such behavior is improbable in the extreme. Our negative response to its falseness, together with its obvious source in Petrarchan convention, constitutes the major obstacle to our acceptance of the *Amoretti* as joyously as we receive their flawless partner the *Epithalamion*. It is here that the *Amoretti* fail for us as fiction; and it is to this failure that apologies for the *Amoretti* have been addressed.

In an English Institute essay,[7] Professor Louis L. Martz undertakes with remarkable skill the defense of the *Amoretti* precisely on the grounds of their probability as realistic fiction. He argues that the most repulsively and improbably abject of the sonnets are playfully ironic allusions to the excesses of the Petrarchan convention. He believes that both the lady and the poet of the sonnets are characterized as being intelligent enough and learned enough in the artificialities of the sonnet tradition to enjoy as amorous play-acting the poet's references to torture, bloodshed, humiliation, captivity, and death, all of which he says he suffers at his lady's hands. In effect, his argument collapses the distinction between the historical Spenser and the speaker of the sonnets by attributing to the fictional characters the sophisticated understanding that could exist only between a real poet and his mistress. Both the poet and his mistress find delight in comparing their actual situation to the absurd inversion of it which is represented in the sonnets. In this view the poet-lover-worshipper of the *Amoretti* is either Edmund Spenser himself or a fictional character as nearly like Spenser as an aesthetic representation could be.

In the remainder of this essay I should like to propose a third alternative for understanding the *Amoretti* in particular and the Renaissance lyric in general, one which I believe accords better with other forms of aesthetic representation in Renaissance art than do the approaches to the *Amoretti* as autobiography or as realistic fiction. I wish to argue that, in general, the late medieval and Renaissance lyric is closer in method to allegory than to realism, and that any attempt to make the *Amoretti* palatable to modern taste by asserting their direct representation of actual experience becomes as hopelessly involved in historical anachronism as would a similar assertion offered in defense of the *Faerie Queene*.

His sonnets are not the only poems in which Spenser refers to himself. The most famous example is the opening of the *Faerie Queene:*

> Lo I the man, whose Muse whilome did maske,
> As time her taught, in lowly Shepherds weeds.

Here is both a factual reference to the historical Edmund Spenser's composition of the *Shepheardes Calender* and a literary allusion to the opening of Vergil's *Aeneid* as it appeared in Renaissance texts.[8] Critics are used to observing that in this instance the poet's life was as much *fashioned* by art as it was *imitated* by it: in order to begin an epic as Vergil had begun his it was necessary first to sit down and actually make one's self into a pastoral poet. Spenser was far from unique in subordinating his own personal inclination to the requirements of the myth of the poet. Hallett Smith has advanced the proposition that it was at least in part the Renaissance poet's aspiration to write *epic* poetry which was responsible for the large amount of *pastoral* poetry that was necessarily generated in the attempt.[9] Also in the Vergilian manner are Spenser's thinly masked personal allusions in *Colin Clouts Come Home Againe* and some of the dialogues of the *Shepheardes Calender.*

I have mentioned that Spenser would have found personal allusions in Chaucer. There is the Geoffrey in the *Hous of Fame,* the author of *Troilus* who appears in the Prologue to the *Legend of Good Women,* the Chaucer who is mentioned in the Introduction to the *Man of Law's Tale,* and there are allusions to Chaucer's friends in the Envoy to *Troilus* and elsewhere. These Spenserian and Chaucerian allusions to themselves as poets and to their friends are direct and undisguised. They are quite unlike such references to the poet's self as we might find in post-Augustan poetry. They are allusions to the poet as public figure, not as individual private man. The *Amoretti* allude to the speaker's authorship of the *Faerie Queene.* The *Faerie Queene* alludes to the narrator's authorship of the *Shepheardes Calender.* And the *Shepheardes Calender* alludes, with the ready assistance of E. K., to still earlier works. The Prologue to the *Legend of Good Women* and the Introduction to the *Man of Law's Tale* allude to the whole Chaucerian canon. Such allusions do little to increase verisimilitude. If anything, they work in the opposite way, reminding us that we are reading a literary construction.

Insofar as the actual life of a medieval or Renaissance poet is reflected in his poetry, it is only so much of the life as has already been molded by art, transmuted from actuality into myth. Even Dante, Petrarch, and Boccaccio were the heirs of a two-hundred-year-old tradition in which the lyric poet was a public figure. The names of over four hundred Provençal troubadours have been preserved from the twelfth and thirteenth centuries. Personal exploits, on the pattern of Jaufré Rudel's fateful (but fictional) journey to die in the arms of the Countess of Tripoli, whom his biographer identified with the "far away love" of his famous poem, were conventionally associated with specific poems.[10] Amorous adventures in particular were invented, exaggerated, and idealized with the effect that the personal life of the poet was absorbed into the fictional world of his own and of others' invention which surrounded his poems. This extra-textual fictional world mediates between the speaker or narrator of a Renaissance fiction and the "real" man who stands behind the work as author.

Of Boccaccio's Fiametta we know a great deal, but all of it from the poet's books. The Laura of Petrarch is similarly unknown to history. Dante alone so thoroughly fused the personal with the traditional, the profane with the sacred, the actual with the ideal, that one shrinks from applying any easy generalization to his art. Of the intimate, day-to-day events of his life we hear nothing in his poetry, only of the great public friendships and debates. If ever we do learn to state the peculiar nature of the personal reference in Renaissance and late medieval poetry, Dante may well emerge as the epitome of a characteristic imaginative impulse of that time to synthesize the personal with the mythic, the individual with the universal, a synthesis which eventually led Western man to formulate what we now, centuries later, understand as the self.

The fictional poet of the *Amoretti* can be identified with the actual Edmund Spenser only insofar as the particular events of Spenser's life may have corresponded to the conventional elements in the life of the mythic Renaissance poet. We may be closest to the truth when we think of the poet of the *Amoretti,* Spenser's particular manifestation of the mythic poet, as Colin. It is he whom G. W. I. addresses in the commendatory sonnet:

> Ah Colin, whether on the lovely plaine,
> Pyping to shepherds thy sweete roundelaies:

> Or whether singing in some lofty vaine,
> Heroick deedes, of past, or present daies.
> Or whether in thy lovely mistris praise,
> Thou list to exercise thy learned quill,
> Thy muse hath got such grace, and power to please,
> With rare invention bewtified by skill.

The plot of the *Amoretti,* the implied story of Colin's courtship, is less significant than are the fictional poet's attempts to formulate and visualize his thoughts and passions during the courtship's evolution. Both the plot and the dramatic aspects of Colin's inner struggle to achieve an appropriate poetic vision, in other words the major elements of the fiction, are vehicles for Spenser's doctrine of love. This is the respect in which the *Amoretti* are nearly akin to allegory in method. Spenser himself did not experience the full force of the inarticulate passions experienced by Colin—at least not when he was forty years old. The experience is typical and mythical, not individual and historical. Given a turn in his own personal affairs that would permit his mythical Colin to woo and marry, Spenser could not find a more congenial expression of his philosophical view of the nature of love than by combining the Petrarchan sonnet sequence with the classical epithalamion. Colin, like Guyon and Red Cross, is not a character whose thoughts and actions are meaningful primarily in terms either of the actual world or of a fictional world which operates under the same laws as those governing the actual world. When their thoughts or actions depart from the probable it is up to us to determine the doctrinal (i. e., allegorical) significance of such thoughts and actions. It is rarely appropriate to dismiss them out of hand as either satire or a failure of fictional art. Not as a record of his own *actual* experience, nor even as the fictional representation of Colin's *typical* experience, but primarily as the imaging forth of an *ideal* experience, Spenser brought the conventions of erotic poetry to the service of his essentially allegorical art. The technique of the *Amoretti,* with their wealth of Petrarchan conceits, is in many ways analogous to that of the *Faerie Queene,* "a continued Allegory, or darke conceit."

The conceit, or, as we might call it, the pattern of metaphor, is the central structure for controlling the thought of a Pertrarchan sonnet. When in Sonnet 10 of the *Amoretti* the poet speaks of his mistress as "the Tyrannesse" and asks the lord of love to enroll her faults in his black book that she might be brought to justice, we recognize the ideas as a highly figurative way of saying that the poet wishes that for once his mistress could feel how it is to be subject to a strong and humiliating passion. Our main objection to this kind of conceited writing is that it disguises good honest thought and emotion under a conventionalized crust of clichés. It is commonly felt that the liberation of Western love poetry from the artificiality of Petrarchan conceits liberated emotion likewise from the bonds of cliché. Almost the opposite point can be advanced in defense of conceited writing, however.

Even the elaborate, far-fetched conceit was more than mere ornamentation of a thought. Its metaphorical imagery permitted Renaissance poets to explore areas of human emotion and thought which were otherwise inaccessible to them. The Renaissance had neither the vocabulary nor the philosophical and psychological orientation for a more straightforward analysis of the extremely complex form of idealized eroticism that was coming to be known in Western culture as "love." To cite only a single example of the degree to which Renaissance philosophers of love were dependent upon essentially fictional modes of thought we could consider Marsilio Ficino's enormously influential Commentary on Plato's *Symposium*. In Chapter 5 of the Sixth Speech, Tommaso Benci describes the Ἔρωτες (a near equivalent to the Italian *amoretti,* or love-gods) which shoot arrows into the men who are captured by Love (a personified god in Ficino).[11] In Chapter 11 he refers to the beautiful object of love who does not return it as a thief and a murderer, for he takes both the soul and control over the soul's possessions away from the lover. He concludes a description of the lover whose affection seems to grow and decrease alternately by observing:

> Poor wretch, you seek yourself outside yourself, you cling to your captor so that you may recover your captured self. You do not wish to love madly because you do not wish to die; but you are unwilling not to love, because you think you must pay service to this image of heaven.[12]

The elaborate conceits of the love lyric were also the conceits of philosophical discourse. They were not cumbersome descriptions of a well-known emotion. Rather they were the instruments by which our Western conception of love was invented and given form. As allegory in narrative fiction was a method of consciously controlling the meaning of mythical and romantic narrative and of making genuine discoveries about the ethical and spiritual nature of man, so the metaphorical conceit in lyric poetry was an instrument for disciplining and controlling the utterances of blind and unselfconscious emotion. Allegory and conceit were the instruments for both the rational analysis of myth and the rational analysis of the real world and the real self.

In the twentieth century we feel we suffer from a deficiency of unrationalized myth and emotion. Our naïve reaction to allegory and the conceit is one of boredom with its conventionality. The later Middle Ages and the Renaissance faced an opposite cultural situation: poets longed to bring to the surface *for analysis and interpretation* the urgings of both the passionate human nature and the images of their most persistent dreams and visions. Allegory and the conceit do not hide or veil or conceal meaning: they are rationalizing and analyzing devices without which Western man could not have illuminated the dark secrets of his own nature, a nature which, nostalgically perhaps, we now wish were once again hidden beneath the veil of unrationalized myth and emotion.

"Unquiet thought," says the poet in Sonnet 2 of the *Amoretti,*

> Breake forth at length out of the inner part,
> In which thou lurkest lyke to vipers brood.

In Sonnet 3 he complains,

> So when my toung would speak her praises dew
> It stopped is with thoughts astonishment:
> And when my pen would write her title true,
> It ravisht is with fancies wonderment:
> Yet in my hart I then both speake and write
> The wonder that my wit cannot endite.

These early sonnets, in which we find the fictional poet concerned with the fiction he is writing, contain several examples of the "inexpressibility topos." [13] Or else, as in Sonnet 9, the conventional search for a suitable expression will constitute the whole conceit.

> Long-while I sought to what I might compare
> Those powrefull eies, which lighten my dark spright,

he begins. After a search through the usual celestial and mineralogical catalogues, he concludes,

> Then to the Maker selfe they likest be,
> Whose light doth lighten all that here we see.

Like nearly all conceits in Renaissance love poetry, Spenser's are conventional. Only the seasoned expert is willing to label a given image or phrase as "original." Also like other conceits, Spenser's are based on what can be thought of as sets of traditional "parodies." These metaphor sets, or parodies, provided both the rules and the raw material for generating an almost endless flow of metaphorical images with which to explore the relationship between traditional literary myth and the newly developing conception of the self. One such parody was the medieval literary convention of the Court of Love, which saw a quasi-judicial procedure as the pattern for all relationships between the sexes. Presiding over the court was the Lord of Love (he of the black book in Sonnet 10). The unfairly handled lover could have his mistress haled before the court of love for judgment; she could be in contempt of court; the lover could serve a sentence in prison; the lover could call upon an advocate to plead his case; and so on endlessly through an infinite number of metaphorical definitions of love. Here we see another similarity between allegory and conceit. The metaphor set or parody, which in the conceit is capable of generating infinite individual conceits, is capable in allegory of generating a sustained narrative in which the fiction bears a metaphorical relationship to the allegorical significance.

Another parody visualized love as an armed conflict, with siege engines, truces, captives, generals, and so forth. This parody generates a number of the conceits in the early part of the *Amoretti* which are most objectionable to modern taste and to the decorum of literary realism. By far the most important, and most difficult for the modern reader to understand, was the convention of love as a parody of the Christian religion. Because of the close similarity between the poetry of religious worship and poetry of idealized sexual love, the two traditions are almost impossible to disentangle. Religious writing used parodies of legal procedure and of military combat—and had since St. Paul. It even parodied sexual love in the passionate poetry inspired by such biblical texts as the Song of Songs. If erotic poetry parodied religion, religious poetry parodied sexual love, and the two traditions continued their mutual dependence until long after Spenser's time.

The physical description of the poet's mistress in the early sonnets of the *Amoretti* is close to the description of Belphoebe in Book II of the *Faerie Queene* (iii. 22–30). The pride and haughtiness of Belphoebe and the mistress imply a Trompart's-eye view of them both. As the fictional poet's vision matures, his mistress loses her aristocratic and military aspect, becoming both more physical and more spiritual. In terms of the *Faerie Queene,* she changes from Belphoebe to Amoret. The source of the conceits changes from the parody of social institutions to a parody of nature. In Sonnet 63 the mistress's embrace becomes a "happy shore." Her kiss in 64 brings perfumes sweeter than those of a garden. In 67 the poet invokes the ancient religious and erotic conceit of the beloved as a tame deer. A similar idea is found in the spider and the bee conceit of 71. He returns in 76 to the conceit of "thought's astonishment" that had first appeared in Sonnet 3 when his tongue was unable to frame his mistress's praise. But by now his thoughts have themselves become graceful *amoretti:*

> Fayre bosome fraught with vertues richest tresure . . .
> How was I ravisht with your lovely sight,
> And my frayle thoughts too rashly led astray!
> Whiles diving deepe through amorous insight,
> On the sweet spoyle of beautie they did pray;
> And twixt her paps like early fruit in May,
> Whose harvest seemd to hasten now apace,
> They loosely did theyr wanton winges desplay,
> And there to rest themselves did boldly place.
> Sweet thoughts I envy your so happy rest,
> Which oft I wisht, yet never was so blest.

Remembering that the sequel to the *Amoretti* is the *Epithalamion,* we recall that the penultimate image of the whole book is the fruitful marriage bed, presided over by Genius, while the final image is that of the generation of new souls to increase the count of saints in heaven. The Spenserian conception of overcoming the wretched and destructive humiliation of erotic passion through the loving body and soul is neither strictly Petrarchan nor Neoplatonic. It is more profoundly spiritual than the former and more physical than the latter. If originality is to be sought in the form of the *Amoretti* at all, it will be found in the details with which conventional elements are recombined to constitute an appropriate vehicle for the strikingly original Spenserian synthesis of spirit, flesh, and imagination in his doctrine of love. Among the details of Spenser's fiction are the figure of the loving poet who must somehow find expression for "the wonder that my wit cannot endite" (Sonnet 3) and the conceits with which he does finally overcome his thought's astonishment. Mediating between the fictional story of the *Amoretti* and the actual experience of the "real" Edmund Spenser is the larger cultural fiction of the poet Colin, a poet whose life story was composed in part by Vergil, Petrarch, and the troubadours of medieval Provence. Spenser's contribution to the Renaissance love lyric rests only indirectly on the quality of his own personal experience as religious worshipper, lover, and poet. It rests instead on his more general imaginative assertion of the doctrine that in the highest civilization the three persons are ideally one.

Notes

1. The commentary reprinted in the *Variorum Edition,* VIII, 631–38, is typical. However, Lee, Draper, and especially Renwick caution against too literal a reading of the sonnets as autobiography.

2. That Spenser married Elizabeth Boyle seems beyond doubt, but neither the date of the composition of the *Amoretti and Epithalamion* nor the date and place of Spenser's wedding are known with any certainty.

3. All quotations of Spenser's text are taken (slightly normalized) from *The Poetical Works of Edmund Spenser,* eds. J. C. Smith and E. de Selincourt (Oxford, 1912).

4. Plato in the *Phaedrus* distinguished four kinds of divine madness: poetry, love, prophecy, and mystery. The latter two correspond to my "religious." See Northrop Frye, "The Imaginative and the Imaginary," in his *Fables of Identity* (New York, 1963), p. 154.

5. "There is no use in singing if the song does not spring from the heart," text and translation in *The Songs of Bernart de Ventadorn,* eds. Stephen G. Nichols, Jr. *et al., University of North Carolina Studies in the Romance Languages and Literatures,* No. 39 (1962), pp. 80–82.

6. Assuming that he was sixteen years old when he matriculated at Cambridge on May 20, 1569.

7. "The *Amoretti:* 'Most Goodly Temperature,' " in *Form and Convention in the Poetry of Edmund Spenser: Selected Papers from the English Institute,* ed. William Nelson (New York, 1962), pp. 146–68.

8. "Ille ego qui quondam gracili modulatus avena / Carmen . . ."

9. *Elizabethan Poetry* (Cambridge, Mass., 1952), p. 1.

10. For a brief account of the debt of the *Vida* to Jaufré's poems, especially his *Languan li jorn son lonc en may,* and for the texts of both, see Alfred Jeanroy, ed. *Les Chansons de Jaufré Raudel* (Paris, 1924).

11. Sears Reynolds Jayne, ed. and trans., *Marsilio Ficino's Commentary on Plato's Symposium,* University of Missouri Studies, XIX, No. 1 (1944), 187.

12. Jayne, p. 202.

13. For the term, see Ernst Robert Curtius, *European Literature and the Latin Middle Ages,* trans. Willard R. Trask (New York, 1953), pp. 159–62.

Thomas M. Greene

Spenser and the Epithalamic Convention

WHEN SPENSER wrote his *Epithalamion* in 1594, he was acutely conscious that his poem was conventional—that is, that it stood in a given relationship to certain past poems and, once published, would be assimilated with them in their relationship to future poems. His conception of past epithalamia was different from his conception, for example, of the sources of the *Prothalamion,* a title which he invented. He would have been aware, moreover, that not all poems for weddings were epithalamia, and that not even all the poems entitled "Epithalamion" fitted strictly into the convention. I shall here sketch briefly the history of the genre, describe the convention as Spenser received it, and attempt to show what in his poem is conventional and what is not, adding interpretative comments that seem relevant.

Although descriptions of a wedding procession involving songs appear in Homer (*Iliad,* XVIII) and Hesiod (*The Shield of Herakles*), the ancestry of the epithalamic convention goes back to Sappho.[1] There is evidence that earlier Greek poets, such as Hesiod and Alcman, wrote nuptial poems; but Sappho's fragments are the earliest which have survived. Brief nuptial songs appear in Aristophanes' *Peace* and *The Birds,* and in other Greek plays, but the next true epithalamion is the eighteenth eclogue of Theocritus, written for the wedding of Helen and Menelaus.

Latin poets adopted the genre but did not immediately alter it radically. Catullus introduced native wedding customs into the first of his three nuptial poems, the beautiful *Epithalamium* (No. 61) for Vinia Aurunculeia and Manlius Torquatus, the single most influential poem of antiquity upon the Renaissance epithalamists. His other two nuptial poems are No. 62, the *Carmen Nuptiale,* a much briefer song in the form of a dialogue between choruses of youths and maidens, written for no specific occasion, and No. 64, a long narrative *epyllion* written for the legendary wedding of Peleus and Thetis. After Catullus, Ovid is said to have written an epithalamion which has been lost; the first chorus of Seneca's tragedy *Medea* may be based upon it.

With the *Epithalamium in Stellam et Violentillam* of Statius (written about A.D. 90), the genre entered a new stage which was to influence the Renaissance far less than the Sapphic-Catullan type (to be described below). Statius' poem, which was imitated by Claudian and several other late Latin epithalamists, consisted of a rather wooden mythological narrative centering around Venus and Cupid. After Statius, the only interesting nuptial poetry is found in the lyrical *Fescennina* which precede one of Claudian's two formal epithalamia. Interest in the genre may have been stimulated in late antiquity by rhetoricians such as Dionysius of Halicarnassus, Menander, Himerius, and Choricius of Gaza, who wrote prescriptions for or examples of wedding orations. In the Middle Ages Latin devotional poems entitled *Epithalamium* were written, but they had virtually nothing in common with the classical genre.

In the fifteenth century the genre was revived by neo-Latin poets and became so familiar that it could be satirized playfully by Erasmus in his *Colloquia* ("Epithalamium Petri Aegidii"). The best of the fifteenth-century epithalamists was Giovanni Pontano, who wrote nuptial poems, among others, for the marriages of two daughters. The practice of writing neo-Latin epithalamia was carried on by Ariosto and lasted through most of the sixteenth century; the best-known examples are the atypical erotic poem of Johannes Secundus and the patriotic celebration of Mary Stuart's first marriage by the Scottish poet George Buchanan.[2]

The genre was neglected by quattrocento poets writing in Italian. Torquato Tasso may have been correct in stating that a poem written by his father Bernardo in 1531 was the earliest in the language, although the primacy is hard to establish with certainty.[3] Examples can be found in anthologies such as Domeniche's *Delle rime di diversi nobilissimi et eccellentissimi autori* (Venice, 1550) and Atanagi's *De le rime di diversi nobili poeti toscani* (Venice, 1565). The genre really flowered in Italy, however, only with Tasso and

Marino, neither of whom was truly conventional. Tasso wrote no formal "epitalamio," but he did write thirteen nuptial poems entitled simply "Nelle nozze di . . ." or "Per le nozze di . . ." These poems did not adhere strictly to the traditional Catullan pattern but borrowed elements freely from that pattern. One of them, written for the wedding of Marfisa d'Este with her cousin Alfonsino, has been ranked among Tasso's finest lyrics.[4] Marino wrote ten epithalamia which differed greatly among themselves in structure and style and which represented even more of a break with the Catullan convention than Tasso's poems.

In France the history of the genre, in vernacular language, really begins with Ronsard, although Eustache Deschamps had written two nuptial *ballades,* and Marot two genial and intimate poems for the marriages of royal princesses.[5] Marot's poems contain occasional borrowings from Catullus, but in tone as well as content they are worlds away from the convention. Ronsard's *Epithalame* (written in 1548), on the other hand, clearly falls within the convention, though it depends more on Theocritus than on Catullus. It was published in Book IV of the *Odes* and prepared the way for a flood of other epithalamia. All but one of the Pléiade poets (Pontus de Tyard) wrote epithalamia, as did most of the other court poets. Among the wealth of examples, Belleau's delicate, lyrical celebration of the princess Claude's wedding in 1558 stands out as particularly attractive. The long *Epithalame* in dramatic form by Du Bellay for the wedding of Marguerite de France, sister of Henry II, is another important example.[6] The convention remained more or less intact in France to the end of the century. In the new literary atmosphere it was virtually abandoned in nuptial poems by Bertaut and Malherbe, and finally parodied out of existence by the zestful indecencies of Scarron.

In England there are few examples before Spenser; after Spenser the genre has an intricate history. Although at least two earlier poets, Lydgate and Dunbar, wrote nuptial poems, Sidney's *Epithalamion* sung by Discus in the third eclogue of the *Arcadia* was the first of its kind. Its composition may possibly have been antedated by a translation by Bartholomew Young of a Spanish poem drawn from Gil Polo's continuation of Montemayor's pastoral romance *Diana.* These are the only two English epithalamia which preceded Spenser's poem, and it is interesting that they are both pastorals. The list of seventeenth-century English poets who wrote epithalamia is a long and distinguished one including Donne, Jonson, Herrick, Crashaw, Marvell, and Dryden.[7] Indeed, to follow the progress of the genre is to follow in microcosm the development of seventeenth-century English poetry. It is remarkable that Spenser's poem did not exhaust the epithalamion in England but seems rather to have given it fresh impetus.

The genre acquired increased status in the Renaissance by the discussion devoted to it in such rhetorical treatises as Scaliger's *Poetices* and Puttenham's *Arte of English Poesie.*[8] These discussions combined historical references to past models with rules governing the genre itself. The characteristics most essential to the Renaissance epithalamic convention are the following:

(1) The principals of the wedding celebrated, when it is not fictive, usually belong to the nobility (this is less true in England than on the continent). The poet of course need not be well born himself but he is with few exceptions financially dependent upon the upper class. The weddings which are distinguished enough to be celebrated in verse are the weddings of people wealthy enough to reward the poet and prominent enough socially or politically to justify, so to speak, his encomia. It follows as a corollary of this patron-poet relationship that the epithalamion must contain praise of the bride and bridegroom. Spenser, himself formerly patronized by noblemen, was so conscious of the comparative social obscurity of his own marriage that the first stanza of his poem announces the reversal of the traditional relationship: "So I unto myself alone will sing." There are a few instances in which the principals belong to the upper middle class. In these cases, shifts in tone and treatment—a curtailment of flattery, greater freedom of allusion, etc.—are usually apparent at once.

(2) The epithalamion must follow classical models, in particular Catullus' No. 61. The specific nature of this influence will be described below. First, however, the functioning of the influence should be understood in terms of literary convention. As the body of Renaissance epithalamia increased, the influence of any single poem decreased; in place of the poem, the epithalamist drew upon a stockpile of *topoi,* commonplaces, similes, epithets, traditional good wishes, common strategies and techniques. The epithalamist seems to have

been aware of the genre, not so much as a number of individual poems among which he could choose his own "source," but rather as a body of poetic material which was itself intricately entangled with borrowings and derivation, a body from which he could draw without necessarily incurring a debt to a given poem. Attempts have been made by scholars to link Spenser's epithalamion to a specific source.[9] But for a student of the convention all such attempts break down because any given *topos* found in Spenser can be found in several earlier epithalamia.

One might define a convention as a set of allusions. A convention exists when the full literary meaning of a word or a line requires a knowledge of many past works in order to be wholly understood. The vocabulary of a pastoral elegy or a Petrarchan sonnet requires a familiarity with comparable works for its allusiveness to be appreciated. It follows that the first example one encounters in a convention cannot be read as the poet expected his work to be read.

(3) The epithalamion implies a social context. It assumes always a wedding attended by guests participating in a commonly shared jubilation. For a wedding without these elements the epithalamion would have to invent them. Apparently the poem was often a literal part of the entertainment accompanying the ceremony, comparable to the music, singing, dancing, and masques which the greatest weddings required.

(4) The epithalamion must refer to a specific day, fictive or real. Poems containing only generalized good wishes for the wedded couple are not epithalamia. To be conventional the poem must be constructed around the events of the wedding day itself—the religious rites, the banqueting, the bedding of bride and bridegroom (itself a ritual), and the sexual consummation. Thus the poem acquires dramatic impetus not from an institution—marriage—but from a series of concrete actions—a wedding. Aristotle, in the *Rhetoric* (I, 3), distinguished ceremonial or epideictic rhetoric from political and judicial in that the first treated of the present, the second of the future, and the third of the past. The epithalamist imitates the classical epideictic orator in assuming the occasion to be at hand.

In antiquity the successive stages of the wedding festivities provided various pretexts for song. There was a song for the wedding procession, a song for the bedding of the couple, the morning song for their reawakening the next day. The word "epithalamion," derived from the Greek *thalamos,* "bed chamber," implies that it was originally only one of these kinds of wedding poems. The Greek generic name for all these songs was *hymenaios.*

(5) The epithalamion involves the fictive poet-speaker in a certain complex and highly stylized role. This role is one of the most distinctive and interesting features of the epithalamic convention. A. L. Wheeler, in *Catullus and the Traditions of Ancient Poetry,* makes the following remarks on the role assumed by Catullus in his epithalamion for Manlius Torquatus (No. 61):

> The Greek element appears most prominently however in matters of technique. The most interesting feature here is the mimetic-dramatic character of the poem—the manner in which the poet represents himself as taking part in the ceremony in the role of a master of ceremonies and chorus leader. It is the poet who invokes Hymen, urges the girls to sing, addresses the bride, apostrophizes the wedding couch, directs the boys to lift their torches and sing, addresses the favorite slave, the groom—all the persons in fact. Sometimes he maintains his individuality . . . sometimes he associates himself with the rest of the company. . . . This is the device which more than anything else gives life to the poem. No other completely extant wedding poem is composed in this way, but the same technique is employed in others forms of poetry, for example in the *Hymns* of Callimachus.[10]

Wheeler is right in saying that no other extant wedding poem of antiquity is written from this assumed role, but there is evidence that Catullus's chief source, Sappho, assumed a role which resembled her imitator's. The evidence is contained in an exemplary wedding oration by Himerius, a Greek rhetorician of late antiquity (315–381 B.C.). In his *Oration for the Marriage of Severus* he recalls the epithalamia of Sappho and says of them:

> It is she [Sappho] who after the mock combats enters the bridal precincts, decorates the room, spreads the couch, marshals the maidens into the bridal chamber, brings Aphrodite in her car of Graces, and a bevy of Loves to play with her. She twines the

> bride's hair with hyacinths . . . but the wings of the Loves and their locks she decks with gold, and dispatches them before the car as an escort waving their torches on high.[11]

This description of the poetess' commanding part in the wedding festivities seems to relate directly to what impresses Wheeler in Catullus' poem. One may conclude from Himerius' evocation that like Catullus Sappho made of herself a kind of mistress of ceremonies, presiding over each successive scene of the wedding pageant and seeming to control its evolution by invocations, apostrophes, and commands. There can be little doubt that Catullus' own mimetic role derives from Sappho.

During the Renaissance the role was accepted almost universally by epithalamists. It is the poet-speaker who makes the wedding arrangements and in the act writes his poem. In some inferior poems he is almost officious, despite his determined high spirits: the chorus of maidens must be out of bed; the correct gods must attend with the correct gifts; the roistering must not prevent the couple from retiring; the sun must now slow his pace; the bride must not be too fearful nor the bridegroom too impetuous. Most epithalamia, like Spenser's, are written chiefly in the second person and in the optative subjunctive. The poet-speaker acts as an advocate for society, assuring the couple that they are fortunate, that they are doing wisely to marry, wishing them the socially valuable blessings of prosperity, harmony, and increase. As a result the typical epithalamion is a ritualistic *public* statement, unconcerned with the actual intimate experience undergone by individuals.

The commands, invocations, flattery, and optatives of the speaker all function to call into being the ideal event which the wedding must be, the ideal as defined partly by the convention, partly by the particular society, partly by the poet. A wedding is an ambiguous enough event to permit many interpretations. Something has happened when the wedding day and night are past, but epithalamists do not agree on the nature of the happening. It may be primarily a sexual event, but it may be also a social event, a religious event, or, at the highest level, a political event. It may even in certain poems be related to the natural macrocosmos and thus become a kind of cosmic event. The epithalamist is able to define the event which has occurred through the commands and injunctions which he chooses to make, through the various actions of the wedding day and night which he chooses to name and evoke. Almost all epithalamia include the bedding of the bride and bridegroom, but even this can be treated in widely different terms.

The underlying optative pressure exerted by the poem, the pressure of the ideal conception upon the actual occasion, is felt throughout. Kenneth Burke has discussed the "magical" use of language as decree.[12] This is the characteristic use of language in the epithalamion. It becomes explicit in the concluding *allocutio sponsalis,* where the couple is addressed directly and the traditional wishes are made for their future, typically in the optative subjunctive.

An eighteenth-century critic wrote this of the genre: "Le but de l'Epithalame est de faire connoître aux nouveaux époux le bonheur de leur union, par les louanges qu'on leur donne successivement, et par les avantages qu'on leur annonce pour l'avenir." [13] To announce to the newly married the happiness of their union—a rhetorical function is involved here which Aristotle, in two separate passages,[14] distinguishes from praise, a function which most Aristotelian translators render as "felicitation" or "gratulation" but which a more courageous translator, W. D. Ross, has rendered, lamely and accurately, as "calling happy." [15] One may recall Dryden: "O happy, happy, happy pair!" The Greek term for this is *makarismos.* The epithalamion can be regarded as a series of invocations to action which will demonstrate the ideal felicity of the wedding and thus function as *makarismos.*

With this background we may turn to Spenser's poem, the one epithalamion besides Catullus' which ranks with the world's great poems. The conventional elements noted above are all present in Spenser, with the exception of the aristocratic milieu. Many conventional *topoi,* moreover, appear in Spenser: among others, the "maske" of Hymen; the attendance of the Graces upon the bride; the praise of the bride's beauty; the impatience with the tardy sun; the greeting of Hesperus; the bedding of the bridal couple, with the injunction to break off the revelry; the concluding invocations which replace the *allocutio sponsalis.*

In the remaining pages of this article I shall discuss ways in which Spenser developed, modified, and broke with the convention.

His first original stroke was to fuse the roles of bridegroom and poet-speaker; to my knowledge no epithalamist had ever done this before. In most respects the device is successful; it makes perfect sense in the poem and confers added motivation for the speaker's injunctions and directions. His invocation to the Muses, nymphs, and Graces who wait upon his bride can be read as tokens of his solicitous regard for her. His praise of her inner and outer beauty in stanzas nine through eleven appear as spontaneous expressions of his love. His command "Pour out the wine . . ." is reasonable because he is the host. And the concluding prayerful invocations gain a particular fervency because they are prayers for the speaker's own marriage.

These invocations are striking examples of Spenser's fine moral taste. One may compare them with the *allocutio* of the *Prothalamion,* which is highly conventional, albeit the only conventional stanza of the poem:

> Joy may you have, and gentle hearts content
> Of your loves couplement;
> And let faire Venus, that is Queene of love,
> With her heart-quelling Sonne upon you smile,
> Whose smile, they say, hath vertue to remove
> All Loves dislike, and friendships faultie guile
> For ever to assoile.
> Let endlesse Peace your steadfast hearts accord,
> And blessed Plentie wait upon your bord;
> And let your bed with pleasures chast abound,
> That fruitful issue may to you afford,
> Which may your foes confound,
> And make your joyes redound
> Upon your Brydale day, which is not long.

In the *Epithalamion* Spenser refrains significantly from asking for joy or conjugal pleasure. He assumes them and does not insult his bride by asking for them. He does refer to Genius who, he says, ensures conjugal chastity and pleasure, but he specifically asks him only for offspring. This is, in fact, the chief gift he asks of all the gods invoked. For his offspring he asks happiness but not the other conventional gifts—fame, heroism, and fertility—nor does he ask that they "confound" his foes; he asks rather that they be permitted ultimate sainthood in Heaven. There are no references in the *Epithalamion* to envy or jealousy, "Loves dislike, and friendships faultie guile," the besetting evils of marriage which were frequently exorcised. These would also be in bad taste where the bridegroom is his own petitioner.

It is only the consummation itself which presents an insuperable problem in tact to the bridegroom-speaker. Spenser, with his delicacy and reverence for his bride, could not have permitted himself any license, license which would be acceptable from a third person. His solution was to divert attention to the ornamental Cupids playing about the bed, a solution not entirely satisfactory. An emotional vacuum is almost created at the point where conventionally emotions are highest. The emotional climax is reserved for the concluding prayers.

The fusion of the bridegroom and speaker roles is not the only original element in the poem. The unconventionality of the bourgeois milieu has already been noted, but some corollary consequences of this might be pointed out. First of all it is interesting that Spenser insists upon rather than veils the provinciality of the occasion. There is a distinctly bourgeois pleasure in the "silken courteins," "odourd sheetes, and Arras coverlets" of the bridal bed, a pleasure which would be unseemly at an aristocratic occasion. The bourgeois world is represented most vividly by the merchants' daughters who watch the bridal procession and attend the feast. The effect of their mediocrity is to render the bride more brilliant. There is a lively humor in the poet's patronizing manner to them, his questioning whether they have ever seen anyone so fair, and why they forget to sing when they see her:

> And stand astonisht lyke to those which red
> Medusaes mazeful hed.

Later in the church they are admonished to learn obedience and humility from the bride. It is they finally who are enjoined to bring the bride to her chamber, breaking off their sports and ceasing to sing: "Enough it is, that all the day was youres." They are associated with the daytime world of activity and festivity which is no longer becoming after the arrival of darkness. With the welcome to night and silence, they disappear from the poem. Conventionally the bride was usually attended by handmaids, but these were never truly realized dramatically.

The bourgeois milieu permits a release of humor which would have been unseemly in the conventional epithalamion. There are a dozen touches of delicate comedy sprinkled through the poem, evidence of the jocularity befitting one's own wedding day. There is the impatient bridegroom's assurance to the sun that his "tired steeds long since have need of rest," a witty way of handling an old *topos*. There is the description of the angels at church who forget to worship out of wonder at the bride's beauty. There is the admonition to the nymphs of Mulla to bind up their hair in order to look their best. There is the wry and realistic allusion to the croking "Quire of Frogs," a reminder of the boggy Irish countryside. There is the tardy regret that the longest rather than the shortest day of the year was chosen for the wedding. There is the admonition to the young men of the town to write down the date lest they forget it. There is even the punning play on "consent" when Spenser avers that the birds, by their harmonious song

> . . . all agree, with sweet consent,
> To this dayes merriment.

These benign and gentle touches represent perhaps the closest approach of the Renaissance epithalamion to the vulgar Fescennine jokes of antiquity.

Another unconventional element lies in Spenser's use of his stanza form. The intricate form was derived by Spenser from the Italian *canzone,* although no Italian poem has been found composed in the identical pattern. Italian epithalamia, including Tasso's nuptial poems, were commonly written in the form of *canzoni,* but of course the form was not limited to epithalamia. Spenser's stanza is unusual in its length, varying as it does from seventeen to nineteen lines, and in its number of recurrences. There are twenty-three stanzas in the *Epithalamion,* whereas the typical Italian *canzone* does not exceed eight or ten. The concluding brief address to the poem, the envoy, was characteristic of the *canzone* and was called technically a *tornata* or *commiato*. On the whole the *canzone* as written by Italian poets tended to be a more static poem than Spenser's. The length and complexity of the stanza tended to strengthen the autonomy of each unit and to render the concluding line more of a conclusion. Spenser's refrain, which is not a characteristic of the *canzone,* renders the conclusion even more emphatic. Thus to write in this form with so strong a narrative element—for the *Epithalamion* is in fact a kind of story—was to demonstrate an audacity of which few Italian poets would have been capable. Spenser's use of the *canzone* was a deformation of its spirit and of its apparent technical limitations.[16]

It has been said that these limitations were in fact too great for Spenser. John Erskine, for example, wrote:

> Strictly speaking, each stanza, with its own inspiration, is a song in itself, and the complete poem is a series rather than an organic whole. But the lyrical emotion aroused by all motives is the same in every case, so that, in the broad sense, it would be difficult to deny unity to the poem.[17]

But it is demonstrably untrue that the emotion of all the stanzas is alike; one has only to compare the fourteenth stanza—"Pour out the wine without restraint or stay"—with the last. Actually the poem is remarkable for its sudden shifts of tone and mood.

If it is true that the poem is only a series of distinct stanzas, then the poem is certainly a failure. Undeniably the individual stanzas of the *Epithamalion,* more than those of most poems, do have a heightened autonomy; the prosodic variations in length and pattern among them tend to increase their distinctiveness. Each makes a fresh beginning; each evolves with a certain spontaneity; each reaches its foreknown conclusion with renewed ingenuity. But to say this is not to admit that the relationship between the stanzas is factitious. The reader is insensitive who does not feel the balance and architecture of the parts, the calculated progression of feeling, the movement forward to a culmination.[18]

Unity is also gained by imagistic motifs which recur frequently enough to be significant. Spenser adopted conventional *topoi,* extended and modified them, and added original inventions of his own to form these harmonious and elegant patterns of description and allusion. Jones[19] has discussed the auditory imagery of the poem, imagery which the refrain requires and emphasizes. Spenser's mastery appears here in the deft suiting of sound to mood at each hour of the day, in the choice of images which echo but also help to create personal emotion. One is also struck by the imagery of light and darkness, an antithesis associated with other antitheses of day and night, harmonious or boisterous sound and precarious silence, rising and dressing on the one hand and retiring and undressing on the other.

The poem is unconventional in the repeated expression it gives to the ominous elements associated with night, the elements which might potentially destroy the joy of the wedding and even the marriage. The induction refers to mishaps raised by "death or love or fortune's wreck" in the lives of those who have appeared earlier in Spenser's poems. The second stanza refers to the vicissitudes of the courtship dramatized in the *Amoretti,* the "pains and sorrows past," and the Muses are asked to sing of "solace" as well as of joy to the bride. At nightfall the appearance of Hesperus, a *topos* which goes back to Sappho, occasions unconventional praise of the star for its guidance of lovers "through the nights sad dread." This "sad dread" is elaborated two stanzas below in the invocation to night:

> . . . in thy sable mantle us enwrap,
> From feare of perrill and foule horror free.
> Let no false treason seeke us to entrap,
> Nor any dread disquiet once annoy
> The safety of our joy;
> But let the night be calme, and quietsome,
> Without tempestuous storms or sad afray . . .

and again in the following stanza which catalogues more fully the disturbances which night might bring:

> Let no lamenting cryes, nor dolefull teares,
> Be heard all night within, nor yet without:
> Ne let false whispers, breeding hidden feares,
> Breake gentle sleepe with misconceived dout.
> Let no deluding dreames, nor dreadfull sights,
> Make sudden sad affrights.

Here quite clearly the night sounds are not only the effects of nightmares or apparition; they are ambiguous enough to suggest by extension the potential suffering which a lifetime of marriage, not only the wedding night, might involve. The "doleful tears," the "false whispers," the "misconceived dout," suggest the jealousies and suspicions which conceivably could threaten the marriage and which must be exorcised. Spenser is too tactful to refer to this possibility directly.[20] After making this veiled allusion, he fills out his catalogue with more fanciful fears—of witches, hobgoblins, ghosts, creatures which the town maidens might believe in—and modulates to a lighter tone with the concluding "quire of frogs still croaking." The ominous associations of darkness are evoked again, however, in the last stanza, where the stars are described as torches in the temple of heaven

> . . . that to us wretched earthly clods
> In dreadful darkness lend desired light.

Here it is not only the marriage but the whole of human experience which is menaced by the night's sad dread. Thus the threat of disaster, the irrational fear of vaguely specified suffering, hovers faintly over the poem, lending particular urgency to the concluding prayers. It is perhaps not too fanciful to relate the wolves of the fourth stanza to this cluster of night associations and to find in the decorative invocation to the "lightfoot maids" an added symbolic nuance:

> And eke, ye lightfoot mayds, which keepe the deere,
> That on the hoary mountayne used to towre;
> And the wylde wolves, which seeke them to devoure,
> With your steele darts doo chace from comming neer;
> Be also present heere . . .

The imagery of light is even more ubiquitous. References to the sun, as well as to the moon and stars, recur repeatedly. The sun is associated with brightness, with beauty, with joyfulness; it presides over the wakefulness and activity of the day. The sunlit day is the time of social joy, ritualistic joy; the night, if it is moonlit and starlit, if it is atypical in its silent tranquillity, is the time of personal intimate joy. Both day and night have their respective culminations: day at the center of the poem, night at the conclusion. The act of dressing, which is emphasized in the poem, suggests the personal preparation to meet the active, social, audible world outside the chamber. Placed in this context, the conventional bedding of the bride, which is also described, suggests the retirement from the social context, from sound, from public ritual, from the "delights forepast" of the merchants' daughters.

The accumulation of subtle and unlabored suggestions like these helps to enrich the meaning with which Spenser informs the wedding event. That meaning is in fact very rich. Ultimately the *Epithalamion* is distinguished by its amplitude. It is in every sense a major poem: by its unusual narrative range, embracing *all* the events of the wedding day, by its emotional range, distinguishing with sensitivity and precision related sets of feelings, and by its allusive range, employing without shock a wealth of pagan figures to orchestrate an essentially Christian statement. The world of the poem may be seen as a series of concentric areas. In the center is the couple, always at the dramatic focus; about them lies the town, the "social context"—the merchants' daughters, the young men who ring the bells, the boys who cry "Hymen" with "strong confused noyce"; beyond lies the natural setting, the woods that echo the jubilation with an answering joy, the "cheereful birds," the Mulla, the hoary mountain, and at night the choir of croaking frogs; vaguely outside of this is the world of classical figures, the Muses and the Graces, Maia and Alcmena, Hera, Cynthia, and Hymen, and "Jove's sweet paradice of Day and Night"; finally above all these realms stretches the thinly disguised Christian Heaven, the "temple of the gods," lending light to wretched earthly clods. The poem begins and ends with the widest perspective; at the center of the poem, during the ceremony, the focus has narrowed to the couple itself. Immediately before and after the ceremony the focus includes the "social context." The opening, with its perspective into the past, is balanced by the concluding perspective into the future. Thus, structurally as well as thematically, the amplitude is complemented with an elegant symmetry and an intricate harmony.

If one asks what ideal event is called into being by Spenser's injunctions, the answer is not simple. The event has been social and religious and sexual, and there are hints of a relationship to nature, of a cosmic dimension also. But the richness of Spenser's interpretation is centered in the personal experience of the bridegroom-speaker; the wedding is above all a private emotional event. Because the two roles are fused, the wedding is seen from within, not without. This kind of unconventionality is the most basic of all. Instead of *makarismos,* the assertion of happiness, Spenser achieves the dramatic realization of happiness.

Notes

1. Psalm 45 (in the Vulgate Psalm 44) is also an epithalamion, apparently for a royal wedding. Given the distance between Hebrew culture and Greek culture, there is a surprising number of elements which the psalm has in common with the convention known to Spenser. Although contemporary scholars do not consider the *Song of Songs* to have been written for a wedding, early in the Christian era it was interpreted as a celebration of an allegorical marriage. Spenser drew upon the *Song of Songs* (see Israel Baroway, "The Imagery of Spenser and the Song of Songs," *Journal of English and Germanic Philology,* XXXIII [1934], 23), but it was not widely influential in the Renaissance, perhaps because it was considered to be too sacred.

2. For texts, see Giovanni Gioviano Pontano, *Carmina,* ed. Soltani (Florence, 1902), II, 160, 164; Ludovico Ariosto, *Lirica,* ed. Fatini (Bari, 1924), p. 217; Johannes Secundus, *Les Baisers* (Latin text ed. and trans. Maurice Rat [Paris, 1938], p. 36); D. A. Millar (ed.), *George Buchanan: A Memorial* (St. Andrews, 1907), p. 300.

3. In one of his *Discorsi del poema eroico* T. Tasso alluded to his father's poem as 'il Epitalamio fatto nelle nozze del Duca Federico, il quale fu peravventura il primo, che si legesse in questa lingua" (*Opere,* ed. Rosini [Pisa, 1821–1832], XII, 16). For the text of this poem see Bernardo Tasso, *De gli Amori* (Venice, 1555), p. 197.

4. See Augusto Sainati, *La lirica di Torquato Tasso* (Pisa, 1912).

5. Eustache Deschamps, *Oeuvres inédites* (Paris, 1849), I, 154; II, 6. Clément Marot, *Oeuvres,* ed. Yve-Plessis and Plattard (Paris, 1875–1931), V, 85, 98.

6. Pierre de Ronsard, *Oeuvres complètes,* ed. Laumonier (Paris, 1914–1949), I, 9. Rémy Belleau, *Oeuvres poétiques,* ed. Marty-Laveaux (Paris, 1878), I, 238. Joachim du Bellay, *Oeuvres poétiques,* ed. Chamard (Paris, 1908–1931), V, 201.

7. The standard, although incomplete, anthology of English epithalamia is edited by Robert H. Chase, *English Epithalamies* (London, 1896). There are two German dissertations which discuss this material: Kurt Wohrmann, *Die englische Epithalamiendichtung der Renaissance und ihre Vorbilder* (Leipzig, 1928); Adelheid Gaertner, *Die englische Epithalamienliteratur im siebzehnten Jahrhundert*

und ihre Vorbilder (Coburg, 1936). The best edition of Spenser's *Epithalamion* is by Cortlandt Van Winkle (New York, 1926).

8. Julius Caesar Scaliger, *Poetices* (Heidelberg, 1617). George Puttenham, *Arte of Englishe Poesie,* ed. Willcock-Walker (Cambridge, 1936).

9. Wohrmann, *op. cit.,* links it with Catullus' No. 61. James A. S. McPeek, in *Catullus in Strange and Distant Britain* (Cambridge, 1939), links it with several "sources" but particularly Marc Claude Buttet's *Epithalame aux nosses de tresmagnanime prince Emmanuel Philibert de Savoie . . .*

10. A. L. Wheeler, *Catullus and the Traditions of Ancient Poetry* (Berkeley, 1934), p. 200.

11. Quoted in *Sappho—Poems and Fragments,* ed. and trans. C. R. Haines (London, 1926), p. 52.

12. Kenneth Burke, *The Philosophy of Literary Form* (Baton Rouge, 1941).

13. Abbé Souchay, "Discours sur l'origine et le caractère de l'épithalame," in *Académie Royale des Inscriptions et Belles Lettres,* IX (1736), 305.

14. "To call any one blest is, it may be added, the same thing as to call him happy; but these are not the same thing as to bestow praise and encomium upon him; the two latter are a part of 'calling happy,' just as goodness is a part of happiness." *Rhetoric,* I, 9. "Clearly what applies to the best things is not praise, but something greater and better, as is indeed obvious; for what we do to the gods and the most godlike of men is to call them blessed and happy." *Nicomachean Ethics,* I, 12.

15. Compare also Hobbes: "The form of speech whereby men signify their opinion of the goodness of any thing, is *Praise*. . . . And that whereby they signify the opinion they have of a man's felicity, is by the Greeks called *Makarismos,* for which we have no name in our tongue." *Leviathan,* ed. Oakeshott (Oxford, 1955), p. 39.

16. Spenser may have been influenced by the Sidney or the Polo-Young epithalamion. Both of these were written in an identical uneven stanza with refrain; neither, however, could be called a *canzone*.

17. John Erskine, *The Elizabethan Lyric* (New York, 1903), p. 189.

18. I am tempted to find more elaborate structural balance than other students have discovered. It has been pointed out that, if the prefatory first stanza is disregarded, the two stanzas describing the church ceremony are exactly central; ten stanzas precede and ten follow. I am inclined to see an ulterior division into three-four-three stanzas of each of these groups of ten. The first group of three consists of injunctions to the Muses and nymphs to attend the bride at her waking. The next group of four, beginning with the line, "Wake now, my love, awake; for it is time," concerns the preparations for the day. The next group of three, beginning with stanza nine, consists of three descriptions of the bride, evoking in turn her immediate beauty as a bride, her physical bodily beauty, and her inner Platonic beauty. After the service three stanzas carry us from the ceremony to nightfall. The seventeenth stanza, beginning "Now ceasse, ye damsels, your delights fore-past . . . Now day is doen, and night is nighting fast," clearly marks a new beginning, and this is emphasized by the shift in the refrain. Stanzas seventeen through twenty form the night group, which is

set off significantly from the preceding daylight stanzas; this group ends the narrative proper. The last three consist of prayerful invocations to the gods.

19. H. S. V. Jones, *A Spenser Handbook* (New York, 1930), p. 354.

20. Sidney, who wrote an epithalamion for a fictive, pastoral marriage, did not need to be so tactful. His poem contains a wry catalogue of marital abuses:

> All churlish words, shrewd answers, crabbed looks,
> All privateness, self-seeking, inward spite,
> All waywardness, which nothing kindly brooks,
> All strife for toys and claiming master's right,
> Be hence, aye put to flight;
> All stirring husband's hate
> 'Gainst neighbour's good for womanish debate,
> Be fled, as things most vain:
> O Hymen, long their coupled joys maintain!

Spenser would have known this catalogue, but his own catalogue of night sounds is the closest approach he makes to it.

Robert Ellrodt

From Earthly Love to Heavenly Love

TO BRING OUT the contrast between the two pairs of *Hymns,* we must know what Spenser intends by earthly love and earthly beauty. Throughout the hymns, beauty, no doubt, is described as a spiritual radiance. But the feeling is evoked by the beauty of *one* woman. It is perhaps more refined and less hyperbolic than in other poets who spoke of their lady as Beauty incarnate,[1] for Spenser, writing a hymn in honour of Beauty, is conscious throughout that the particular beauty of each being is not its own, but a gift of a higher Beauty. Yet, that higher Beauty is described as a source, not as a goal. The lover's aim is the conquest of an earthly beauty, not the vision of Beauty's self; his heart is set on a "handmaid" of *Cytherea,* not on "great beauties Queene" (*H.B.* 26–87). To the "great Soveraine" he proffers homage, after the chivalric and classical tradition; to "*Venus* dearling," the addressee of "these fearefull lines," he proffers love. What kind of love?

The answer is given by the description of Love's "Paradize" in the first hymn. If Spenser meant to describe only the Platonic delights of eye and ear, would he have written these lines, fraught with clear suggestions of fruition?

> There with thy daughter *Pleasure* they doe play
> Their hurtlesse sports, without rebuke or blame,
> And in her snowy bosome boldly lay
> Their quiet heads, devoyd of guilty shame,
> After full joyance of their gentle game. (*H.L.* 287–91)

Moreover, that "Paradize of all delight and joyous happie rest," where the classical Gods and Cupid's daughter, Pleasure, are assembled, is clearly intended to recall Venus' "joyous Paradize," the Garden of Adonis.[2] Spenser was fond of pointing back to his own myths,[3] and we know that all four hymns were written, or, at least, rewritten, after the first six Books of the *Faerie Queene*. Love in the Garden of Adonis has been shown to be the natural instinct, innocent so far as it is indulged in a sinless Eden, or within the sinless bonds of marriage.[4] I therefore think it not improper to read the close of the first Hymne, coming after the *Amoretti* and the *Epithalamion,* as "an apology of the marriage-bed," the interpretation scorned by Dr. Bennett.[4] "Marriage," in a way, may be thought an unnecessary qualification, and, indeed, Spenser refrains from suggesting it as clearly as in the Amoret story. I have shown that the *Fowre Hymnes* were composed at a time. For the sake of the retractation, it was not amiss that a "lewd" construction might be put upon the rhymes ascribed to "greener" years. But I have suggested also that Spenser was anxious to make even the more sensuous lines unobjectionable when properly construed, in order to answer the criticisms of Burghley. He therefore insisted throughout, not only on the ennobling power of love, but on truth and loyalty, feelings which, though they were called for as well by the chivalric romance of adultery, may be taken in Spenser as the ethical standard pointing to married love "devoyd of guilty shame." Besides, his description of the lover's quest is little more than a rather dull narrative of the quest of Scudamour for Amoret "through seas, through flames, through thousand swords and speares." It will be noticed that it does not end when the lover has gained his lady's *grace,* for

> He nathemore can so contented rest,
> But forceth further on, and striveth still
> T'approch more neare, till in her inmost brest,
> He may embosomed bee, and loved best. (*H.L.* 247–50)

The suppressed stanzas on the meeting of Scudamour and Amoret changed into a "faire Hermaphrodite"[5] are a better comment upon the *Hymne in Honour of Love* than the fastidious Platonic interpretation of Dr. Bennett, provided we remember that chaste love, "without rebuke or blame," is implied throughout. Of such a love, not of "brutish" love, will the poet sing "An heavenly Hymne, such as the Angels sing."[6] For such a love did "sweet Angels Alleluya sing," as the bride stood "before the altar."[7]

The first hymn, therefore, leaves us in no doubt that Spenser remains faithful to the conception of love we have traced in the *Faerie Queene.* Since the second hymn is devoted to beauty, and beauty is perceived by the eyes and the ears alone, it is not surprising that only the more Platonic delights should be suggested. The close of the hymn seems distinctly reminiscent of the rhapsody of Gismondo on the pleasures of love in *Gli Asolani:*

> For lovers eyes more sharply sighted bee
> Then other mens, and in deare loves delight
> See more then any other eyes can see. (*H.B.* 232–4)

Non sono, como quelle de gli altri huomini, le viste de gli amanti, o Donne. . . .[8]

Both Spenser and Bembo give prominence to the visual and auditive delights, in accordance with both the Petrarchan and the Platonic code of love. But the English poet ends with the traditional plea for "grace," and the first hymn has shown that the lover, once "grace" is gained, "forceth further on" (*H.L.* 245–50). As to Bembo's spokesman, Gismondo, he praises that *amore humano,* which is content to rest in the senses of sight and hearing. Yet he allows his eyes to rove complacently on the budding charms of a lady's breast while describing the contemplative delights of a lover,[9] and he humourously declines to keep up the pretense to the last. The pleasures afforded by the other senses are not utterly disclaimed. Lovers are only invited to "taste" them sparingly. And though sacrificing in speech to the fashionable convention, Gismondo smilingly confesses his own inability to restrain his appetite,[10] further adding that such advice would ill apply to a bridegroom.[11]

Gismondo, no doubt, is no true Platonist and will be upbraided by Lavinello. He is not given the last word. Yet many *trattati d'amore* could have afforded precedent for a toleration or even a vindication of sexual love. The uncompromising attitude of Pico and Benivieni has already been contrasted with the more moderate views of Ficino. Yet, while refusing to scorn earthly Venus and the desire of generation as base and brutish, while praising marriage as a civil and religious institution, Ficino wisely avoided any attempt to fuse or associate the sexual instinct with the higher Platonic love. Paradoxically, though logically enough when the claims of human nature are considered, an easy-going and sophistical toleration of sensual love, irrespective of matrimony, often appeared among those who professed to follow the philosophy of Pico. A clear instance is afforded by *Il Cortegiano*. The last speech, ascribed to Bembo, is an outright rejection of sexual love in principle. But the speaker's asceticism, modeled on Pico's, is tempered in practice and his very contention implies a qualification since he undertakes to show that "*olde men* may love not onely without slander, but otherwhile more happily than young men." [12] Though the happier love is recommended to old and young alike, Bembo admits that sensual love in young men "deserveth excuse, and [is] perhaps in some case lawfull: for although it putteth them in afflictions, dangers, travels, and the unfortunateness that is said, yet are there many that to winne them the good will of their Ladies practise vertuous thinges, which for all they be not bent to a good end, yet are they good of them selves. And so of that much bitternesse they picke out a little sweetnesse, and through the adversities which they sustaine, in the ende they acknowledge their errour." [13] This is no more than a toleration or a palliation, for the principle is maintained: "sensuall love in every age is naught," and "the coveted ende," not "a good end" in itself.[14] The wiser lover will rest satisfied with "mery countenances, familiar and secret talke, jeasting, dalying, hand in hand," and "may also lawfully and without blame come to kissing," for "a kisse may be saide to be rather a coupling together of the soule, than of the body." [15] But even that love is still subject to the miseries bred by absence and "the trouble to behold the beautie of one bodie alone;" the "not yong Courtier" is invited to press further and "beholde no more the particular beautie of one woman, but an universall, that decketh out all bodies." [16] Love for one woman, therefore, whether sensual or Platonic, is never a satisfying, self-complete experience, even on the human level.

The more fastidious writers of *trattati d'amore* treated Platonism as a beautiful aesthetic creed and a fashionable garb. The more sincere did not hesitate to vindicate the sensual love which others affected to disclaim. They derived their arguments from the Aristotelian and scholastic philosophy which denied that the human intellect could act without the instruments of the senses. But they could also appeal, whether seriously or irreverently, to the Christian conception of man. To the Platonist, the soul was the whole man, but Christianity had always insisted that "the union of body and soul makes the man." [17] Renaissance writers in love who took that stand therefore should hardly be styled Platonists, since they opposed the very spirit of Platonism even while retaining much Platonic material. Equicola no longer let "Plato trim the sails," but was faithful to the principles of Aristotelian philosophy and Christian faith when he did not admit of any separation of body and soul in the experience of love. But he went beyond this and sounded an almost naturalistic note when he argued that spiritual love by itself, when disembodied, could not endure. He who loves permanently, he concluded, must needs love both the soul and the body in the beloved, for the body ministers sensual pleasure to the senses as their own end, while the soul seeks from the soul a love answering hers.[18]

An abler and more mystical defender of this philosophical position, though, was the Hebrew scholar Jehudah Abarbanel, known as Leo Hebraeus or Leone Ebreo. He argued that the union of the lovers' souls was the end of perfect love but could only be fully achieved when the bodies, too, were united: the bodily union therefore made spiritual love more perfect.[19] Not only did he approve of the function of generation, like Ficino, but he claimed that "carnal delectations," when temperate, were good in themselves and belonged with "honest" love.[20] His *Dialoghi d'Amore* were highly praised and immensely popular throughout the sixteenth century. Their influence is traceable in the later vindications of bodily union together with the earlier Aristotelian arguments. One instance from Varchi's *Lezioni sopra alcune questioni d'amore* may suffice:

> È impossibile, che nell' amore umano, cio è, quando alcun uomo ama alcuna donna ancora di buono amore, che cotale amore sia perfetto, se non si congiungano ancora i corpi. Perchè tutto il composto, cioè la forma e la materia ed in somma l'anima e'l corpo sono tanti uniti mentre viviamo, che niuna cosa è piu una,

> che essi si siano; onde come il corpo non fa nulla da sè, non essendo il fare della materia, ma della forma, cosi l'anima, se bene è suo proprio il fare come forma, non pero si puo dire, che faccia da sè cosa niuna, ma tutte insieme col corpo per la colleganza che hanno le sentimenta e tutte le potenze dell'anima insieme.[21]

Spenser's frank acceptance of physical love, therefore, was neither new nor surprising. Yet both his approach to the problem and the compromise he evolved were different from the philosophy of the Italian *trattattisti d'amore*. The characteristic of his attitude, indeed, is that there does not seem to be any problem in his eyes. That the consummation of love between man and woman should be a physical as well as a spiritual union is quietly taken for granted and no dialectical justification is offered nor felt to be required. In a way this allows the poetic imagination to move in a more uniformly Platonic *atmosphere* than the thought of Varchi, or Donne in the *Extasie,* since the poet need not introduce Aristotelian considerations on the union of matter and form, or body and soul. On the other hand, the very conception of "l'amore honesto" suffered a sea-change when the "sage and serious Spenser" identified it with wedded love, either openly as in the *Faerie Queene,* or implicitly as in the *Hymnes*.

I have discovered so far no other instance of this identification in the Neoplatonic literature of the Renaissance but for Le Roy's prefaces to his translation of the *Symposium*. And since the French humanist was addressing a newly-married pair, he could be suspected of a complimentary intention. The other Platonists often urged contradictory opinions in regard to sexual love, but they always kept apart the consideration of marriage and the Platonic philosophy of love. That duality is noticeable in Castiglione's *Courtier*. The treatise on the whole has a high ethical standard. The ideal "gentlewoman" fashioned by the Lord Julian will be truly virtuous. In case she "be not married minding to love, I will have her to love one she may marrie." [22] Once married, she would do herself injury in loving any other beside her husband:

> Yet since not loving is not many times in our will, if this mishappe chaunce to the woman of the Pallace, that the hatred of

> her husband or the love of an other bendeth her to love I will have her to graunt her lover nothing els but the minde.[23]

Platonic notions are not introduced into the portrait of the ideal wife, who is only required to have, with regard to her husband and children, "all those partes that belong to a good huswife." [24] And when "love of the minde," Platonic love, is discussed, it turns out to be, like *amour courtois,* an ideal version of adulterous love. Loving platonically, the Courtier "shall doe no wrong to the husband . . . of the woman beloved." [25] For the ethical advice of the Lord Julian, Bembo substitutes the refinements of the Neoplatonic ladder. But the purposes of generation and married love are no longer taken into consideration. In Italian courtly circles and in the language of fashion, married love and Platonic love indeed were usually contrasted. In his *Trattato del matrimonio* dedicated to the courtesan Tullia d'Aragona on her entering into wedlock, Girolamo Muzio, one of her admirers, could at the same time rhapsodize on marriage and press his own suit, assuring her "che il suo amore per lei non era di quelli volgari, che sogliono concludersi col matrimonio, ma era di quelli spirituali, che non si stancano mai di amar e contemplare la bell'anima dell'amata." [26] Needless to say, such Platonism often proved the cloak of gallantry.

The originality of Spenser's philosophy of love lies in the association of Platonic idealism with an acceptance of bodily union limited by ethical standards. The "Englishness" of this attitude is obvious. It rejected the worldly game and mere pretense of courtly Platonism, but it also excluded the higher flights of mysticism. On the one hand, what had become a mere convention at the hands of *trattatisti* and courtiers, became again a living inspiration and a sincere creed—what it had earlier been for Ficino. Spenser's deep instinct for purity ensured sincerity in his profession of scorn for mere sensual love while the un-Platonic features of his philosophy of love, his apology of fruition, in a way infused new blood to the Platonism it modified. He introduced true passion into an aesthetic and intellectual pastime. But, on the other hand, he turned into an essentially human experience what had earlier been a reaching-out towards the divine in Ficino or Benivieni. What had only been a "step" became with him a self-contained, self-complete experience. The "happie port" was reached with the lover's possession of his mistress.[27] Scudamour wins Amoret; Spenser weds Elizabeth Boyle, and the story ends. Romantic love, contrary to Platonic love, does not transcend itself. This does not mean that it bears no relation to a metaphysical scheme. Love is of heavenly nature, but its consummation is earthly. The process of falling in love may receive a metaphysical justification, but its effects are not different from the phenomenon Stendhal later described as crystallization.[28] Such being his conception of love between man and woman, what kind of relation could the poet establish between human love and divine love?

The relation could not be conceived as a progression, for one does not progress from the enjoyment of a bride, or mistress, to the enjoyment of God. The relation could only be one of analogy or contrast, inclusion or exclusion. Spenser's poetry happens to offer both types of relation. The first is best illustrated by the second Easter sonnet in the *Amoretti* (LXVIII):

> Most glorious Lord of Lyfe that on this day,
> Didst make thy triumph over death and sin:
> and having harowd hell didst bring away
> captivity thence captive us to win:
> This joyous day, deare Lord, with joy begin,
> and grant that we for whom thou diddest dye
> being with thy deare blood clene washt from sin,
> may live for ever in felicity.
> And that they love we weighing worthily,
> may likewise love thee for the same againe,
> and for thy sake that all lyke deare didst buy,
> with love may one another entertayne,
> So let us love, deare love, lyke as we ought,
> love is the lesson which the Lord us taught.

Christ's redeeming love has not only justified sinners; it justifies human love. The love of a bridegroom for a bride, as well as love for our brethren. Nothing could be more alien to the spirit of Platonism. For the Platonist always seeks to divest love of all earthliness. But by the mystery of the Incarnation, God has stooped to earth and consecrated earthly love. The entire contrast between the

Platonic and the Christian conception lies in two words: abstraction, consecration.

If we turn now to the hymns of heavenly love and beauty, we are confronted with an uncompromising rejection of human love. The first two hymns which had praised "true" love—possibly married love in the poet's mind—are characterized as "lewd layes" (*H.H.L.* 8).

> And that faire lampe, which useth to enflame
> The hearts of men with selfe consuming fyre,
> Thenceforth seemes fowle, & full of sinfull blame.
> (*H.H.B.* 274–6)

Christ's redeeming love is celebrated as an invitation to love him again, "then next to love our brethren," but the poet carefully abstains from mentioning or suggesting any other love than Christian charity.[29]

How shall we account for such a difference in the poet's outlook on the relation of earthly love to heavenly love? Spenser's profession of ascetic contempt in the last two hymns is naturally suspect of some exaggeration for the sake of dramatic emphasis. He meant to contrast the two pairs of hymns, and just as he emphasized the profanity of the hymns ascribed to "greener times,"[30] he may have overdone his *contemptum mundi* in the religious hymns. Another explanation would be furnished by a change in the poet's mood. But, on the one hand, two or three years at most had elapsed since the composition of the *Amoretti* sonnet, and at the time when he wrote the *Hymnes,* Spenser, so far as we know, had given no sign of abjuring his earlier ideal of human love.[31] On the other hand, the vanity of "ladies love" in comparison to the love of God had been emphasized as early as the first Book of the *Faerie Queene,* when the Red Cross knight asked the Hermit:

> But deeds of armes must I at last be faine,
> And Ladies love to leave so dearely bought?
> What need of armes, where peace doth ay remaine,
> (Said he) and battailes none are to be fought?
> As for loose loves are vaine, and vanish into nought.
> (I. x. 62)

There is no reason to suspect Spenser's sincerity. In both cases he speaks in perfect accordance with the Christian tradition, and if his contrasted utterances disclose a paradox, it is the time-honored Christian paradox. In a way, the poet's attitude is much more consistent, because much more true to the complexity of human nature, than it would have been without that apparent contradiction. God is love, and all pure love proceeds from God and is approved by Him. Even physical love is the result of his injunction "Be fruitful, and multiply," and the will of God is accomplished in the Garden of Adonis as in the House of Holiness.[32] Love, therefore, is to be experienced by the lovers with the full consciousness of fulfilling the designs of the God of Nature and the God of Love. Human love, not to degenerate into brutish love, must never be experienced apart from the love of God. But the Christian love of God, on the contrary, does not admit of any alloy: it must be experienced in its purity. It does not admit either of any intermediary. It is not impious for a lover to tell his bride: "love is the lesson which the Lord us taught." But it were wrong for a Christian to attempt to reach God through the love of woman, even though the woman were early left behind in the progression. Beauty in the woman is divine, and must be so acknowledged.[33] Even love in the lover is divine and should be so experienced.[34] But both the lover and the beloved, being men, are sinful creatures in the eyes of Spenser. Though love is pure, there will be in *their* love some impurity, as in *her* beauty some imperfection. Now, the mind may proceed from a lesser beauty to a higher beauty, but the heart cannot substitute a purer feeling for a less pure: the feeling of adoration may be more or less intense, but it must be pure from the first. God therefore must be adored apart from woman, though the woman is not to be loved apart from God. Human love is included in divine love, so far as it is humanly experienced; but it must be excluded from divine love, divinely experienced. It is not merely a question of being differently sincere at different times: it may be a simultaneous realization of different orders of reality.

Spenser may not have been fully conscious of the distinction I have drawn. But both his own temper and his Christian inheritance would force upon him that twofold attitude. The Platonic mode of ascent from earthly beauty to heavenly beauty through abstraction and intellectualization did not suit the concrete mind of the poet, and it would be open to suspicion for the Christian, owing to the character of Spenser's own sensitiveness to beauty. The Italian Platonists were able, or pretended they were able, to abstract the sexual element from human love as early as the second step. Ficino's own Platonism was convincing because he was mostly concerned with love-friendship between men, which enabled him to effect a fusion of Platonic love with Christian charity.[35] But Spenser mainly conceived of love as a response to the beauty of woman:

> Why doe not then the blossomes of the field,
> Which are arrayd with much more orient hew,
> And to the sense most daintie odour yield,
> Worke like impression in the lookers view?
>
> (*H.B.* 78–81)

The argument is used as a metaphysical proof of the spiritual nature of beauty, but it affords clear psychological evidence that love to Spenser was essentially a sexual emotion. The contemporary of Montaigne and La Boëtie naturally wrote a Legend of Friendship, and gave the "Zeale of friends combyned with vertues meet" preeminence over "raging fire of love to womankind" (*F.Q.* I.ix.1). But it is characteristic of him that he should have failed to invest his pairs of friends with the poetry and glamour he attached to his pairs of lovers. Obviously his feelings, though sincere, are much more sober: though friends are but "another kind of lovers," he insists on "zeal" and "virtue" rather than on love. The conception is more or less Platonized, but the feeling hardly extends beyond the old chivalric sense of the personal loyalty of man to man. Friendship with Spenser is an ethical, not an aesthetic nor an intellectual emotion as with Ficino. And since he did not separate love from sex in human relations, he could idealize human love after the manner of the poets and the Petrarchans. He could declare it heavenly in his profane poetry, but he could not consider it as a step towards heavenly love in his religious poetry. No clear-sighted and healthy-minded man could treat it so.

Now, precedent for the recantation of the last two hymns will be found, not in consistent and orthodox Platonists like Ficino, Pico or even Castiglione, but in authors still influenced by medieval

Christianity like Bembo, and beyond him, Petrarch. For orthodox Platonism does not call for a recantation, but for a process of elimination; it does not require a turning-away but a passing-beyond. The "conversion," if any, occurs from the very start, when love is defined as a desire for beauty, and beauty declared to be incorporeal: [36] henceforth, the progression is lineal.[37] It has been contended that Pico introduces a "conversion" after the third step, when the soul turns in upon itself and finds within itself the source of the beauty formerly beheld in the sensible object.[38] The process may be described as a conversion, no doubt, but a conversion of an intellectual and mystical type, not the simple religious conversion of Spenser in the *Hymnes*.[39] Besides no break is implied here. What the soul considers is not really a different object. It has turned from the effect to the cause, from the light reflected to the fountain of light, but there is no real discontinuity in the progress, for there is no change in the goal. From the first, the soul had traveled in the direction of God. We may picture it to ourselves as a man who, catching a reflection in a mirror, first moves away from the mirror with his eyes still on it and at a certain point, swings round and beholds the object itself. But Spenser in the first two *Hymnes* had not really moved away from the reflection; he had not even fully taken the second step, since the "wished scope" was still the enjoyment of beauty in the body. In the heavenly hymns, he had to make a fresh start from the lowest stair, as Renwick observes.[40] But the start was in a new direction and from another kind of beauty than the beauty of woman. And, again, he found precedent for it in the Renaissance *trattati d'amore*.

Both Bembo and Leone Ebreo had adopted, instead of the Platonic ladder, the Christian and Biblical mode of ascent: the contemplation of God in his handiwork.[41] Castiglione had also used it, but for a different purpose: to prove "that whatsoever is good and profitable, hath also evermore the comeliness of beautie." [42] For the notion of ascent he closely followed the steps of Pico.[43] Spenser's debt to Bembo's *Asolani* has been strangely neglected. It is not a mere question of source-ascription: the interest lies in the identity of spirit and composition. *Gli Asolani* did not reproduce the continuous Platonic ladder. Gismondo was concerned in his speech with the praise of love and, like Spenser, he fused the first and second steps, the beauty of the body and the beauty of the soul.[44] As in Spenser's first hymns, the feeling remained concrete and personal, not extended to a universal concept of beauty. Besides, as in the last hymns, the speech of the Hermit to Lavinello did not invite the lover merely to take a new step beyond earthly love and earthly beauty, but first to abjure them, and entertain an entirely different love by contemplating not the beauty of woman, which awakes desire, but the beauty of the creation, which awakes love for the Creator.

This meant a clean break with both Perotino's and Gismondo's conceptions of love. The attribution of the speech to a hermit made the contrast the more emphatic. Like Spenser within the diptych of the *Fowre Hymnes,* Bembo within the triptych of *Gli Asolani* worked by opposition, not by continuous progression as Ficino, Pico, Benivieni, and Castiglione had done in their consistent expositions of the Platonic *scala.* Each speech was self-ended, and each made a fresh start in the contrary direction to the preceding.[45] With a writer like Bembo, more concerned with art than philosophy, it is not easy to say whether the composition commanded the thought, or the thought governed the composition. Spenser, too, was a poet first. Had he hesitated between Platonic continuity and Christian duality, artistic reasons would have swayed his mind and determined his choice.[46] But was any choice offered to his mind? By temper and tradition he was bound to reject or modify the Neoplatonic ladder. He had petrarchized Platonism in the first hymns. The turning away from earthly to heavenly love was not to be described as the turning inward of the soul and the discovery of intellectual beauty. It was to be the common Petrarchan recantation of loose loves and lewd rhymes (*H.H.L.* 8–21). Not that the love earlier praised had been loose, nor the rhymes lewd.[47] The poet, like Petrarch, might even have pleaded with himself that his earthly love had truly inspired him with the love of virtue and the love of God. If he did, he probably gave himself the answer which Petrarch had received from Augustine in the *Secretum:*

> Thou hast perverted the order, for, whereas thou oughtest to have loved the creature for the sake of the Creator, captured by the charms of the creature, thou hast loved the Creator, but not in the way thou shouldst have loved him.[48]

Notes

1. E.g., Lorenzo in the *Selve d'Amore,* Pt. I, stanzas 27–28, quoted by Robb, *Neoplatonism of the Italian Renaissance* (London, 1935), pp. 105–106, or Sidney in *Astrophel and Stella,* Sonnet XXV.

2. *F.Q.* III.vi.29. See also the paradise of lovers in the Temple of Venus, *F. Q.* IV. x. 23 ff.

3. In *Colin Clout* (l. 804), he reminded the reader of his own "gardens of Adonis."

4. J. W. Bennett, "Spenser's *Fowre Hymnes:* Addenda," *SP,* XXXII (1935), 138–57.

5. *Variorum F.Q.,* III, pp. 181–82.

6. *H.L.* 302. "Do the angels sing the praises of sensual or beastly love?" (Bennett). Obviously not, but (1) Spenser means that he would praise Love ("my God") as the Angels praise God, a commonplace of profane love-poetry, medieval or Renaissance; (2) he has in mind not "beastly love," but a love "bred in spotlesse brest" (*Amoretti,* LXXXIIII).

7. *Epithalamion,* l. 240. Hebe is present both in *H.L.* 284 and *Epith.* l. 405.

8. *H.B.* 232 ff; Pietro Bembo, *Gli Asolani* (Vinegia, 1558), p. 135: "Nor is the sight of lovers like that of the other men. . . ." See also the description of "amourous eye-glaunces": "O mirabile forza degli amorosi risguardamenti . . . dolcezze, che al core li passano per le luci" (p. 139) and compare *H.B.* 235 ff.

9. *Asolani,* p. 138.

10. *Asolani,* pp. 158–59. "Quantunque io per me non mi seppi far mai cosi savio; che io a quella guisa ne conviti d'Amore mi sia saputo rattemperare."

11. *Asolani,* p. 159: "Nor would I counsel our inexperienced bridegroom that when love puts upon the board that final course which he has not tasted yet, he like one contented with his previous fare, should merely sample this before he let it be removed: he might repent his moderation afterwards," tr. Rudolf B. Gottfried (Bloomington, 1954), p. 134.

12. Baldassaro Castiglione, *The Book of the Courtier,* tr. Sir Thomas Hoby (London, 1928), p. 303.

13. *Ibid.,* pp. 306–307. Cf. p. 312: "I say therefore, that since the nature of man in youthful age is so much enclined to sense, it may be granted the Courtier while he is young to love sensually. . . . Such love in young men deserveth more to be pitied than blamed."

14. *Ibid.,* p. 306.

15. *Ibid.,* p. 315.

16. *Ibid.,* pp. 317–18.

17. Donne's words in "Death's Duell," *Complete Poetry and Selected Prose,* ed. John Hayward (London, 1929), p. 746.

18. Mario Equicola, *Di Natura d'Amore* (Venice, 1563), p. 381. "Concludiamo qualunche si sia, che permanente ama, amar l'animo e'l corpo insieme, dico amar necessariamente & per vigor naturale l'uno & l'altro, & afferma che l'uno dall'altro in tal amore non patisce separatione: i sensi dell'amante dall'amato corpo ricercan volutta sensuale come suo fine: l'animo di vero amante dell'amato animo amor richiede, & esser riamato."

19. *Dialoghi,* ed. S. Caramella (Bari, 1921), p. 50.

20. "FI. Di questa sorte di dilettationi non ho detto mai che fussero cattive, & solamente buone in apparentia, anzi t'affermo che sono veramente buone. SO. Sono pur dilettationi carnali, & l'amor loro e dalla parte del dilettabile. FI. Sono ben carnali dilettationi, ma non sono puramente della specie del dilettabile, anzi sono veramente di quella dell' honesto, quando, comme dissi, sono temperate quanto si richiede al bisogno della sostentatione dell' individuo, & conservatione della specie." *Dialoghi* (Venice, 1558), fol. 229v.

21. "Lezione Seconda, Quistione Quinta": "It is impossible in human love, that is, when a man loves a woman even though with the right love [spiritual love], that such a love should be perfect if the bodies too be not joined. For the whole compound, that is form and matter, which are the soul and body, is of such unity as long as we live that nothing could be more one than these are together. Hence, as the body does nothing by itself since action is no attribute of matter but of form, so the soul, although her property as form is to act, nevertheless cannot be said to do anything by herself, but does everything together with the body on account of the interconnection of the sense impressions and of all the faculties of the soul." Benedetto Varchi, *L'Ercolano e Lezioni Quattro sopra Alcune Quistioni d'Amore* (Milan, 1880), p. 310.

22. *Courtier,* p. 240.

23. *Courtier,* p. 239.

24. *Courtier,* p. 190.

25. *Courtier,* p. 317.

26. [". . . that his love for her was not of that common sort that usually ends in marriage, but of the spiritual kind that never tires of loving and contemplating the beautiful soul of the beloved"—ed.] L. Savino, *Studi di letteratura italiana* (Napoli, 1909–1914), X, 306.

27. *H.L.* 298.

28. *H.B.* 218–31. I have shown that the "fancy" is mainly involved in the process, the stage of pure concept not being reached.

29. *H.H.L.* 190–217. Cf. *Amoretti,* LXXII, 9–14, quoted above.

30. In *H.H.L.* 8–21 and in the Dedication. The hymns themselves are not more profane than Colin's praise of love and other poems.

31. The sixth book of the *Faerie Queene,* probably completed in 1594, has delightful idylls. Part of Colin's praise of love seems to have been inserted before publication in 1595, and the proem to Book IV of the *Faerie Queene,* probably written before publication in 1596, is a vigorous defence of love. *The Prothalamion* composed in November, 1596, though an occasional piece, affords

further evidence that no marked change had come over the poet's mind since the day when he wrote his own *Epithalamion.*

32. *F.Q.* III. vi. 34 and I. x.

33. "T'adore thing so divine as beauty were but right" (*F.Q.,* III. vii. 11).

34. Cf. *F.Q.* III. iii. 1 and *T.M.* 387–90.

35. See P. O. Kristeller, *The Philosophy of Marsilio Ficino,* tr. Virginia Conant (New York, 1943), pp. 277–85.

36. Ficino, *Discours de l'honneste amour sur le Banquet de Platon,* tr. Guy Le Fèvre de la Boderie (Paris, 1588), I. iv. fol. 11 r°; IV. iii. fol. 66v°.

37. See the paraphrase of Diotima's speech in Ficino, *Discours,* VI. xviii, fol. 141 v°.

38. J. W. Bennett, "The Theme of Spenser's *Fowre Hymnes, SP,* XXVIII (1931), 18–57.

39. For the enlightenment of the reader, I reproduce Pico's words: "El quarto grado è che lalma considerando la operatione sua, vede se conoscere la natura della bellezza universalmente, & non ristretta ad alcuna particolare, & conosce che ogni cosa che è nella materia fondata è particolare, di che conclude questa tale universita non dallo objetto esteriore sensibile, ma dallo intrinseco suo lume, & dalla sua virtù procedere, & infra se stessa dice, se nelli adombrati specchi de phantasmati materiali per vigore della mia luce mi si representa questa bellezza, certo è ragionevol cosa che nello specchio della mia sostantia dogni nube materiale spogliata riguardando, debba ogni simil cosa assai piu chiaramente vedere & cosi in se conversa vede la imagine della beltà ideale à lei dalla intelleto participata." (Pico della Mirandola, *Commento* on Benivieni, in Benivieni, *Opere* (Venice, 1524), fols. 64v–65.)
The *Hymne of Heavenly Love* is devoted not to the turning inward of the soul, purged of all sensible representations, but to the coming down of Christ on earth to take a body. One can hardly imagine a sharper contrast.

40. W. L. Renwick, ed., *Daphnaida, and Other Poems* (London, 1929), p. 212. See also F. M. Padelford, "Spenser's *Fowre Hymnes,*" *JEGP,* XIII (1914), 418–33.

41. *Gli Asolani,* pp. 211 ff.; *Dialoghi di Amore* (Venetia, 1558), fol. 166v.

42. *Courtier,* p. 309.

43. *Courtier,* pp. 317–19.

44. *Asolani,* p. 186: "For as that body whose members are proportionate is beautiful, so is that mind whose virtues meet in harmony. . . . So virtuous love is a desire for beauty of mind no less than body; and in order to reach that end and object of its longing, love spreads and beats its wings" (tr. Gottfried, p. 157).

45. Perotino had discoursed on the bitterness of (vulgar) love. Gismondo extols the pleasures of love (Petrarchan, with Platonic overtones). Lavinello and the Hermit repudiate human love to praise divine love, both Christian and Platonic.

46. Spenser was partial to symmetrical arrangements, and symmetry invites contrast or identity rather than development.

47. Padelford has observed that Spenser in the *Dedication* styled the two sisters, his patrons, "the most excellent and rare ornaments of *all* true love and beautie, *both in the one and the other kinde,*" that is, both of earthly and heavenly love and beauty. This had been a strange compliment, had the first hymns been seriously considered "lewd." (F. M. Padelford, "Spenser's *Fowre Hymnes:* A Resurvey," *SP,* XXIX (1932), 207–32.

48. "De Contemptu Mundi," *Opera* (Basel, n.d.), I, 355–56.

V. *The Faerie Queene*

Richard Hurd

"Gothic Unity in *The Faerie Queene*"

SPENSER, tho' he had been long nourished with the spirit and substance of Homer and Vergil, chose the times of chivalry for his theme, and Fairy Land for the scene of his fictions. He could have planned, no doubt, an heroic design on the exact classic model: Or, he might have trimmed between the Gothic and Classic, as his contemporary Tasso did. But the charms of *fairy* prevailed. And if any think, he was seduced by Ariosto into this choice, they should consider that it could be only for the sake of his subject; for the genius and character of these poets was widely different.

Under this idea then of a Gothic, not classical poem, the *Faerie Queene* is to be read and criticized. And on these principles, it would not be difficult to unfold it's merit in another way than has been hitherto attempted. . . .

It is certain much light might be thrown on that singular work, were an able critic to consider it in this view. For instance, he might go some way towards explaining, perhaps justifying, the general plan and *conduct* of the *Faerie Queene,* which, to classical readers has appeared indefensible.

I have taken the fancy, with your leave, to try my hand on this curious subject.

When an architect examines a Gothic structure by Grecian rules, he finds nothing but deformity. But the Gothic architecture has it's own rules, by which when it comes to be examined, it is seen to have it's merit, as well as the Grecian. The question is not, which of the two is conducted in the simplest or truest taste: but, whether there be not sense and design in both, when scrutinized by the laws on which each is projected.

The same observation holds of the two sorts of poetry. Judge of the *Faerie Queene* by the classic models, and you are shocked with it's disorder: consider it with an eye to it's Gothic original, and you find it regular. The unity and simplicity of the former are more complete: but the latter has that sort of unity and simplicity, which results from it's nature.

The *Faerie Queene* then, as a Gothic poem, derives it's METHOD, as well as the other characters of it's composition, from the established modes and ideas of chivalry.

It was usual, in the days of knight-errantry, at the holding of any great feast, for Knights to appear before the Prince, who presided at it, and claim the privilege of being sent on any adventure, to which the solemnity might give occasion. For it was supposed that, when such a *throng of knights and barons bold,* as Milton speaks of, were got together, the distressed would flock in from all quarters, as to a place where they knew they might find and claim redress for all their grievances.

This was the real practice, in the days of pure and antient chivalry. And an image of this practice was afterwards kept up in the castles of the great, on any extraordinary festival or solemnity: of which, if you want an instance, I refer you to the description of a feast made at Lisle in 1453, in the court of Philip the Good, Duke of Burgundy, for a crusade against the Turks: As you may find it given at large in the memoirs of *Matthieu de Conci, Olivier de la Marche,* and *Monstrelet.*

That feast was held for twelve days: and each day was distinguished by the claim and allowance of some adventure.

Now laying down this practice, as a foundation for the poet's design, you will see how properly the *Faerie Queene* is conducted.

—"I devise," says the poet himself in his Letter to Sir W. Ralegh, "that the Faerie Queene kept her annual feaste xii days: upon which xii several days, the occasions of the xii several adventures hapened; which being undertaken by xii several knights, are in these xii books severally handled."

Here you have the poet delivering his own method, and the

reason of it. It arose out of the order of his subject. And would you desire a better reason for his choice?

Yes; you will say, a poet's method is not that of his subject. I grant you, as to the order of *time,* in which the recital is made; for here, as Spenser observes (and his own practice agrees to the Rule) lies the main difference between *the poet historical, and the historiographer:* The reason of which is drawn from the nature of Epic composition itself, and holds equally, let the subject be what it will, and whatever the system of manners be, on which it is conducted. Gothic or Classic makes no difference in this respect.

But the case is not the same with regard to the general plan of a work, or what may be called the order of *distribution,* which is and must be governed by the subject-matter itself. It was as requisite for the *Faerie Queene* to consist of the adventures of twelve knights, as for the *Odyssey* to be confined to the adventures of one Hero: Justice had otherwise not been done to his subject.

So that if you will say anything against the poet's method, you must say that he should not have chosen this subject. But this objection arises from your classic ideas of Unity, which have no place here; and are in every view foreign to the purpose, if the poet has found means to give his work, tho' consisting of many parts, the advantage of Unity. For in some reasonable sense or other, it is agreed, every work of art must be one, the very idea of a work requiring it.

If you ask then, what is this *Unity* of Spenser's Poem? I say, It consists in the relation of it's several adventures to one common *original,* the appointment of the Faerie Queene; and to one common *end,* the completion of the Faerie Queene's injunctions. The knights issued forth on their adventures on the breaking up of this annual feast; and the next annual feast, we are to suppose, is to bring them together again from the atchievement of their several charges.

This, it is true, is not the classic Unity, which consists in the representation of one entire action: but it is an Unity of another sort, an unity resulting from the respect which a number of related actions have to one common purpose. In other words, It is an unity of *design,* and not of action.

This Gothic method of design in poetry may be, in some sort, illustrated by what is called the Gothic method of design in Gardening. A wood or grove cut out into many separate avenues or glades was amongst the most favourite of the works of art, which our fathers attempted in this species of cultivation. These walks were distinct from each other, had, each, their several destination, and terminated on their own proper objects. Yet the whole was brought together and considered under one view by the relation which these various openings had, not to each other, but to their common and concurrent center. You and I are, perhaps, agreed that this sort of gardening is not of so true a taste as that which *Kent and Nature* have brought us acquainted with; where the supreme art of the Designer consists in disposing his ground and objects into an *entire landskip;* and grouping them, if I may use the term, in so easy a manner, that the careless observer, tho' he be taken with the symmetry of the whole, discovers no art in the combination:

> In lieto aspetto il bel giardin s'aperse,
> Acque stagnanti, mobili cristalli,
> Fior vari, e varie piante, herbe diverse,
> Apriche Collinette, ombrose valli,
> Selve, e spelunche in UNA VISTA offerse:
> E quel, che'l bello, e'l caro accresce à l'opre,
> L'Arte, che tutto fà, nulla si scopre.[1]
>
> Tasso. C.xvi. S. ix.

This, I say, may be the truest taste in gardening, because the simplest: Yet there is a manifest regard to unity in the other method; which has had it's admirers, as it may have again, and is certainly not without it's *design* and beauty.

But to return to our poet. Thus far he drew from Gothic ideas, and these ideas, I think, would lead him no farther. But, as Spenser knew what belonged to classic composition, he was tempted to tie his subject still closer together by *one* expedient of his own, and by *another* taken from his classic models.

His *own* was to interrupt the proper story of each book, by dispersing it into several; involving by this means, and as it were intertwisting the several actions together, in order to give something like the appearance of one action to his twelve adventures. And for this conduct, as absurd as it seems, he had some great examples in the Italian poets, tho' I believe, they were led into it by different motives.

The *other* expedient which he borrowed from the classics, was by adopting one superior character, which should be seen throughout. Prince Arthur, who had a separate adventure of his own, was to have his part in each of the other; and thus several actions were to be embodied by the interest which one principal Hero had in them all. It is even observable, that Spenser gives this adventure of Prince Arthur, in quest of Gloriana, as the proper subject of his poem. And upon this idea the late learned editor of the *Faerie Queene*[2] has attempted, but I think without success, to defend the Unity and simplicity of it's fable. The truth was, the violence of classic prejudices forced the poet to affect this appearance of unity, tho' in contradiction to his Gothic system. And, as far as we can judge of the tenour of the whole work from the finished half of it, the adventure of Prince Arthur, whatever the author pretended, and his critic too easily believed, was but an after thought; and at least with regard to the *historical fable,* which we are now considering, was only one of the expedients by which he would conceal the disorder of his Gothic plan.

And if this was his design, I will venture to say that both his expedients were injudicious. Their purpose was to ally two things, in nature incompatible, the Gothic, and the classic unity; the effect of which misalliance was to discover and expose the nakedness of the Gothic.

I am of opinion then, considering the *Faerie Queene* as an epic or *narrative* poem constructed on Gothic ideas, that the Poet had done well to affect no other unity than that of *design,* by which his subject was connected. But his poem is not simply narrative; it is throughout *Allegorical:* he calls it *a perpetual allegory or dark conceit:* and this character, for reasons I may have occasion to observe hereafter, was even predominant in the *Faerie Queene.* His narration is subservient to his moral, and but serves to colour it. This he tells us himself at setting out. "Fierce wars and faithful loves shall *moralize* my song," that is, shall serve for a vehicle, or instrument to convey the moral.

Now under this idea, the *Unity* of the *Faerie Queene* is more apparent. His twelve knights are to exemplify as many virtues, out of which one illustrious character is to be composed. And in this view the part of Prince Arthur in each book becomes *essential,* and yet not *principal;* exactly, as the poet has contrived it. They who rest in the literal story, that is, who criticize it on the footing of a narrative poem, have constantly objected to this management. They say, it necessarily breaks the unity of design. Prince Arthur, they affirm, should either have had no part in the other adventures, or he should have had the chief part. He should either have done nothing, or more. And the objection is unanswerable; at least I know of nothing that can be said to remove it but what I have supposed above might be the purpose of the poet, and which I myself have rejected as insufficient.

But how faulty soever this conduct be in the literal story, it is perfectly right in the *moral:* and that for an obvious reason, tho' his critics seem not to have been aware of it. His chief hero was not to have the twelve virtues in the *degree* in which the knights had, each of them, their own; (such a character would be a monster) but he was to have so much of each as was requisite to form his superior character. Each virtue, in it's perfection, is exemplified in it's own knight: they are all, in a due degree, concenter'd in Prince Arthur.

This was the poet's *moral:* And what way of expressing this moral in the *history,* but by making Prince Arthur appear in each adventure, and in a manner subordinate to it's proper hero? Thus, tho' inferior to each in his own specific virtue, he is superior to all by uniting the whole circle of their virtues in himself: And thus he arrives, at length, at the possession of that bright form of *Glory,* whose ravishing beauty, as seen in a dream or vision, had led him out into these miraculous adventures in the land of Faery.

The conclusion is, that, as an *allegorical* poem, the method of the *Faerie Queene* is governed by the justness of the *moral:* As a *narrative* poem, it is conducted on the ideas and usages of *chivalry.* In either view, if taken by itself, the plan is defensible. But from the union of the two designs there arises a perplexity and confusion, which is the proper, and only considerable, defect of this extraordinary poem.

Notes

[1] [When they had passed all those troubled ways,
  The garden sweet spread forth her green to show,
The moving crystal from the fountains plays,
  Fair trees, high plants, strange herbs, and flow'rets new,
Sun-shiny hills, dales hid from Phoebus' rays,
  Groves, arbors, mossy caves, at once they view;
And that which beauty most, most wonder brought,
Nowhere appear'd the art which all this wrought.
(Fairfax translation)—ed.]

[2] [John Upton—ed.]

John Upton
Preface to The Faerie Queene

'TIS NOT MY INTENTION in this place to enter into a particular criticism of any of our poet's writings, excepting the *Faerie Queene;* which poem seems to have been hitherto very little understood; notwithstanding he has opened, in a great measure, his design and plan in a letter to his honored friend Sir W. R. How readily has every one acquiesced in Dryden's opinion? "That the action of this poem is not one [1]—that there is no uniformity of design; and that he aims at the accomplishment of no action." [2] It might have been expected that Hughes, who printed Spenser's works, should not have joined so freely in the same censure: and yet he tells us "that the several books appear rather like so many several poems, than one entire fable: each of them having its peculiar knight, and being independent of the rest." [3]

Just in the same manner did the critics and commentators formerly abuse old Homer; his *Iliad,* they said, was nothing else, but a parcel of loose songs and rhapsodies concerning the Trojan war, which he sung at festivals; and these loose ballads were first collected, and stitched,[4] as it were, together by Pisistratus; being parts without any coherence, or relation to a whole, and unity of design.

As this subject requires a particular consideration; I desire the reader will attend to the following vindication of Homer and Spenser, as they have both fallen under one common censure.

In every poem there ought to be simplicity and unity; and in the epic poem the unity of the action should never be violated by introducing any ill-joined or heterogeneous parts. This essential rule Spenser seems to me strictly to have followed: for what story can well be shorter, or more simple, than the subject of his poem?—A British Prince sees in a vision the Fairy Queen; he falls in love, and goes in search after this unknown fair; and at length finds her.—This fable has a beginning, a middle, and an end. The beginning is, the British Prince saw in a vision the Fairy Queen, and fell in love with her: the middle, his search after her, with the adventures that he underwent: the end, his finding whom he sought.

But here our curiosity is raised, and we want a more circumstantial information of many things.—Who is this British Prince? what adventures did he undergo? who was the Fairy Queen? where, when, and how did he find her? Thus many questions arise, that require many solutions.

The action of this poem has not only simplicity and unity, but it is great and important. The hero is no less than the British Prince, Prince Arthur: (who knows not Prince Arthur?) The time when this hero commenced his adventures is marked very exactly. In the reign of Uther Pendragon, father of Prince Arthur, Octa the son of Hengist, and his kinsman Eosa, thinking themselves not bound by the treaties which they had made with Aurelius Ambrosius, began to raise disturbances, and infest his dominions. This is the historical period of time, which Spenser has chosen.

> Ye see that good King Uther now doth make
> Strong warre upon the paynim brethren, hight
> Octa and Oza, whom hee lately brake
> Beside Cayr Verolame . . . (B. iii. C. 3. St. 52.)

Could any epic poet desire a better historical foundation to build his poem on? Hear likewise what he himself says on this subject, "I chose the history of K. Arthur, as most fit for the excellency of his person, being made famous by many mens former works, and also furthest from the danger of envy and suspicion of present time." I much question if Virgil's *Aeneid* is grounded on facts so well supported. Beside a poet is a *Maker;* nor does he compose a poem for the sake of any one hero, but rather he makes a hero for the sake of his poem: and if he follows fame, whether from the more authentic relation of old chronicles,[5] or from the legendary tales of old romances, yet still he is at liberty to add, or to diminish: in short, to speak out, he is at liberty to *lie,* as much as he pleases, provided his lies are consistent, and he makes his tale hang well together.

Prince Arthur saw in a vision, and seeing fell in love with the Fairy Queen, just about the time that she held her annual festival, when her knights had their various adventures assigned them. From either of these periods an historian might begin his narration; but a poet must begin from neither: because 'tis his province to carry you at once into the scene of action; and to complicate and perplex his story, in order to shew his art in unraveling it. The poet therefore might have opened his poem either with Prince Arthur, now actually set out on his quest, or with one of the knights sent from the Court of the Fairy Queen: by which means the reader is introduced into the midst of things; taking it for granted, that he either knows, or some way or other will know, all that preceded. 'Tis from the latter of these periods, namely from one of the Fairy Knights, who is already rode forth on his adventure, that Spenser opens his poem; and he keeps you in suspense concerning his chief hero, Prince Arthur; 'till 'tis proper to introduce him with suitable pomp and magnificence.

Homer sings the anger of Achilles and its fatal consequences to the Grecians: nor can it be fairly objected to the unity of the *Iliad,* that when Achilles is removed from the scene of action, you scarcely hear him mentioned in several books: one being taken up with the exploits of Agamemnon, another with Diomed, another again with the successes of Hector. For his extensive plan required his different heroes to be shown in their different characters and attitudes. What therefore you allow to the old Grecian, be not so ungracious as to deny to your own countryman.

Again, 'tis observable that Homer's poem, though he sings the anger of Achilles, is not called the Achilleid, but the *Iliad;* because the action was at Troy. So Spenser does not call his poem by the name of his chief hero; but because his chief hero sought for the Fairy Queen in Fairy Land, and therein performed his various adventures, therefore he intitles his poem *The Faerie Queene.* Hence it appears that the adventures of Prince Arthur are necessarily connected with the adventures of the knights of Fairy Land. This young Prince has been kept hitherto in designed ignorance of what relates to his family and real dignity: his education, under old Timon and the magician Merlin, was to prepare him for future glory; but as yet his virtues have not been called forth into action. The poet therefore by bringing you acquainted with some of the heroes of Fairy Land, at the same time that he is bringing you acquainted with his chief hero, acts agreeably to his extensive plan, without destroying the unity of the action. The only fear is, lest the underplots, and the seemingly adscititious members, should grow too large for the body of the entire action: 'tis requisite therefore that the several incidental intrigues should be unraveled, as we proceed in getting nearer and nearer to the main plot; and that we at length gain an uninterrupted view at once of the whole. And herein I cannot help admiring the resemblance between the ancient father of poets, and Spenser; who clearing the way by the solution of intermediate plots and incidents, brings you nearer to his capital piece; and then shows his hero at large: and when Achilles once enters the field, the other Greeks are lost in his splendor, as the stars at the rising of the sun. So when Prince Arthur had been perfected in heroic and moral virtues, and his fame thoroughly known and recognized in Fairy Land; Him we should have seen not only dissolving the inchantment of the witch Duessa (an adventure too hard for the single prowess of St. George) but likewise binding in adamantine chains, or delivering over to utter perdition that old wizard Archimago, the common enemy of Fairy Knights, whom no chains as yet could hold: in short, him should we have seen eclipsing all the other heroes, and in the end accompanied with the Fairy Knights making his solemn entry into the presence of Gloriana, the Fairy Queen: and thus his merits would have intitled him to that Glory, which by Magnificence, or Magnanimity, the perfection of all the rest of the virtues, he justly had acquired.

It seems, by some hints given us by the poet, that he intended likewise an Heroic Poem, whose title was to be *King Arthur;* and the chief subject of the poem, the wars of the King and Queen of Fairy Land (now governed by Arthur and Gloriana) against the Paynim King: the chief Captains employed were to be those Fairy Knights, whom already he had brought us acquainted with: and the historical allusions undoubtedly would point, in the allegorical view, at the wars that Q. Elizabeth waged with the K. of Spain; as the Fairy Knights would typically represent her warlike Courtiers. This seems plain from what St. George says to Una's parents, in B. i. C. 12. St. 18.

> I bownden am streight after this emprize . . .
> Backe to retourne to that great Faery Queene,
> And her to serve sixe yeares in warlike wize
> Gainst that proud Paynim King that works her teene.

And plainer still from what the poet says in his own person, in B. i. C. 11. St. 7.

> Fayre goddesse, lay that furious fitt asyde,
> Till I of warres and bloody Mars doe sing;
> And Bryton fieldes with Sarazin blood bedyde,
> Twixt that great Faery Queen and Paynim King.

Dryden tells us in his preface to the translation of Juvenal, that he had some thoughts of making choice for the subject of an heroic poem, King Arthur's conquests over the Saxons: And hinting at the same design in the preface to his Fables says, "That it was not for this noble knight (meaning Sir R. Blackmore) that he drew the plan of an epic poem on King Arthur." Milton likewise had the same intention, as he intimates in a Latin poem to Mansus.

> Si quando indigenas revocabo in carmina reges,
> Arturumque etiam sub terris bella moventem;
> Aut dicam invictae sociali foedere mensae
> Magnanimos heroas; et, O modo spiritus adsit,
> Frangam Saxonicas Britonum sub Marte phalanges.[6]

We have shown that the action of the *Faerie Queene* is uniform, great and important; but 'tis required that the fable should be probable. A story will have probability, if it hangs well together, and is consistent: And provided the tales are speciously told, the probability of them will not be destroyed, though they are tales of wizards or witches, monstrous men and monstrous women; for who, but downright miscreants, question wonderful tales? and do you imagine that Homer, Virgil, Spenser, and Milton, ever thought of writing an epic poem for unbelievers and infidels? But if after all the reader cannot with unsuspecting credulity swallow all these marvelous tales; what should hinder the poet, but want of art, from so contriving his fable, that more might be meant, than meets the eye or ear? cannot he say one thing in proper numbers and harmony, and yet secretly intend something else, or (to use a Greek expression) cannot he make the fable allegorical? Thus Forms and Persons might be introduced, shadowing forth, and emblematically representing the mysteries of physical and moral sciences: Virtue and Truth may appear in their original ideas and lovely forms; and even Vice might be decked out in some kind of dress, resembling beauty and truth; lest if seen without any disguise, she appear too loathsom for mortal eyes to behold her.

It must be confessed that the religion of Greece and Rome was particularly adapted to whatever figurative turn the poet intended to give it; and even philosophers mixed mythology with the gravest subjects of theology. Hesiod's *Generation of the Gods,* is properly the generation of the world, and a history of natural philosophy: he gives life, energy, and form to all the visible and invisible parts of the universe, and almost to all the powers and faculties of the imagination; in a word his poem is "a continued allegory." When every part therefore of the universe was thought to be under the particular care of a tutelar deity; when not only the sun, moon, and planets, but mountains, rivers, and groves; nay even virtues, vices, accidents, qualities, etc. were the objects of veneration and of religious dread; there was no violation given to public belief, if the poet changed his metaphor, or rather continued it, in an allegory. Hence Homer, instead of saying that Achilles, had not wisdom checked him, would have slain Agamemnon, continues the metaphor; and consistent with his religion, brings Minerva, the goddess of wisdom, down from heaven, on purpose to check the rage of the angry hero. On the same system is founded the well-known fable of Prodicus: and the picture of Cebes is a continued allegory, containing the most interesting truths relating to human life.

Notes

1. Dryden's dedication of the translation of Virgil's *Aeneid.*

2. See his dedication of the translation of Juvenal.

3. In the preface to his edition.

4. Hence called rhapsodies.

5. Our poet follows Jeffry of Monmouth, the British historian; and the old Romance intitled, *The History of Prince Arthur and his Knights of the Round Table:* or *La Mort d'Arthure,* as intitled at the end, and so cited by Ascham in his *School-Master*, p. 87, who mentions it as a favorite author in his time.

6. ["If ever I shall summon back our native kings into our songs, and Arthur, waging his wars beneath the earth, or if ever I shall proclaim the magnanimous heroes of the table which their mutual fidelity made invincible, and (if only the spirit be with me) shall shatter the Saxon phalanxes under the British Mars!"—ed.]

Graham Hough

Allegory in *The Faerie Queene*

I

> The Last Judgement is not Fable or Allegory, but Vision. Fable or Allegory are a totally distinct and inferior kind of Poetry. Vision or Imagination is a Representation of what Eternally Exists, Really and Unchangeably. Fable or Allegory is formed by the Daughters of Memory . . . Note here that Fable is seldom without some Vision. Pilgrim's Progress is full of it, the Greek poets the same; but Allegory and Vision ought to be known as two distinct things, and so called for the Sake of Eternal Life.[1]

So Blake wrote in reference to one of his own paintings. And what Blake wished to distinguish for the sake of eternal life has since been distinguished in the name of literary criticism. The distinction between allegory and some other mode, usually seen as more authentic and more reputable, has attained the status of a dogma from the Romantic age on. The term opposed to allegory is not always Blake's "vision"; symbol or symbolism is the opposite most employed by later criticism. Coleridge in *The Statesman's Manual* draws the contrast in this way:

> Now an allegory is but a translation of abstract notions into a picture-language which is in itself nothing but an abstraction from objects of the senses; the principal being even more worthless than its phantom proxy. . . . On the other hand a symbol . . . is characterized by a translucence of the special in the indi-

> vidual, or of the general in the special, or of the universal in the general, above all, by the translucence of the eternal through and in the temporal. It always partakes of the reality which it renders intelligible; and while it enunciates the whole, abides itself as a living part in that unity of which it is the representative.[2]

Yeats quotes the Blake passage, and then identifies Blake's vision with the symbolic imagination; and uses symbol as his opposite to allegory thereafter:

> A symbol is indeed the only possible expression of some invisible essence, a transparent lamp without a spiritual flame; while allegory is one of many possible representations of an embodied thing, or familiar principle, and belongs to fancy and not to imagination: the one is a revelation, the other an amusement.[3]

And C. S. Lewis in *The Allegory of Love* draws a similar contrast between allegory on the one hand, and symbolism or sacramentalism on the other:

> On the one hand you can start with an immaterial fact, such as the passions you actually experience, and can then invent *visibilia* to express them . . . this is allegory. . . . But there is another way of using the equivalence, which is almost the opposite of allegory, and which I would call symbolism or sacramentalism. If our passions, being immaterial, can be copied by material inventions, then it is possible that our material world in its turn is the copy of an invisible world. . . . The attempt to read that something else through its sensible imitations, to see the archetype in the copy, is what I mean by symbolism or sacramentalism.[4]

Blake's "vision" is not quite the same thing as the "symbol" of Coleridge, and Professor Lewis's "symbolism" is slightly different again: vision for Blake is an intuitive and immediate view of super-sensible reality, symbolism for Professor Lewis is an attempt at spelling this out; and Coleridge's symbol seems to embrace Professor Lewis's, with a number of more commonplace operations as well, including even synecdoche—"the translucence of the general in the special." But in all cases the root of the antithesis is the same—it is the contrast between allegory as a kind of picture-writing, a translation into visible form of concepts that were formulated in advance, and some other process in which an object perceived is taken as a revelation of some super-sensible reality not previously apprehended. Yet different as they appear to be in value and direction, Blake says that there is seldom allegory without some vision, and Professor Lewis adds that symbolism and allegory are closely entwined.

Setting aside the depreciation of allegory in Blake, Coleridge and Yeats (to depreciate allegory is not Professor Lewis's business) the distinction seems to be mainly one of priority and direction. If the concept comes first and is then translated into a visible equivalent, this is allegory. If the visible object comes first and an immaterial reality is seen behind it or through it, this is symbolism. Clear enough; but it hardly seems weighty enough to account for the strong emotional coloring of the language in which the distinction is generally made. Literary distinctions do not commonly arouse much passion unless there is some other factor at work. Perhaps there is one here. It is plain, I think, that allegory, on our present definitions, does not require any particular view of the world; it is a rhetorical device, quite compatible with the blankest positivism. One could write an allegory of Dialectical Materialism (probably somebody has), or the Business Cycle. But with symbolism the case is different. If we start with the material world and see in it "the copy of an invisible world" (Lewis), if what we perceive in symbol is "the translucence of the eternal through and in the temporal" (Coleridge) it is implied that the invisible and the eternal really exist. We are not adopting a manner of speech, we are seeing something that we believe to be really there. For the Jewish people and for the Christian Middle Ages history was the sensible embodiment of the actual intentions of God. For Baudelaire nature is the partial evidence of a mysterious system of correspondences that actually pervades the universe. Ultimately, symbolism as generally described is compatible only with some kind of belief in the supernatural, or at least some kind of idealism. For the materialist there is no invisible or eternal world that the object could be a symbol of.

In fact a metaphysical spectre has been lurking behind the allegory-symbolism distinction. Allegory is an inferior mode because it is a pragmatic device, compatible with a purely empirical cast of mind. It abstracts certain qualities from experience, and then looks for sensible images, mere conventions of presentation, to bring them vividly to the mind of the reader. Symbolism at least sets our foot on the platonic ladder that leads from sense experience to the ideal world, at best takes us up to the top rung in one instantaneous leap. (The social superiority of idealists to other forms of life has long been acknowledged in literary circles.) Or if we employ Coleridgean terms, allegory is a product of the mechanical fancy, symbolism of the intuitive imagination. And even if, as with Professor Lewis, there is no animus against allegory, it yet turns out to be a mere rhetorical device as against a whole mode of apprehension.

But ideally the literary critic should have no metaphysical or epistemological axes to grind. He is concerned with images used in literature, and certain ways of using them. Whether the images represent what eternally exists is not a matter on which he can form any opinion, as long as he confines himself to criticism. (As a man, of course, he is entitled to any opinion he likes.) Dante's hell was for Dante a representation of what eternally exists; for most of his modern readers it is not. But the literary phenomena remain the same. The questions the critic should ask are how the allegory-symbolism opposition works out for literature; whether it is valid, if he can decide this point; how far it is useful, if he cannot. At once he meets a peculiar feature in this case. Allegory and symbolism are irrevocably opposed, yet we are told there is seldom allegory without some symbolism (or vision), the two are closely intertwined. If this is so it is natural to ask how far it is going to prove possible to distinguish them. What principle have we for deciding whether the image or the concept came first? Nevill Coghill has recently argued that as far as *Piers Plowman* is concerned we cannot decide, unless we happen to have some quite fortuitous external evidence.[5]

And surely the opposition between the two has been made too absolute? There is a third possibility. The poet may present an object or an event or a series of events in the material world, and without predicating or supposing anything about an invisible world beyond them, he can see a pattern in them—a pattern which he can recognize as having occurred before in other objects and events, and as likely to occur again. In fact he sees it as typical. Any *Rake's Progress* or tale of virtue rewarded will afford an example. The moral extracted from it is irrelevant; the point is that the individual tale is seen as a type; and it is often impossible to say which is primary, the pattern or the events in which it is embodied. Here we seem to have something intermediate between allegory and symbolism as defined up to now. Perhaps if the matter were pursued further we should find that there was not one intermediate but an indefinite number of gradations.

As it happens, this suggestion, or something very like it, has been made by Northrop Frye, in the "Theory of Symbols" essay of his *Anatomy of Criticism:*

> Within the boundaries of literature we find a kind of sliding scale, ranging from the most explicitly allegorical, consistent with being literature at all, at one extreme, to the most elusive, anti-explicit and anti-allegorical at the other. First we meet the continuous allegories, like *The Pilgrim's Progress* and *The Faerie Queene,* and then the free-style allegories just mentioned (works of Ariosto, Goethe, Ibsen). Next come the poetic structures with a large and insistent doctrinal interest, in which the internal fictions are exempla, like the epics of Milton. Then we have, in the exact centre, works in which the structure of imagery, however suggestive, has an implicit relation only to events and ideas, and which includes the bulk of Shakespeare. Below this, poetic imagery begins to recede from example and precept and become increasingly ironical and paradoxical.[6]

Here we have a graduated scale, whose earlier gradations at any rate seem on the face of it accurately descriptive. But what has happened to symbolism? It seems to have dropped out altogether, unless it is included under "ironical and paradoxical" imagery—terms which, I confess, in this context I do not fully understand.

In all these formulations there is one conspicuous lack. There is no mention of plain, straightforward, univocal mimesis, innocent as far as may be of conceptual or typical suggestion altogether. Surely if allegory has a polar opposite, this must be it. I shall call it realism, not because I like the term, but because I cannot find any other. At one extreme, then, the simplest kind of allegory in which the interest of the objects and events is entirely subordinate to that of the concepts; at the other, realism, in which the interest of the concepts is entirely subordinate to that of the objects and events. It will be evident by now that I have my own formula to propose. Deprecation and persuasive rhetoric are omitted to save time; but what is said dogmatically should be read simply as suggestion towards the solution of an obviously large and complex question.

Allegory in its broadest possible sense is a pervasive element in all literature. Unlike scientific or discursive writing, literature hardly finds it possible to present actions, events, objects or characters without at least an implied reference to some wider pattern of human experience. (This is said purely empirically, not as a deduction from the nature of literature, but as an observation of the way works of literature actually behave.) Sometimes this reference is explicit and dominant, and at the extreme of this kind of literature we are aware of allegory as a formal constituent of the work. Sometimes this reference is obscured and recessive, and we shall not be inclined to use the term allegory at all, though quasi-allegorical implications are always likely to make their appearance in commentary and criticism. Allegory is naturally most at home in fictional literature (works in which there are internal characters besides the author); but it is not impossible elsewhere. The description of a landscape, for example, can be allegorical. At this point we need some technical terms. I shall use "theme" for the moral or metaphysical "abstract" element in allegory, and "image" for the "concrete" characters, actions or objects in which it is embodied.

We have then two extremes, literature in which theme is dominant, and literature in which image is dominant; and a number, perhaps a large number, of gradations in between. It is probable that the relations between theme and image vary in other ways too, besides this simple quantitative way. We have two kinds of literature, for example, in which theme and image seem equally balanced; first, that represented by Shakespeare in which the two seem completely fused and can only be separated by an act of critical violence; and second what we have vaguely called symbolism, where theme and image are separable, but where image, to use Coleridge's phrasing, "always partakes of the reality which it renders intelligible, and while it enunciates the whole, abides itself as a living part in that unity of which it is the living representative." This suggests that we might look not for a linear arrangement, but for a circular one, in which through one half of the circle we recede from simple allegory to the opposite extreme of realism, while in the other half we return towards simple allegory again, by another route.

I believe that such a circular arrangement represents the nature of the case better than any other. It can be represented diagrammatically; and since we need some means of notation for the various phases I will use the familiar figures of the clockface for this purpose. The four key points are at twelve, three, six, and nine. I shall proceed clockwise round the circle, and for each quarter I shall isolate the key point first, and then fill in the intermediate stages.

At twelve o'clock we have naïve allegory. (I borrow this term, and much of the description through the first quarter of the circle, from Northrop Frye. Indeed this whole essay is in the nature of a footnote to his treatment of the subject, to which anyone who thinks at all on these matters must be deeply indebted.) In naïve allegory theme is completely dominant, image merely a rhetorical convenience with no life of its own. In its pure form it is, as Frye puts it, "a disguised form of discursive writing, and belongs chiefly to educational literature on an elementary level: schoolroom moralities, devotional exempla, local pageants, and the like." It is properly described in the terms which anti-allegorical critics use of allegory in general—a picture-writing to transcribe preconceived ideas. Where theme is so completely dominant, image tends to become incoherent, insipid or characterless; and we are on the verge of passing out of literature altogether, into moral suasion, political propaganda or what not. Naïve allegory appears in literature proper mainly in the form of small patches in long and complex works conceived on other lines; and they cannot sustain more than a very limited amount of it.

At three o'clock we have the kind of literature best represented by the work of Shakespeare, in which theme and image are completely fused and the relation between them is only implicit, never open or enforced. We have not yet found a name for this. For want of a better I shall call it incarnation (without any theological implication). Incarnational literature is that in which any "abstract" content is completely absorbed in character and action and completely

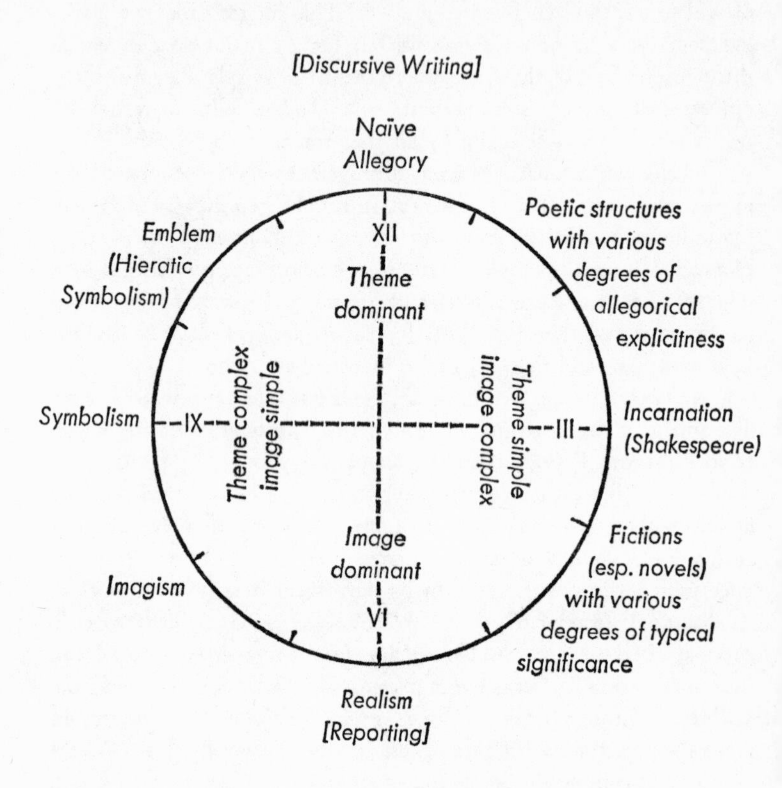

expressed by them. Between twelve and three lie various forms of literature in which the relation between theme and image is of varying degrees of explicitness. At about one o'clock we have allegory proper. This differs from naïve allegory in that, though theme is still dominant, image now assumes a vitality and interest of its own. Here we find the continuous formal allegories, like *The Pilgrim's Progress* and Book I of *The Faerie Queene*. (I cannot agree with Frye, or

Spenser himself for that matter, that *The Faerie Queene* as a whole is continuous allegory.) Between one and three, between allegory and incarnation, there is a continuous gradation in which close scrutiny would doubtless be able to distinguish many forms. Briefly, at half past one we could situate "humor" literature and the romance of types. A good deal of Jonson's comedy comes here, and the romance episodes in *The Faerie Queene* that have a moral and typical significance but fall short of pure allegory. At two are what Frye calls the freestyle allegories, poetic fictions like those of Ariosto, Ibsen, and Goethe, in which allegorical significance is picked up and dropped at will. At half past two we have (I quote Frye again) "the poetic structures with a large and insistent doctrinal interest, in which the internal fictions are exempla, like the epics of Milton." These are the closest to incarnation at three o'clock.

This completes the first quarter of our circle, and I now desert Northrop Frye's formulation to follow up the rest of the circumference in different terms. At six o'clock, opposed to naïve allegory, we find what I have called realism. Here image is predominant and theme at a minimum. That literature which presents itself as the direct mimesis of common experience comes here—realist and quasi-documentary fiction, descriptive writing, and so forth. And just as naïve allegory is on the edge of passing out of literature into discursive writing, so this is on the edge of passing out of literature into reporting. Literary realism is in fact a highly unstable compound. As soon as it ceases to be mere factual reporting, that is as soon as it becomes literature at all, the element of theme tends to grow unconsciously and turn it into something else. Zola, the great naturalist, has had a comeback in this century as a sort of symbolist; and no doubt this critical vagary corresponds to a tendency really present in his work. In the quarter between three and six we have again a densely populated gradation of forms with a gradually increasing dominance of image over theme. This is preeminently the territory of the novel, a kind which can only live by the vitality and integrity of the image, but can accommodate very various proportions of theme. Nearest to Shakespeare we should find Tolstoy, both hedgehog and fox, moralist and observer, in still undissolved alliance. In the middle of the quarter, at half past four, is Fielding, in whom thematic interest is still strong, but beginning to come apart from his structure of images, and decidedly overshadowed by their interest and variety. With him I suppose would go most of the traditional English novelists—Dickens and Thackeray and a number of lesser Victorians. At five o'clock we pass to the professed "realists," Flaubert and his disciples; and from there to six, "pure" realism, the last hundred years will provide innumerable examples. But this is a crowded and complex area, although so much of it seems plain sailing. The decorum of the novel, the relation of theme and image within it, still requires a long discussion to itself.

The next quarter, from six to nine, is a difficult one, for it includes forms that, though much discussed in recent years, have not had the prolonged and familiar attention that has been given to those of the first quarter. Realism is a *ne plus ultra;* any farther in that direction takes us outside literature altogether. So now the literary circle begins to return towards allegory. At nine o'clock we find symbolism, like incarnation a form in which theme and image have equal weight, but opposed to incarnation because the relation between the two elements is different. In symbolism there is none of the harmonious wholeness of incarnational literature. Theme and image are equally present, they assert their unity, but the unity is never achieved, or if it is, it is only a unity of tension. The archetype for incarnational literature is the union of soul and body in the human person, but symbolism resists this human and accessible integrity. It seeks for the union of theme and image not through the representation of living, acting, and suffering human beings, but through words as talismans, *alchimie du verbe,* or through direct visionary experience. It seems to divide itself into two realms, one a realm of stratagems and devices, *dérèglement de tous les sens,* things seen as the equivalent of concepts, fragments that mysteriously contain wholes; the other an attempt like that of Blake to *see* the invisible with all the concreteness of sense-experience.

We can understand this more clearly if we look at an intermediate phase. Between realism at six o'clock and symbolism at nine stands imagism. Realism attaches value to the thing itself rather than to the verbal image of it; it is often associated with coarseness of style and a relative indifference to verbal art. In a period when realist influence is strong an empirical, material, brass-tacks attitude is hard to escape from—we see it in Pound's early criticism. When this attitude prevails in writers whose verbal, "poetic" interests are also strong the natural response is imagism. Here the image itself begins to acquire special value, rather than the thing that it is the image of. At the same time theme is still depreciated; it is regarded as something vague and "abstract." There is a growing belief that all the work of literature is done by images, not by syntax or dianoia. Poetry is "thinking in images." (We recognize the clichés of yesterday's criticism.) There is a tendency to regard images atomically and disjunctively, and the longer poetic units try to make their effect by the juxtaposition of images—like *The Waste Land* or Pound's *Cantos*—theme is only allowed to make its appearance surreptitiously. We are presented simply with petals on wet black boughs and must make what we can of them.

This is the intermediate stage, somewhere about half past seven, between realism and symbolism. (I am aware that this is not the historical sequence.) But imagism, like realism itself, is an unstable compound. When brooded over to this degree images tend to acquire magical properties. They engage in mysterious correspondences and enter into occult relations with vision. When this happens imagism passes over into symbolism. And with symbolism we enter the last quarter and are already well on our way back to naïve allegory again.

But as before there is an intermediate stage. Half-way between symbolism and naïve allegory we have what I will call emblem or hieratic symbolism. It exists largely outside literature—its special field is iconography and religious imagery. There is a tendency for symbolism to become fixed; the image shrinks and becomes stereotyped, and theme expands. We think of emblems like the cross or the marriage ring, heraldic devices or of various sacramental objects—baptismal water, oil of consecration. There is perhaps no literature written entirely in this mode, unless some of the more gnomic sacred scriptures, wisdom of the East, etc. But in much literature, especially of an occult kind, it is a strong element. Yeats uses imagery in this way. The scope of emblem or hieratic symbolism is both limited and inflexible. Its strong thematic interest, as far as literature is concerned, is always likely to carry it over into naïve allegory where image is more flexible and obedient. And so by a commodious vicus of recirculation we come back to our starting point.

II

With this armament at our disposal we can look more closely at the allegory of *The Faerie Queene.* We can I think determine Spenser's field of operation. It extends from eleven o'clock to two—from hieratic symbolism through naïve allegory, allegory proper, and the romance of types to the freestyle allegory where thematic significance is picked up and dropped at will. Its center is in allegory proper. There is a little hieratic symbolism, in the heraldic devices borne by the knights—the red cross, the figure of Cupid in Scudamour's shield and in some of the pictorial set-pieces such as the procession of the seven deadly sins. There are patches of naïve allegory, as in the castle of Alma and a number of minor figures. On the other hand much of Book IV is less explicit than allegory proper; it consists of romance stories with a typical significance: and in the pastoral episodes of Book VI allegory is only faintly and intermittently present and often seems to disappear altogether. But we rightly feel that these are the outlying areas of *The Faerie Queene.* Its core is in the long sustained allegorical portions—Books I and II and the central narrative threads of Books III and V. However near Spenser may come to "humanizing" his characters (and he sometimes comes very near) he never touches the confines of incarnational literature—he never embodies his themes in the completely rounded and individual representation of a human person. And on the other side, symbolism, in either the verbal or the visionary sense, is quite alien to Spenser's mode of perception.

All this is quite unhistorical. Since Spenser is a conscious and acknowledged allegorist it is now appropriate to inquire how he himself conceived of allegory, or is likely to have conceived of it. Apart from the internal evidence of *The Faerie Queene* itself we have a little Spenserian documentation, in the letter to Ralegh, and a great deal of documentation derived from contemporary critical works and from Spenser's earlier models.

In the letter to Ralegh, Spenser calls *The Faerie Queene* "a continued Allegory, or darke conceit." "Dark" in Elizabethan literary discourse steadily means obscure; and "conceit" in this context means conception, idea, thought. Allegory then is an obscure conception that needs explanation. And Spenser "knowing how doubtfully all Allegories may be construed" sets out in the letter "to discover unto you the general intention and meaning, which in the whole course thereof I have fashioned, without expressing of any particular purposes or by-accidents therein occasioned." Courthope acutely points out that in fact he hardly does this.[7] Most of the letter is far more concerned with plan and narrative structure than with allegorical intention as such—that is, more concerned with the disposition of the images than with discovering the theme hidden behind them. Here at the beginning we get a strong though unintentional hint that as far as the structure of *The Faerie Queene* as a whole is concerned allegory is not so decisive a factor, theme not so dominant over image, as we have sometimes been led to expect. This is reinforced by the conclusion we reached in the previous chapter—that the conventions of romantic epic, the desire to reconcile the antique unity with modern variety, had a great deal to do with giving the poem its general shape. And this has nothing to do with allegory at all.

Nor is the central idea as the letter expounds it expressly allegorical: "To fashion a gentleman or noble person in vertuous and gentle discipline," and to present this "coloured with an historical fiction," is the announced "generall end" of all the book; that is to portray the ideal knight in the person of Prince Arthur. This is no more allegorical than the *Aeneid;* and in what sense the *Aeneid* is allegorical we shall have to inquire in a moment. But then Spenser goes farther. Besides choosing Prince Arthur for historical and heroic (and Tassonian) reasons, "as most fitte for the excellency of his person, being made famous by many men's former workes, and also furthest from the daunger of envy, and suspition of present time," he has chosen him to represent Magnificence, that virtue which "according to Aristotle and the rest" is the sum and perfection of all the virtues. We may then be permitted to ask in what sense Arthur represents magnificence. Surely not in the same sense as Ate represents strife, Furor anger, or Despair despair. These personages carry their *significatio* in their names and have no other function but to illustrate it. Ate and Furor are figures of naïve allegory, or something not much more advanced; Despair, splendidly and somberly dramatized, is a figure of true allegory at its richest and most expressive. All three are created out of thematic needs. But Arthur is not of this kind. His existence as a mythico-historic figure, a perfect knight, a wise leader, and a British leader at that, is logically anterior to the thematic idea of magnificence. The process by which the Arthur-Magnificence fusion is created is surely more akin to the *allegorizing* of an existing story than to allegory in its pure form. Does anyone feel when Arthur sets off in pursuit of Florimell (III. i. 18) that Magnificence is about to succor Distressed Beauty? Not in the least. A knight is going to the rescue of a lovely lady, inspired by the usual mixed chivalric motives. We can see that they are mixed because they are contrasted with those of Britomart, which are not, in the next stanza—

> The whiles faire Britomart, whose constant mind,
> Would not so lightly follow beauties chase,
> Ne reckt of Ladies Love, did stay behind.

There is nothing blatantly incompatible with Arthur's ascribed character here, but he is not really behaving like Magnificence; he is behaving like Rinaldo in the first canto of the *Furioso*. And even in less unguarded moments he never seems to represent Magnificence in any explicit fashion. A brave knight, able to succor the other knights in times of distress by his courage and military prowess; and that is all.

Red Cross on the other hand stands for Holiness, Guyon for Temperance, and Artegall for Justice in quite a different way. We see each vanquishing the temptations appropriate to his condition. Red Cross has to face the dangers that beset the religious life—Pride and Despair; Guyon the seductions of the flesh and the passions; Artegall battles with unjust external foes. We never see Arthur in any distinct moral relation at all. What we seem to find is a number of local allegories of considerable clarity embedded in a framework that is only allegorical in a vaguer and more general sense. This may amount to a "continued Allegory, or darke conceit"; in Spenser's estimation it apparently did; but it certainly does not justify what is sometimes attempted—an unremitting allegorical interpretation, conducted on the same level throughout.

A better illustration would be the figure of Britomart, since she is far more fully drawn than Arthur and we see more of her. She is the titular hero of a book, and with her magic lance, her invulnerability, and her ability to rescue other lovers in distress or failure she is a worthy representation of Chastity—chastity in Spenser's special sense of faithful, pure and honorable love. When she passes through the flame that guards the house of Busirane (III. xi), the flame that Scudamour, the less perfect, the merely erotic lover is unable to pass, she is behaving allegorically. I shall try to avoid making too many direct translations of image into theme, for the proper way to read allegory is the same as the proper way to read any other literature—to apprehend as far as may be, the living whole; but here it is necessary to make my point. And surely the thematic meaning here is that a wholly pure and selfless love is immune to sensual obstacles and disturbances that can be fatal to even a devoted love of a lesser kind. But in III. ii we see Britomart portrayed in quite another way. She has seen the vision of Artegall in the magic mirror, she has fallen in love with him, she pines, and her nurse tries to comfort her. But she will not be comforted.

> These idle words (said she) doe nought asswage
> My stubborne smart, but more annoyance breed,
> For no no usuall fire, no usuall rage
> It is, O Nurse, which on my life doth feed.
>
> Sithens it hath infixed faster hold
> Within my bleeding bowels, and so sore
> Now ranckleth in this same frail fleshly mould,
> That all mine entrailes flow with poysnous gore,
> And th'ulcer growth daily more and more;
> Ne can my running sore find remedie,
> Other then my hard fortune to deplore,
> And languish as the leafe falne from the tree,
> Till death make one end of my dayes and miserie.
>
> (III. ii. 27–29)

This is no representation of chastity; it is a proud girl in the grip of what she fears is a disastrous passion. And in V. vi. 12–14, when she hears of Artegall in the power of Radigund, she is plainly a jealous young woman, and she is compared to a froward child who "kicks and squals, and shriekes for fell despight."

We then remember Britomart's literary ancestry. She is a reincarnation of Bradamante of the *Orlando Furioso,* one of a long line of warrior maidens who love and fight through the romantic epic—romantic heroines, not allegorical personifications; and Britomart partakes of their nature, whatever her activities as a type of chastity. We begin to suspect that allegory was conceived by Spenser in a more relaxed and intermittent way than many of his modern interpreters would have us suppose.

This suspicion is confirmed when we look at the contemporary interpretations of Ariosto. There are of course a few passages in Ariosto that are overtly allegorical—the Alcina and Logistilla episodes, for example, with their antithesis of passion and reason; and the passage in XIV. 76 seq. where Silence and Discord are summoned to bring aid to Charles besieged in Paris. They are few, comparatively short, and quite distinct in method from the general run of the narrative. But a very few years after the appearance of the *Furioso* we find that the poem as a whole, including some of the most obviously romantic and fantastic episodes, begins to be subjected to allegorical interpretation. This is simply the continuation of a very old practice, nearly as old as epic poetry itself, by which all the great epics were read as allegories. This habit of mind is foreign to us, and we must again diverge from *The Faerie Queene* itself in order to understand the tradition in which Spenser was working.

III

The allegorizing of Homer [8] goes back as far as the pre-Socratics. As early as the sixth century B.C. protests were made against the fanciful and immoral Homeric mythology. Defenders of Homer replied by saying that the superficial sense was not the true one, there was a deeper meaning (ὑπόνοια, it was not called "allegory" till some centuries later). Theagenes (fl. 525 B.C.) suggested a twofold allegory, moral and physical. The names of the gods express either mental faculties in man or the elements in nature—Apollo is fire, Poseidon water, Pallas wisdom, Hermes intelligence. This is perhaps little more than an attempt to exorcize the more inconveniently human aspects of the gods by identifying them with their functions. Other allegorizations were more far-fetched. Anaxagoras early in the fifth century saw an elaborate emblem of the rules of dialectic in the web of Penelope. His pupils interpreted the Homeric myths in a moral sense. Cleanthes of Assos at the end of the third century found fanciful allegories in Homer, and his is the earliest known use of the word ἀλληγοριχός.[9] With Plato the moral objections to the mythology of Homer revived, and in the Republic there is no other remedy but censorship. Among the Neoplatonists, however, allegorical interpretations were proposed. The discourse of Porphyry (A.D. 233–301) *On the Cave of the Nymphs* is an elaborate commentary on *Odyssey* XIII, 102–12, in which the cave is treated as an allegory of the universe and the fate of the soul within it. In most of these cases the purpose is to give an acceptable meaning to something that was on the face of it either indecorous or morally neutral. In Porphyry, as is usual with Neoplatonists on poetry, we find rather the construction of a free philosophical fantasia, using the poem as the merest pretext.

By the time commentaries on Vergil begin to make their appearance the allegorizing of heroic poetry was already well established. Allegorical commentaries on the *Aeneid* were produced by Donatus in the fourth century, by Servius and Macrobius in the fifth. There is not the same necessity to excuse Vergil for the immorality of his tales about the gods; but for the early Christian centuries the same sort of problem appears in another form. How is the Christian to be excused for reading these false pagan fables? The answer is that they conceal a store of moral and religious truth. The most elaborate allegory is that of Fulgentius, *Virgiliana Continentia* (*c.* 530); and the allegorical interpretation was accepted by Bernardus Silvestris, John of Salisbury, as well as by Dante. Nor was it abandoned during the Renaissance. Cristoforo Landino, a member of the famous Platonic academy of Florence, wrote the *Disputationes Camaldulenses* about 1470. In Books III and IV Alberti, a fellow academician, is represented as producing an elaborate allegory of the first six books of the *Aeneid*.[10] It is a lengthy argument explaining the travels of Aeneas as an allegory of the soul, forsaking all earthly passions, symbolized by Troy, struggling with the perturbations of the senses and passions, and ultimately arriving in the true heavenly kingdom. There are two loves, a true and divine one, and a false and earthly one. Paris gives himself to the false love and perishes with Troy, Aeneas gives himself to the true celestial love, and *si non recta navigatione (id enim humanae conditioni, aut nunquam, aut raro conceditur, ut eodem tempore et stulticiam exuat, et sapiens efficiatur) tamen post multos errores, in Italiam ad veram sapientiam pervenit.*[11] Much is made of the antithesis between heavenly and earthly love; the authority of Plato is constantly cited, sometimes in the same breath with that of St. Paul and Dionysius the Areopagite—in short this is a typical Renaissance Neoplatonic document. And yet when all is said the extravagant platonizing only extracts the archetypal pattern that actually underlies the story—the leaving of a city of destruction, the perilous voyage, the coming to a land of promise. With this plot, so naturally analogous to the story of Israel, captive, wandering, and restored, or to the individual pilgrim's progress, it can never have been hard to turn Vergil into an honorary Christian poet.

About fifty years later than Landino, Ariosto was writing the *Furioso,* in the last days of Italian freedom, and in the last days of Renaissance liberty of expression. The carefree atmosphere of the court of Ferrara was not long to subsist. Within thirty years of the publication of the poem, Counter-Reformation rigidity and the fear of ecclesiastical authority had already begun to make some excuse for its irresponsibility and license seem desirable. And of course the time-honored remedy was applied—the poem was an allegory. There are indeed considerable areas of explicit allegory in the *Furioso.* What we are discussing now is something different. It is the deliberate allegorizing of that far more extensive part of the poem where the unsophisticated reader would see only simple romance. From the fifteen-forties [12] on almost every edition of the poem appears "con le allegorie," "con le nuove allegorie," "con l'allegorie a ciascun canto di Thomaso Porcacchi," and the more popular allegorical annotations were reprinted many times. In addition, separate commentaries on the poem were published. Two were available by Spenser's time—Fornari's *Spositione sopra l'Orlando Furioso* (1549) and Toscanella's *Bellezze del Furioso* (1574).[13]

Toscanella has not a great deal to say about allegory, but he provides at the beginning a list of the allegorical equivalents of the principal characters, and some allegorical suggestions in the introductions to the several cantos. Fornari's [14] work is in two parts; the first is a minute commentary, mainly mythological and historical; in the second (1550) he undertakes the allegorical explanation of the poem. An introduction *Agli Studiosi Lettori* explains that all through nature the most precious things are hidden, like jewels in the earth; so it is with the meanings of the poets. According to Anaxagoras, the Pythagoreans, and the Platonists, things above correspond with things below, and the poets in describing material and earthly things often signify heavenly ones. It is right and sanctioned by ancient usage to hide the most precious thoughts from the unworthy in this way; besides, by this means sound doctrine is insinuated under the delights of fiction. Coming to Ariosto in particular, as he need give way to none of the ancient poets in ingenious and delightful inventions, so in moral fiction he surpasses and leaves behind all others. The parts of the poem most suited for this kind of interpretation are the stories of Ruggiero and Astolfo, which Fornari then proceeds to expound.

It is impossible to say how much of this exegesis Spenser used, but that he did use it, and turn it to good purpose, is quite clear from internal evidence. Editions with allegories were also very much more numerous than those without. Some writers have suggested that it was a sort of British or puritan obtuseness in Spenser that made him read the irresponsible Ariosto as allegory. This is mere ignorance. Spenser read Ariosto in the manner of the Italians of his time. So, it would appear, did others. Harington, who cannot be suspected of undue rigor, who is quite capable of producing a slyly tolerant defence of the poem, also regards it as allegorical, on more than one level.[14]

When in the *Orlando Furioso* we meet Bradamante, with her high spirit, her devotion, and her very human jealousy, she does not appear to be an allegorical character at all. However, for Fornari she represents sacred or spiritual love; for Porcacchi she is *pudicizia;* for another anonymous allegorist (Venice, 1588) she is *virtù congiunto con la ragione;* while for Toscanella she is simply a portrait of an affectionate and devoted wife. It is easy to see how these suggestions, or some of them, or others like them, could combine to produce Britomart, the brave, loving, and devoted girl who is at the same time the symbol of chastity—in Spenser's special sense of honorable love. I am inclined to believe that he used Porcacchi, for with his frequent vagueness in rendering abstract terms from other languages (his temperance is Aristotle's continence, his magnificence is Aristotle's megalopsychia) *pudicizia* could easily have been translated by the not very distant chastity.[16] Similarly Atlante the enchanter, from whose castle Bradamante liberates prisoners as Britomart liberates Amoret, represents Lust for Fornari, Love for Toscanella and Porcacchi—and for Porcacchi, love described specifically as an *appetito*. Here we have clearly the origin of Busirane and his house. (Professor Lewis identifies Busirane with Courtly Love.) The suggestion must come from the commentators, for in the poem itself it is by no means plain that Atlante has anything to do with sensual appetite at all.

It is noticeable that these allegorical commentaries are extremely arbitrary and capricious. Toscanella in the "allegory of the proper names" at the beginning of the *Bellezze* equates Atlante with Love; but in the commentary to Canto IV he identifies him with Time, and gives quite a different explanation of the whole canto. The choice of passages for allegorical interpretation also seems largely fortuitous, and other parts of the narrative are left unexplained. In the commentary on Canto I, for example, Porcacchi concentrates on the perturbation of Rinaldo, Ferraù, and Sacripante at not being able to enjoy Angelica, and says that it shows how often the heavens are contrary to the desires of men. He then goes on to explain (very feebly) the two fountains of love and disdain. Toscanella and an anonymous allegorist of 1588, on the other hand, are struck by the pride and ingratitude of Angelica in refusing worthy suitors; and say nothing about the fountains at all. Fornari confines his allegorizing to two parts of the plot—the first, Ruggiero's story, being obviously a moral allegory; the second a fantastic tale easily susceptible to recondite explanation. And he particularly deprecates the industrious extracting of allegories from unpromising places. Often the alleged allegories are mere statements of the most obvious implications of the narrative. Rinaldo is angry and in love, he therefore represents anger and the effects of love. Medoro and Cloridano are devoted to their lord and to each other; they therefore represent feudal and mutual devotion; and so on. I deduce from this that in reading Ariosto as he did Spenser must have become completely habituated to *discontinuous* allegory, which can be picked up and dropped at will; and to a conception of allegory that is often enough fulfilled by the simplest moral implications drawn from a pre-existing romantic tale.

The allegorical interpretation of Tasso followed a different course. He wrote the allegory for the *Jerusalem Delivered* himself.[17] He suffered great anxiety about the orthodoxy of his poem and constantly suspected that it was about to be condemned by the Inquisition; and the allegory is an afterthought designed to vindicate the purity of his intentions. It is far more complete and consistent than the allegorizings of Ariosto, and aims at exhibiting the whole poem as a "continued allegory or dark conceit," showing that it was all informed by a single idea. Tasso sees all earlier epic poetry as conceived in this way. The *Odyssey* and the *Comedy* of Dante are types of the life of the contemplative man; civil life is "shadowed" in the *Iliad;* and the *Aeneid* shows a mixture of the active and the contemplative. For his own poem Tasso establishes a hierarchy of the virtues on Platonic lines. "The army compounded of divers princes, and of other Christian soldiers, signifieth Man, compounded of soul and body, and of a soul not simple, but divided into many and diverse powers." Goffredo signifies the Understanding, "lord over the other virtues of soul and body." Rinaldo stands for the Ireful Virtue, next in dignity to the virtue of reason itself; since "Rinaldo, which in Action is in the second degree of honour, ought also to be placed in the Allegory in the answerable degree." The other Princes are in lieu of the other powers of the soul, and the body is figured by the less noble soldiers. The resemblance to the Arthur passages in the letter to Ralegh can hardly be missed; and though Tasso adheres to Plato not Aristotle it is surely here rather than in any authentic inspiration from Aristotle that we are to look for the source of the idea of Magnificence and the twelve virtues. If this is so, our suspicion that this part of the plan is a second thought finds confirmation. Spenser cannot have known Tasso till after *The Faerie Queene* had been begun.

There are other likenesses too between Spenser's allegory and Tasso's. We have in both the same sense that the romantic and sentimental episodes tend to escape from the allegory altogether, the same sense of a mind that is deeply desirous of unity of being, but still in some degree divided between the erotic and sensuous on the one hand, the moral and spiritual on the other. But Spenser is less inclined to psychologize than Tasso, and his vast varied composition is far more recalcitrant to such a process. We could at a pinch concede that the *Jerusalem* might be taken to represent the structure of the soul—the hierarchy of the Christian army typifying the hierarchy of mental powers, the external war representing the internal psychomachia. But even in the Letter Spenser hardly insists on the figures of Arthur and the knights as internal constituents of the soul. They rather seem to represent their several virtues as active in the world. This way of interpreting epic narrative as typical psychology is Neoplatonic. We find it in Porphyry and Landino. But I can see no sign that Spenser had read Landino at all. The lofty Platonic tone, lifting the true meaning of a poem above the sphere of earthly experience altogether, is not that of *The Faerie Queene*. Love in *The Faerie Queene,* however nobly and tenderly idealized, remains love that hopes for an earthly fruition; it cannot be translated into the heavenly love which *ad divinam nos pulchritudinem rapiat;* nor does Spenser suggest that it should. For this reason the comprehensive metaphysical-psychological allegory that we find in Landino and Tasso is not really his chosen method. The mazy diversity of actual moral and erotic experience is his field, and the discontinuous, capricious allegorizing of the commentators on Ariosto was more influential with him.

IV

Other forces may have been at work in the same direction. Allegory is a standard rhetorical term in Spenser's day. It is one of the tropes defined in all the rhetoric books. It is true that the definitions are not particularly illuminating; but they do give us a general sense of what the word meant to the sixteenth century. It always means something very short, and is always closely connected with metaphor. The most compendious statement I have found is in Peacham's *Garden of Eloquence:*

> Allegoria, called of Quintilian, Inversio, is a Trope of a sentence, or forme of speech which expresseth one thing in words, and another in sense. In a Metaphore there is a translation of one word only, in an Allegorie of many, and for that cause an Allegorie is called a continued Metaphore.[18]

Like the other English rhetoricians Peacham is derivative. He draws his material from Susenbrotus, Melanchthon, and Robert and Henry Etienne; so it is not surprising that the same sort of definition and the same relation to metaphor is found in the other English rhetorical writers. Angel Day in *The English Secretarie* defines allegoria as:

> . . . a kind of inverting or change of sense, as when we shew one thing in words, and signify another in meaning: a Trope most usual among us, even in our common speaking, as when we say, Bow the with while it is green, meaning to correct children whilest they be young: or, There is no fire without smoake, meaning that there is no ill conceipt without occasion: or, I smell a Rat, that is, I know your meaning.[19]

And he makes the distinction from metaphor simply that metaphor is a "Trope of words," that is, it is confined to a single word, while allegory extends through a whole sentence. And rather earlier Puttenham had written at great length in the same sense:

> *Allegoria* is when we do speake in sence translative and wrested from his own signification, nevertheless applied to another not altogether contrary, but having much conveniencie with it as before we said of the metaphore: as for example if we should call the common wealth a ship; the Prince a Pilot, The Counsellors mariners, the stormes warres, the calm and haven peace, this is spoken all in allegorie: and because such inversion of sence in one single worde is by the figure *Metaphore,* of whom we spake before, and this manner of inversion extending to whole and large speeches, it maketh the figure *allegorie* to be called a long and perpetuall Metaphore.[20]

The most notable feature of these definitions is that allegory is typically considered to be a matter of a single sentence. Puttenham, who gives it the widest range, allows it to extend to "whole and large speeches." But the rhetoricians' definitions never consider allegory as the informing principle of a whole work. They also insist that it is a common feature of our ordinary discourse—"a trope most usual among us in our ordinary speaking" (Day); or as Puttenham puts it, "The use of this figure is so large, and his vertue of so great efficacie as it is supposed no man can pleasantly utter and persuade without it." How can we suppose Spenser to have been affected by this conception of allegory? First, apart from the idea of an allegorical structure underlying a whole poem, there would have been present to his mind the normal rhetorical conception of allegory as a short form; and when he speaks of *The Faerie Queene* as a "continued allegory" a good deal of stress should fall on "continued." He is aware that he is making a more extended use of allegory than the normal. As allegory is a continued metaphor, *The Faerie Queene* is a continued allegory. But this need not mean continuous and uninterrupted—simply that he is using allegory continually, in our popular sense of the word "continually," to mean "repeatedly" or "pervasively." And the general insistence on allegory as a common feature of all discourse would allow for a great deal of only half conscious, "natural" allegory, no more deliberate than the ordinary use of metaphor in ordinary speech. I do not wish to make too much of this, but I think we can derive from the rhetorical definitions a useful warning against pressing too hard on Spenser's allegorical purpose, against the relentless discovery of deliberately inserted allegorical intentions at every point. The consistency we are to expect is the kind of consistency we should expect from the metaphors in a long poem—that various in kind and material as they may be, they should all subserve a consistent tone and purpose. And as in the metaphorical content of a long poem we should expect a good many "accidents" as well as "intendments," so we should in the allegorical content of *The Faerie Queene;* particularly since Spenser has expressly told us to do so.

V

We have been speaking up to now of the formal principles of allegory in *The Faerie Queene* and have said little or nothing about its actual content; for this is almost coextensive with the poem itself and is so shifting and various that it can only be discussed in direct commentary on the several books. But there is one constant preoccupation among the scholiasts on Spenser that can be discussed briefly now, both in its formal and material aspects; and some of it put out of the way for good. This is the so-called historical allegory. It has given rise to voluminous and unhelpful commentary, it is a stumbling block to most readers of the poem, as far as they allow themselves to consider it; yet it is indubitably there, and it is necessary to realize the limits of its importance.

In the first place the poem is called *The Faerie Queene,* and by that Faerie Queene, Spenser tells us in the Letter, he means glory in general intention, "but in my particular I conceive the most excellent and glorious person of our soveraine the Queene, and her kingdom in Faery land." Queen Elizabeth, then, is the eponymous heroine, and a romantic glorification of the Queen and her England is very near to Spenser's central intention—however little she may appear in the structure as it stands. Spenser also tells us that she is otherwise "shadowed" as Belphoebe; and though he does not tell us this, she appears equally clearly as the Mercilla of Book V. Britomart is among her ancestors, and may, if we care, be supposed to bear among other attributes a foreshadowing of her qualities. Nor is this all. The announced general hero is Arthur, the legendary embodiment of the glory of Britain, in love with the Faerie Queene, and again one of the historical Queen Elizabeth's putative forebears. So, even though it is not clearly apparent in the existing narrative structure, the spirit of dynastic and national panegyric pervades the whole poem. It would be strange if it did not. Besides all that we know of the expanding national consciousness of Spenser's time, we must add that it is part of the genre in which he is writing. As Northrop Frye has put it, the centripetal gaze, directed to a court or a sovereign, is the typical note of the high mimetic style. To be more specific, it goes back at least as far as the *Aeneid* with its glorification of Augustus; and both Ariosto and Tasso are celebrating, in their several ways, the glories of the house of Este. Legendary genealogies, mythical history, and visionary anachronistic links between past and present are the ordinary procedure of such things.

Secondly there is, very unevenly distributed, a good deal of intermittent allusion to contemporary persons and events. Its extent and importance has been much disputed, but there are places where it is unmistakable. What is called the historical allegory therefore divides itself into two aspects, one the general encomium on England and her Queen, the other an occasional specific comment on current affairs. There can be little doubt that the first is the more important of the two.

For his general glorification of England Spenser employs what may be called the political mythology of his day. It is now well known that part of the elaborate apparatus of history and legend by which the Tudors established their dominance over the English imagination was their claim to be descendants of the ancient kings of Britain. The matter is illustrated at length in Greenlaw's *Studies in Spenser's Historical Allegory*,[21] and it is discussed by Dr. Tillyard in his book on Shakespeare's histories. Not only did Henry VII in his person unite the rival roses and bring to an end a long period of civil strife, but he fulfilled an old prophecy. The case is summarily stated in Hall's chronicle:

> It was by a hevenly voice reveled to Cadwalader last kyng of Brytons that his stock and progeny should reigne in this land and beare dominion again: Whereupon most men were persuaded in their awne opinion that by this heavenly voice he [i.e. Hy vii] was provided and ordeined long before to enjoye and obteine this kyngdome.[22]

Henry in fact, according to this story, was the heir of Brut, grandson of Aeneas, the mythical founder of Britain; and even more important for Spenser's purpose, he was the heir of Arthur. Henry himself recognized the political value of this by giving his eldest son the name of Arthur. This Prince Arthur died young, but the legendary succession was easily transferred to his brother, Henry VIII, who was in fact hailed as Arturus Redivivus. This return of the ancient line of Arthur was an important topic for the Tudor chroniclers and antiquaries, and was frequently celebrated in pageants and royal entertainments in Queen Elizabeth's reign. The prime source for the history of the ancient British kings is Geoffrey of Monmouth, their story had been elaborated by later chroniclers, and the more striking parts of it were taken over by the poets and dramatists. The history had also been attacked, notably by Polydore Vergil in Henry VII's reign, who is scornful of Geoffrey and distinctly ironical about the story of Arthur. This un-British scepticism

(Polydore was an Italian) called forth a strong response from the traditionalists—chroniclers, antiquaries, and poets; and to their party Spenser naturally belonged.[23] In making Arthur the hero of his poem he was not only celebrating the legendary British hero, but the supposedly historic ancestor of the Tudor line.[24]

Had Queen Elizabeth been a king his course would have been simple; Prince Arthur would simply have been the type of his sixteenth-century successor. But a queen cannot be personally Arturus Redivivus; she must then become his destined bride. And this introduces an additional element of romantic vagueness into Spenser's honorific genealogies. In II. x Arthur at the house of Alma reads the book called *Briton Moniments,* and in it traces his own ancestry down to the time of Uther Pendragon his father. His exclamation at the end of the recital shows the spirit in which we are to read it:

> At last quite ravisht with delight, to heare
> The royall offspring of his native land,
> Cryde out, Dear countrey, O how dearely deare
> Ought thy remembrance, and perpetuall band
> Be to thy foster Childe, that from thy hand
> Did commun breath and nouriture receave?
> How brutish is it not to understand,
> How much to her we owe, that all us gave,
> That gave unto us all, what ever good we have.
>
> (II. x. 69)

In III. iii Britomart is shown by Merlin the tale of her descendants; a place is ingeniously found for her and Artegall in the succession (she is inserted into the chronicle history, without authority from the chronicles, just after Arthur) and from their offspring the line continues down to the time of Elizabeth herself.

> Then shall a royal virgin raine, which shall
> Stretch her wide rod over the Belgicke shore,
> And the great Castle smite so sore withall,
> That it shall make him shake, and shortly learn to fall.
>
> (III. iii. 49)

On the other hand the Faerie Queene, who is also Elizabeth, is provided with a purely fanciful genealogy. While Arthur is reading his *Briton Moniments* in II. x Guyon is equally eagerly devouring a book called the *Antiquitie of Faerie Land,* which traces the forebears of Tanaquil-Gloriana from the original Elf and Fay through such monarchs as Elfin, Elfinan, and Elfinell—all apparently creatures of Spenser's own fancy, though clear enough glances at Henry VII (Elficleos), the young prince Arthur (Elferon), and Henry VIII (Oberon) occur at the end of the story (St. 75).

So Queen Elizabeth is furnished with two genealogies, one supposedly historic, through the British kings, and one purely in the fairy line. In the face of this it is surely impossible to distinguish clearly (as Greenlaw and others try to do) between British and fairy knights, or to see any subtle significance behind the distinction between Britain and Fairy Land. The Britain of *The Faerie Queene* is England, and so is Fairy Land. British knights are symbolically English champions, and fairy knights no less. Gloriana stands for Elizabeth the historic Tudor princess, on the one hand; and on the other for Elizabeth the half-magical object of a nation's devotion. And this is hardly *allegory* at all. It is a piece of legendary and historical machinery, immensely important in most epic poetry, which links the supposed time of the story both backward to a still remoter past and forward to the present. It gives *The Faerie Queene* its extremely un-Italian, autochthonously British air, while at the same time assimilating it in spirit to the Latin and Italian poems that were its forerunners.

The second element in the historical "allegory" (if we are to call it allegory) is the intermittent allusion to contemporary events and persons. It has been a happy hunting ground for fruitless and misguided ingenuity. Some of the allusions were naturally recognized in Spenser's own day; but the idea that all the principal knights are contemporary portraits has no Elizabethan authority; it goes back no further than Dryden. Dryden, in the *Discourse on the Original and Progress of Satire* in 1693, said that "the original of every knight was then living in the court of Queen Elizabeth; and he attributed to each of them that virtue which he thought most conspicuous in them." Dryden must have got the idea from Spenser's dedicatory sonnets to *The Faerie Queene,* in which a number of famous persons are promised immortality by the poet. But carefully read, the sonnets do not bear this interpretation. The immortality promised by the poet is guaranteed by the rehearsing of these distinguished names in the sonnets themselves, and by their association with so great a subject. However, the idea of *The Faerie Queene* as a historical and political *roman à clef* was continued by Warton, by the early editors Upton and Todd, and confirmed by Sir Walter Scott. The principal modern monument of this line of thinking is Miss Winstanley's edition of Book I, which treats the whole book as a disguised transcript of Tudor history. And there is a mass of what I suppose must be called scholarship, aimed at identifying the principal characters, of a particularly contentious and inconclusive kind.

Let us admit that an element of allusion to contemporary history is inescapable in reading the poem. The identification of Duessa with Mary Queen of Scots was made in Elizabethan times. There are prolonged and unmistakable references to events in Ireland and the Low Countries in Book V. Less certainly, but still fairly obviously, the Timias-Belphoebe story seems both to present a somewhat idealized version of the Queen's displeasure with Sir Walter Ralegh; and to suggest a happy termination. But to pursue such identifications very far is both uncertain and poetically unilluminating. Some of Artegall's enterprises clearly glance at the those of Lord Grey in Ireland. Some on the other hand do not; they refer to the wars in the Low Countries in which Leicester and not Lord Grey was engaged. If we care to think that Leicester is somewhat allusively celebrated in Arthur, Sidney in Calidore, we may. But if we try to multiply and elaborate these allusions we shall find ourselves taken farther away from the poem, not closer to its heart. Those who go too far find themselves near the territory inhabited by measurers of the Great Pyramid and discoverers of cryptograms in Shakespeare.

Glorification of England and her queen through history and legend, passing allusions, sometimes more sustained, to the splendors and miseries and conflicts of the day—all this is a part of the intricate web of *The Faerie Queene*. But it is not a sustained historical allegory. If it is to be called allegory at all it is only an intermittent and occasional strain. But a better term, as Greenlaw has suggested, would be historical allusion. And the best way to deal with it is to appreciate it where it is evident, for what it is worth, as part of a crowded and complex pattern, one of the elements which helps to give such density to the whole; and to be at no great pains to look for it where it does not make its presence plain.

VI

In speaking of the structure of *The Faerie Queene* we have compared its organization to that of a dream; we must now continue this argument into the allegory. If we believe that dreams have meaning at all (as by now we surely must), there is an obvious parallel between dream and allegory. The *dream-content,* as Freud calls it (the manifest content), is used to represent in a disguised form the *dream-thoughts* (latent content).[25] Thus the dream-content corresponds to what in allegory we have called image, the dream-thoughts to what we have called theme. In much allegory however the relation between the two elements is quite unlike that found in dreams. In naïve allegory, and even in developed religious allegory like *Everyman* or *The Pilgrim's Progress,* the image is a simple translation of the theme, by a series of one-to-one correspondences: one element in the theme corresponds to one in the image. (*The Pilgrim's Progress* escapes from naïve allegory not because of any complex relation of theme to image, but because the image-sequence has so much vitality and coherence of its own.) This is not the relation in dreams. One of the principal dream-mechanisms recorded by Freud is *condensation:* one single element in the dream-content corresponds to more than one in the dream-thoughts. To transfer this to our terms for allegory one element in the image refers to more than one element in the theme. Even from the limited observations we have made already it will be apparent that Spenser often proceeds in this way. I will now try to illustrate this in more detail.

The most obvious illustration is that in so many places there is a double reference—to the moral or psychic life in general, and to particular historical events. The attempt to read Book I as a transcript of Tudor history is strained and uncertain; but clearly a strong strain of allusion to the English reformation runs through it. The Red Cross Knight is Holiness, fighting against the temptations and errors that must universally beset such a virtue. But he is also, more intermittently and imprecisely, English religion (why else should he bear St. George's cross?) struggling against the conspiracies and misdirections of the time, as Spenser saw them. But he is not always Holiness as an achieved state; he is often the universal *miles Christianus,* the militant Christian who must struggle and learn and seek to perfect himself in his journey through the world. Similarly, three themes (not unrelated but certainly distinct) stand behind the figure of Arthur—Magnificence, the historic might and glory of Britain, and the Earl of Leicester. Artegall's adventures are sometimes those of an abstract and general justice, sometimes those of Lord Grey in Ireland.

We have already spoken of the ambiguity of Britomart in another context—of her way of stepping beyond her allegorical role. But what is her allegorical role? She represents Chastity, in Spenser's special sense of the word, but not exclusively that. She represents also a quite complex Renaissance ideal of female *virtù* (*virtù* meaning strength and energy, not virtue) which Spenser was familiar with through the virago heroines of the Italian epic, and which has nothing to do with chastity at all.

We are of course meant to admire both equally; but there are times when this kind of dual or multiple significance can introduce a moral ambiguity as well. Duessa in Book I is the embodiment of falsehood, outwardly fair but in reality hideous and deformed. When she reappears in Book V a whole cluster of notions connected with Mary Queen of Scots has become attached to her. She is still falsehood, and still to be rejected, but she is also misguided beauty, and a decided element of sympathy for the unhappy queen as a woman has crept into the *significatio.* I do not wish to enter into the vexed question of the Bower of Bliss at this point, except to remark that it cannot represent a simple concept. The idea sometimes put forward that Spenser was secretly on Acrasia's side is obviously wrong; but it could hardly have arisen if the allegory of the bower were a totally unambiguous affair. There *is* an element of indulged and happy voluptuousness in the description of Acrasia's abode, that takes us back to Tasso's Armida, Spenser's principal source. And Armida at the end of the *Gerusalemme Liberata* is not rejected but forgiven.

Frequently, then, more than one theme lies behind the same image, and this is one of the features of *The Faerie Queene* that assimilates it most closely to the dream. "The construction of collective and composite personages is one of the principal methods of dream-condensation," as Freud puts it. I do not believe that we should avert our eyes from this, or try to explain away any ambiguities to which it may give rise. Spenser's moral attitude as a man may have been unambiguous enough, but an element of ambiguity is an essential part of his imaginative procedure. This means in fact that there is a far greater quantity of psychic material behind Spenser's romance-figures than a simple translation of them into the obvious moral terms would suggest.

It is worth noting that Spenser's multiple significance is quite unlike the medieval four levels of meaning as applied to the interpretation of Scripture, and Spenser shows no sign of being aware of this tradition.

> Littera gesta docet,
> Quid credas allegoria,
> Moralis quid agas,
> Quo tendas anagogia.

The literal sense, that is, is concerned with historical facts, the allegorical with belief, the moral with right action, and the anagogical with man's last end. Now Spenser's literal sense is not historical; his historical allusions are always concealed. He is concerned with *quid credas* only in Book I; and even there it is *how* we should believe, and how act on our belief, rather than *what* we should believe that is his main subject. The whole book is based on the necessity of cleaving to truth, and what happens when we depart from it; but truth is never given any doctrinal content. The moral sense, *quid agas,* is of course omnipresent; the right conduct of life in this world is Spenser's real field. But anagogia, *quo tendas,* man's last end, only appears directly in the vision of the heavenly city in I. x, and in the two lovely closing stanzas at the end of the Mutability cantos. The grades of reference for Spenser's allegory are not the medieval ones, they are the romantic, the historical, the moral and the psychological. And in the simpler and less developed parts, that is in the minor characters who are mere narrative or thematic conveniences—Sansfoy, Sansjoy and Sansloy, Furor, Occasio, etc.—the underlying sense is always the moral one.

A second feature of the dream-process mentioned by Freud is

the converse of condensation—it is that an individual dream-thought may be represented by several different elements in the dream-content. Or again to translate this into terms of allegory, a single theme can issue in several images. Freud is not particularly clear about this in *The Interpretation of Dreams;* but he illustrates an aspect of it more fully in the essay "Character Types in Analytic Work" in Vol. IV of the *Collected Papers;* and any student of recorded dreams will be familiar with the way that a single idea appears in the dream under various guises. This happens in Spenser too, and it has sometimes disquieted his commentators. Legouis remarks that Red Cross, who is Holiness, goes to the House of Holiness; that Guyon who is Temperance goes to the Castle of Temperance. Pride appears twice over in Book I, as Lucifera and Orgoglio. True we can explain this if we will; Red Cross and Guyon, besides standing for their respective virtues, are also their yet imperfect human embodiments; Lucifera and Orgoglio are two different kinds of pride. But the resemblance to the dream-mechanism can hardly be missed.

Often in the dream a single character is split up into its several components, who are exhibited in the dream-content as separate figures. There are places where Spenser seems to be working on the same lines. It is often remarked that it is not easy to give any simple allegorical interpretation of the principal woman-figures in Books III and IV. This is probably because they are dissociated parts of the total image of woman. The most obvious dissociated character of this kind is Amoret-Belphoebe. Twin sisters given totally opposite educations, one brought up by Venus, the other by Diana, they stand for two opposed aspects of womanhood—woman as the overflowing fountain of love, and woman as the virgin, the solitary, the untouchable. Their sisterly relationship makes this particularly clear; but I should be inclined to go farther and include Florimell in this group-figure—Florimell who stands for woman as the object of desire, and who herself splits into two; the true Florimell, the right object of love; and the false Florimell, its factitious and deceiving semblance. We could include Britomart too—the active virtue of womanhood; and perhaps we should; all that forbids it is that she is a so much more developed figure in her own right.

Amoret, Belphoebe and Florimell are all aspects of the idea of woman. They do not represent virtues; they cannot be translated into clear-cut moral qualities at all. They are both more and less than that; more because they represent the unconscious, unformulated psychic background, out of which morals and virtue are yet to be developed; less because they are severally incomplete. They are a composite portrait of the anima, and they have their curious, unseizable charm not because they are romance-heroines, or not mainly for that reason, but because each is a glimpse and only a glimpse of the total image of womanhood that dominated Spenser's imagination.

Lastly (for I wish to make these dream-analogies suggestive rather than exhaustive) Freud inquires how logical relations can be represented in dreams. "What representation," he asks, "do 'if,' 'because,' 'as though,' 'although,' 'either-or,' and all the other conjunctions without which we cannot construct either a phrase or a sentence, receive in our dreams?" And he finds that the dream has no direct means of exhibiting these. Causal relations are expressed in dreams by mere succession; alternatives by taking both members of the alternative into the same context. In fact the ample array of logical relations is reduced to a simple parataxis; apparently discrete events simply occur one after another. This is of course characteristic of romance-literature in general. Malory's typical conjunction is "and." But Malory's "and" rarely means anything more; Spenser's temporal sequences often do imply more—or to put it in a fuller form, what appears as temporal sequence in the image conceals another relation, usually causality, in the theme. Immediately after the Red Cross Knight is separated from Una or Truth (I. i) he meets with Duessa or Falsehood. This appears as mere temporal sequence in the story, but thematically it is a matter of cause and effect. It is *because* he has been separated from Truth that the knight falls into the company of Falsehood. We take the meaning without noticing the mechanism because the narrative sequence is so much the expected one; having lost one lady the romance-hero naturally meets another one. Sometimes however the sequence of images conceals a thematic meaning that is less obvious. It is on her wedding day "before the bride was bedded" (IV. i. 3) that Amoret was stolen away from Scudamour by Busirane. Busirane has never cherished any designs on Amoret before; in the image-sequence this appears as an uncaused, inconsequential calamity. Thematically it means that *because* of the wedding she was stolen away; it is *because* their consummation is so much desired and is so close that the lady is tortured and her lover frustrated by the perverse cruelty of amour-passion.

Other relations similarly find expression in dream-fashion. *Although* Guyon is attracted by the loveliness of the Bower of Bliss he knows it must be destroyed and destroys it. The "although" hardly finds expression in the narrative; there is simply an abrupt temporal transition, astonishing to most readers, from the manifest seductions of the bower (II. xii. 70–78) to its sudden, hastily described overthrow (83). Alternatives likewise: woman's beauty as the object of desire can be either true beauty (the outward expression of gentleness, innocence, and chastity), or its false simulacrum (the outward covering of flightiness, greed, and untruth); and this is expressed by the two Florimells, absolutely indistinguishable in appearance. What appears then in *The Faerie Queene* as the simple alogical sequaciousness of naïve romance conceals a wealth of more complex thematic relations; and meaning must be sought almost as often in these relations as in the isolated signification of individual figures.

. . . To make an end of this general discussion we should try to sum up the special distinguishing characters of Spenser's allegory. In the first place, it *is* allegory, not symbolism in either a Blakean or a Mallarmean sense; nor fully incarnate literature like Shakespeare. It is of very varying degrees of explicitness, ranging from naïve allegory to romance with only the vaguest thematic significance. It is discontinuous—the general directing allegory announced in the Letter is only faintly developed, and the greatest allegorical intensity is reached in certain of the local stories. And as we have seen there were models of this kind near to Spenser's hand in the allegorizing of Ariosto. The allegory is in the most important places multivalent; it is on the whole only the minor characters who have a single simple allegorical significance. And last, in some ways most important, and to some readers most difficult to accept, it proceeds by loosely associative, half-unconscious methods like those of the dream, rather than by the rigorous translation of clearly formulated conceptual ideas. All the thematic content of *The Pilgrim's Progress* could have been as easily formulated in a sermon. This is true of parts of *The Faerie Queene,* but in all the best parts the thematic content finds its only possible embodiment in the actual image-sequence that the poem presents. And the poem is both—theme and image in perpetually shifting relations, variously interwoven, sometimes perceived separately, often talked of separately as a matter of expository convenience; but ultimately indissoluble.

Notes

1. *Poetry and Prose of William Blake,* ed. Geoffrey Keynes (1927), p. 810.

2. Appendix B to *The Statesman's Manual* (1816).

3. *Essays* (1924), p. 142.

4. *The Allegory of Love* (1936), p. 44.

5. *Some Figures in Langland's Vision.* Paper given at the Conference of the International Association of University Professors of English, Lausanne, 1959. I have only seen an abstract of this.

6. Northrop Frye, *The Anatomy of Criticism* (Princeton, 1957), p. 91.

7. W. J. Courthope, *History of English Poetry,* II (1897), 248.

8. See S. E. Sandys, *History of Classical Scholarship,* I (1903), 29 *seq.;* and E. R. Curtius, *European Literature and the Latin Middle Ages,* tr. Willard Trask (1953), pp. 203–207.

9. Sandys, *op. cit.,* p. 147.

10. *In P. Virgilii Maronis Allegorias,* printed with Hortensius *In Virgilium* (Basel, 1577), p. 3000 *seq.*

11. *Ibid.,* p. 3007.

12. The first edition with "allegories" attached was published at Venice in 1542.

13. These allegorizers of Ariosto are discussed by S. J. McMurphy in *Spenser's Use of Ariosto for Allegory* (Seattle, 1924). Miss McMurphy was in error in supposing that Porcacchi's allegories came too late to be used by Spenser. They first appeared in 1568, and were several times reprinted. Oratio Toscanella's *Bellezze del Furioso* was printed at Venice in 1574.

14. Simone Fornari, *La Spositione sopra l'Orlando Furioso* (first part Florence, 1549; second part Florence, 1550).

15. Sir John Harington, *Orlando Furioso in English heroical verse* (1591). See the preface "or rather a Briefe Apologie of Poetry" prefixed to the translation, and the Allegory of the Poem appended to it. This latter is mostly from Fornari. The preface is also reprinted in G. Gregory Smith's *Elizabethan Critical Essays* (1904).

16. Though in fact *pudicizia* appears as Shamefastness in the House of Alma.

17. I quote from Fairfax's translation of *G.L.* (1600). The Allegory is to be found on p. 436 *seq.* of Henry Morley's edition of Fairfax (1890).

18. Henry Peacham, *The Garden of Eloquence* (1593), p. 25. (This is the second edition.)

19. Angel Day, *The English Secretarie* (n.d., but actually 1595), Part II, p. 79.

20. G. Puttenham, *The Art of English Poesie* (1589), Book III, Chap. XVIII. The whole chapter is relevant.

21. Edwin Greenlaw, *Studies in Spenser's Historical Allegory* (Baltimore, 1932).

22. Quoted in Greenlaw, p. 9.

23. Greenlaw, Chap. I.

24. It is noticeable that though Malory was read, he exerted little influence in Tudor times. It is the historical British Arthur, not the hero of French romances, that the Elizabethans cared for. Hence the absence of direct debt to Malory in Spenser.

25. All the features of the dream-process referred to here are described in Chapter VI of Freud's *Interpretation of Dreams.* I have used A. A. Brill's translation (1913).

A. C. Hamilton

The Nature of Spenser's Allegory

. . . I SHALL ANALYZE . . . from Spenser's poem . . . the opening episode in which the Red Cross Knight defeats Error. I shall compare it, since we have been considering the art of reading allegory, to the opening episode of Dante's *Commedia*. These are the only two major classics in modern literature which were conceived by their authors as allegories; yet, strangely enough, they have never been brought into any significant relationship.

Studies in the allegory of each work proceed independently, and what we understand by Dante's claim that his poem is polysemous has not been related to Spenser's similar claim that his poem is "a continued Allegory, or darke conceit." Our most distinguished Dante critic, C. S. Singleton, turns to the *Romance of the Rose* and Ariosto, he even puts Bunyan and Milton together in the vain effort to get Dante's kind of allegory and ignores Spenser.[1] Yet Dante's "allegory of theologians," for which he argues so cogently, is uniquely paralleled by *The Faerie Queene* Book I. Spenser's critics, on the other hand, have considered only Dante's possible influence upon him, finding nothing sure. In the past there have been strong reasons for failing to connect the two poets, though they should not prevail now. Earlier critics made a barrier of age, the historical watershed dividing the medieval Catholic world from the Protestant Renaissance. Now we recognize that the watershed comes later, between us and the two poets. A stronger reason has been the differences between their traditions: Dante writes within a medieval theological tradition, Spenser within a Renaissance humanist tradition of the rediscovered classics. Though these differences are real, Spenser's tradition, as expressed in Sidney's *Apology,* regards Dante as the ideal poet. In defining the right poet as one who creates a golden world, Sidney cites Dante as one "hauing all, from . . . his heauen to hys hell, vnder the authoritie of his penne."[2] But more important, each poem makes an imaginative leap from anything that comes before. It was a leap which makes comparison of Dante with the *Romance of the Rose* ineffectual, and of Spenser with Ariosto mockery. Even with their own previous allegorical works, the *Convivio* and *The Shepherds Calender,* there is a difference of kind. I believe that it is a leap which brings them together.

Unless these poets write a common language of allegory, there is little we may ever understand about the genre; but if they do, comparison of the opening episodes of each poem should be mutually illuminating. At first the differences in matter and method may seem too striking. Dante's Wood is nasty, brutish, rough (to adapt Hobbes's relevant phrase), and fills his heart with fear; Spenser's is a pleasant Wood where the knight and his lady are beguiled with delight. Dante describes in concrete and very real terms a man of flesh and blood who is defeated by fear and doubt until Virgil aids him; Spenser uses allegorical devices of a chivalric combat between an armed knight and a monster which personifies Error. But such differences are not essential. Spenser's Wood is also dark, for the enshrouding trees "heauens light did hide, / Not perceable with power of any starre" and leads to the monster's "darksome hole."[3] That Beatrice sends Virgil to aid Dante, and that Una accompanies her knight, reflect rather differences of religious faith than of poetical method. (The differences of method are more apparent than real, but I leave this point until later.) Moreover, these differences do not rule out striking similarities. In larger terms each episode presents an image of one lost in a Wood where he confronts certain monsters (Dante's three beasts, Spenser's threefold enemy in the woman-serpent with her brood) and is overcome by error and doubt. Dante is driven back into the dark pass where he struggles with death until Beatrice aids him: Spenser's knight wanders until he comes to the dark den where he is almost slain before Una aids him. (The *donna . . . beata e bella* and the "louely Ladie" clearly suggest God's grace.) Then both begin their Exodus—the one treading that pass which had allowed none to go alive ("che non lasciò già mai persona viva") and the other taking by-ways "where neuer foot of liuing wight did tread" (I. vii. 50)—until they are restored to the heavenly Jerusalem. Essentially, then, each episode is an initiation: the candidate wanders in a labyrinth or maze which prepares him for his salvation. It initiates the poet also by committing him to his kind of allegory. Further, it initiates the reader by offering a brief allegory of what is to come, and by teaching him the art of reading allegory.

The literal level of an allegory seems the most difficult to read properly. Does the fiction exist in its own right, or is it a veil which must be torn aside to reach the allegorical levels beneath? The latter has been the usual fashion in which to read not only Spenser, as we have seen, but also Dante. Modern Dante criticism recognizes, however, that the *Commedia* does not respond to such allegorizing. On this subject Professor Hatzfeld writes:

> In passages where . . . the allegorical sense *is* the literal one, the reader is even less entitled to ask extratextual and biographical questions, such as whether the dark wood means heresy, or fornication, or pursuit of worldly honors in Dante's life, or whether the leopard means Florence and the lion Charles of Valois. These questions refer only to potentialities, namely, Dante's life as raw material, and abandon the actually achieved world of Dante's poetical symbolism. In other words, the new Dante interpretation makes a strong point of the fact that Dante in his poetry (not in his prose) overcomes the usual mediaeval allegorism and fuses personal, theological, political, moral, even astronomical elements into symbols of a decidedly poetical and not didactic quality.[4]

But not modern Spenser criticism where, as we have seen, the poem's literal level is still translated into moral precept and historical example. We are told that in the episode of the Wandering Wood, the knight is Holiness, Una is Truth, Error is obvious error: *ergo,* the episode means that Holiness defeats Error with the aid of Truth. We are told this by the critics, not by Spenser who does not name the knight, nor the lady, and describes the monster in very real terms. Again without support from the text, we are told that the knight is England, Una is the true Church, Error is the Church of Rome: *ergo,* the episode means that England passed successfully through the dangers of Reformation.[5] Since both poems share a similar critical history—contemporary praise for their profound meaning, the neoclassical eclipse, the romantic age's rejection of the allegory for lyrical beauty (Livingston Lowes on Spenser, Croce on Dante), and yesterday's search for hidden meanings—probably Spenser criticism needs to catch up.

What seems so perverse about translating the literal level is that Spenser, like Dante, labors to render the fiction in its own right. It is an image presented in realistic and visual detail. There is the precise detail of the monster's huge tail wound about the knight's body, his strangling her gorge, her filthy vomit, the serpents swarming about his legs, and the final gruesome beheading. There is the exact rendering of the monster "vpon the durtie ground," her brood "sucking vpon her poisonous dugs," her vomit "full of great lumpes of flesh and gobbets raw." The details are immediately repulsive to all the senses: to the *sight* with the monster half-serpent, half-woman, and her deformed brood sucking up her blood; to the *hearing* with the monster's loud braying and her brood "groning full deadly"; to the *smell* with the "deadly stinke" of her vomit; to the *taste* with the violent spewing of the flood of poison; and to the *touch* with the monster's tail strangling him. The realism of the episode is enforced by its dramatic action: the monster's brood creeping into her mouth "and suddain all were gone," her rushing forth and retreating before the knight, the brilliant chiaroscuro effect of the knight's armor which casts "a litle glooming light, much like a shade" into Error's dark hole, the brood with "bowels gushing forth." This monster has all the terrible reality of a nightmare, and even Fuseli who saw the nightmare could complain that "when Spenser dragged into light the entrails of the serpent slain by the Red Knight, he dreamt a butcher's dream and not a poet's."[6] Clearly the poet labors to make us see. His whole effort is to render a clearly-defined, exact, and visual image. No less than with Dante, Spenser's reader must respect the primacy and integrity of the poem's literal level.

Whatever the differences of their critical traditions, both poets clearly demand that the reader focus upon this literal level. For Dante it may be enough to point (as Mr. Singleton does) to Holy

Scripture with its insistence upon the literal level. For the Renaissance poet there is the classically-derived doctrine that the poet gathers precept and example into a poetic image which he makes us see; and behind this doctrine is the Neoplatonic faith that if man once sees virtues and vices, he will embrace the one and shun the other. For the Protestant poet there is also the renewed emphasis upon the Bible's literal sense. But they may share a simpler basis for insisting upon the literal level of their poems. Ever since Plato, poets have recognized that they deliver fiction rather than truth or morality. In the *Convivio* Dante claims that "the literal sense ought always to come first, as being that sense in the expression of which the others are all included, and without which it would be impossible and irrational to give attention to the other meanings, and most of all to the allegorical." Further, the highest allegorical sense, the anagogic, sustains and illuminates the literal by seeing in it the poem's total meaning: "this occurs when a writing is spiritually expounded, which even in the literal sense by the things signified likewise gives intimation of higher matters belonging to the eternal glory." [7] The corresponding Renaissance claim is Sidney's doctrine that "in Poesie, looking but for fiction [that is, *only* for fiction and not allegorical truth], they [the readers] shal vse the narration but as an imaginatiue groundplot of a profitable inuention." [8] Since the fiction is the groundplot for readers of both Dante and Spenser, to strip it away leaves the poem barren. As readers we must respect what they have given us. To read their allegories we must accept as given that Dante's matter is a history of what happened to him, and that Spenser's "History" (he insists upon the term) is "matter of iust memory" (II. Pr. 1).

But how may we understand their opening episodes? Not according to the usual medieval or Renaissance theories of allegory: these, with their stress upon levels of allegorical meaning, only distract. If we seek more clear authority for the art of reading than the *Letter to Can Grande* and the *Apology for Poetry* provide, we must begin with the poems themselves, with the fact that each within its tradition is a separate kind of allegory which demands its own kind of reading. And this provides the clue we need. The opening episode of each poem defines the art of reading the allegory. The initiation which is described here both separates and joins: it separates the candidate from us, from our way of life, and enters him upon a pilgrimage which is treated in the rest of the poem. It follows that there are two ways of understanding. The first is outward, that extrinsic meaning which relates the episode (and the poem) to our world; the second is intrinsic, that inner coherence which binds all parts of the poem. Allegory's unique power is achieved through the contrapuntal relationship between the poem's world and our world, and by the centripetal relationship of its parts. More comprehensively and significantly than other genres, it points beyond itself and also to itself. The brazen world of fallen nature and the poem's golden world, reality and the ideal, fact and fiction become united in our reading.

In their opening episodes both poets exploit the metaphor of the labyrinth or maze, of one wandering lost in a Wood where he encounters beasts. Dante's source has been found in Horace's *Satires*,[9] Spenser's in medieval romance; but the more likely source is Holy Scripture. There we learn that Wisdom (with whom Beatrice and Una are identified) "wil walke with him [her lover] by crooked waies, and bring him vnto feare, and dread, and torment him with her discipline vntill shee haue tried his soule, and haue proued him by her iudgementes. Then will she returne the streight way vnto him, and comfort him, and shew him her secrets." [10] But the metaphor is universal, too centrally archetypal to be traced to any source. Or if any, it is that of Christ who, after His baptism, entered the Wilderness where He was with the wild beasts during his initiation into the role of Redeemer. (Dante's baptism is signified by the metaphor of the lake in which he struggles, the knight's baptism by the spiritual armor which he dons.) The Renaissance poet may mingle classical myth with Scripture: the labyrinthine wood with the monster in the middle invokes the myth of Theseus who enters the labyrinth to slay the Minotaur in the middle, and is guided out by Ariadne's thread. He may do so because Christ is the true Theseus who slew monsters, and the Word is "the thread that will direct us through the winding and intricate labyrinths of this life." [11]

Singelton has shown Dante's complex use of this metaphor, how it is designed to locate us by showing the way of our life.[12] It is *our* life, as Dante's opening line suggests, but his experience in the Wood is unique. He becomes lost only when he separates himself from the common herd, from our life, through love of Beatrice. As Christian alone in the City of Destruction knows that he bears upon his back the burden which plunges him deeper into hell, Dante in the Dark Wood is forced by the beasts back into the darkness.[13] In the beginning when he is with us, he is nameless; he may begin to find himself only by losing himself, that is, by finding himself lost; and finally Beatrice will restore him to himself, and name him Dante. As in Bunyan where the pilgrim in our city is anonymous—after he enters the way of salvation he is named Christian—and in Spenser where the knight is not named until after he endures the first test. We may say, then, that Dante's poem arises out of its opening episode: once he realizes the horror of our way of life, he is prepared to be initiated into a new way of life.

Spenser also exploits the metaphor in order to locate us within our world. When the knight has been chosen by Una and the Faery Queen, he goes out "to winne him worship, and her grace to haue" until the tempest drives every one into hiding: "euery wight to shrowd it did constrain, / And this faire couple eke to shroud themselues were fain." All seek the shady grove where "all within were pathes and alleies wide, / With footing worne, and leading inward farre." The ominous phrase, "so in they entred arre," announces the beginning of his initiation (literally, *inire,* to enter in). Within the Wood they no longer lead their way, but passively are led: "led with delight" they "wander too and fro in wayes vnknowne":

> That path they take, that beaten seemd most bare,
> And like to lead the labyrinth about;
> Which when by tract they hunted had throughout,
> At length it brought them to a hollow caue,
> Amid the thickest woods.

This is the path which "euery wight" takes, but none returns. In the first stage of the initiation the candidates (both Dante and Spenser's knight) wander as we do in our life.

In the second stage they are proven worthy of being chosen. To pass this test separates them from us. In Canto II Dante's spirit is so overwhelmed by cowardice that he withdraws from what he has begun. Virgil abjures him:

> L'anima tua è da viltate offesa,
> La qual molte fiate l'omo ingombra,
> Sì che d'onrata impresa lo rivolve,
> Come falso veder bestia, quand' ombra.

Dante is freed from all doubts of his worthiness only after he is told by Virgil how Beatrice cares for him. Only through faith in her compassion may he enter upon his journey. (These doubts recur at the beginning of his final ascent, the "dubbi" of *Paradiso* IV, but Beatrice herself is there to resolve them.) In Spenser the knight wanders lost (that is, he is overcome by Error) and in doubt—"the place vnknowne and wilde, / Breedes dreadfull doubts"—until he so persists that he sees Error herself. The battle with this monster is described in terms of her labyrinthine tail which "her den all ouerspred, / Yet was in knots and many boughtes vpwound, / Pointed with mortall sting," for this is the labyrinth which he must overcome. In the encounter his courage is first overcome—l'anima tua è da viltate offesa—and he retreats. Only when the lady intercedes with the injunction: "add faith vnto your force, and be not faint," does he slay the monster. Then the brood, the doubts bred by the earlier experience in the Wood, "him encombred sore"—la qual molte fiate l'omo ingombra—but with the death of Error they cannot hurt him and only destroy themselves. Spenser's remark during the battle, "God helpe the man so wrapt in *Errours* endlesse traine," points to our life here: this monster will devour us, as she devours all who take the beaten path to her den, unless God helps us. But when God intercedes through the Lady, the knight may go "forward on his way (with God to frend)." Then he is no longer led by the path, but keeps it:

> That path he kept, which beaten was most plaine,
> Ne euer would to any by-way bend,
> But still did follow one vnto the end.

(The straight march of the concluding line demonstrates his victory over the labyrinth.) In Una's address to him:

> Well worthy be you of that Armorie,
> Wherein ye haue great glory wonne this day,
> And proou'd your strength on a strong enimie,
> Your first aduenture,

the repetition of "you" and "your" emphasizes that the battle proves him worthy his armor.[14] (Yet worthy only within his armor: "that Armorie, / *Wherein* ye haue great glory wonne": at first he uses "all his force" to free himself from the monster, but defeats her only when he "strooke at her with *more then manly force.*") His worthiness which is sealed by his faith sets him apart from us, even as Dante is commended by the Virgin as "il tuo fedele." Through this victory over the world, that is, over our way of life, both Dante and Spenser's knight are initiated into their pilgrimage.

Dante's poetic method may seem to differ radically from Spenser's. Dante renders the experience directly as his own; he describes dramatically and concretely the fear and agony which he suffers in the Wood. In contrast, Spenser leaves the given for the less real: rather than describe a man in error and doubt, he shows a wandering knight battling with Error. These are the terms in which C. S. Lewis has taught us to regard allegory.[15] And such abstract personification, we say, is alien to the reality of Dante's poem. But what, in fact, does Spenser do? In similarly dramatic and concrete terms, he shows a man confronting a monster; and in the immediate visual terms which we have noted earlier, he describes the physical impact of the battle. His "Allegoricall deuices" serve to sharpen the sense of reality; they add to it; and render it more "real." Spenser's metaphor is overt: to yield to the world is to wander in an enchanting Wood; to seek the way out—how difficult it is to avoid metaphor!—is to battle a woman serpent. Dante's metaphor is half-submerged, but it is no less present. Beatrice sees Dante struggling with death: "non vedi tu la morte che 'l combatte / Su la fiumana ove 'l mar non ha vanto." This is the sea which Dante struggles to leave:

> E come quei che, con lena affannata,
> Uscito fuor del pelago a la riva,
> Si volge a l'acqua perigliosa e guata;

and Virgil, in the lines quoted previously, sees Dante's spirit *encumbered* with cowardice, *stricken* by doubts. Once Dante accepts Virgil as his guide, the beast no longer forces him back into the dolorous pass. In effect he has "slain" the beast. Metaphorically? yes. But it is all metaphor: the Dark Wood, the beasts, even (though in a different way) Hell itself, the Wandering Wood, the monster with her brood, the dungeon of Orgoglio. Dante's three beasts are emblems of the three stages of his journey through Hell. Spenser's monster is an emblem of Error; but what does Error signify? Not vice, nor any simple psychological state such as we meet in the personifications of other poets. Error is all that which stands between the knight and his entering upon his salvation, that is, Hell itself and the death which he must suffer before he may be reborn. The dragon-figure suggests this all-encompassing significance, as it does again in the knight's final antagonist. More simply, Error is what Dante means by the Dark Wood and the three beasts.

Spenser's treatment is more sophisticated largely because his age allowed him to be.[16] For one thing, his knight is more obviously an ideal pattern of what man should be. His entrance into the enchanting wood where he slays the woman-serpent invokes the analogy to Adam who, at the beginning of his quest, centered the Garden of Eden where the enchantress Eve joined with the serpent conspired his fall. (Eden was traditionally linked with the labyrinth,[17] and in medieval-Renaissance iconography the woman-serpent is the common emblem for Satan.) As Adam was tempted by the fruit of the knowledge of good and evil, the knight is first overcome by the serpent's vomit "full of bookes and papers." [18] Through faith, however, the knight defeats the serpent-Eve and enters the path which leads to his salvation. But in one way Spenser's treatment is more primitive than Dante's. He uses the symbol of the cave which traditionally signifies rebirth. Yet surely Dante's metaphor of the struggle in the water suggests another primitive metaphor, such as that used in *Beowulf* where the hero grapples with the sea monster.

Besides this significant pointing to our world, the initiation described in the opening episode of each poem points inward to the poem's world. In Dante, as Mr. Singleton has shown, it serves as prologue.[19] The three beasts represent the three stages of descent into Hell, Beatrice reveals the role which the poem fulfills, and Dante's journey here corresponds to his journey through Hell. Thus it stands by itself as a brief epic, a "dumb show" revealing the argument of the drama which will unfold. Virgil saves Dante from the beasts, as later he will guide him through Hell. It is Beatrice who persuades him to begin his journey, as later she brings him to his final salvation. Spenser's opening episode points inward in the same significant way to the world of his poem. The woman-serpent is later revealed as Duessa, the "goodly Lady" with "her neather partes misshapen, monstruous," and by the composite symbol of Duessa upon the Dragon. The knight's victory over Error is an emblem, then, of his final victory over Duessa and the Dragon. Here Una reveals the role which the poem fulfills, as later she prepares the knight to battle the Dragon by leading him to the house of Holiness where he is confirmed in faith. As Dante leaves the labyrinth to enter the descending circles of Hell, the knight leaves the Wood only to lose faith in Una through Archimago's false vision, and to wander lost, "all in amaze" upon that path which leads him into Orgoglio's dungeon. After his rescue by Arthur, as he girds himself for the second stage of his journey—it is also an ascent through Purgatory—he meets Despair. By using the same allegorical language, Spenser places the two scenes in close correspondence. As Error is "a monster vile, whom God and man does hate," Despair is "a man of hell," a "Snake in hidden weedes." The one lives in a "darksome hole" in the thickest woods, the other in a "darkesome caue" among "old stockes and stubs of trees." [20] Again the knight must enter the cave and fight the monster. But while the first struggle was outward and physical, this is inward and spiritual. It takes place within his conscience; therefore the labyrinth he treads is intellectual. Error's vomit of books and papers appears in Despair's learning. Earlier he wanders in a maze until Error's "huge traine / All suddenly about his body wound," now he wonders in amazement until Despair's arguments charm him in "his guilefull traine." [21] Against Error Una urges him to "shew what ye bee": now she reminds him what he is, one chosen by God. As before, she offers faith, that is, faith in God's mercy. Each encounter tests the knight: the earlier proves him worthy his armor, the later to be worthy as one chosen by God.

More than this, we may say, in Singleton's phrase, that Spenser's opening scene also "figured and forecast, as well as any single scene might do, the whole configuration of the journey beyond." The knight's token entrance into the cave—he only looks in—is fulfilled later when he descends into the dark depths of Orgoglio's dungeon. Through Una's intercession again, he is redeemed when Arthur makes his deep descent to restore him to light. Later he pays tribute to her "whose wondrous faith, exceeding earthly race, / Was firmest fixt in mine extremest case." Then in his last battle he "descends" into the cave: his sword plunges into the Dragon's mouth which "wide gaped, like the griesly mouth of hell." As he slays Error by adding faith to his force, here his "baptized hands" wielding "his godly armes" defeat the Dragon. The first battle against the Dragon initiates his fall: this last battle initiates him to that restored state signified by his marriage to Una. In the cycle of fall and ascent he progresses from light to darkness to light. But with this difference: that "his glistring armor made / A litle glooming light, much like a shade" as he peers into Error's cave, while at the end "those glistring armes . . . Heauen with light did fill" (I. xi. 4). The opening episode which shows his primal state of innocence becomes a measure of his later descent into sin, and a promise of his final ascent.

The two kinds of reading which we have applied to Dante and Spenser, the one pointing outward to our world, and the other turning inward to the poem's world focus in our single vision of the poem as fiction. That fiction is "an ideal space," as Curtius terms Dante's poem,[22] or a "golden world" in Sidney's phrase. Though allegory usually suggests a way of writing in which one thing is said but another is meant, our poets tell "of Forests, and inchantments drear, / Where *more* is meant then meets the ear."[23] We read the fiction not by translating, but by retaining the fiction as metaphor. Earlier poets had written fiction, but for Dante and Spenser both the matter and form of their poetry were transformed by Holy Scripture. Mr. Singleton has convinced us that Dante imitates Scripture: "the literal sense is given as an historical sense standing in its own right, like Milton's, say—Not devised in order to convey a hidden truth, but given in the focus of single vision."[24] Here Spenser's kind of allegory may seem antithetical to Dante's. Dante moves towards greater reality as his poem proceeds: Spenser moves in an unreal world of giants and dragons where Dr. Johnson would never stub his toe. But what does this difference amount to? Dante's fiction is that his matter is fact; Spenser's fiction is that his matter is romance. The one establishes the illusion of historical reality, the other of faery land. For both poets, their fiction is a metaphor of Holy Scripture. Dante's position is clear; but what of Spenser? To consider briefly the knight's final battle against the Dragon. We say that here Spenser exploits the allegorical devices of the armed knight facing a fire-breathing Dragon while his lady retires to a hill. But where is the truth of this fiction? It is not the moral truth that Holiness defeats Sin or Death, or the historical fact that England defeats the powers of Antichrist. Its truth is given by Holy Scripture. The knight's three-day battle in Eden against the Dragon in order to release Una's parents, Adam and Eve, imitates Christ's harrowing hell, His three-day descent through which mankind is restored to the Tree and Well of Life. The fiction of both poets, then, whether it is given as an historical sense or as romance, is a metaphor of Holy Scripture. Once we see that each poet writes metaphor, then one poem becomes a metaphor of the other. And it is this fact which allows them to be compared.

Once we allow that in reading Spenser's poem we should focus upon the image, rather than upon some idea behind the image, our understanding gathers around our response to the poem's literal level because it arises from it. Our sense of that other reality to which the poem points, by first pointing to itself, grows from our sense of the poem's reality. We may be said to understand—literally to under-stand—the poem because we bear the whole poem in our response. That response is integrated because the intense delight given by the poem determines, at the same time, our understanding of its meaning. Our delight and understanding being integrated, our awareness of the literal and allegorical levels is continuous and simultaneous, and our vision of the poem whole. This simple, yet radical, alteration of focus may be achieved by reading the poem not for its hidden truth but rather for its fiction. Instead of treating the narration as a veil to be torn aside for the hidden meaning, we should allow Sidney's art of reading poetry by using the narration "but as an imaginatiue groundplot of a profitable inuention." Once we allow this art of reading, then Spenser's allegory need not be read as a complicated puzzle concealing riddles which confuse the reader in labyrinths of error, but as an unfolding drama revealing more and greater significance as it brings the reader full understanding of its complex vision.

Notes

1. *Dante Studies,* I (Harvard, 1954), 13. In commenting upon the Error episode, Upton notes: "I must not forget that Dante opens his poem with this very same allegory." *Spenser's Faerie Queene* (London, 1758), II, 339.

2. Ed. J. Churton Collins (Oxford, 1907), p. 22.

3. All references are to the opening episode of each poem, unless indicated otherwise. For Dante, I cite the edition of *La Divina Commedia,* ed. C. H. Grandgent (New York, rev. ed., 1933).

4. Helmut Hatzfeld, "Modern Dante Criticism," *Comparative Literature,* III (1951), 297–98.

5. See *Variorum Spenser,* I, 422 f., 449 f.

6. See E. C. Mason, *The Mind of Henry Fuseli* (London, 1951), p. 217.

7. *Convivio,* tr. W. W. Jackson (Oxford, 1909), p. 74. See also his letter to Can Grande in *The Letters of Dante,* tr. Paget Toynbee (Oxford, 1920).

8. See the Ponsonby edition, whose version is here less elegant but more explicit, ed. A. S. Cook (Boston, 1890), p. 36.

9. J. H. Whitfield, *Dante and Virgil* (Oxford, 1949), p. 74. Cf. Upton: "What are these trees and labyrinths [of the Wandering Wood], but the various amusements and errors of human life? So Horace and Dante apply the similitude." *Spenser's Faerie Queene,* II, 339.

10. Eccles. iv. 17–18, the Genevan version (London, 1580) which I cite throughout this study. The tropological significance of Spenser's episode, then, is that given by Fulke Greville to Sidney's *Arcadia:* "His end in them was not vanishing pleasure alone, but morall Images, and Examples (as directing threds) to guide every man through the confused *Labyrinth* of his own desires, and life." *Life of Sir Philip Sidney,* ed. Nowell Smith (Oxford, 1907), p. 223.

11. Alexander Ross, *Mystagogus Poeticus* (London, 1647), p. 254.

12. *Dante Studies,* p. 7.

13. Francis Fergusson acutely remarks of Dante's experience: "Once in the terror of the Dark Wood, he had to explore the full import of that experience

before his spirit was free to take another direction." *Dante's Drama of the Mind* (Princeton, 1953), p. 5.

14. It is evident that the episode also proves Spenser worthy of his role as England's heroic poet. The catalog of trees which he so carefully elaborates in stanzas 8 and 9 imitates Chaucer's *Parlement of Foules,* 169–82. It indicates that he now wears the mantle as England's poet. Behind both poets' use of the catalog is Ovid's account of Orpheus, the archetype of the inspired poet, moving trees with his music. The power of Orpheus descends now to Spenser as he begins to create his faery land. Spenser's imitation of Chaucer is all the more apt since the poet in the *Parlement* enters a delightful Wandering Wood where he is overcome by error: "no wit hadde I, for errour to chese, / To entre or flen, or me to save or lese" (146–47). Cf. Affrican's rebuke in 155–56. Since Chaucer is indebted to Dante's opening episode (see J. A. W. Bennett, *The Parlement of Foules* [Oxford, 1957], pp. 63–65), there is a nice historical connection between Spenser and Dante.

15. *The Allegory of Love* (Oxford, 1936), pp. 44 f.

16. His elaborate personification follows Renaissance convention, and in this matter it is pertinent to refer to Harington's preference for Ariosto's personification over Dante's. "This description of the monster of covetousnesse, is (in my fancy) very well handled by mine Author, far beyond the like in *Dant* who maketh her onely like a Wolfe, pined with famine; But *Ariosto* goeth farder, and more significantly, describing her first to be ugly, because of all vices it is the most hatefull; eares of an asse, being for the most part ignorant, or at the least carelesse of other mens good opinions; a Wolfe in head and breast, namely ravenous and never satisfied; a Lions grisly jaw, terrible and devouring; a Foxe in all the rest, wyly and craftie, and timerous of those that are stronger then himselfe; all which applications are so proper and so plaine, as it is needlesse to stand upon them." *Orlando Furioso* (London, 1634), p. 213.

17. Cf. Bartas' account of Adam in the Garden of Eden: "musing, anon through crooked Walks he wanders,/ Round-winding rings, and intricate Meanders,/ False-guiding paths, doubtfull beguiling strays,/ And right-wrong errors of an end-less Maze." *Divine Weekes and Workes,* tr. Sylvester (London, 1633), p. 86. Milton's Adam relates how he "stray'd I knew not whither" at his creation until in vision God comes as his "Guide/ To the Garden of bliss." Once in the garden he is so overcome by its delight that "here had new begun/ My wandring, had not hee who was my Guide/ Up hither, from among the Trees appeer'd/ Presence Divine." *Paradise Lost,* viii. 283, 298–99, 311–14. This is the Red Cross Knight's state of innocence in which he conquers the labyrinth "with God to frend."

18. That human knowledge comes from Satan is Agrippa's argument, and one passage from the *De Vanitate* serves as motto for the Error episode: "Nothinge can chaunce vnto man more pestilente then knowledge: this is the very pestilence, that putteth all mankinde to ruine, the which chaseth awaie all Innocencie, and hath made vs subjecte to so many kindes of sinne, and to death also: whiche hath extinguished the light of Faith, castinge our Soules into blinde darkenesse: which condemninge the truethe, hath placed errours in the hiest throne" (p. 4^r).

19. *Dante Studies,* pp. 5–6.

20. Cf.I.i.13 and I.ix.28; I.i.14 and I.ix.34, 35. After the knight defeats Error, "then mounted he vpon his Steede againe": after he defeats Despair, "vp he rose, and thence amounted streight" (I.i.28; I.ix.54).

21. I.i.18 and I.ix.31.

22. E. R. Curtius, *European Literature and the Latin Middle Ages,* tr. Willard Trask (New York, 1953), p. 18.

23. *Il Penseroso,* 119–20.

24. *Dante Studies,* p. 15.

Frank Kermode

The Cave of Mammon

THE OBJECT of this essay is to expound the seventh Canto of the Second Book of *The Faerie Queene*. There is little agreement as to its interpretation, so the topic has its own interest. But it cannot be treated in isolation from the Second Book as a whole; and since the relation between this mysterious episode and the remainder of the Legend of Temperance seems to be characteristic of Spenser's method throughout *The Faerie Queene,* what I have to say, insofar as it is correct, has a bearing upon the conduct of the entire poem, and in the long run upon certain obscure aspects of Renaissance poetry in general. So I begin with some remarks on that larger topic.

Any reader who has even a slight familiarity with Renaissance allegorical habits will see at a glance that Spenser's epyllion *Muiopotmos* is concerned with the descent of the soul into the captivity of matter as a result of sensuality. He may see other related meanings, some of them debatable; but I think he will not have any doubt about this one. On the other hand, a reader who has no such familiarity will be quite in the dark. He will see, of course, that the story must be allegorical, but at best will invent some sort of historical key for it; as a matter of fact, commentary on *Muiopotmos* was, until quite recently, of this kind. With *The Faerie Queene* the position is incalculably more difficult; there is historical allegory; there is very simple allegory as in the House of Alma and the Castle of Medina passages in this Second Book; but there is also allegory of the kind represented by the Temple of Isis in Book V, the Garden of Adonis in Book III, and the Cave of Mammon. These are not "face-value" allegories, and the confusion of commentary is adequate testimony to the fact. Spenser seems to be assuming a special kind of reader, or rather a special kind of information, and he may also be held to believe that even this community of information will not, however complete and subtle, provide absolute explanations, full translations of image into discourse. The efforts of poets who wrote like this were not merely to discover wisdom but to create it—not merely to benefit by the power of extant mythologies, but to make significant myths of their own. It is a mythopoeic power that we must deal with; if we cannot see Spenser as a myth-maker we shall make very little of his poem. It is all the more important to see this need because Spenser, though he characteristically refers to his whole work as a "dark conceit," does not, like Chapman, boast of the secrecy of his meanings.

Yet, he is, in his way, an esoteric poet; like all poets in the Neoplatonic tradition, not only the guardian of secrets but the creator of new secret wisdom. The position is one that was so familiar to Renaissance poets that to put it out of one's mind is almost certainly to distort one's reading not only of a Chapman or a Spenser but even in some degree of Shakespeare; for it was taken for granted that one of the properties of a fiction, however esoteric it might appear, was the possession of occult significance. This will not seem strange to anyone who considers the currency, the commonplaceness indeed, of commentaries on the Scriptures—the myriad works on Genesis, the expositions of the Psalms and Job and the Song of Songs—that strike the modern eye as merely curious or fantastic. Given certain assumptions about its relation to revealed truth, these methods of allegoresis were equally applicable to pagan wisdom. On the boundary between the two stood the always influential Macrobius, who deplored fables as a means of entertainment, but believed *narratio fabulosa* to be a proper means of veiling holy truths:

> A frank, open exposition of herself is distasteful to Nature, who, just as she has withheld an understanding of herself from the uncouth senses of men by enveloping herself in variegated garments, has also desired to have her secrets handled by more prudent individuals through fabulous narratives. Accordingly, her secret rites are veiled in mysterious representations so that she may not have to show herself even to initiates.[1]

The extant Pythagorean *logia* are an instance, nonsense phrases which preserved wisdom *a vilitate secretam,* for *amat divina natura celari.*[2] Such phrases have a skin everybody can see and a marrow a few can extract; they are not meant for the profane. *Sub verborum tegmine vera latent,* in John of Salisbury's words.[3] This is a twelfth-century Platonist; in the Renaissance such views grew in strength and complexity. How could Erasmus say that a pagan fable, allegorically interpreted, might be more valuable than scripture read literally (*si consistas in cortice*)? [4] How could Ronsard speak of ancient poetry as "une Theologie allegorique, pour faire entrer au cerveau des hommes grossiers par fables plaisantes et colorees les secrets qu'ils ne pouvoient comprendre, quand trop ouvertement on descouvroit la vérité"? [5] Or Chapman plant obscurity at the core of his fictions? "Obscuritie in affections of word, & indigested concets, is pedanticall and childish; but where it shroudeth it selfe in the hart of his subject . . . with that darknes will I still labour to be shaddowed . . ." (Dedication of *Ovids Banquet of Sence*). Were they not aware that there was an inherent contradiction in making public what they wished to keep secret? Even Chapman, with his talk of writing for two or three only, sought publication. And this is, as Wind points out, "the basic paradox of cryptic art . . . it frequently addresses itself to the very audience from which it professes to be hidden" (Wind, pp. 157 and 20; Seznec, pp. 102–103). But the paradox ceases to be troublesome if provision can be made for two classes of reader, one which stops at the skin, the other which penetrates to the marrow.

Of the complex tradition of secret ancient wisdom, much has recently been written, not only in learned papers on the *icones symbolicae,* Orphism, and the like, but also in the authoritative general studies of Seznec and Wind. The earlier *Genealogia* of Boccaccio was supplemented in the middle of the sixteenth century by the manuals of Giraldi, Conti, and Cartari, and these became the source of a great many allegorical programmes, both pictorial and literary. The medieval element, as Seznec shows, remains in all these works; but there was some attempt, however perfunctory, to use ancient texts (Philostratus, Pausanias) and ancient coins and statues. And the Orphic strain in Renaissance Neoplatonism ensured a respect for mystery as well as straightforward allegory. We have also to remember the syncretism of the movement; Christian themes could be given pagan expression, Ovid was habitually moralized, the view that Plato had learned the wisdom of Moses opened a path to the most elaborate discoveries of truth in ancient mythology and religion. Christian truth is hidden in pagan story. "But have a care in speaking of these things. They should be hidden in silence as are the Eleusinian mysteries; sacred things must needs be wrapped in fable and enigma" (Mutianus Rufus, quoted in Seznec, p. 99). *"Universam poesim aenigmatum esse docet plenam decet Plato."*

It is a short step from this creative exploration of mythology to the new making of enigmatic myths. The differences between a modern and Renaissance view of the ancient world and its divinities are vast. As D. J. Gordon has said of Chapman's having invented mythological deities such as Teras, Eronusis, and Ceremony, his was not the familiar Olympic pantheon:

> The elaborate abstractions of late antiquity were far more familiar to sixteenth century writers than they are to us. The syncretism of Plutarch in his *Isis and Osiris,* and the mixture of Greek and Egyptian cults in Diodorus Siculus were as present to their minds as the marbles of the Olympians. . . . A glance through the pages of Cartari or at the illustrations to his text is enough to show how wild, how "unclassical" . . . this pantheon was.[6]

When a man set out to imitate antique models—and that was the key to most Renaissance artistic activity—he assumed the right to amplify and to change the model. He would *invent,* though in the Renaissance sense of the word; he would create new figures and new meanings by adapting and recombining any fragmentary or scattered evidence he could find. He would make new mysteries, and the material of them would be "classical" in his sense; their meaning would be of universal import because, in so far as they were authentic, truth lay enigmatically within them. Such are Wind's "Pagan Mysteries of the Renaissance." Such are the "programmes" of Renaissance art, recombinations of old myth and allegory to reveal truth. The material may derive from well-thumbed manuals, the contributory themes from the allegorical fantasies of Platonic academists; but the result will be an enigma calling for explication by adepts. So, for example, with the still-disputed interpretation of Botticelli's *Primavera.*[7]

My assumption is that the Cave of Mammon had such a programme and that it is similarly enigmatic; that it is an invention of this kind, requiring the sort of attention given by art historians to the *Primavera.* One may make this assumption without at all disputing that Spenser's allegory is frequently medieval, that he is staid, "churchwardenly," openly didactic. Underneath all that, there is a profounder mythopoeic activity; the great allegorical centers of his poem are planned like enigmatic pictures. The audience of an epic is likely to be uneven in learning:

> While it was no doubt best for people as a whole to continue to accept the traditional teachings with naïve faith, learned men . . . should be able to discern the inevitable part played in Christianity, as in pagan belief, by the weaving of fables (Seznec, p. 99).

The marrow of a Spenserian allegory is designed to be extracted by the same enlightened method as that of an Orphic mystery, an Egyptian hieroglyph, a Renaissance emblem, or indeed an ancient epic.

Guyon is the hero of the legend of Temperance. In the sixth Canto he is parted from his guide, the Palmer, but resists the temptations of Phaedria, "immodest Mirth." He then proceeds, though without his Palmer, "as Pilot well expert in perilous wave" through a wilderness. After a long journey during which he comforts himself with reflecting upon his own virtues, he comes to "a gloomy glade" where, in the darkness sits "an uncouth, salvage, and uncivile wight." This is Mammon. All about him are heaps of gold, which, at the sight of Guyon, he pours down a hole into the earth. Guyon, however, stops him, and asks him who he is. After complaining of Guyon's presumption, Mammon explains that he is "God of the world and worldlings," dispenser of everything for which men "swinck and sweat incessantly":

> Riches, renowne, and principality;
> Honour, estate, and all this worldes good.

He offers Guyon limitless wealth if he will serve him. Guyon rejects this "worldly mucke." Mammon points out that money is a way to greatness; but Guyon scorns him, and attributes much of the world's misery and wrongful government to the love of money. He will not in any case "receave / Thing offred till I know it well be got." Guyon then asks in what secret place all this mass of treasure is kept; and Mammon leads him down through a hole into the earth. Soon they come to "an ample plaine" through which runs "a beaten broad high way" that leads "to Plutoes griesly raine." Beside this road sit Pain and Strife, Revenge, Despight, Treason, Hate, Gealosie, Feare, Sorrow, Horrour with Owls and Night-ravens, and "sad *Celeno*" a harpy, to signify rapacity, but sitting and singing as she does in *Aeneid* III. They arrive at a "little dore . . . that to the gate of Hell . . . was next adjoyning." This is the house of Richesse. Before it sits "selfe-consuming Care." The door opens, and they enter, Guyon undismayed by the darkness and danger. As soon as he gets in, and thenceforth during his stay, he is followed by a monstrous fiend; if Guyon should covet anything or lay hand or lip or lustful eye on anything, or sleep, so transgressing "the fatall *Stygian* lawes," this fiend that hovers over him, would rend him in pieces. The house is full of gold, roofed over by a spider's web and covered in dust; there is but "a faint shadow of uncertain light, / Such as a lamp, whose life does fade away." The skulls and bones of dead men lie around. They pass through an iron door, Guyon not speaking, and find there a show of riches such "As eye of man did never see before"—all the wealth of the world, above and below ground: "Loe here the worldes blis, loe here the end, / To which all men do ayme." Guyon rejects it:

> Another blis before mine eyes I place,
> Another happinesse, another end.

Mammon gnashes his teeth; Guyon has escaped. But he takes him into his furnace room, where fiends make gold; "Here is the fountaine of the worldes good." Guyon easily rejects him.

Now Mammon leads the knight to the Temple of Philotime, which is guarded by Disdayne. In a large room supported by golden pillars, all inscribed with emblems of mortal glory, sits Philotime, surrounded by her adorers. Her beauty is great, but "wrought by art and counterfetted shew":

> Nath'lesse most heavenly faire in deed and vew
> She by creation was, till she did fall.

She holds a chain stretching from heaven to hell and called Ambition, upon which men fight for advantage. Mammon explains that Philotime is his daughter, and that

> Honour and dignitie from her alone
> Derived are, and all this worldes blis.

She has been thrust out of heaven from envy; and he offers her to Guyon, who politely refuses, calling himself unworthy, but also explaining that he has plighted his troth to another lady.

Mammon, inwardly angry, now conducts him down a somber path into a garden full of black flowers and fruit: Cypress, Gall, Heben, Poppy, Hellebore, Cicuta (the hemlock of Socrates). This is the Garden of Proserpina. In an arbor in the midst she has a silver seat, and beside it is a tree laden with glistering fruit. This tree is the source of certain mythological apples: those of the Hesperides, that by which Atalanta was defeated, that which Paris awarded to Venus. The boughs overhang Cocytus, in which stream groan the damned. Two of these are described: Tantalus, who begs drink and is sternly refused it by Guyon; and Pilate. Mammon roughly asks Guyon to eat of the fruit and rest on the silver stool; should he do either the fiend would rend him in pieces. But he does not suffer "lust his safetie to betray." By now he is weak for lack of food and sleep; he has been with Mammon for three days. He requests immediate escort back to "living light"; Mammon has to grant it, as no man may spend more than three days below the earth. Guyon at once falls into a deep faint. There ends the seventh Canto. The eighth opens with the famous "And is there care in heaven?" giving praise for God's mercy in sending angels "to serve to wicked men." A voice summons the Palmer, who finds sitting beside the prostrate Guyon an angel sent to save him from a threatening danger.

This is the picture. It makes much allegorical sense without elaborate explanation; I have mentioned a great many simple personifications with an obvious function in an allegory of this kind. But there is evidently something pretty mysterious about some details; and these are so important that commentators disagree radically about the true meaning of the allegory, and its place in the second Book as a whole. For example, there is a general dispute as to whether Guyon stands for Aristotle's Temperance or his Continence; more particularly, whether his going with Mammon in the first place is not parallel to the Red Cross Knight's submission to Pride and Despair in the first Book. Thus V. K. Whitaker sees the significance of the events in the separation from the Palmer (Prudence), after which Guyon "is tempted by Phaedria [and] weakened almost to death by Mammon."[8] Harry Berger, in his recent impressive study of Book II, argues that Guyon descends of his own free will, and is guilty of curiosity. Once in the cave, he has no difficulty with Mammon's crudely material enticements; he surveys them all coldly, with scientific detachment. His faint is a direct result of his mental intemperance (*curiositas*) for he has neglected his human needs in order to serve it (H. Berger, *The Allegorical Temper,* 1957, pp. 17 ff.). The more general view is, roughly, Milton's, though he made the odd and famous mistake of sending the Palmer into the cave with Guyon:

> . . . our sage and serious Poet *Spencer,* whom I dare be known to think a better teacher then *Scotus* or *Aquinas,* describing true temperance under the person of *Guion,* brings him in with his palmer through the cave of Mammon, and the bowr of earthly blisse that he might see and know, and yet abstain.[9]

So Ernest Sirluck, seeking to reestablish the contact, which some recent speculation has questioned, between *Faerie Queene* II and the *Nicomachean Ethics,* finds that Guyon here represents "the virtuous man with reference to wealth and honour" as part of Spenser's larger purpose, which is to show the good life with reference to moral virtue, just as in the first Book he showed it with reference to faith.[10]

These wide disagreements do not, however, preclude general consent that the ordeal in the cave is the crisis of Guyon's quest, the character of which is to be understood in accordance with the interpretation placed upon the crucial seventh Canto. It is argued, for instance, that Guyon overgoes Achilles in the first half of the book by demonstrating the conquest of wrath, and Ulysses in the second by his conquest of concupiscence;[11] or that he moves out of the sphere of Fortune into that of creative love, so dramatizing the insufficiency of Aristotelian temperance—"the innocence and limited wisdom resulting from reflexes so easy"—in comparison with the Christian temperance—"supernaturally infused, accessible to all, but gained by each with difficulty" (Berger, pp. 62–63). It is, at all events, essential to understand what is meant by the Cave of Mammon passage if one is to get Book II right.

Is Guyon in the cave committing a sin, merely resisting temptations which are scarcely troublesome to the habitual temperance of Aristotle, or undergoing some kind of initiation? I shall argue for the last of these interpretations. To begin with, what precisely does Mammon offer Guyon? The usual answer is Wealth, or perhaps, Wealth and Honor. Mammon offers the inducements of the World, as against those of the flesh and the Devil. And this is, doubtless, a good explanation, *si consistas in cortice;* the fact that it is insufficient is amply shown by the allegorical details it leaves unexpounded, and notably by the Garden of Proserpina, the final stage of Guyon's temptation, which has indeed never been explained. I hope to show that the temptation, understood as a whole, is of a kind that makes it certain that the Canto does in fact describe an initiation, and that what Guyon undergoes is a *total* temptation parallel to that of Christ in the wilderness.

Mammon is not merely a money-god; in *Paradise Lost,* for instance, Milton associates him with vainglory as well as money (II. 229 ff.) and elsewhere, speaking of the Cave of Mammon with Spenser in mind, he expressly adds to these venal learning (*Animadversions on the Remonstrant's Defence to Smectymnuus,* xiii). Now commentators have noticed, without explaining, certain similarities between Spenser's Cave and the temptations in *Paradise Regain'd.* There Christ rejects a magic banquet of potent appeal to the senses; and then, in turn, temptations of wealth, power, honor, and forbidden learning. Satan at this point is "quite at a loss, for all his darts are spent" (*Paradise Regain'd,* IV. 366). According to exactly this scheme Marvell constructed his "Dialogue between the Resolved Soul and Created Pleasure." Each sense is tempted in turn and the temptation rejected on the ground that the reward of abstinence will be superior. There is a break in the poem there, marked by a chorus, and the tempter passes on to the temptation of female beauty, rejected by Satan as unlikely to succeed with Christ; the temptations of gold, military and civic glory, and finally of knowledge. These resisted, the Chorus proclaims the soul triumphant. "The World has not one Pleasure more." This insistence on the totality of the temptation as set forth in a literary scheme is ultimately based on Luke, iv.13, "And when the devil had ended *all* the temptation, he departed from him for a season." In the normal intensity of biblical commentary the word *all* becomes significant; accordingly Augustine in his remarks on the text, writes as follows:

> . . . these three kinds of vice, namely, the pleasures of the flesh, and pride, and curiosity, include all sins. And they appear to me to be enumerated by the Apostle John, when he says, *Love not the World: for all that is in the world is the lust of the flesh, and the lust of the eyes, and the pride of life.* For through the eye especially prevails curiosity. To what the rest indeed belong is clear. And that temptation of the Lord Man was threefold: by food, that is, by the lust of the flesh, where it is suggested, *command these stones that they be made bread:* by vain boasting, where, stationed on a mountain, all the kingdoms of the earth are shewn Him, and promised if He would worship; by curiosity, where, from the pinnacle of the temple, He is advised to cast Himself down, for the sake of trying whether He would be borne up by angels. And accordingly after the enemy could prevail with Him by none of these temptations, this is said of Him, *When the devil had ended all his temptations.*

This occurs in the Homily on Psalm 8,[12] in which, incidentally, occur the words, "What is man that thou art mindful of him? or the son of man, that thou visitest him?" to which Spenser alludes in the opening of Canto viii when treating of Guyon's angelic helper. An understanding of this would have saved much bewildered commentary.

The Cave of Mammon Canto is not concerned with the concupiscence of the flesh; that is dealt with in the Phaedria episode. It provides the remainder of the total temptation. Guyon is offered and rejects money, even as a means to greatness. Milton's Christ, who will accept benefits only insofar "as he likes the giver" (*Paradise Re-*

gain'd, II, 321–22) is anticipated in the refusal of Guyon to "receave thing offred till I know it well be got." Spenser intensifies the temptation of riches by leading up to a point where Guyon is offered literally all the riches of the world, as the demon hovers over him. But he knows of a higher reward "another bliss, another happiness, another end." He then rejects Philotime, the daughter of Mammon. Since Mammon was equated with Pluto by the mythographers,[13] Philotime is the daughter of Dis and Persephone, and virtually the same person as Pride in I. iv (Lucifera, daughter of Pluto and "sad *Proserpina* the Queene of hell") patroness of the other deadly sins. Her beauty is counterfeit, because she stands for an earthly idea of honor not a heavenly; the honor of the pagans which resides in human values, not those of the Christian which go by "perfect witness of all-judging Jove." Behind this choice of a heavenly honor there lies the authority of St. Augustine; for reasons connected with the whole design of *The City of God* he spent much time on the antithesis between the two honors. The pagan, even at its most virtuous, rests on Opinion, not Truth. The exalted Roman honor commended by Sallust, for instance, and exemplified by Scipio Africanus, is only a shadow of the Christian honor, which is achieved more by suffering than by action, and rewarded in the next world, not this.[14] Guyon, then, temperately rejects the false honor in favor of the true, the earthly in favor of the heavenly city. The Christian honor depends upon self-conquest. In Marvell's poem, Pleasure offers Glory:

> Wilt thou all the Glory have
> That War or Peace commend?
> Half the World shall be thy Slave,
> The other half thy Friend.

But the reply of the Resolved Soul is clear as to the falsity of the thing offered:

> What Friends, if to myself untrue?
> What Slaves, unless I captive you?

If the analogy with Marvell and Milton is correct, Spenser should include a temptation to vain learning. And this brings us to the Garden of Proserpina, the unexplained part of the Mammon episode.

The principal literary sources of this Garden are *Odyssey,* x. 509 ff., and Claudian, *de Raptu Proserpinae,* where Pluto consoles his captive with talk of the benefits she will enjoy in his realm:

> est etiam lucis arbor praedives opacis
> fulgentis viridi ramos curvata metallo
>
> (II. 290–91)

("And there is a rich tree in the dark groves, the curving branches of which gleam with bright gold"). The spider also derives from Claudian, perhaps by way of *Muiopotmos.* But Spenser, as Warton noticed, omits the beautiful flowers and fruits of Claudian's garden, and instead combines this tree of golden fruit with the Homeric Grove of Persephone. The result is a picture like that of Polygnotus in the Lesches at Delphi, to which I shall recur, and which shows the grove of Proserpina as a place where "black poplars and willows grow" (Pausanias, *Description of Greece,* x. 30). Homer does not say they are black. The herbs in Spenser's garden are all deadly poisons, appropriate to Proserpina in her character as Hecate, patroness of poisons (Natalis Comes, *Mythologia* (Frankfurt, 1588, p. 570). One of these, Cicuta, killed Socrates, devotee of true knowledge.

What is the meaning of the apples on Spenser's tree? They are in the first place the fruit that must not be eaten in the underworld; and insofar as they represent a temptation to be resisted under severe penalties, they are related to Eve's apple, which was eaten out of appetite, vainglory, and curiosity. But Spenser complicates this by saying that all the famous apples of mythology grew on this tree. So they mean rather more than merely *mala Punica.*[15] The apples mentioned are related: those with which Hippomenes deceived Atalanta were said to be Hesperidean (Comes, p. 637) and given to him by Venus, who also, according to Ovid, gave Acontius his apple (*Heroides,* XXI. 123–24). Whatever they signify it is not avarice, as the commentators say; we have left that behind. The apples of the Hesperides were emblems of astronomical knowledge. The story of Atalanta was sometimes interpreted as a warning against blasphemy, since she desecrated the shrine of the Great Mother (Comes, p. 738). Comes says that the apple offered by Discord to the goddesses was the symbol of an insane contempt for the divine wisdom (p. 670).

For the apple of Acontius I can find no mythographical source; this may be one that Spenser made up himself. Acontius, enamored of Cydippe, won her by a trick. He wrote on an apple, "I swear by Artemis that I will marry Acontius" and threw it in the girl's way. She picked it up and read the message aloud; and as she did so in the precincts of the temple of Artemis the words had the force of a solemn oath. Attempts to marry her to another man were thwarted by the gods, and in the end she married Acontius. It may be this trifling with an oath that made the story seem to Spenser another illustration of the danger of blasphemy; certainly the apple-stories all indicate intemperance of mind not body.

Spenser's Cocytus contains many sinners, but only two are named. The first is Tantalus. He is normally taken as a type of avarice, not without support from the mythographers; but he is much more certainly a type of blasphemous or intemperate knowledge. "Lo, Tantalus, I here tormented lye: Of whom high Jove wont whylome feated bee." Tantalus served the gods with a dish made of the body of his son Pelops; as Fulgentius says, in order to test their immortality (*Fabularum liber,* ed. Helm, 1898, p. 57)—a *curious* thing to do. Others, with Pindar, say that being a guest of Jove, Tantalus grew arrogant, and reported to men the secrets of divine knowledge. Comes says he suffers *"ob loquacitatem, quia secreta Deorum mortalibus diuulgaveret"* ("for his loquacity, in that he revealed to mortals the secrets of the Gods" [pp. 633 ff.]), and quotes Cornelius Gallus saying that Tantalus "published what should not be spoken." "Why," asks Comes, "was Tantalus called a son of Jupiter? Because he was held to be a man deeply versed in divine and natural knowledge, and this, as the Pythagoreans understood, is not every man's having, but pertains only to those whose souls have been especially summoned from the sphere of Jupiter to inhabit these bodies" (Comes, p. 637). Tantalus, in short, revealed to the profane the innermost secrets of religion. Similarly Ovid says that Tantalus was punished for revealing or despising the Eleusinian mysteries, and got an appropriate punishment for his fault (*Ars Am.,* II. 601–606); and Pausanias in the account of Polygnotus' painting shows Tantalus suffering in hell among those who showed disrespect for these mysteries (X. xxxi). Guyon refusing him help, says he must be an example of the *mind's* intemperance, not the body's. Tantalus, like the apples, stands for a blasphemous ambition of divine knowledge, a subject both traditional, and, in Spenser's time, acutely topical, for the limits of permitted enquiry were a matter of interest to theologians, scientists, and magicians alike.

The companion of Tantalus is Pontius Pilate, and one confesses to feeling less certain here. He calls himself "the falsest judge alas, and most unjust" and certainly as a magistrate he corrupts the purposes by falsifying the law. As an archetype of judicial corruption he was presented in the Towneley plays as a questmonger, an unambiguously vile and corrupt lawyer.[16] Here he admits that he "delivered up the Lord of life to die, And did acquite a murder felonous, The whiles my hands I washt in puritie." His question, "what is truth?" would in the circumstances fall under the Augustinian *curiositas;* and he abuses knowledge.[17]

There is small doubt, then, that Guyon undergoes the temptations of wealth, glory, and inordinate or blasphemous curiosity. There remains, at this stage, one obscure and important detail, Proserpina's silver seat or stool, in which Mammon urges the weary knight to rest and eat an apple. Had he done so, the fiend would have seized him. What are we to make of this stool? It cannot be, in common sense, what the commentators say, an invitation to sloth. Upton wrote an interesting but unsatisfactory note relating the stool to the seat upon which Theseus sits for ever in *Aeneid,* VI: *Sedet, aeternumque sedebit / Infelix Theseus* (617–18). This is traditionally moralized in the manner of Tertullian: "to sit too long is laborious in itself; the poet Virgil treats it as a punishment . . ." (quoted in Gronovius, *Thesaurus,* X, 16). And Spenser alludes to Theseus in *F.Q.* (I. v. 35) describing the damned in the course of his passage on Aesculapius in the underworld: "Theseus condemned to endlesse slouth by law." But Theseus was condemned *to* sloth, not *for* sloth; in fact he had just been attempting with some vigor the rape of Proserpina. Upton gets nearer the point when he adds, "This stoole, on which it was unlawful to sit, our poet imaged from the forbidden seat in the Eleusinian mysteries"; and he refers us to the standard seventeenth-century work on these mysteries, the *Eleusinia* of J. Meurs or Meursius, and to Warburton's famous disquisition on the sixth *Aeneid* in *The Divine Legation of Moses,* adding, "Our knight has now gone through a kind of initiation, and passed all the fiery trials;

and comes out more temperate and just, as silver tried in the fire" (*Variorum,* Spenser, II. 239).

I think Upton was right about the stool, and about the initiatory nature of Guyon's ordeal; but the points need proving. The Homeric *Hymn to Demeter* has a stool covered with a silver fleece, on which Demeter, after Iambe has made her smile, consents to sit; but the Hymn was not known, save for a few lines, until 1780. However, as Allen points out in his edition (p. 151), this seat was often related to the sorrowful stone, *agelastos petra,* on which Ceres sat by a well on the road to Eleusis; and this stone has a well-established place in the ritual as a forbidden seat. Clement of Alexandria knew that the *mystes* might not sit in a certain seat, "lest they should appear to be imitating the mourning Ceres" (*Protrepticon*), and Meursius repeats this "*. . . ne lugentem imitari viderentur*" (*Eleusinia* (1619), p. 10). This forbidden seat of the mysteries was associated with Theseus, who, either by his descent or in the course of a preparatory initiation like that of Hercules, had violated the secret knowledge they confer. He duly appears in the Polygnotus painting, in his Chair of Forgetfulness, as it was called; he is to pass eternity forgetting what it would have been better for him not to know (Pausanias, xxix. 9). I should like to produce, but cannot, Spenser's immediate source for this placing of a punitive chair of oblivion in the garden of Proserpina;[18] it is in Meurs—too late, of course, and in a scholium on Aristophanes, perhaps too obscure. However, it seems certain enough that this Chair or stool fits the general pattern of the Garden temptations; they are all associated with the sin of forbidden knowledge, and the related sin of revealing or perverting divine knowledge.

In its general conception, the underworld in which this total temptation is enacted derives from *Aeneid,* VI, of which a normal Renaissance allegorical interpretation was that Aeneas underwent certain trials to strengthen his own virtues that they might collaborate with divine grace in bringing him to a final spiritual consummation.[19] But Spenser drew also on Homer and Claudian; and he seems to me to have used also the Delphic murals as described by Pausanias. These were an important source of Renaissance mythography (Seznec, pp. 232 ff.), and contain, as does Claudian, Eleusinian elements. For example, Polygnotus depicted the basket of Demeter which was an important ritual object; he showed, as we have seen, the fate of the profaner of the mysteries. Pausanias gives a detailed account of the fiend Eurynomus (X. xxviii) amplified by Cartari in his *Imagini de i Dei,* a standard manual (1581 ed., p. 235). Cartari describes the practice Eurynomus had of tearing his victims to pieces, and he seems to be the same fiend described by Spenser as continually threatening Guyon. In the Eleusinian rite the suppliant was followed by a fury, and was forbidden to turn round.[20] There is a concurrence of detail to suggest that Spenser was doing what had been done before; so Michelangelo in his *Bacchus* may have celebrated the mysteries of Dionysius (Wind, pp. 147 ff.) suggesting an initiatory rite based upon ancient mysteries.

There is, naturally, an ambiguity in the attitude of the Renaissance to these mysteries. They were pagan, and the early fathers strenuously condemned them; but the Neoplatonists valued them highly, and their influence in Spenser's day was powerful. Even Clement, an important source of information on Eleusis, saw that they were in some respects parallel to Christian teaching (*Stromata,* V. ii); an initiate exchanges a human for a divine *phronesis;* he spends three days in "hell." Tertullian, commenting on the rite in which Mithraic initiates were offered, and were required to refuse, a crown, the ceremony taking place in a cave, argued that this was the devil imitating divine things (*De Corona,* xv). The celebrated initiation of Apuleius was regularly given a Christian application,[21] and Meurs himself insists, as do many others, that the aim of the mysteries was the correction of life, the achievement of a perfection which would bring happiness in this life and honor in the next (Meursius, pp. 12, 47; taking the hint from Cicero, *De Legibus,* xi). The Platonic interpretation of the rite as representing the descent of the soul into matter and its liberation therefrom was not hostile to Christian teaching, especially under the conditions I described earlier; the veiling of truth under the shows of pagan myth and religion is assumed in allegories of Spenser's kind, and it seems likely that he has reinforced the theme of Guyon's initiation with a series of occult allusions to the Eleusinian rite.

What makes this the more likely is the fact that Hercules was an Eleusinian initiate; he had to be, before he could descend to the underworld for Cerberus—a labor allegorized as the conquest of the passions (Meursius, p. 12). There is no space to speak of the strong element of Hercules in Guyon, as in most of Spenser's knights. It is another subject. Suffice it that Guyon even in his lapse when he sees the nymphs in the fountain, is imitating Hercules, who had become as a result of the allegorization of his Choice and his Labors, a type of heroic virtue, and indeed of Christ.[22] There is nothing to be wondered at in the consequence of what I have argued: that Guyon in the Cave is imitating both Hercules and Christ, particularly in their initiatory ordeals.

I return now to the original total temptation of Christ in the desert. We have seen that Guyon's corresponds in its general pattern; but a consideration of a few more aspects will suggest an answer to the questions, What is Guyon initiated into? How is he different when he comes out of the Cave? Let us take up the resemblances between his temptation and that of Christ.

Christ wished to be tempted "that he might strengthen us against temptations" (*Summa Theologica,* III. 41. 1); this was, as St. Gregory said, "not unworthy" in him, and Guyon's openly encountering Mammon is parallel. Christ's resistance is exemplary; so is Guyon's. "Christ of his own freewill exposed himself to be tempted by the devil . . . the devil prefers to assail a man who is alone . . . And so it was that Christ went out into the desert, as to a field of battle, to be tempted there by the devil." So Aquinas, adding that Christ actually provoked the devil. The distinction between a proper avoidance of the occasion of sin and a proper acceptance of the good temptations which strengthen a man for great achievements is as clear in Spenser, who makes Occasio a character in the Second Book, as it is in Aquinas. The difference is between an external temptation, like Job's or Christ's, and a temptation caused internally by concupiscence. The former variety is without sin (Heb., 4. 15: Christ "was *in all points* tempted like as we are, yet without sin"). "And hence," adds St. Thomas, "Christ wished to be tempted by an enemy, but not by the flesh." The proper resistance to such temptation is *passive.* This is the familiar paradox of Christian warfare, that the soldier puts on the whole armour of God, but merely suffers himself to be tempted; and this disposes of Berger's objection, that Guyon is quite untroubled by Mammon's inducements and merely pandering to his own vanity (Berger, pp. 17 ff.). Augustine had distinguished at length between the passive Christian and the active pagan heroism; Aquinas reaffirms this in the present context: "Christ came to destroy the works of the devil not by powerful deeds, but rather by suffering" (*S.T.*, III. 41. 1). Milton says he conquered "by humiliation and strong sufferance"; his Christ replies "temperately," "sagely," "unmoved," etc., to all temptation, and defeats the final temptation of violence by complete immobility on the pinnacle.

Christ's temptation took place at the end of his time in the wilderness; so did Guyon's. He allowed this because at such a time the devil would dare to approach him; he "abandoned his manhood to its nature" that he might conquer the devil "not by God, but by the flesh" (*S.T.*, III. 41. 4). Similarly Guyon undertakes Mammon as natural man (without his palmer) and vanquishes him "not as by God, but as by man" (*S.T.*, III. 41. 4). After the temptation, Christ, in the weakness of his human nature, receives the ministrations of angels; so does Guyon. According to Luke, 4.13, the devil then "departed from him for a time," and this was interpreted as meaning "until his Passion." Guyon's next temptation is at the climax of his quest in the Bower of Bliss. After his Herculean faltering over the nymphs [23] in the fountain he proceeds to the active destruction of the evil Acrasia. Milton undoubtedly thinks of the temptation in the wilderness as a kind of initiation; having passed through it, say the angels, Christ is now ready for his work:

> Queller of Satan, on thy glorious work
> Now enter, and begin to save mankind.
>
> (*P.R.*, IV. 634–35)

Hercules, after his own (passive) initiation, became actively heroic and dragged Cerberus, the passion, from hell. Hercules was the pagan type of heroic virtue, and, as I have said, he was Christianized. If Guyon's temptation was a prelude to an active heroic virtue, we should now ask what this virtue was.

The classic exposition is in a book upon which Spenser certainly drew, the *Nicomachean Ethics*. Aristotle, at the end of his Sixth

Book, distinguishes between "natural" and "proper" virtue; we are born with the first, but the second is what we aspire to, and it cannot exist without prudence. Book VII, which is mostly about the lower virtue Continence, opens with some distinctions. Three things are to be avoided; vice, incontinence, brutality. The contraries of the first two are virtue and continence; the contrary of the third is Heroic Virtue, which places men above others, in the likeness of gods. Aristotle says very little about Heroic Virtue but it is enough, in the context of so famous a book, to have provoked a long debate, in which the virtue of Hercules also plays its large part. Augustine made it a suffering virtue; Isidore of Seville applied the idea to poetry. Milton has the virtue in mind when he writes in *Areopagitica* of the true warfaring Christian as one who, like Hercules, "can apprehend and consider vice with all her baits and seeming pleasures, and yet abstain" (*ed. cit.*, p. 514); and *Paradise Lost,* IX opens with an excursus on his "Sad task, yet argument / Not less but more Heroic then the wrauth / Of stern *Achilles,*" and a defence of a new kind of heroism—not of wars, "hitherto the onely Argument / Heroic deem'd" but "the better fortitude / Of patience and Heroic Martyrdom." The frontispiece of Sandys' *Ovid* and the verses prefatory to the work illustrate the association of Heroic Virtue with Pallas Athene and the control of appetite, as against voluptuous indulgence as represented by Circe or, in some manifestations, Venus: choose Heroic Virtue and you undertake "the Path and Toyles of *Hercules*." The formal confrontation of pagan and Christian heroic virtue may be found in Dryden, where it occurs at length in a debate between St. Catherine and a heathen philosopher Apollonius in *Tyrannic Love,* II. iii. And, more remarkably, Dryden uses the idea of Christianized heroic virtue elliptically in a witty passage of *Annus Mirabilis*. Prince Rupert, refusing the tactical bait by which the Dutch admiral tried to lead him on to the sandbanks, refuses the engagement and joins the main fleet instead.

> Heroic Virtue did his Actions guide,
> And he the substance not th'appearance chose. (l. 166)

In this instance the normally impetuous Rupert displayed the true heroism of abstinence, which incidentally requires the ability to distinguish between apparent and real goods.

The idea, then, is common enough, especially in an age ambitious of Christian epic. The reconciliation of Aristotle's Heroic Virtue with Christianity had been undertaken by Aquinas and elaborated in the process of distinguishing between the virtues and the gifts of the Holy Ghost (*S.T.*, III. 68. 1):

> The virtues perfect man according as it is natural for him to be moved by his reason in his interior and exterior actions. Consequently man needs yet higher perfections whereby to be disposed to be moved by God. These perfections are called gifts, not only because they are infused by God, but also because by them man is disposed to become amenable to the Divine inspiration. . . . Even [Aristotle] says that for those who are moved by Divine Instinct, there is no need to take counsel according to human reason, but only to follow their inner promptings, since they are moved by a principle higher than human reason. . . . The gifts perfect men for acts which are higher than acts of virtue. . . . Hence Aristotle above virtue commonly so called, places a kind of *heroic* or *divine* virtue.

This reconciliation of Aristotle's Heroic Virtue with the gifts is brought about partly through the agency of a third party unnamed, Macrobius, whose treatment of the Virtues in the *Commentary* on Cicero's *Somnium Scipionis* was the second great ancient source for medieval and Renaissance treatments of the subject. Following Plotinus (*Enn.*, I. ii) the Commentary "arranges the grades of the virtues according to a proper and natural classification: the first, political virtues, the second 'cleansing' or purgatorial virtues; the third the virtues of the purified mind, the fourth, the exemplary virtues. Virtues of the first grade are proper to man as a social animal; virtues of the second type are found only in the man who is capable of attaining the divine, 'the man who has resolved to be purged of all contamination with the body,' and by an escape from mortal things, as it were, to mingle solely with the divine." In this grade, Temperance is abstinence "from everything that the habits of the body seek, as far as nature will permit." The third type "includes the virtues of the purified and serene mind, completely and thoroughly cleansed from all taint of this world." The fourth type is inaccessible to men, consisting of the virtues "that are present in the divine mind itself." Macrobius sums up: "The first type of virtues mitigates the passions, the second puts them away, the third has forgotten them, and to the fourth they are anathema."

When Aquinas speaks of "those who are moved by Divine Instinct"—the most striking example of this kind of heroic virtue in literature is Milton's Samson at the end of his life—he presumably has in mind the man who possesses the Macrobian virtues of the third type. One may see the conflation of Aristotle and Macrobius in Benedict XIV's treatment, which the *Catholic Encyclopedia* calls "classical," of heroic virtue: "a habit of good conduct that has become a second nature, a new motive power stronger than all corresponding inborn inclinations, capable of rendering easy a series of acts each of which, for the ordinary man, would be beset with great, if not insurmountable, difficulties." And Benedict distinguishes between the "social virtues," which are the political virtues of Macrobius related to Matthew, v. 48, and the exemplary or divine virtues, adding that "it is . . . necessary to posit certain intermediate virtues which are between the social, which are human, and the exemplary, which are divine. These intermediate virtues are of two degrees of perfection; the lesser in the soul still struggling upwards from a life of sin to a likeness with God—these are called the purifying virtues (*virtutes purgatoriae*): the greater in the souls which have already attained to the divine likeness—these are called the virtues of the purified soul (*virtutes jam purgati animi*) . . . this is a perfection rare in this life." The distinction between heroic virtue, so Christianized, and sanctity, is a fine one; but it is demonstrated in the parallel careers of Guyon and the Red Cross Knight. The progress of Guyon towards heroic virtue is from *virtutes purgatoriae* to *virtutes jam purgati animi;* and the inclusive temptation of the Cave of Mammon is a divine aid to this progress.

To bring the matter of the virtues nearer to Spenser, one may mention Tasso's brief and direct treatment of it in his discourse *Della Virtù Heroica e della Carità*. Cicero, he says—but he means Macrobius—placed above the moral virtues "le purgatorie, e quelle d'anima giàpurgata, e l'esemplari." He places Heroic Virtue as far above the moral virtues as heroes are above men, between the human and the divine. Aristotle he finds in some ways unhelpful, since there must be more to say about the virtue than that it is abstention from vice and bestiality; indeed he was wrong to call it a mediocrity. It is a perfection of good, and it has its own *soggetto,* as temperance has pleasure and fortitude danger. It contains all the other virtues, as the heavens the elements, in a nobler and more eminent mode. The nearest of the virtues to the Heroic is Magnanimity; heroic virtue is to magnanimity as glory is to honor. Above all the other virtues it involves prudence. Is it a way of keeping the affections in bounds, or does it on occasion use their vehemence? It both reins and employs the passions; for, as Plato says, "anger is the warrior of the reason." It has to do more with action than speculation. Finally, it resembles Charity in that Charity contains the other theological virtues; and it has no limited end; and controls the affections efficaciously; and looks for the reward of glory. But Heroic Virtue is inferior to Charity not only in that the hero is inferior to the martyr in fortitude, but in its end; for it achieves acts of fortitude, whereas Charity benefits others (*Opere di Torquato Tasso* (1823), xi. 169 ff.). Elsewhere, Tasso calls proper to heroic poetry the virtues acquired by long exercise and also those infused by divine grace (xii. 7). The *Aeneid* is the pagan model of an epic in which both kinds of virtue are represented; and it is balanced on the mysterious sixth book, in which Aeneas descends into Hell.

Guyon is concerned with Heroic Virtue, as the Red Cross Knight with Charity. In the course of his quest, the Red Cross Knight errs, suffers, is purged, and attains to sanctity and a vision of the Heavenly City. Guyon passes from the lower temperance of natural habit to the virtue of a hero, which includes all the cardinal virtues. His achievement is active, indeed destructive; he makes his anger the warrior of his reason. He passes not from temperance to continence, as they argue who relate Spenser too narrowly to the *ipsissima verba* of Aristotle, but through a purgatorial process from human to semidivine virtue, from a human to a divine *phronesis.* He becomes one of the purified souls described by Benedict, rare in this life; not a saint but a hero, like Hercules after his initiation. But the initiation of Guyon is modeled upon the temptation of the great exemplar of Christian heroic virtue, Christ in the wilderness. After his succor by the angels he can proceed, "all his great work before him set." He destroys the Bower without reflection, as if by an inner prompting. His initiatory temptation in the Cave of Mammon is the necessary preparation for his assault on Acrasia, just as the temptation of Christ was the necessary prelude to the final victory over Satan.

The Cave of Mammon is a mystery of the sort that labours to be shadowed with obscurity. We have first to see that the temptations to which Guyon is subjected are tacitly based upon those of Christ, and that they represent all possible temptations. The passive resistance of Guyon is related, by a typical syncretist device, to the pagan mysteries as well as to Christ as hero. Guyon undergoes, like Aeneas in the allegorized *Aeneid,* a purgatorial experience, and emerges no longer a knight of mere temperance but an exemplar of heroic virtue and direct instrument of providence. At the beginning of Book II, there is a meeting between the Red Cross Knight and Guyon. When they part the Palmer says:

> Joy may you have, and everlasting fame,
> Of late most hard atchiev'ment by you donne,
> For which enrolled is your glorious name
> In heavenly Registers above the Sunne,
> Where you a Saint with Saints your seat have wonne:
> But wretched we, where ye have left your marke,
> Must now anew begin, like race to runne.

"Like race"—it is notorious that the two Books run in parallel. That is because of the parallelism between Charity and Heroic Virtue. The trials of each knight differ in accordance with their ends; but each is tried and purged. As Upton said, "Our knight has now gone through a kind of initiation, and passed all the fiery trials: and comes out more temperate and just, as silver tried in the fire." The state into which he passes is that of heroic virtue; he is no longer a temperate man but an active instrument of God.

Notes

1. *Commentary on the Dream of Scipio,* tr. W. H. Stahl (1952), pp. 85–87.

2. L. G. Gyraldus, *Philosophi Pythagorae Symbolorum Interpretatio,* in *Opera Omnia* (1696), pp. 637–38; see further Edgar Wind, *Pagan Mysteries of the*

Renaissance (New Haven, 1958), Chap. I, and for "screening allegories . . . coined to hide from exoteric view the facts of an esoteric rite, while suggesting symbolically the rite's spiritual sense" in primitive societies, see Joseph Campbell, *The Masks of God* (1959), pp. 96 ff.

3. *Entheticus,* quoted in Curtius, *European Literature and the Latin Middle Ages,* tr. Willard Trask (New York, 1953), p. 206.

4. *Enchiridion militis Christi,* quoted in Jean Seznec, *The Survival of the Pagan Gods,* tr. Barbara F. Sessions (New York, 1961), pp. 98–99.

5. *Abbregé de l'Art Poetique Francoys* (1565), quoted by D. P. Walker, "The *Prisca Theologia* in France," *Journal of the Warburg and Courtauld Institutes,* XVII (1954), 224.

6. "Chapman's *Hero and Leander,*" *English Miscellany* (1954), pp. 53–54; see also p. 42, and Seznec, p. 321.

7. See E. H. Gombrich, "Botticelli's Mythologies," *Journal of the Warburg and Courtauld Institutes,* XVII (1954), 7–60; Seznec, pp. 112 ff., and Wind, pp. 100 ff.

8. *That Soueraine Light: Essays in Honor of Edmund Spenser, 1552–1952,* ed. W. R. Mueller and D. C. Allen (Baltimore, 1952), p. 77.

9. *Areopagitica, Complete Prose Works,* ed. Sirluck, II (1959), 516. Sirluck argues that Milton's own convictions led him unconsciously to revise Spenser's passage, which must have seemed to him to place too much confidence in the Aristotelian doctrine of habitual temperance. This assumes that the Palmer is Reason. If he were Prudence, another common interpretation, one might equally expect him to go with Guyon into the Cave, since Prudence is *conduttrice delle virtù morali.*

10. "*The Faerie Queene,* Bk. II, and the *Nicomachean Ethics,*" *Modern Philology,* XLIX (1952), 73–100.

11. A. C. Hamilton, "A Theological Reading of *The Faerie Queene*, Book II," *English Literary History,* XXV (1958), 155–62.

12. *Enarrationes in Psalmos; Exposition of the Book of Psalms,* tr. Tweedy, Scratton, and Wilkins (1847), I, 70 ff. Aquinas, citing Ambrose, also asserts the inclusiveness of the temptation (*S.T.,* III. 41. 4), and Lancelot Andrewes said that "under these three heads come all temptations." *The Wonderfull Combate . . . between Christ and Satan* (1592), p. 23.

13. See Gyraldus, p. 202; Ben Jonson, "Love Restored," *Workes* (1640), pp. 203 ff.; H. G. Lotspeich, *Classical Mythology in the Poetry of Edmund Spenser* (Princeton, 1932), p. 20.

14. *City of God,* V. xii–xx; see F. Kermode, "Milton's Hero," *Review of English Studies,* IV (1953), 317–30.

15. The pomegranate, associated with Proserpina and the food of the dead, was widely diffused in Greek myth and folklore, and the motif exists also in Celtic folklore.

16. Arnold Williams, "The Characterization of Pilate in the Towneley Plays."

17. Spenser's Pilate cries out in the manner of Vergil's Theseus, "*discite ustitiam moniti et non temnere divos,*" *Aeneid,* VI. 620.

18. Persephone is represented visually as sitting on a silver chair holding up a pomegranate. V. Magnien, *Les Mystères d'Eleusis* (1950), p. 136.

19. As in the *Disputationes Camuldulenses* of Landino, of the Florentine Academy; see M. Y. Hughes, *Virgil and Spenser* (University of California Publications in English, 1929), pp. 263–418, especially pp. 399 ff.

20. Iamblichus, *Protrepticon,* p. 340; see also Lucian, *Cataplus.*

21. See the commentary of Beroaldus; and A. D. Nock, *Conversion* (1933), Chap. IX.

22. See M. Y. Hughes, "The Christ of *Paradise Regained* and the Renaissance Heroic Tradition," *Studies in Philology,* XXXV (1938), 254–77; also Hallett Smith, *Elizabethan Poetry* (Cambridge, Mass., 1952), pp. 290 ff. That Guyon could partake simultaneously of the nature of Christ and Hercules is suggested by this observation of Comes (*ed. cit.,* p. 1056), "In order to show that wisdom is the gift of God, and that there can be no virtue without this divine will, they [the ancients] feigned that Hercules, that is to say fortitude and honesty and greatness of soul in overthrowing vice and trampling down pleasures, was the Son of God."

23. Guyon (unlike his colleague in Book V) does not succumb to pleasure as Hercules did to Omphale. On this aspect of Hercules, cf. Comes, p. 713, "Magis periculosum est ne voluptatibus, quam difficultatibus, plerumque vincamur," which is echoed by Spenser in the opening of the sixth Canto of Book II:

> A Harder lesson to learn Continence
> In joyous pleasure, then in grievous paine.

Thomas P. Roche, Jr.

The Image of Britomart

My Dear One is mine as mirrors are lonely,
And the high green hill sits always by the sea.

—AUDEN

We cannot love your love till she take on
Through you, the wonders of a paragon.
Sing her triumphant passage to our land,
The sun her footstool, the moon in her right hand. . . .
Sing her descent on the exulting shore
To bless the vines and put an end to war.

—AUDEN

The image of Britomart, presented to us in the third and fourth books of *The Faerie Queene,* is a more dramatic characterization than any other in the poem. We see her puzzled and disturbed in the first throes of love and comforted by the protective antics of Glauce. The whole flashback of the inception of the love is treated with extraordinary delicacy and homeliness. Similarly we are always totally unprepared for Britomart to tease Amoret at the beginning of Book IV after the harrowing experience of Busyrane's castle, nor are we prepared for her almost girlish nervousness when she recognizes the subdued Arthegall. But these details are part of the image of chastity. In Britomart Spenser was able to make his allegorical method subsume the smaller, more human details of psychological realism. As the ancestress of Elizabeth she embodies the conflicting claims of idealism and reality that the Queen herself embodied for Spenser the courtier.

Despite these touches of realism Britomart is not more "real" than the other characters in the poem. To treat Britomart as if she were a character in a drama or a novel is to deny the psychological validity of the allegorical method, and no patient reader of Spenser will allow this. In the literature of psychological realism—let us say a novel by Virginia Woolf or D. H. Lawrence—something more is gleaned from the details, some new insight into the subtle shifts of personality, some further evidence of the kind of person we are reading about. Conditioned as we are by the novel, we might expect Spenser's details to suggest some shift from the psychology of the virgin to the psychology of the wife. This Spenser does not give us, for it is not the way of allegory. Surface realism is no indication of the symbolic significance of character or action in *The Faerie Queene.* We learn as much about Britomart as we need to know, but we shall never know her so well as we do Mrs. Dalloway. In fact, Britomart is hardly a character in our modern sense of that word; she is an image that Spenser uses to lead us to an increased awareness of the concept of chastity. The development of her character is not "dramatic" or "novelistic"; it is thematic and allegorical.

Britomart is Spenser's allegorical representation of love directed by the virtue of chastity. The stages in her quest for Arthegall are marked by those who accompany her. She sets out with Glauce her nurse, the figure of protection in childhood, who accompanies her until her trial in the House of Busyrane. This is the end of her preparation, and Glauce must be left outside the wall of flame while Britomart endures alone the trial of perverted love. The original ending of Book III made Britomart merely the champion of married love; the second installment carries the quest to its fulfillment, in which chastity is not only the champion of married love but also becomes married love. Britomart's companion until her encounter with Arthegall is Amoret; her companion after this encounter is Scudamour. From the point of view of the action Amoret's disappearance before the encounter is annoying, but it does allow the thematic development of Britomart's character. It would be untrue to say that this encounter is the symbolic analogue of a consummated marriage, but it does exchange the shadow with which Britomart started for the reality that she sought. In this sense the shift from Amoret to Scudamour symbolizes what she has gained from her encounter with Arthegall, a new and more complete realization of that love which is the moving spirit of her quest. This is the kind of development that Spenser gives to his image of Britomart; we look in vain for evidence to show this development "within" the character itself. . . .

Although Britomart's name clearly suggests her function as the warrior maiden of Britain, it even more precisely symbolizes her function as the knight of chastity. Merritt Y. Hughes has pointed out that the source of the name is Vergil's *Ciris* and that Spenser has emphasized his source by making the dialogue between Britomart and Glauce in Book III, Canto ii, little more than a translation of a similar dialogue in Vergil's poem.[1]

The *Ciris* is a poem about the passion of Scylla, daughter of King Nisus, who betrays her father's kingdom to obtain the love of Minos his enemy. The portion that Spenser imitated is the long discussion between Scylla and her nurse Carme, who tries to help Scylla in her unfortunate love. Carme already knows the power of Minos, for to escape the love of Minos her own virgin daughter Britomartis fled into the sea, for which act of heroic virtue she was rescued and made a goddess by Diana.

> . . . ut quid ego amens
> te erepta, o Britomarti, mei spes una sepulchri,
> te, Britomarti, diem potui producere vitae?
> atque utinam celeri nec tantum grata Dianae
> venatus esses virgo sectata virorum,
> Gnosia nec Partho contendens spicula cornu
> Dictaeas ageres ad gramina nota capellas![2]

Carme's lament is undoubtedly the source of Spenser's name, but he has transferred the name of the chaste daughter to the passionate foster-child of Carme. Britomart then has the name of a dedicated virgin and the passion of a love-sick maiden who brings destruction to herself and to her kingdom.

The fusion of the two young women in Spenser's image of Britomart is more appropriate than might at first sight appear. Britomartis resists love; Scylla yields. They represent the two extremes of dedicated virginity and lust, extremes that lead to a godlike transmutation or to a debasement of humanity, bringing with it political as well as personal ruin. Spenser, like Vergil, sees love as a force that can destroy nations as well as individuals, and as a result his Britomart shares qualities with both Britomartis and Scylla. Her chastity is derived from Britomartis, but it is a chastity that springs from a love as passionate as Scylla's. Spenser makes it quite clear that this kind of love is the foundation of both political and personal integrity: "such loue not lyke to lusts of baser kynd,/ the harder wonne, the firmer will abide" (*Am.,* VI). The element of restraint is always evident in Spenser's examples of the proper use of love. In chaste love the strength of the passion is moderated by the virtue of the loved one.

> You frame my thoughts, and fashion me within,
> you stop my toung, and teach my hart to speake,
> you calme the storme that passion did begin,
> strong thrugh your cause, but by your vertue weak.
> (*Am.,* VIII)

But even in chaste love there must be an eventual surrender. Amoret, though reluctant, does leave the Temple of Venus, and Britomart is finally won by Arthegall. To surrender one's self to love is either to lose one's integrity or to transmute it into a higher unity. The legend of Britomart is an exemplum of this transmutation, not in the manner of Britomartis, but in the "famous Progeny" of her union with Arthegall.

Spenser images the eternal battle of pleasure and virtue, fought anew in every love, in the traditional Petrarchan metaphor of love as war. The metaphor is so common that it has almost ceased to be metaphorical. We may be describing the psychomachia of pleasure and virtue, the winning of a rose, a Game of Chess, the Rape of a Lock, or the Battle of the Sexes, but somehow the imagination of Western civilization images the relation of man and woman in terms of a game, a chase, or a battle, and for good reason. How else are the two to become one? For Spenser, as for many Elizabethans, the metaphor is grounded in a metaphysics of creation. Out of the discord of chaos came the concord of creation, out of the discord of the Fall came the concord of the Redemption, out of the discord of man's disordered passions comes the concord of love and propagation. We have already seen that Spenser allegorizes the *discordia concors* of the world in the story of Cambell and Triamond, and we shall see that all the good loves of Books III and IV emerge from an initial conflict of man with woman, woman with man. With the love that moves the sun and stars as example Spenser cannot view chaste love in any other way.

The theme of *discordia concors* is everywhere implicit in the image of Britomart. We see the ambiguity in her name. We see it in the Saxon armor that clothes this British maiden. We see it in the fact that Spenser reverses all the details taken from Arthurian romance. We see it as the major narrative episode in the middle books, where the culmination of Britomart's quest leads her to battle with the man she loves. We see it in the imagery used consistently to describe her.

The metaphor of love as war emphasizes the duality of man and woman as it emphasizes the element of restraint in a chaste love affair, but Spenser's image of love is more elemental, more unified and bears with it the stamp of its divine origins. To complement the metaphor of love as war and to symbolize the singular power of chastity as a positive force Spenser uses the image of light breaking through an obscuring veil.[3] At every point in the poem where Britomart removes her armor the effect of her beauty and chastity on her companions is described in images that make her virtue apparent to the reader as a visible force. In Castle Joyous Britomart lifts only the visor of her helmet,

> And so did let her goodly visage to appere.
> As when faire *Cynthia,* in darkesome night,
> Is in a noyous cloud enueloped,
> Where she may find the substaunce thin and light,
> Breakes forth her siluer beames, and her bright hed
> Discouers to the world discomfited;
> Of the poore traueller, that went astray,
> With thousand blessings she is heried;
> Such was the beautie and the shining ray,
> With which faire *Britomart* gaue light vnto the day.
>
> (III.i.42–43)

Again in Canto ix when she removes her helmet,

> Her golden locks, that were in tramels gay
> Vpbounden, did them selues adowne display,
> And raught vnto her heeles; like sunny beames,
> That in a cloud their light did long time stay,
> Their vapour vaded, shew their golden gleames,
> And through the persant aire shoote forth their azure streames.
>
> (III.ix.20)

Likewise, in Book IV, Canto i, after defeating the "Younker" she enters the castle, removes her helmet and is compared to

> . . . the shining skie in summers night,
> What time the dayes with scorching heat abound,
> Is creasted all with lines of firie light,
> That it prodigious seemes in common peoples sight.
>
> (IV.i.13)

At the climax of her encounter with Arthegall, her "ventail" has been "shared away":

> With that her angels face, vnseene afore,
> Like to the ruddie morne appeard in sight,
> Deawed with siluer drops, through sweating sore,
> But somewhat redder, then beseem'd aright,
> Through toylesome heate and labour of her weary fight.
>
> (IV.vi.19)

In each instance the comparison is based on light breaking through an obscuring veil. The image is appropriate on these occasions when Britomart reveals herself—light, goodness, beauty, truth breaking through darkness, evil, ugliness, or falsity,[4] but in particular these similes symbolize the force of her chastity. Neither the image nor its consistent use is of especial novelty to readers brought up on the analysis of image patterns, but a word of caution should be spoken at this point about Spenser's use of consistent image patterns.

Modern criticism generally teaches that the coherence of an image pattern is part of the formal structure of the poem, and very often the shorter forms of poetry do conform to this criterion. We may even find the criterion met in such long poems as *Paradise Lost,* where the enormously rich image patterns are part of the formal structure, but the modern teaching falls short of the mark when we read the great invocation to light at the beginning of *Paradise Lost,* III. It does form part of the pattern of light and dark imagery, it is consistent; but here Milton is not simply using images, he is invoking the source of the image. He has pushed us past the confines of verbal coherence, in which images of light and dark are part of a verbal pattern, and is asking us to pass from the sign to the thing signified. If this were not the case, the invocation would be pointless.

Spenser has been criticized for his failure to form coherent image patterns, but the fact that he does not conform to modern usage in this matter is not a sign that he has failed but that he is making his images do something else. The point is all the more important when we do find him using consistent image patterns as in the similes describing Britomart, for I think that Spenser was not intending us to read them primarily as part of the formal structure of his poem. These similes bear more resemblance to Milton's images in his invocation to light. Their primary allegiance is not to the verbal pattern of which they are a part but to the fundamental energy of which they are a sign. They have the startling simplicity of such lines as Nashe's "Brightness falls from the air" and Lovelace's "But shake your head and scatter day." No amount of verbal analysis will *elucidate* these images so much as the immediate human response to that "something far more deeply interfused" investing the images themselves. Similarly Spenser's images ask us to turn from epistemology to ontology to find our criterion for judging their goodness.[5] In these similes Spenser is invoking another realm of being to invest his image of chastity with analogical significance. They do not depend for their validity on what Rosemond Tuve calls the criterion of sensuous vividness; they are patently artificial. Rather the image of Britomart as Spenser's image of chastity attracts to it that image of light which best characterizes its inner qualities and for the Neoplatonist best symbolizes its ultimate source. The primal nature of these similes rather than their exfoliation in the verbal pattern of the poem is more characteristic of Spenser: significant intensity rather than formalistic extension.

Thus the Temple of Isis episode in Book V identifies Britomart and Arthegall with Isis and Osiris. Earlier in the canto we learned that "*Isis* doth the Moone portend; Like as *Osyris* signifies the Sunne. For that they both like race in equall iustice runne" (V.viii.4). This is the imagistic core (to expropriate Professor Lewis' term) of the light imagery associated with Britomart. It is not so much a culmination as an intensification of that imagery which has been generally used to describe her. Reading through the poem, one finds that the identification presented in this episode has been anticipated. Arthegall first appears to Britomart in Venus's mirror "as *Phoebus* face out of the east . . ." (III.ii.24). Glauce explains to Merlin, "Now haue three Moones with borrow'd brothers light, / Thrice shined faire, and thrice seem'd dim and wan," since a "sore euill" took hold on Britomart (III.iii.16). Britomart, as she listens blushing to the prophecy of Merlin, is described "As faire Aurora rising hastily . . ." (III.iii.20), and it is from a window "that opened West, / Towards which coast her loue his way addrest" (V.vi.7) that she sees Talus approaching to tell her of Arthegall's subjection by Radigund.

It would be unfair to call these occurrences of light imagery an image pattern. To do so is to attribute to Spenser aims he either did not foresee or carried off rather badly. He is not trying to make the kind of coherent pattern of sun and moon images that we find in *Henry the Fourth, Part I,* but neither is he trying to obliterate all trace of associations that, consciously or unconsciously, he is moving toward in the Temple of Isis episode. Part of Spenser's pictorialism is due to the fact that he restrains his descriptive talents until he reaches a place where he can utterly concentrate and intensify those images that he might have been weaving into the texture of his narrative. Much of the power of the great set pieces comes from this intensification of the imagery into great, simple iconographic symbols.

Nevertheless Spenser uses again and again the sequence of time as a symbol and organizing force; the calendar device in *The Shepheardes Calender,* the movement from morning to night in *Epithalamion,* the faint pattern of the church year in *Amoretti,* and the cycle of the months in the *Mutabilitie Cantos*—all these emphasize the profoundly simple devices that Spenser used to obtain some of his most brilliant effects. To see in the descriptions of Britomart and Arthegall a submerged metaphor of the journey of the sun from east to west, to see in Britomart a light, at first obscured by a veil, progressively realizing itself, occasionally breaking through the veil as beauty or the power of chastity, until the moment of revelation occurs, when she and Arthegall meet and recognize, when her quest is completed—to see this is only to enrich the poem, to give due praise to Britomart and Arthegall as the founders of the line that was to produce Elizabeth,

> . . . Goddesse heauenly bright,
> Mirrour of grace and Maiestie diuine,
> Great Lady of the greatest Isle, whose light
> Like *Phoebus* lampe throughout the world doth shine. . . .
> (I.Proem.4)

But images of light are not the only means that Spenser uses to create his image of Britomart. Spenser's chronicle of British kings in Book II stresses the importance of racial conflicts later resolved by national unification. This *discordia concors* works not only in the total plan of the poem, but also in the details Spenser employs to create Britomart, his invented British queen. Immediately after Merlin's prophecy Glauce the old nurse suggests the "bold deuise" of setting out on their quest disguised as knights. The time is very carefully specified.

> Ye see that good king *Vther* now doth make
> Strong warre vpon the Paynim brethren, hight
> *Octa* and *Oza,* whom he lately brake
> Beside *Cayr Verolame,* in victorious fight,
> That now all *Britanie* doth burne in armes bright.
> (III.iii.52)

This was no ordinary battle but the great victory of Uther over the Saxons. This battle and Uther's affair with Igerne are often the only details given in the chronicler's accounts. The time is particularly appropriate in light of the Saxon's eventual victory as foretold in Merlin's prophecy, but Spenser carefully shows that this later British defeat is only a necessary stage in the unification of Briton and Saxon. Glauce reminds Britomart of the armor of a Saxon virgin warrior that now hangs in her father's chapel.

> Ah read, (quoth *Britomart*) how is she hight?
> Faire *Angela* (quoth she) men do her call,
> No whit lesse faire, then terrible in fight:
> She hath the leading of a Martiall
> And mighty people, dreaded more then all
> The other *Saxons,* which do for her sake
> And loue, themselues of her name *Angles* call.
> Therefore faire Infant her ensample make
> Vnto thy selfe, and equall courage to thee take.
>
> (III.iii.56)

Angel, Angle, England—we are reminded of the Pope's pun on first seeing the fair Angles. The names themselves suggest the unity Britomart's offspring will create from the diversity of Saxon and Briton. The armor of this Saxon warrior, the best example of her people, becomes the protection of Britomart in her search for Arthegall and a symbol of the eventual unity of the best of Saxon and Britain in that greater warrior and queen, Elizabeth. It is in this armor that we first see Britomart in the opening episode of Book III, as she rides along with Arthur, Guyon, and their squires.

The moral implications of both the light imagery and the armor are brought to bear on Britomart's role in British history in Book III, Canto ix, where she hears Paridell's story of the fall of Troy. The whole Malbecco episode provides a fit background for a retelling of the Troy story, since it is itself a reenactment. The interplay of the themes of love perverted and society destroyed depends for its success on the correspondence between the love of individuals and the welfare of the body politic. Britomart, whose progeny will create a new Troy, is receiving a negative exemplum of the government of self and state. It is particularly appropriate for Paridell to tell of Troy, for he is about to take another Helen from another Menelaus. Paridell's story is a version slanted to suit his personality. To him

Troy is now "but an idle name," which is in entire accord with the *ubi sunt* motif of Troy moralized, but Paridell sees in the fall of Troy not an exemplum of human misgovernment but a "direfull destinie" from "angry Gods and cruell skye." Paridell's blindness is shown in his description of Paris:

> Most famous Worthy of the world, by whome
> That warre was kindled, which did *Troy* inflame,
> And stately towres of *Ilion* whilome
> Brought vnto baleful ruine. . . . (III.ix.34)

Just as Paris and Helen are unaware of the claims of the body politic, Paridell is unaware of their moral responsibility in causing the ruin he so lightly describes. Paridell then identifies himself as the descendant of Paris and Oenone. She, deserted, named her son Parius.

> Who, after *Greekes* did *Priams* realme destroy,
> Gathred the *Troian* reliques sau'd from flame,
> And with them sayling thence, to th'Isle of *Paros* came.
>
> That was by him cald *Paros,* which before
> Hight *Nausa,* there he many years did raine,
> And built *Nausicle* by the *Pontick* shore,
> The which he dying left next in remaine
> To *Paridas* his sonne. (III.ix.36–7)

Parius, the son of Paris's true marriage, sets off like the other Trojan exiles to establish a new city. Upton was unable to find Nausa among the names given to Paros and conjectured that the myth of Paros and Parius was Spenser's own. This is very probably true. The Greek word *nausa* means ship. In this city founded by Paris's son we are to see the countless voyages clustered around the Troy story—the ship that bore Paris from Oenone to Helen, the ship that bore Paris and Helen to Troy, the ships of the Greeks, the ships of the wandering Ulysses and the Trojans in exile. These are the ships of discord and the ships that will bring the concord of new cities from the fall of Troy.

> From whom I *Paridell* by kin descend;
> But for faire Ladies loue, and glories gaine,
> My natiue soile haue left, my dayes to spend
> In sewing deeds of armes, my liues and labours end.
>
> (III.ix.37)

But Paridell's departure from Paros is another sign of his inheritance from Paris: the ability to ignore the higher allegiance to one's country in favor of a personal passion. He like Britomart is on a quest, indeed, a quest of love, but his aim is a succession of Helens and the purpose of his deeds of arms is personal glory, not the furtherance of civil life. His quest becomes the inversion of Britomart's quest for Arthegall, as we can see from her response to his story.

> She was empassiond at that piteous act,
> With zelous enuy of Greekes cruell fact,
> Against that nation, from whose race of old
> She heard, that she was lineally extract:
> For Noble *Britons* sprong from *Troians* bold,
> And *Troynouant* was built of old *Troyes* ashes cold.
>
> (III.ix.38)

Opposed to his selfish view of Troy as "but an idle name" Britomart thinks of the famous town "in one sad night consumd,"

> What stony hart, that heares thy haplesse fate,
> Is not empierst with deepe compassiowne,
> And makes ensample of mans wretched state,
> That floures so fresh at morne, and fades at euening late?
>
> (III.ix.39)

Troy as example of the mutability of this life has moved Britomart, "For nothing may impresse so deare constraint, / As countries cause, and commune foes disdayne." In asking him to turn back his course to the story of Aeneas, Britomart, probably unaware, is asking for the story of the Trojan who gave up love for the higher destiny of founding the second Troy. But even here Paridell's personality intervenes. Significantly his story does not mention Dido, the one episode in Aeneas's life that repudiates Paridell's wantonness. Paridell brings his story to the time of Romulus's founding of Rome.

> There there (said *Britomart*) a fresh appeard
> The glory of the later world to spring,
> And *Troy* againe out of her dust was reard,
> To sit in second seat of soueraigne king,
> Of all the world vnder her gouerning.
> But a third kingdome yet is to arise,
> Out of the *Troians* scattered of-spring,
> That in all glory an great enterprise,
> Both first and second *Troy* shall dare to equalise.
>
> It *Troynouant* is hight, that with the waues
> Of wealthy *Thamis* washed is along,
> Vpon whose stubborne neck, whereat he raues
> With roring rage, and sore him selfe does throng,
> That all men feare to tempt his billowes strong,
> She fastned hath her foot, which standes so hy,
> That it a wonder of the world is song
> In forreine landes, and all which passen by,
> Beholding it from far, do thinke it threates the skye.
>
> (III.ix.44–45)

Britomart is aware of the past as it is relived in the present, and her praise of the third Troy provokes Paridell to recall the story "whilome I heard tell / From aged *Mnemon;* for my wits bene light." His tale is that of Brute's journey to Britain and his founding of Troynouant,

> . . . so heard I say
> Old *Mnemon*. Therefore Sir, I greet you well
> Your countrey kin, and you entirely pray
> Of pardon for the strife, which late befell
> Betwixt vs both vnknowne. So ended *Paridell*.
>
> (III.ix.51)

The encounter of these two descendants of Troy presents the basic problem facing Britomart as progenitrix of Troynovant and as knight of chastity. The history that Paridell relates is at times distorted by his own selfish interests. His forgetfulness and omissions reveal to the reader his essential lack of understanding of his lineage. His apology and lip service at the end of his tale refer to his overthrow by Britomart outside the wall of the little Troy represented by Malbecco's castle. Despite the apparent amity Britomart will ride off in the morning, and Troy will fall again. Unlike their prototypes the easy love of Paridell and Hellenore will not destroy any state but the inverted world of Malbecco. Of this fall Britomart need not know. Her love is to be hard won. As with Rome and Troynovant it is to be a concord won from discord, climaxed in the fight between Arthegall and Britomart in Book IV, Canto vi, and reinforced throughout the poem by the Vergilian source of her name, by the lineage of her armor, and by the light imagery consistently used to describe her.

Notes

1. Merritt Y. Hughes, "Virgil and Spenser," *University of California Publications in English* II (1929), 348–54. The parallels are *FQ,* III. ii. 30, ll. 220–28; 32, ll. 232–35; 34, ll. 250–52; 35–36, ll. 257–62; 40–41, ll. 237–49; 47, ll. 251–52; 48, ll. 349–54; 50–51, ll. 369–76.

2. "Why have I, frenzied one, when thou, Britomartis, thou Britomartis, the sole hope of my tombe, wert torn from me—why have I been able to prolong my day of life? And would that thou, maiden so dear to fleet Diana, hadst neither pursued, a maiden, the hunt that belongs to men, nor, aiming Gnosian shafts from Parthian bow, hadst driven the Dictaean goats to their familiar meadows!" Vergil, *Ciris,* ll. 294–300.

3. Britomart's removal of her helmet at IV. i and IV. vi as a symbol of concord has been pointed out by Calvin Huckabay, "The Structure of Book IV of *The Faerie Queene,*" *Studia Neophilologica,* XXVII (1955), 56, 59, 63.

4. Similes of light occur at III.i.43, III.iii.20, III.iv.13, III.ix.20, III.i.25, IV.i.13, IV.iv.47, IV.vi.19. The comparison is not always so simple as those quoted. It becomes clear that the veil as well as the light can be part of the description, e.g., III.iv.13 and IV.iv.47.

5. It seems to me significant that Spenser separates the images from an intimate metaphoric connection with his narrative by isolating them in epic similes.

Sherman Hawkins

Mutabilitie and the Cycle of the Months

> . . . we all beholde as in a mirrour the glorie of the Lord with unveiled face, and are changed into the same image, from glorie to glorie, as by the Spirit of the Lord (II Cor. 3.18).

Critics of the Mutabilitie Cantos have sometimes felt that, although Nature silences Mutabilitie, her verdict comes from Spenser's heart rather than his head. The Cantos express his despair, confronted by the universal rule of change,

> Which makes me loath this state of life so tickle,
> And loue of things so vaine to cast away.[1]

But these lines come at the end of the Mutabilitie Cantos, and if we take them as expressing the mood and meaning of the entire poem, there is danger we will read it backwards. The pessimistic interpretation involves two other mistakes, it seems to me. The first of these is the tacit assumption that constancy means changelessness, and that all change therefore is inconstancy. This is a conceptual error. The second error is structural, and consists in ignoring the symbolic center of the Cantos, the pageant of the months and seasons. This pageant is introduced by Mutabilitie as final proof of her claims, and here, if anywhere, the evidence for Nature's verdict will be found.

Let us look at the conceptual problem first. What does Spenser mean by mutability and constancy? C. S. Lewis, I think, goes too far in equating Mutabilitie with sin and corruption.[2] The Titanesse is blamed for death and old age and the fall of man, but she also causes changes as innocent as the random movements of fish, of wind and water, and as desirable as spring or growing up. She is, then, simply what Spenser calls her in his proems, "Change" or "Alteration." As child of Titan and Earth and granddaughter of Chaos, she is allied on the mother's side with inchoate matter, and on the father's with rebellious pride, for Spenser associates the Titans with the giants who revolted against Jove. But we notice that Mutabilitie's sisters, who share this sinister parentage, have received great power and high authority from Jove. Hecate and Bellona—or Fortune and War—work as parts of the divine plan administered by Jove, though their working may seem dark and inexplicable to human eyes. A similar function is open to Mutabilitie. But she refuses to "seeke by grace and goodnesse to obtaine / That place from which by folly *Titan* fell." Mutabilitie is not sin, but it is sin which sends her in revolt against the gods, repeating the error of her father, the primal rebel. Yet this rebellious creature is described as beautiful—

> Beeing of stature tall as any there
> Of all the Gods, and beautifull of face. . . .

This beauty stays the Thunderbearer's hand, "Such sway doth beauty euen in Heauen beare," and Spenser's insistence on the beauty of change underlies all the intellectual complexities of the Cantos.

Mutabilitie claims the sovereignty of heaven and earth both *de jure* and *de facto,* in Canto vi by right of lineage, in Canto vii as an accomplished fact. Jove, she complains, has superseded the older line of Titan, and thus we have the delightful spectacle of Mutabilitie indicting mutability and Change railing against change. But primacy in metaphysics does not depend on priority in time. Though chaos precedes order, it has, as a principle, no greater reality or right. Thus Spenser makes Hate the elder brother of Love:

> Yet was the younger stronger in his state
> Then th' elder, and him maystred still in all debate.
>
> (IV.x.32)

Jove does not justify his rule by temporal priority but by conquest and "eternall doome of Fates decree." In other words, order has "maystred" chaos, and this change, decreed even before time, represents the will of Providence. In this instance, there is meaning in mutability.

This is the very point which Mutabilitie challenges in Canto vii. She claims to rule the world, and she easily proves that all things change. No one disputes that. But the change she pictures is a denial of purpose and law. Change is a law unto itself—indeed, the only law governing the phenomenal world. All things, including man, change simply for the love of changing, for "all that moueth, doth mutation loue." Now the universe envisaged by Spenser's contemporaries is indeed a world in motion, and it is love which moves this world—but not the love of moving. The Elizabethan concept of motion is philosophic and not scientific, explaining movement by its goal rather than its source: it is the difference between a physics of push and a metaphysics of pull. All things, Richard Hooker explains, have an "appetite or desire" for perfection, and thus they move and change towards an end, the perfection peculiar to their natures.[3] Since God, the first mover, is absolute perfection, they seek to participate in Him as far as their natures permit. Law is not opposed to change, but regulates its mode and force. Love gives change direction; law gives it settled course. Nature's choice, then, is not between changelessness and change, but between the aimlessness of change for its own sake, and the constancy of movement directed by love and law towards a perfect goal. Nature gives her verdict without hesitation: things are not changed from their first estate

> But by their change their being doe dilate:
> And turning to themselues at length againe,
> Doe worke their owne perfection so by fate:
> Then ouer them Change doth not rule and raigne;
> But they raigne ouer change, and doe their states maintaine.

In other words, all things conquer change by achieving a perfection implicit in their origin; they finally become what they were first created to be. Since God is the source and end of this movement, its efficient and its final cause, the movement is a circle. For creatures lacking reason, this is a natural process; their cycles are controlled by destiny. But since man used his freedom to violate the law of his nature, he must now seek his end by a "way which is supernaturall,"[4] the way of grace opened to him in the Incarnation. He too moves in a circle, working to restore in himself the original righteousness of Adam, but now in the more perfect image of Christ. The fall has made this a cycle of labors: but if man is constant to the law of his supernatural way, he too can make his circle just and end where he began. And this suggests the irony which Spenser intends in presenting the cycle of the months and their labors as proof of the aimlessness of change.

What of Nature and Jove, the other major figures in the Cantos? Nature is here, I think, the Wisdom or Sapience which, in the "Hymne of Heauenly Beautie," rules all things so that they "do in state remaine, / As their great Maker did at first ordaine."[5] Nature, like Wisdom in Apocrypha, is more beautiful than the sun: her face cannot be seen "but like an image in a glass."[6] In his "Hymne," Spenser explains that we cannot endure the direct brightness of God's face, but we can behold its image in the looking-glass of his created works. Then by degrees of contemplation we rise to look upon the "celestiall face" of Sapience.[7] In the same way, the creatures at Arlo Hill, not yet ready to look on Nature's face unveiled, may yet behold the works of Wisdom in the labors of the months—like an image in a glass. Wisdom, the ordering power which creates and sustains the universe, appears to them in the guise of Nature. And the name of the judge defines the area in dispute. Mutabilitie claims to rule both nature and man, and we notice that although the months are human beings, they are workers in the fields and vineyards, who labor to bring the fruits of earth to their perfection. The dispute is over man in nature, and Spenser does not dissociate the way of grace by which man attains salvation from the natural movement of the rest of creation. Both together constitute the "nature" Mutabilitie claims to rule, and her claim is therefore judged by the power Spenser calls the "God of Nature." It could be argued that the meaning of the Cantos would be different if Spenser named his umpire Jove, or Grace, or simply God.

Wisdom is that stability of the divine thought which orders all change and generation. As referred to God, this stable order is called Providence; as referred to his creatures and acting in time, it is called Destiny. This distinction, familiar from Boethius to Richard Hooker, is lucidly explained by Justus Lipsius in his *Two Bookes of Constancie.* Destiny operates within the created order: it is the *"immoueble decree of Prouidence inherent in things mooueable."* But Destiny represents only one aspect of Necessity. The other is a "naturall propertie to all things created, to fall into mutabilitie and alteration." [8] Thus Lipsius helps us understand the functions of Spenser's principal characters. Nature corresponds to Providence, the divine Wisdom that decrees; Jove and the planets represent Destiny, which executes these decrees in the temporal world; while Mutabilitie is that tendency to change inherent in all created things, which is the other aspect of Necessity. Langius, the instructor of Lipsius in the dialogue, runs through all the evidence of change: like Mutabilitie herself, he shows that the stars have varied their fashion and their course; that the air, the waters, and earth are altered; that there is war among the elements; that every man passes through youth and strength to old age and death. Lift up your eyes, he urges Lipsius: behold the alterations in all human affairs and "let this wheel of changeable things run round, so long as this round world remayneth." Dismayed by the vanity of human life, Lipsius breaks into tears: What are these things for which we toil? he cries. *"Man is a shadowe and a dreame."* But Langius replies: "Imprint CONSTANCIE in thy mind amid this casuall and inconstant variablenesse of all things. I call it inconstant in respect of our vnderstanding and judgment: for that if thou looke vnto God and his prouidence, all things succeed in a steddy and immoueable order." The necessity of change, which seems the evidence of disorder and decay, actually testifies to this immovable order. "Thinkest thou that CHAVNCE or FORTVNE beareth any sway in this excellent frame of the world? . . . I wot well thou thinkest not so, nor any man els that hath either wisdome or wit in his head." The voice of nature itself, wheresoever we turn our eyes or minds, cries out that there is an eternal spirit we call God "which ruleth, guideth and gouerneth the rolling Spheares of heauen, the manifolde courses of the Stars and Planets, the successiu alterations of the Elements, finally, al things whatsoeuer in heauen and earth." [9] Thus Lipsius shows how the whole of Mutabilitie's argument for change fits into a larger argument for constancy. It would seem that Spenser's solution comes from his head as well as his heart.

This hierarchy of powers—Nature, Jove, and Mutabilitie—suggests a triple interpretation of constancy as a virtue of the intellect, the affections, and the will. All constancy ultimately depends on the stability of the divine understanding, working by a law which Hooker tells us can "haue no shew or cullor of mutabilitie." [10] Constancy, then, is first of all an intellectual virtue, finding stability in contemplation of the wisdom of Providence, represented here by Nature. Secondly, constancy in relation to the passions is steadfast fortitude, whose patient endurance remains unmoved by Mutabilitie and her wheel of change. Thirdly, as a virtue of the active will, it is perseverance, the unswerving pursuit of the course of Destiny, here figured by Jove and the other planets. This is virtue in motion, and, like natural law, it attains stability in its unchanging direction and its changeless end. As Nicholas Breton writes in his "Praise of Constancie,"

> It set the course of Wisedomes cariage,
> And neuer further then affection went:
> It is the state of all perfections stay,
> And Times all euerlasting holy day.[11]

I should now like to turn from the conceptual problem to more concrete problems of tone and structure. The obvious fact about the tone of the Cantos is its variety. Spenser's mimic world is inclusive and hospitable. His Grecian myth triumphantly assimilates its Irish setting: the imagined reality finds room for both the crystal pillars of Diana's palace and the salmon swimming in the Shure. Yet this variety is without confusion. The entire natural creation gathers at Arlo Hill: it is Nature's sergeant, Order, who finds each creature his due place in his degree. Spenser's delight in the fertile variety of things, and his deep confidence in the order which underlies variety, account for the varied texture of the Cantos and the unusual solidity of the objects they contain. The tone, as C. S. Lewis points out, is infinitely flexible: it rises to Olympian councils and descends without faltering to the rustic humors of foolish god Faunus.[12] And though it is flexible, it is firm: the sure and gracious movement of the verse seems to preclude the possibility of aimlessness in the poet's creation and in the greater creation which the poet imitates.

A definite purpose directs these changes of tone. We noticed that Spenser makes Mutabilitie responsible both for degeneration and decay and also for changes which are quite harmless and innocent. He does not distinguish between the ideas that "all things change" and that "all things change for the worse." This deliberate ambiguity permits him to alter his tone subtly but definitely in the course of the Cantos. He states the darkest implications of Mutabilitie at the very beginning: here she is associated with Adam's fall, Satan's rebellion, and the gradual decay of the world. But in Canto vii, when Mutabilitie presents her own case, she is associated with morally neutral mutations of creatures, elements, and times. This transition from "unnatural" to natural change alters our conception of change itself from our fallen predicament to our natural condition, and prepares us for the pageant of months, in which change becomes almost our opportunity.

The structure of Cantos vi and vii is markedly symmetrical. In each, an abstract debate is followed by a more concrete pictorial episode, the interlude of Faunus and Molanna, and the pageant of the times. Both episodes are relevant and functional. The buffoonery of the pastoral interlude is a parody of Mutabilitie's revolt. Thus in both halves of the sixth canto, a demigod assaults Diana. This is appropriate, for Diana is an emblem of constant inconstancy. Below the moon all things change; above it circle the unchanging heavens; the lunar sphere is the border between mutability and the immutable. The moon, which monthly changes in its circled orb, is a type of all inconstancy, "So that *as changefull as the Moone* men vse to say," and Spenser notes that Cynthia "neuer still did stand." Her very identity is triple in heaven, on earth, and in the underworld, and her changes are directly responsible for the changing months of the next Canto. On the other hand, as goddess of chastity, Diana is a type of constancy. Cynthia is a name for the Virgin Queen, whose motto was *Semper eadem,* always the same.[13] The parallel invasions of Canto 6 are directed against Diana in her double role: Mutabilitie attacks the divine power who is most changeable, while Faunus attempts the type of virgin constancy.

Faunus, half god, half goat, is closely related to Pan, whose dual nature was allegorized as the heavens and earth which make up the universe. His goatish legs, says Abraham Fraunce, betoken the crooked course of things under the moon, for these observe no immutable order. Pan pursues the spotless virgin Syrinx because universal nature desires a "celestiall and perpetuall constancy in these inferior bodies." [14] So we can see how the story of Faunus' lust for the goddess of chaste constancy fits into a debate on mutability. But plot and subplot are closely modeled on other classical myths. Mutabilitie's invasion of the skies recalls Phaeton, who also invaded heaven to demand his birthright, while Faunus recalls Actaeon, who was likewise hunted as a deer after he saw Diana bathing. Spenser uses these myths, I think, to hint at the primary myth of the fall. Phaeton is a type of pride, and Mutabilitie's ambitious revolt suggests the intellectual pride which made man aspire to be as God. Faunus represents the other aspect of the fall, the element of animal concupiscence: Actaeon torn by his hounds is man devoured by his animal passions. Mutabilitie's hybris is the stuff of tragedy, but the follies of the flesh are theme for comedy, so Spenser abates the sternness of his style in relating them. But the fall is essential to an account of mutability, and very lightly, very allusively, Spenser reminds us of its reality. Faunus tempts Molanna with "Queene-apples, and red Cherries from the tree"—the analogies with the Eden story are obvious enough. Faunus, like Satan, is punished in animal guise, while Molanna, like Eve, is sentenced to death for her inconstancy. But the episode is allusive and resists strict allegory. If Faunus' role as tempter recalls Satan, his subservience to appetite suggests Adam, as does his hunger for forbidden knowledge. The Actaeon story, according to Fraunce, teaches that "we ought not to be ouer curious and inquisitiue in spying and prying into those matters, which be aboue our reache." [15] Both Mutabilitie and Faunus break in upon assemblies of the gods, and finally Nature must appear, like Diana, without a veil to satisfy the Titanesse. But Diana, when she is spied upon, abandons Arlo Hill, a motif recalling the departure of Astraea at the end of the first golden age. Thus abandoned by its deity, the paradise of Arlo Hill falls prey to wolves and thieves.[16] The same wolves lurk in the pastoral landscape of "Lycidas," and we have not done with them yet, for we are all "in-dwellers" of that fallen country, and Spenser's myth, as he himself declares, is "too-too true." But at the beginning of the seventh canto, we see the coming of a divinity greater than Diana for a final judgment, and now Arlo is transfigured like Mount

Thabor in a second golden age. What seemed a triumph of mutability turns out to be a cycle, ending in greater perfection than before: the episode repeats the meaning of the whole.

Faunus also marks a new stage in our understanding of nature, for nature, like mutability, is a concept which changes and develops in the poem. As we first see it, the fair frame of the universe is so perverted that "all this world is woxen daily worse." This state of decay and disorder seems inimical to Diana and the constancy she represents. Faunus, whose form reflects a doubleness in nature, is one step closer to order. Certainly he is anything but hostile to Diana, but he represents an unshaped world of impulse and appetite, incapable of either love or law. The divine beauty which lures him produces neither reverence nor real desire—only an inchoate excitement which breaks out in laughter. Contrast the response of the created world to Nature herself in Canto vii. At her bright coming the earth puts forth voluntary flowers, and all creatures are ranged in order by her decree. The natural world is now seen as orderly and fertile, though fertility remains dominant. Even old Father Mole has changed his grey attire to green, "As if the loue of some new Nymph late seene, / Had in him kindled youthfull fresh desire." At this level of barely sentient life, response to the divine does not distinguish between worship and desire, goddess and nymph. But the joy of the old mountain and the flowering earth is instinct with reverence: the divine and the natural are in harmony as once before on Haemus hill at the marriage of Peleus and Thetis, the union of god and man, where Phoebus sang the "spousall hymne full cleere." We hardly need the *Ovide moralisé en prose* to identify that marriage feast with the *paradis terrestre* in which man lived before the apple thrown by Discord, that *diable d'enfer,* began our woe.[17] And it is against this background of natural harmony, of paradise regained, that Mutabilitie introduces the conflict of the elements as evidence of change. Actually it is, both traditionally and elsewhere in Spenser, an argument for concord and stability, and we begin to suspect that Mutabilitie is the victim of a vast dramatic irony.

This is, in fact, the case; but Spenser is a poet, not a philosopher: he gives us his essential realities in images, not arguments. As the pageant of the months bursts upon us, logic gives way to picture. It is easy for us to lose the argument in the profusion of sensuous imagery, but pictures spoke for the Elizabethans. They were accustomed to interpret such rich disguisings, where more is meant than meets the eye. The entrance of the months and seasons resembles the climax of a masque: we have had the allegorical *débat* and the comic antimasque: now in glorious procession the masquers march before us. The Jonsonian masque is, of course, a later development; but, like Jonson, Spenser uses the revelation of his "masquers" to mark the turning point, the defeat of the forces of disorder, the establishment of harmony in color, music, and motion. Spenser feels no need to interpret his pageant: the splendor of the vision, its order and its perfect rightness, should suffice.

But the modern reader needs to be reminded that Spenser's imagery belongs to a very old iconographical tradition. For centuries the months and their labors appeared over and over again in calendars and books of hours, above the portals of cathedrals, in handbooks and encyclopedias, signifying that the divisions of time—winter and summer, seedtime and harvest, days and years—are part of the divine plan, and that by labor man works out his own place in it. The medieval man who paused to contemplate the great stone calendar over a church door found various meanings there, according to Emile Mâle—and all of them apply to Spenser's calendar. The laborer recognized his own unceasing round of work, but the statue of the Savior looking down on these things of earth reminded him that he did not work without hope. The churchman, knowing that each month in the church calendar marks some event in the life of Christ or some great saint, saw them as a sequence of heroic acts: to him the year seemed like a garland of the virtues. The mystic saw in time the shadow of eternity and the year itself as a figure of Christ.[18] No doubt sheer repetition often obscured this complex of meanings and the labors of the months were reproduced as ornaments or mere conventions. Indeed, the modern reader is likely to assume either that such highly conventional figures can have no special meaning in Spenser's poem or that Spenser was simply repeating some explicit and generally accepted symbolism. Neither assumption is correct. It was not difficult for a fourteenth-century allegorist like Pierre Bersuire to translate the months, complete with etymologies, labors, and zodiacal signs, into elaborate symbols of twelve vices and virtues. The just man, perfected in all these virtues, is like the tree of life in

Revelation which bears twelve manner of fruit and yields her fruit each month.[19] Bersuire shows how far the symbolic interpretation of these stereotyped figures could be carried. But his systematic and detailed medieval allegories differ from Spenser's both in method and result. Spenser aims neither to repeat nor to invent. He is a traditional poet in a sense we have almost forgotten: he strives to penetrate and revive the central meaning in these images, so profoundly suggestive and so old, to recreate this meaning for a specific poetic purpose. The result is a genuine act of creative imagination, which can be understood only in the double perspective of a long history and an immediate poetic context. And the details of this poetic context require careful scrutiny.

At first glance Spenser's seasons seem to favor Mutabilitie. Rabanus Maurus tells us that spring represents the resurrection and renewal of life. Summer symbolizes the warmth of charity and prefigures the joys of the blest. Autumn, season of harvest and grape-gathering, refers to the Last Judgment, and winter signifies tribulation and the end of mortal life.[20] But these meanings are not active here—at least not yet. Spenser's Ovidian images of the seasons are brilliant but rather blank. Like the ages of man which represent them, the seasons seem to move in cycles without a goal: youth, maturity, decay, followed by the spring of another generation, another year. But there is regularity here: Spring does not follow Summer, nor Autumn Spring. The seasons are marshaled by Order, who is Nature's sergeant, and this order, this regular and repeated sequence, scarcely supports the claims of restless and uncertain change, self-fed and self-consumed.

Spenser begins his months with March. The choice, though commonplace, is significant. After Julius Caesar reformed the calendar, the secular year always began on January 1. This remained New Year's Day throughout the Middle Ages and the Renaissance. But it was originally a pagan festival. The Church remembered that the world was created in March, and that after the Exodus, God had designated this month as the beginning of months, the first of the year (Exodus 12.2). When dating from Christmas and Easter proved impractical, the Church began the year on March 25, or Lady Day. This was the date of the Annunciation, the beginning of the Christian era, and therefore the proper beginning for what came to be called the "Year of Incarnation" or the "Year of Grace." The year *ab incarnatione Domini* thus coincided with the year *a passione Domini,* since that event too was thought to have occurred on March 25. The cycle was perfect. Though January continued to be the first month in calendars and almanacs, all official documents in England followed the dating of the "Year of Grace" until the middle of the eighteenth century.[21]

The Year of Grace offered several advantages to Spenser. Most obviously, it matched the sequence of his months with that of the seasons. It also allowed him to suggest religious implications which would be obscured in the cycle from January to January. He had used this cycle in *The Shepheardes Calender,* but the symbolism had to be explained by E. K. in bald prose:

> . . . we mayntaine a custome of coumpting the seasons from the moneth Ianuarye, vpon a more speciall cause, then the heathen Philosophers euer coulde conceiue, that is, for the incarnation of our mighty Sauiour and eternall redeemer the L. Christ, who as then renewing the state of the decayed world, and returning the compasse of expired yeres to theyr former date and first commencement, left to vs his heires a memoriall of his birth in the ende of the last yeere and beginning of the next . . . ("The generall argument of the whole booke").

This symbolism was inherent in the very structure of the Year of Incarnation. Finally, beginning with March allowed Spenser to harmonize nature and grace as he had already done in the figure of Nature herself.[22] This calendar synchronizes the life of Christ with the progress of the seasons, the cycle of grace with the cycle of nature, "renewing the state of the decayed world" in both a spiritual and a physical sense. The same Providence is at work in the cycle of natural time and in the progress of redemptive history.

As the months march past, we note that almost all of them are laborers. Most of them carry farming tools: so eager is Spenser to make his point that July, who has cast away all his garments for the heat, nevertheless wears a sickle beneath his belt. Even old January's hands are numbed

> . . . with holding all the day
> An hatchet keene, with which he felled wood,
> And from the trees did lop the needlesse spray. . . .

This work moves with the steady rhythm of the seasons, the quickening and decay of all green things. We are watching man in nature, but we notice that man uses nature for his human ends. The burgeoning of spring is directed towards a harvest. And when that harvest is in, it is time to begin planning for the coming year: February has with him

> His plough and harnesse fit to till the ground,
> And tooles to prune the trees, before the pride
> Of hasting Prime did make them burgein round . . .

Man's foresight imposes a direction on the cycle of the months. Yet we are not made to feel that man is "above" nature or that he violates its meaning. His purposes are immanent in the natural processes themselves, so that man's end and nature's seem the same. December's feasting is what the harvest and its fruits are for.

This suggests another point. The labor is not felt as a burden. It is hard work, and November's brows "reek and steem" with sweat. Even the player, "iolly *Iune*," has with him his plough irons, and "in his time, he wrought as well as playd." Yet we are always conscious of the rewards of labor, and of a strong current of joy and affirmation that bears the months along. This is the joy of that strong generative power which impels the endless succession of seeds and sexes, the bull all garlanded with flowers and horned with golden studs, his sides wet with the waves "through which he waded for his loues delight." It is the joy of sheer abundance, of the harvest riches which fill December's "broad deepe boawle" and turn October's totty head with "ioyous oyle, whose gentle gust / Made him so frollick and so full of lust." It is the quick joy of life itself, which dances at the very sight of May:

> Lord! how all creatures laught, when her they spide,
> And leapt and daunc't as they had rauisht beene!

And there are hints of another kind of joy, which is harder to define, in the picture of August with his "garment all of gold downe to the ground" and in that Lady he leads by the hand. But even when joy is past, when January shivers in the cold, still there is work to do, and a reason and a will to do it.

Labor, we remember, is one of the punishments of Adam's sin, and his sons win their bread by the sweat of their brow. But these sowers and harvesters and grape gatherers recall the Biblical parables in which men labor for a different wage. According to Augustine, there are two kinds of work. "For it is on account of the love of this world that men labor in all their affairs: but do you labor in all good works, not for the love of this world, but for the eternal rest which God promises."[23] What of Spenser's laborers? Do they work for the world and for the world's bread? Or do they labor in all good works towards the endless rest when "no more *Change* shall be"?

The answer is to be found in five months, some having no labors of their own, which suggest the values that inspire and sanction the labors of the others. April clearly represents fertility: he is "full of lustyhed" and "wanton as a Kid" and he is mounted upon Europa's bull. In May fertility evolves into love: May is a lovely girl, borne on the shoulders of the Gemini and strewing flowers from her lap. To make sure we do not miss the point, Spenser adds a Cupid, fluttering about her, "all in greene."

The fertility of seedtime ripens into August, the month of harvest. He leads forth Virgo, "the which was cround / With eares of corne, and full her hand was found." Paradoxically, it is Virgo who brings fertility to consummation. She represents the temperance without which abundance grows to wilderness, the chastity without which love is an expense of spirit in a waste of shame. This is justice as principle of nature; the "righteous Virgin" is, of course, Astraea. The paradox is only apparent: the laws of proportion and restraint are for Spenser and Milton as natural as the generative power itself. And just as the fertility of April develops into human love in May, so the natural justice of August becomes human and social justice in September. He carries a pair of scales with which he measures out the harvest, "And equall gaue to each as Iustice duly scann'd." They are Astraea's scales, for "next her selfe her righteous ballance hanging bee" (V.i.11.9).

Thus in Spenser's calendar, April and May are balanced by August and September: seedtime and harvest represent the poles on which the Spenserian system turns. A central problem in the *Faerie Queene* (it is also a central problem in Chaucer and Milton) is the reconciliation of fertility and order, love and law. But here we see these powers cooperating harmoniously in a cycle which brings man and natural things to their perfection. This—and much more—is summed up in the figure of Astraea.

Spenser tells us in Book V that Justice ruled man and nature as they were first created:

> Peace vniuersall rayn'd mongst men and beasts,
> And all things freely grew out of the ground:
> Iustice sate high ador'd with solemne feasts,
> And to all people did diuide her dred beheasts.
>
> (V.Proem.9)

But when the world fell from this perfection, Astraea departed. Now she returns, led by August.[24] This second coming of Justice at the harvest season suggests that greater harvest, that final judgment, of which the season is a type. But the golden age which finally begins with that act of judgment has already begun for Christians in the Incarnation, in an act of love. This too Astraea signifies, for in her return, the Renaissance believed that Vergil had seen the coming of Messiah: "Iam redit et Virgo; redeunt Saturnia regna." In that event the Christmas psalm proclaims that law and love are reconciled: mercy and truth are met together; justice and peace have kissed each other. The function of Astraea in the cycle of the months is clear. She stands for the advent of the divine Love, the divine Justice into our world of history, the presence of God in the beginning and end and in the midst of times. So August prepares us for December.

For human love and human justice and human labor are not sufficient to their end. The center must intervene in the circle, the timeless come into time. It is the Incarnation which gives meaning to the cycle of time and direction to man's striving. All things would stray to their confusion, as Boethius writes, but that God's purpose draws them back, "by love retorned," to their source and goal. So the circle is made perfect: "Alle thinges seken ayen to hir propre cours, and alle thynges rejoysen hem of hir retornyge ayen to hir nature."[25] Thus Spenser shows us the Incarnation not in itself but in man's joyous response to it: December forgets the year's labors and the cold, "His Sauiors birth his mind so much did glad." This is the gladness of the old collect for Christmas—"God, which makest us glad with the yerely remembraunce of the birth of thy onely sonne"—but here it issues in bonfires and merriment and feasting. The advent of grace is manifest in the rejoicing of nature. The toil of the harvest months, with their counterpoint of food and drink—corn and oil, hogs and wine—culminates in December's "merry feasting" and his "broad deepe boawle." Though there is nothing symbolic, nothing sacramental about that feast and that cup, they are literally eucharistic: within the order of nature, they stand for remembrance, for thanksgiving, for peace among those men of good will who are December's "peeres." And in the midst of this human feasting, recalling its sanction and its source, we have the shaggy-bearded goat—

> The same wherewith Dan Jove in tender yeares,
> They say, was nourisht by th'Idaean mayd.

Thus that far-off divine event, with its earthly "mayd" and infant god, takes its place in the natural calendar of works and days. Remembering it, we, like December, forget the cold. Winter wins in the order of time. In January and February we see the triumph of the cold—tribulation and the end of life. But behind the triumph of death, and after the end of time, a greater year begins. There can by definition be no symbol for that final spring in the temporal procession of the months; we glimpse it only in the last stanza of the poem.

Spenser's vision of time embraces its entire course from beginning to end. The six days of creation are repeated in the six ages of history: the sixth age is the period from the Incarnation to the present, and thus the birth of Christ occurs proportionally in history at almost precisely the same point as in Spenser's year.[26] January and February are the age we know, a wintry and declining time of tribulation and death. But we can look forward from the sixth age to the seventh, the great sabbath of God's rest, and looking back we can survey and understand the whole pattern of God's redemptive plan. The circle, like the zodiac, is the emblem of perfection; it is also a symbol of eternity. In the circle of Spenser's calendar, with its counterpoint of labors and virtues, we see the eternal purpose incarnate in time.[27]

But revelation demands response. The plough and hatchet which January and February carry remind us of our obligation to bring the golden age to pass. This ethical lesson is repeated even in the signs of the zodiac. Several are fertility symbols (fish, flood, bull). Others are dangerous or evil (lion, scorpion, crab). These "eyressh bestes" are ridden or led—and hence controlled—by the human figures of the months like July:

> Vpon a Lyon raging yet with ire
> He boldly rode and made him to obay . . .[28]

This stress on order and control persists in the stanzas on Day and Night, and those on the Hours, who in spite of their loveliness were "Virgins all, and loue eschewed" lest they slight their duties at heaven's gate

> Which they did dayly watch, and nightly wake
> By euen turnes, ne euer did their charge forsake.

Duty and regularity, responsibility and discipline: the recurrent themes are unmistakable. Even Death is insubstantial; the reality is Life, "Full of delightfull health and liuely ioy." But this is not the joy of idleness—his are wings "fit to employ."

At this point Jove, who (unlike many critics) has scrutinized the pageant carefully, asserts that if time changes, it also keeps a course, and demands

> . . . who is it (to me tell)
> That *Time* himselfe doth moue and still compell
> To keepe his course? Is not that namely wee . . . ?

His question is echoed and answered by Hooker: "Who [is] the guide of nature but only the God of nature? *In him wee liue, moue, and are.*"[29] Mutabilitie gives a different reply. It should not be read as a tragic revelation of disorder in the heavens, with the new astronomy calling all in doubt. Spenser does not risk stating the graver implications of his theme so near its resolution: for that we must turn to the Proem of Book V. Mutabilitie's gleeful allusions to Sir Saturn and Dan Jove and Venus, "that goodly Paragone," give her speech a playfullness which prevents our taking the indictment seriously. Spenser's real concern is to disable the astrological notion of the stars as fate: their eccentricities cause star-gazers to "damne their lying bookes." Moreover, Jove is a mortal, born on earth. In other words, the stars are parts of the natural creation; they influence it only as agents of a higher power. And as Mutabilitie turns to that higher power, her tone, with its triumphant hybris, should warn us that her downfall is at hand.

Nature delivers her verdict in a stanza and a half. No more is needed: the evidence which Mutabilitie presents refutes her. All things change, but they change according to a providential law, the law of love which guides them to the perfection of their first estate. Thus they undo the fall, the work of Mutabilitie. The symbolic months represent the values which direct the labors of the rest: Love, Justice, Chastity, and Holiness, the virtues triumphant throughout the *Faerie Queene*.[30] Thus through the labors and disciplines of change, the creation prepares itself for

> . . . that same time when no more *Change* shall be,
> But stedfast rest of all things firmely stayd
> Vpon the pillours of Eternity. . . .

For labor and change are not the ultimate realities, and Spenser's emblem has another meaning. To the Middle Ages and the Renaissance, the cycle of months suggested the vanity of temporal things no less than their purpose and their order. The power of Spenser's emblem is in part this paradox: it inculcates both commitment and withdrawal. As the figures of the months glide by, we feel their transience as well as their constancy, and we are prepared, half-consciously, for the last stanzas, in which Spenser turns from change and toil to a vision of rest with God. The labor and the rest are not opposed, for the rest is the motive of the toil. "There remaineth . . . a rest to the people of God," writes Paul, "Let us labour, therefore, to entre into the rest. . . ."[31] In the two stanzas of Canto viii, the laborer looks up from his work to its reward, and in the last change in this poem of changes, we move from time to eternity, from action to contemplation.

The developing concepts of Mutabilitie and Nature give to the Cantos their intellectual action: by a kind of ultimate decorum they *enact* the meaning of change and constancy by the steady development and definition of these concepts. Here the very numbering of the Cantos is suggestive.[32] In Canto vi, the sixth age of trial and confusion, Mutabilitie appears to mean flux, disorder, and decay. But in the next Canto, the pageant of the months reveals the beauty of constancy within the wheel of change. This is the seventh Canto of the seventh book, and the number—itself a symbol of God's immutability and of eternal rest—recalls the stability and repose which completed the labors of creation and pronounced it good. Then, in the eighth Canto, we look beyond creation and its weeks to the sabbath which is both the seventh day of rest and the eighth day of resurrection, the glory of which Gloriana's feast is but a type.[33] In the steadfast brightness of eternity, the radiance of the months seems dark indeed. There is a suggestive parallel in the "Hymne of Heauenly Beautie." There we behold God's image in the mirror of his work, rising in contemplation from the beauty of earth and sea up to the heavens and the fixed stars. Finally we behold the face of Wisdom herself; then—and only then—do we realize that earthly beauty is meaningless compared to this. It is the vision of "that soueraine light" which "loathing brings / Of this vile world, and these gay seeming things."[34] Thus in Canto viii, Spenser can echo the claim of Mutabilitie herself, declaring that he loathes this state of life so fickle where "all that moueth, doth in *Change* delight." These lines have often been read as expressions of personal disillusionment and despair. But it is important to realize that here, as elsewhere in the opening stanzas of a book or canto, Spenser speaks in the role of the Poet, the Narrator, the Presenter, that his sentiments on these occasions are dictated by decorum and serve to define or emphasize his theme.[35] Here, extolling the divine changelessness, the poet repudiates all change. His naïve dismay at the prospect of a world of transience and toil is not intended to define our response to what has gone before but to introduce what follows. It directs us towards the final vision of a transcendant stability and repose, just as the conventional wording, the lapsing, hesitant rhythms, and feminine rhymes of the first stanza prepare us for the superb climax of the final lines. This vision does not cancel the beauty that has gone before, but offers a final qualifying perspective on it. The revelation of a transfigured nature is at the center of the Mutabilitie Cantos, and its meaning is declared by a higher authority than the poet. At the end of the seventh Canto, Nature has put aside her veil, for the creatures are described as "looking in her face." As she pronounces sentence, we see the purpose and meaning of Nature, no longer in the dark glass of her created works or in the veiled allegory of the months, but explicitly and simply, face to face. The reader, like Solomon, has been instructed by Wisdom herself in "the true knowledge of the things that are . . . The beginning and the end, & the middes of the times: how the times alter, and the changes of the seasons, The course of the yere, the situacion of the starres." [36]

Read in this way, the Mutabilitie Cantos take their due place as Spenser's "Legend of Constancy." As decorum requires, we find the virtue of the book exemplified in many aspects of the poem. We find it symbolized in the circular garlands which deck Molanna and her father Mole, in the star Vesper which guides the mutable moon in its course, "And ioy to weary wandring trauailers did lend"—note the pun on "trauailers." We find it in allusions like the marriage of Peleus and Thetis, for Peleus won his divine bride by clinging to her through all her changing shapes. We see it in Jove settling himself to meet his foe (his sitting posture, writes Abraham Fraunce, betokens his immutability),[37] and in the aspect of Nature herself, "Still mooning, yet vnmoued from her sted." We watch it prevailing in the action, in the cycles which restore Molanna to Fanchin and bring a goddess once again to Arlo Hill. Thus the Cantos exemplify and define constancy, and it is not what we supposed, for Spenser has the power of genius to surprise. It is not, in this world at least, a power "contrayr" to Mutabilitie. It is a purpose persisting through mutability, redeeming it. It combines the energy of love with the stability of law; it is not a denial of change but a direction for work.

We hardly need the rest of the seventh book to exemplify its virtue. For the central emblem of the Cantos is the cycle of twelve months, which for Bersuire symbolize the twelve virtues or works of the just man. And the *Faerie Queene* itself, aiming to "fashion a gentleman or noble person in vertuous and gentle discipline," is also planned as a cycle of the twelve private moral virtues. Each knight repeats this cycle in twelve cantos, beginning as the bare title of a virtue, but laboring till it becomes his very nature. The virtue of the seventh book is not without a champion, for each of Spenser's knights in turn becomes the type of constancy, quitting the Eden of the Faerie Queene to work his own perfection in the realms of Mutabilitie.

Notes

1. Quotations are from the Johns Hopkins Variorum Spenser and, unless otherwise noted, from the Mutabilitie Cantos. My obligations to Professors Bennett, Bush, Cumming, Stirling, and Tuve are obvious, as are my differences and agreements with other scholars. I am indebted to Dr. Richard Stockton's dissertation, "The Christian Content of Edmund Spenser's 'Mutabilitie' Cantos" (Princeton, 1954) for my interpretation of Nature, and to Dr. Thomas Roche for help in interpreting the Faunus episode and the mythological figures.

2. *The Allegory of Love* (Oxford, 1938), p. 354.

3. *Of the Lawes of Ecclesiasticall Politie* (London, 1594–1597), p. 57. The argument of this paragraph is drawn largely from Hooker's first Book. For the figure of the circle, see Pierre de la Primaudaye, *The French Academie,* tr. T.B.C. (London, 1618), p. 647.

4. Hooker, p. 81.

5. "An Hymne of Heauenly Beautie," ll. 200–201.

6. See Wisdom 7.29, 26: Wisdom is "more beautiful then the sunne," the "brightnes of the euerlasting light, the vndefiled mirroure of the maiestie of God." Biblical quotations follow the Geneva version of 1560 excepting the substitution of "unveiled" (Revised Standard Version) for "open" in the epigraph, and "labour" (1611) for "studie" in Hebrews 9.11.

7. "An Hymne of Heauenly Beautie," l. 242.

8. *Two Bookes of Constancie, Written in Latine by Iustus Lipsius,* tr. Sir John Stradling, ed. Rudolf Kirk (New Brunswick, N.J., 1939), pp. 118, 106.

9. Lipsius, pp. 110–11, 102.

10. Hooker, p. 51.

11. "The Praise of Constancie," in *The Soule's Immortall Crowne* (1605) in *The Works in Verse and Prose of Nicholas Breton,* ed. A. B. Grosart (2 vols., Edinburgh, 1879), I, 20 B2v. Compare Spenser's Nature to Breton's Wisdom ("Vpon the Praise of Wisedom," *ibid.,* pp. 20 Bv–20 B1).

12. Lewis, pp. 356–57.

13. Hence when Sir Henry Lee presented before her "An excellent Dialogue betweene Constancie and Inconstancie," the outcome was a foregone conclusion: Inconstancie finds herself drawn by the Queen's power "from the circle of my fancies, to the center of constant loue," and "changed to that estate which admitteth no change," to "be my selfe as she is, *Semper eadem.*" *The Phoenix Nest, 1593,* ed. Hyder E. Rollins (Cambridge, Mass., 1931), pp. 28–29. *The Phoenix Nest* assigns the last two phrases to *Const*[*ancie*], but two MSS give them to her opponent (pp. 137, 139, 141). For the association of Elizabeth, the moon, and constancy in motion, see also Endimion's disquisition on Cynthia in *Endimion,* I.i.30 ff., in *The Complete Works of John Lyly,* ed. R. W. Bond (3 vols., Oxford, 1902), III, 22, especially ll. 34–36: "Is shee inconstant that keepeth a settled course, which since her first creation altereth not one minute in her mouing?" The whole passage is significant for Spenser's argument.

14. *The Third Part of the Countess of Pembrokes Yuychurch* (London, 1592), pp. 10v–11.

15. Fraunce, p. 43.

16. For Eden as a pastoral hill, comparable to other hills of legend, sacred and profane, see "Iulye" ll. 57 ff., and E.K.'s gloss. The parallelism between Arlo and Acidale is surely no accident: one is the favorite haunt of Diana, the other of Venus; Calidore, like Faunus, intrudes on naked goddesses; the Graces, like Diana, quit the mountain of their choice. The analogy suggests close connections between the Legends of Courtesy and Constancy: indeed, Calidore's abandonment of his quest raises the very problem to be resolved in the Cantos.

17. *Ovide moralisé en prose,* ed. C. DeBoer, in *Verhandelingen der Koninklijke Nederlandse Akademie van Wetenschappen,* LXI, No. 2 (1954), 288.

18. Emile Mâle, *The Gothic Image,* tr. Dora Nussey (New York: Harper Torchbooks, 1958), p. 66.

19. Pierre Bersuire, *Opera Omnia,* 6 vols. in 3 (Cologne, 1730), I, 247–48; II, 127–29; V, 42.

20. *Patrologia latina*, CXI, 302–303.

21. This paragraph is drawn from Sir W. W. Greg, "Old Style—New Style," in *Joseph Quincy Adams Memorial Studies,* ed. James G. McManaway, *et al.* (Washington, 1948), pp. 563–69, and Reginald L. Poole, "The Beginning of the Year in the Middle Ages," *Proceedings of the British Academy,* X (1921–1923), 113–37.

22. To distinguish the religious from the natural year as Spenser does in the *Calender* fits a more dualistic view of nature than I find in the Mutabilitie Cantos and helps explain the darker tone of the earlier poem. Cf. Robert Allen Durr, "Spenser's Calendar of Christian Time," *ELH,* XXIV (1957), 269–95.

23. *PL,* XXXVIII, 85. For a series of sixteenth-century paintings and engravings which merge the labors of the months with the parables of Christ, see Pierre Marie Auzas, "Les douze mois de Grimmer," *Pro Arte,* XVII (1948), 3–16.

24. In the satirical *Mother Hubberds Tale,* ll. 1–3, August is the month in which Astraea *leaves* the world. For full discussion of Astraea, see Frances A. Yates, "Queen Elizabeth as Astraea," *Journal of the Warburg and Courtauld Institutes,* X (1947), 27–82.

25. *De Consolatione Philosophiae,* IV, m. 6; III, m. 2, in *The Works of Geoffrey Chaucer,* ed. by F. N. Robinson, 2d ed. (Cambridge, Mass., 1957), pp. 371, 343. The collect quoted below appears in the first Communion for Christmas in the 1549 Prayer Book of Edward VI. It was omitted in the Prayer Book of 1552.

26. The ages of the world were also analogous to the ages of man: see Rabanus Maurus, *PL,* CVII, 726–28, and Bede, *PL,* XC, 288. For an iconographical representation of the six ages of history as a circle, see British Museum Royal MS 19 C 1 f.58ᵛ.

27. The figure of the circle dominates the Cantos from the "euerwhirling wheele / Of *Change*" in the first stanza to the great cycle of time in Canto 7: the changing significance of the figure reflects the development of the argument. Compare the emblem of a compass tracing a broken circle with the motto, "Labore et Constantia," in George Wither, *A Collection of Emblemes* (1635), reproduced in Rosemary Freeman, *English Emblem Books* (London, 1948), opposite p. 147. The emblem appears earlier on the title pages of Geoffrey Whitney, *A Choice of Emblemes* (London, 1586) and Alciati's *Emblemata* (Antwerp, 1581). Note the star-gazers in the background of Wither's version.

28. Compare the familiar political interpretation of the Phaeton story in which the "Bulls, Centaurs, Lyons, Scorpions, and such like" of the zodiac are interpreted as evil and seditious subjects (Fraunce, p. 35ᵛ). In an unusual fourteenth-century almanac (Vienna Nat. Bibl. Codex 1921), the signs of the zodiac attack or menace human figures—even the fish are shown biting a swimmer. But the zodiacal signs, like the months, were conventional figures capable of fresh interpretation: for examples of novel religious symbolism (Aries suggests the Paschal Lamb; Aquarius, the Baptist), see "The Columnes," ll. 520–49, in *Du Bartas His Second Weeke,* in *The Complete Works of Joshuah Sylvester,* ed. A. B. Grosart (2 vols., Edinburgh, 1880), I, 158–59.

29. Hooker, p. 54.

30. If a man loves righteousness, declares Solomon in the 1611 version, the labors of Wisdom are virtues: temperance and prudence, justice and fortitude (Wisdom 8.7).

31. Hebrews 4.9, 11.

32. I am assuming that this numbering is Spenser's, and that the Legend of Constancy follows that of Courtesy.

33. Spenser's sabbath, like the modern Sunday, combines the Jewish seventh day of rest with the Christian eighth (or first) day celebration of the resurrection of Christ. These correspond to the seventh age of the world, representing the repose of just souls, and the eighth age, representing their final resurrection (see

Rabanus Maurus, *PL,* CVII, 726–28 and CXI, 299–300). For the symbolic values of seven and eight, see Pietro Bongo, *Mysticae Numerorum Significationis Liber* (Bergamo, 1585). According to Hugh of St. Victor, numbers have significance by extension: thus seven beyond six represents rest after work, and eight beyond seven represents eternity after mutability. Vincent F. Hopper, *Medieval Number Symbolism* (New York, 1938), p. 101.

34. "An Hymne of Heauenly Beautie," ll. 295, 298–99

35. Compare the beginning of Canto vii, where the poet's awe at the "too high flight" which he must undertake serves to emphasize the hardihood of Mutabilitie, the vain curiosity of Faunus. These utterances of the poet help direct the reader's attitude. We too are permitted to enter the councils of the gods, but Spenser warns us that the secrets of Providence are to be approached in the humility that waits upon divine illumination, not in the spirit of a prying astrologer or a rebellious titan. See Lipsius, p. 104: "The Auncientes haue fayned that Gyantes aduanced themselues against God, to pull him out of his throne. Let vs omitte these fables: In very trueth you querulous and murmuring men be these Gyantes." Compare Boethius, III, pr. 12, pp. 356–57.

36. Wisdom 7.17–19.

37. "*Iupiter* is commonly pictured sitting, sith the eternall Monarch of heauen, and earth, is alwaies immutable, one, and the same, and neuer subiect to any alteration" (Fraunce, p. 13). See also Vincenzo Cartari, *The Fountaine of Ancient Fiction,* tr. Richard Linche (London, 1599), sig. K2.

Selected Bibliography

(This bibliography provides a basic list of reference works, editions, and studies. The studies are principally recent ones of general interest. Specialist students should consult the Bibliographies listed in Section I. Books and articles represented in the present collection are omitted here.)

I. Works of Reference

Atkinson, D. F. *Edmund Spenser, A Bibliographical Supplement.* Baltimore, 1937. (Supplement to Carpenter's *Reference Guide,* below.)

Carpenter, F. I. *Reference Guide to Edmund Spenser.* Chicago, 1923.

Jones, H. S. V. *A Spenser Handbook.* New York, 1930.

McNeir, Waldo, and Provost, Foster. *Annotated Bibliography of Edmund Spenser, 1937–1960.* Pittsburgh, 1962.

Wurtsbaugh, Jewel. *Two Centuries of Spenserian Scholarship (1609–1805).* Baltimore, 1936.

II. Editions

The Poetical Works of Edmund Spenser. J. C. Smith and E. de Selincourt (eds.). Oxford, 1912. (Includes the Spenser-Harvey Letters.)

The Works of Edmund Spenser: A Variorum Edition. Edwin Greenlaw, Charles Grosvenor Osgood, Frederick Morgan Padelford, and Ray Heffner (eds.). 10 vols. Baltimore, 1932–1957.

Works. W. L. Renwick (ed.). 4 vols. London, 1928–34. (Omits *The Faerie Queene.*)

Books I and II of The Faerie Queene, The Mutability Cantos and Selections from the Minor Poetry. Robert Kellogg and Oliver Steele (eds.). New York, 1965.

III. *Critical Studies*

A. General

Berger, Harry, Jr. "The Prospect of Imagination: Spenser and the Limits of Poetry," *Studies in English Literature,* I (1961), 93–120.

Bush, Douglas. "Spenser," in *Mythology and the Renaissance Tradition in English Poetry.* Minneapolis, 1932. Reprinted 1963.

Davis, B. E. C. *Edmund Spenser: A Critical Study.* Cambridge, 1933.

Freeman, Rosemary. *Edmund Spenser.* London, 1957.

Lotspeich, H. G. *Classical Mythology in the Poetry of Edmund Spenser.* Princeton, 1932.

Mueller, William R., and Allen, Don Cameron (eds.). *That Soveraine Light: Essays in Honor of Edmund Spenser, 1552–1952.* Baltimore, 1952.

Mueller, William R. (ed.). *Spenser's Critics: Changing Currents in Literary Taste.* Syracuse, 1959. (An anthology of critical essays.)

Smith, Hallett. *Elizabethan Poetry.* Cambridge, Mass., 1952.

Whitaker, Virgil K. *The Religious Basis of Spenser's Thought.* Stanford, 1950.

B. *The Faerie Queene*

Alpers, Paul J. "Narrative and Rhetoric in *The Faerie Queene,*" *Studies in English Literature,* II (1962), 27–46.

Bennet, J. W. *The Evolution of The Faerie Queene.* Chicago, 1942.

Berger, Harry, Jr. *The Allegorical Temper: Vision and Reality in Book II of Spenser's "Faerie Queene."* New Haven, 1957.

Durling, Robert M. "Spenser," in *The Figure of the Poet in Renaissance Epic.* Cambridge, Mass., 1965.

Greenlaw, Edwin. *Studies in Spenser's Historical Allegory.* Baltimore, 1932.

Hoopes, Robert. " 'God Guide Thee, *Guyon*': Nature and Grace Reconciled in *The Faerie Queene,* Book II," *Review of English Studies,* V (1954), 14–24.
Hughes, Merritt Y. "The Arthurs of *The Faerie Queene,*" *Études Anglaises,* VI (1953), 193–213.
Kermode, Frank. "Spenser and the Allegorists," *Proceedings of the British Academy,* XLVIII (1962), 261–79.
Lewis, C. S. *The Allegory of Love.* Oxford, 1936. Reprinted 1958.
Nellish, B. "The Allegory of Guyon's Voyage: An Interpretation," *ELH,* XXX (1963), 89–106.
Parker, Pauline. *The Allegory of The Faerie Queene.* Oxford, 1960.
Sirluck, Ernest. "*The Faerie Queene,* Book II, and the Nicomachean Ethics," *Modern Philology,* XLIX (1951), 73–100.
Stampfer, Judah L. "The Cantos of Mutability: Spenser's Last Testament of Faith," *University of Toronto Quarterly,* XXI (1951–1952), 140–56.
Williams, Kathleen. *Spenser's World of Glass: A Reading of The Faerie Queene.* Berkeley and Los Angeles, 1966.
Woodhouse, A. S. P. "Nature and Grace in *The Faerie Queene,*" *ELH,* XVI (1949), 194–228.
——, "Nature and Grace in Spenser: A Rejoinder," *Review of English Studies,* VI (1955), 284–87.

C. The Minor Poems

Allen, Don Cameron. "Muiopotmos, or the Fate of the Butterflie," in *Image and Meaning: Metaphoric Traditions in Renaissance Poetry.* Baltimore, 1960.
Hamilton, A. C. "The Argument of Spenser's *Shepheardes Calender,* *ELH,* XXIII (1956), 171–82.
Hieatt, A. Kent. *Short Time's Endless Monument.* New York, 1960. (On the "Epithalamion.")
Lever, J. W. *The Elizabethan Love Sonnet.* London, 1956.
McLane, Paul E. *Spenser's Shepheardes Calender: A Study in Elizabethan Allegory.* Notre Dame, 1961.
Smith, Hallett. "The Use of Conventions in Spenser's Minor Poems," in *Form and Convention in the Poetry of Edmund Spenser,* Selected Papers from the English Institute, ed. William Nelson. New York, 1961.
Stein, H. *Studies in Spenser's Complaints.* New York, 1934.
Wrenn, C. L. "On Re-Reading Spenser's *Shepheardes Calender,*" *Essays and Studies by Members of the English Association,* XXIX (1943), 30–49.

Biographical Notes

Samuel Taylor Coleridge (1772–1834) devoted himself as much to criticism and literary theory as to the writing of poetry. Coleridge's criticism of Spenser survives only in the imperfectly reported lectures on the English poets given at the Royal Institution in 1818.

Abraham Cowley (1618–1667), poet and dramatist, was among the last practitioners of the "metaphysical" school of poetry, though he wrote epic, satiric, and pastoral verses as well.

Sir William Davenant (1606–1668), poet and dramatist, became Poet Laureate in 1638. The Preface to his epic poem, *Gondibert,* surveys the history of epic poetry, and in its criticism of Spenser's extravagance anticipates the neo-classical principles of the succeeding age.

Edward Dowden (1843–1913) was Professor of English Literature at Trinity College, Dublin. His essay on Spenser appeared as part of the prefatory material in Grosart's edition of Spenser's *Works* in 1884.

Michael Drayton (1563–1631) was one of the most prolific of Elizabethan poets. "To Henery Reynolds" is a verse letter containing Drayton's critical estimates of other poets.

John Dryden (1631–1700) has several discussions of Spenser in his voluminous critical works. Dryden is thought to have been one of the editors of the 1679 edition of Spenser's *Works.*

John R. Elliott, Jr. (1937–   ) was educated at Harvard and the University of California, Berkeley. He has taught at the University of North Carolina and the University of Virginia, and is currently Assistant Professor of English at the University of California, Santa

Barbara. He is the author of several articles on Shakespeare and is preparing a book on Shakespeare's History Plays.

Robert Ellrodt (1922–), a French scholar, is head of the Department of English at the University of Nice. From 1961–1966 he held the Professorship of Seventeenth-Century English Literature at the Sorbonne. He is the author of *Les poètes métaphysiques anglaises* (Paris, 1960), a three-volume study of metaphysical poetry.

Thomas M. Greene (1926–) is Professor of English and Comparative Literature at Yale, and is the author of *The Descent from Heaven: A Study in Epic Continuity* (Yale University Press, 1963).

Joseph Hall (1574–1656), poet and clergyman, included poets and poetry among the targets of his satire in his English adaptation of Juvenal, *Virgidemiae.*

A. C. Hamilton (1921–) is Professor of English at the University of Washington. He is currently preparing an annotated edition of *The Faerie Queene.*

Gabriel Harvey (1545?–1630), scholar, poet, and pamphleteer, became Spenser's friend at Cambridge. He published his correspondence with Spenser, probably without his approval, in 1580.

Sherman Hawkins (1929–), Associate Professor of English at the University of Rochester, was educated at Harvard, Oxford, and Princeton, and has taught at Princeton and Bryn Mawr. He is currently preparing a book on religion and Renaissance tragedy.

William Hazlitt (1778–1830), essayist, critic, and periodical reviewer, was one of the most voluminous and systematic of the Romantic literary critics. He wrote essays applying the principles of Romanticism to nearly every major poet from Spenser to his own time.

Graham Hough (1908–), Fellow of Christ's College, Cambridge, is the author of a number of books on English poetry. He has been a Visiting Professor at Johns Hopkins and Cornell.

Leigh Hunt (1784–1859), poet, critic, and editor, wrote several essays on Spenser. Together with Hazlitt, Hunt was chiefly responsible for the establishment of the Romantic view of Spenser.

Richard Hurd (1720–1808), Bishop of Lichfield and Coventry, was one of the earliest champions of "gothic" and romantic literature in the eighteenth century.

Ben Jonson (1572–1637), poet and playwright, made his famous criticism of Spenser's style in his chief critical work, *Timber,* which also contains Jonson's strictures of Shakespeare.

John Keats (1795–1821) first read *The Faerie Queene* at the age of sixteen, going through it, according to Cowden Clarke, "as a young horse would through a spring meadow—ramping!" Keats's earliest known poem is an imitation of the Spenserian stanza.

Robert Kellogg (1928–) is Professor of English at the University of Virginia, where he has taught since receiving his doctorate from Harvard in 1958. He is coeditor with Oliver Steele of an edition of Books I and II of *The Faerie Queene* (Odyssey, 1965) and coauthor with Robert Scholes of *The Nature of Narrative* (Oxford, 1966).

Frank Kermode (1919–) is Lord Northcliffe Professor of English in University College, London. He has formerly taught at the Universities of Manchester and Bristol. Professor Kermode has written widely on Renaissance literature, particularly on Shakespeare, Donne, and Milton.

James Russell Lowell (1819–1891), Professor at Harvard and editor, in succession, of the *Atlantic Monthly* and the *North American Review,* was perhaps the most influential American critic of the nineteenth century.

Louis L. Martz (1913–), Douglas Tracy Smith Professor of English and American Literature at Yale University, is a specialist in seventeenth-century poetry. He is the author of *The Poetry of Meditation* (New Haven, 1954) and an accompanying anthology, *The Meditative Poem* (Doubleday-Anchor, 1963).

John Milton (1608–1674) acknowledged Spenser as his poetic master, much as Spenser regarded Chaucer. Spenser's influence is especially evident in Milton's early poems, such as *Comus.* Milton also referred directly to Spenser in *Il Penseroso* and the *Apology for Smectymnuus.*

Thomas Nashe (1567–1601), pamphleteer, novelist, and playwright, spent much of his literary efforts on vituperative controversies with Spenser's friend, Gabriel Harvey, and other literary figures. Spenser was one of the few to escape the vitriol of Nashe's pen.

William Nelson (1908–) is Professor of English at Columbia University, where he has taught since 1949. In addition to his study of Spenser, he is the author of books on John Skelton and Alexander Barclay. He is currently Executive Director of the Renaissance Society of America.

Alexander Pope (1688–1744), while perhaps the least Spenserian of English poets, paid tribute to Spenser in a letter to John Hughes upon the publication of Hughes's edition of Spenser in 1715.

Sir Walter Ralegh (1552?–1618), courtier, adventurer, and poet, was a close friend of Spenser. Two of the commendatory sonnets prefixed to the 1590 edition of *The Faerie Queene* were written by Ralegh.

W. L. Renwick (1889–) is Regius Professor Emeritus of Rhetoric and English Literature in the University of Edinburgh. He has edited Spenser's minor works (4 vols., 1928–1934), and is the author of the volume covering the period 1789–1815 in the *Oxford History of English Literature.*

The Return from Parnassus, Part II, is the last of a trilogy of plays produced in Cambridge from 1598–1601, dealing with the tribulations of poets and scholars in the England of the 1590's. It contains references to Marlowe, Shakespeare, and Jonson, as well as to Spenser.

Thomas P. Roche (1931–) is Associate Professor of English at Princeton, where he has taught since 1960. He was educated at Yale, Pembroke College, Cambridge, and Princeton, and has also taught at Williams College.

Sir Philip Sidney (1554–1586), Elizabethan poet, scholar, soldier, and courtier *par excellence,* was a friend of Spenser. Spenser dedicated *The Shepherds Calender* to Sidney.

John Upton (1707–1760) was born into a family of classical scholars and published books on Epictetus and Shakespeare, in addition to his edition of Spenser.

Thomas Warton (1728–1790) was Professor of Poetry at Oxford and Poet Laureate. His *Observations on the Faerie Queene of Spenser* (1754) was the first comprehensive critical analysis of *The Faerie Queene.*

William Webbe (fl. 1568–1591) was a member of St. John's College, Cambridge, where he may have known both Harvey and Spenser. Nothing else is known of his life.

Virginia Woolf (1882–1941), English novelist and essayist, left her essay on *The Faerie Queene* among her papers at her death. It was published posthumously by her husband, Leonard Woolf.

William Wordsworth (1770–1850) shared the admiration of other Romantic poets for Spenser. His "Essay Supplementary" is a survey of English poetry from Spenser to his own time, stressing the critical vicissitudes suffered by great poets.

William Butler Yeats (1865–1939), Irish poet and dramatist, published an anthology of excerpts from Spenser's poetry in Edinburgh in 1902.

Index